CELEBRATE!
Young Poets Speak Out

West – Spring 2006

Creative Communication, Inc.

CELEBRATE!
Young Poets Speak Out
West – Spring 2006

An anthology compiled by Creative Communication, Inc.

Published by:

CREATIVE COMMUNICATION, INC.
1488 NORTH 200 WEST
LOGAN, UT 84341

ISBN 10: 1-60050-052-8
ISBN 13: 978-1-60050-052-7

Foreword

Welcome! Thank you for letting us share these poems with you.

This last school year we surveyed thousands of teachers asking what we could do better. We constantly strive to be the best at what we do and to listen to our teachers and poets. We strongly believe that this is your contest. Several changes were made to this anthology as we adapt to what was requested.

In this and future editions of the anthology, the Top Ten winners will be featured on their own page in the book. Each poet that is included in this book is to be congratulated, however, the Top Ten Poets should receive special recognition for having been chosen as writing one of the best poems. The Top Ten Poems were selected through an online voting system that includes thousands of teachers and students. In a day and age where television programs use viewer voting to determine which contestant is the winner, it is appropriate that our poetry winners are chosen by their peers.

Over the years we have had many parents contact us concerning the privacy of their children. The comments focus on the fact that publishing a poet's name, grade, school name, city and state with each poem is too much information. We want to address these concerns. In the Fall 2005 edition of the anthology, we made the decision to only list the poet's name and grade after each poem. Whereas we received many calls and letters concerning the issue that we were publishing too much information, we received thousands of calls and letters requesting that we again publish more information to include a student's school name and state with each poem. Therefore, for this and future editions we will publish each student's name, grade, school name and state unless specifically instructed not to include this information. Just as this information is included in a school yearbook, we provide this information in this literary yearbook of poetry. This decision hopefully makes it easier to find classmates in the book and brings appropriate recognition to the schools.

We are proud to provide this anthology. In speaking to the poets in our anthologies we have found that our anthologies are not stuffy old books that are forgotten on a shelf. The poems in our books are read, loved and cherished. We hope you enjoy reading the thoughts and feelings of our youth.

Sincerely,
Gaylen Worthen, President
Creative Communication

WRITING CONTESTS!

Enter our next POETRY contest!
Enter our next ESSAY contest!

Why should I enter?

Win prizes and get published! Each year thousands of dollars in prizes are awarded in each region and tens of thousands of dollars in prizes are awarded throughout North America. The top writers in each division receive a monetary award and a free book that includes their published poem or essay. Entries of merit are also selected to be published in our anthology.

Who may enter?

There are five divisions in the poetry contest. The poetry divisions are grades K-3, 4-6, 7-9, 10-12, and adult. There are three divisions in the essay contest. The essay division are grades 4-6, 7-9, and 10-12.

What is needed to enter the contest?

To enter the poetry contest send in one original poem, 21 lines or less. To enter the essay contest send in one non-fiction, original essay, 250 words or less, on any topic. Each entry must include the writer's name, address, city, state and zip code. Student entries need to include the student's grade, school name and school address. Students who include their teacher's name may help the teacher qualify for a free copy of the anthology.

How do I enter?

Enter a poem online at:
www.poeticpower.com

or

Mail your poem to:
Poetry Contest
1488 North 200 West
Logan, UT 84341

Enter an essay online at:
www.studentessaycontest.com

or

Mail your essay to:
Essay Contest
1488 North 200 West
Logan, UT 84341

If you are mailing your poetry entry, please write "Student Contest" at the top of your poem if you are in grades K-12. Please write "Adult Contest" at the top of your poem if you are entering the adult division.

When is the deadline?

Poetry contest deadlines are December 5th, April 5th, and August 15th. Essay contest deadlines are October 17th, February 15th, and July 17th. You can enter each contest, however, send only one poem or essay for each contest deadline.

Are there benefits for my school?

Yes. We award $15,000 each year in grants to help with Language Arts programs. Schools qualify to apply for a grant by having a large number of entries of which over fifty percent are accepted for publication. This typically tends to be about 15 accepted entries.

Are there benefits for my teacher?

Yes. Teachers with five or more students accepted to be published receive a free anthology that includes their students' writing.

For more information please go to our website at **www.poeticpower.com**, email us at editor@poeticpower.com or call 435-713-4411.

Table of Contents

Poetic Achievement Honor Schools   1

Language Arts Grant Recipients   5

Young Poets Grades 10-11-12   9
    Top Poems   10
    High Merit Poems   20

Young Poets Grades 7-8-9 105
    Top Poems 106
    High Merit Poems 116

Index 219

Spring 2006 Poetic Achievement Honor Schools

* Teachers who had fifteen or more poets accepted to be published

The following schools are recognized as receiving a "Poetic Achievement Award." This award is given to schools who have a large number of entries of which over fifty percent are accepted for publication. With hundreds of schools entering our contest, only a small percent of these schools are honored with this award. The purpose of this award is to recognize schools with excellent Language Arts programs. This award qualifies these schools to receive a complimentary copy of this anthology. In addition, these schools are eligible to apply for a Creative Communication Language Arts Grant. Grants of two hundred and fifty dollars each are awarded to further develop writing in our schools.

Alta High School
Sandy, UT
Arna Clark
Sally Wilde*

Buhl High School
Buhl, ID
Trish Wetzstein*

Canfield Middle School
Coeur d'Alene, ID
Jodi Booth
Jody Hiltenbrand

Central Davis Jr High School
Layton, UT
Tiffany Ralphs*

CLASS Academy
Portland, OR
Teresa Cantlon
Justice Evans
Leslie Huffman*

Covenant High School
Tacoma, WA
Douglas Bond*

Culver Middle School
Culver, OR
Peni Hendryx
Kimberly Kaylor*

Eagle Point Middle School
Eagle Point, OR
Sammie Eaton
Lee Shupe
Rick Taylor*

Elk Ridge Middle School
South Jordan, UT
Stephanie Nicolaides*

Emery High School
Castle Dale, UT
Diane Carter
Valene Wakefield
Wendy Whittle*

Kearns Jr High School
Kearns, UT
Pamela Carson*

Kodiak High School
Kodiak, AK
Mrs. Herbert
Ben Jackson
Mike Sirofchuck
Mrs. Thomas

Komachin Middle School
Lacey, WA
Evan Furtick
Annette Wells*

La Center High School
La Center, WA
Heather Grotte*

Mears Middle School
Anchorage, AK
Mrs. Haynes*

Morgan Middle School
Ellensburg, WA
Sara Eubanks*

Mount Si High School
Snoqualmie, WA
William E. Dillon*
Chris Jackson

Mountain Crest High School
Hyrum, UT
Sue Hodgkinson*

Mountain Ridge Jr High School
Highland, UT
Mrs. Chynoweth
Marjorie Eddy
Rachel Kelson*

Mt Olive Lutheran School
Las Vegas, NV
Mr. Rosenbaum*

Nampa Sr High School
Nampa, ID
A. Patterson*

Oak Harbor High School
Oak Harbor, WA
Erik Christensen*

Ogden Middle School
Oregon City, OR
Leslie Bennett-McCue*
Maureen Davis*
Bobbi Snider*

Orem High School
Orem, UT
Neil K. Johnson*

Pocatello Sr High School
Pocatello, ID
Marie Fairchild*

Preston High School
Preston, ID
Julie Tueller
Kaye Woodward*

Rancho High School
North Las Vegas, NV
Ms. Axt
Ms. Doyel
Danielle B. Ristow

Reid School
Salt Lake City, UT
Kim Aulbach
Meagan Black
Paulette Evans
Jill Gammon
Cheri Israelsen
Mindyn Mullinix
Rose Palmer
Michelle Peterson
Shauna Tateoka

River HomeLink Program
Battle Ground, WA
Tonia Albert
Ryan Anderson
Sherri Gassaway
Julie Sperry

South Jordan Middle School
South Jordan, UT
  Sandra L. Watts*

St Anne School
Seattle, WA
  Shannon Sifferman*

St Mary's Elementary School
Kodiak, AK
  Sr. Angela Goedken*

St Patrick's Catholic School
Pasco, WA
  Michelle Good
  Ms. Lampson*

Sunnyside Christian Elementary School
Sunnyside, WA
  Diane Groenewold*

Sylvester Middle School
Burien, WA
  Ms. Michelson
  Shawna Moore*

Thomas Edison Charter School
North Logan, UT
  Tanya Bidstrup
  Mr. Packard
  Mären Wendel*
  Lee Ann Wilkins*

Union High School
Union, OR
  Vivian Matthews
  Kristy E. Romer*

W F West High School
Chehalis, WA
  Patty Howard*

Walker Middle School
Salem, OR
  Amy Baldwin
  Lisa Hughes
  Susan Lovelace

Wasatch Jr High School
Salt Lake City, UT
  Ann Florence*

Language Arts
Grant Recipients
2005-2006

After receiving a "Poetic Achievement Award" schools are encouraged to apply for a Creative Communication Language Arts Grant. The following is a list of schools who received a two hundred and fifty dollar grant for the 2005-2006 school year.

Acushnet Elementary School – Acushnet, MA
Admiral Thomas H. Moorer Middle School – Eufaula, AL
Alta High School – Sandy, UT
Alton R-IV Elementary School – Alton, MO
Archbishop McNicholas High School – Cincinnati, OH
Barbara Bush Elementary School – Mesa, AZ
Bellmar Middle School – Belle Vernon, PA
Bonham High School – Bonham, TX
Cool Spring Elementary School – Cleveland, NC
Douglas Elementary School – Liberty, KY
Dumbarton Middle School – Baltimore, MD
Edward Bleeker Jr High School – Flushing, NY
Emmanuel/St. Michael Lutheran School – Fort Wayne, IN
Floyds Knobs Elementary School – Floyds Knobs, IN
Fox Creek High School – North Augusta, SC
Friendship Jr High School – Des Plaines, IL
Gibson City-Melvin-Sibley High School – Gibson City, IL
Hamilton Jr High School – Hamilton, TX
John F. Kennedy Middle School – Cupertino, CA
John Ross Elementary School – Edmond, OK
MacLeod Public School – Sudbury, ON
McKinley Elementary School – Livonia, MI
Monte Cassino School – Tulsa, OK
New Germany Elementary School – New Germany, NS
North Beach Elementary School – Miami Beach, FL
Paradise Valley High School – Phoenix, AZ
Parkview Christian School – Lincoln, NE
Picayune Jr High School – Picayune, MS
Red Bank Charter School – Red Bank, NJ
Sebastian River Middle School – Sebastian, FL
Siegrist Elementary School – Platte City, MO

Language Arts Grant Winners cont.

Southwest Academy – Baltimore, MD
St. Anthony School – Winsted, CT
St. John Vianney Catholic School – Flint, MI
St. Paul the Apostle School – Davenport, IA
St. Rose School – Roseville, CA
St. Sebastian School – Pittsburgh, PA
Sundance Elementary School – Sundance, WY
Thorp Middle School – Thorp, WI
Townsend Harris High School – Flushing, NY
Warren Elementary School – Warren, OR
Washington High School – Washington Court House, OH
Wasilla Lake Christian School – Wasilla, AK
Woodland Elementary School – Radcliff, KY
Worthington High School – Worthington, MN

Young Poets
Grades 10-11-12

Note: The Top Ten poems were finalized through an online voting system. Creative Communication's judges first picked out the top poems. These poems were then posted online. The final step involved thousands of students and teachers who registered as online judges and voted for the Top Ten poems. We hope you enjoy these selections.

Top Poem Grades 10-11-12

The World Is My Playground

The world is my playground
I do as I please
I jump from the swing of dependability
Independence is my trapeze

The world is my playground
Though I "Shoot for the Stars"
Achievement and success
Are my monkey bars

The world is my playground
I replay my memories past
As the carousel of life turns
Boy, I had a blast!

Jeff Andersen, Grade 10
Puget Sound Adventist Academy, WA

Top Poem Grades 10-11-12

The Fruit Not Tasted

The tree, it stood, in a sparkling glen,
Its fair leaves and bark untouched and pure,
Its glory and beauty unknown to men.
My hands unable, forsaken to pen
Of the magnificence I so adore.

On trembling limbs, I approach the tree.
I stare in wonder, regarding its fruits
That shine with brightened luster and gleam.
The tree tempts my hand, beseeching me
To partake of its poisonous loot.

And perish at its deadly kiss
To let death live and life be wasted?
No! I declare, defying all bliss.
And sadly sighing, seeing its beauty amiss,
I turn away from the fruit not tasted.

Jessica Bland, Grade 11
Mountain Crest High School, UT

Top Poem Grades 10-11-12

With Each Setting Sun

With each setting sun I'll remember the way we both shared the sight of the sea;
the way that you watched me with eyes aglow when you thought I didn't see.

With each setting sun I'll remember your laugh as the wind viciously whipped at my hair,
and the way you shivered when you draped me with your coat, but didn't seem to care.

With each dying of day I'll see us again, as silhouettes against the sun,
and the way that the silence stole us away, and you seemed to be the only one.

I may never see another horizon blazing hues of crimson against skies of blue
without having to close my tear-filled eyes against the images of you.

I will still feel the pain at the memory, and the heartache will seem cruel and unfair,
and not one sunset will not whisper your name, and make me wish that you were there.

But I also know that with each setting sun, for a time there will be tears in my eyes,
but this darkness that comes will soon fade away, and the sun will once again rise.

Kayla Gilbert, Grade 10
Granite Falls High School, WA

Top Poem Grades 10-11-12

My Story

My hands tell my story.
Each wrinkle has a line.
And when they are put together
the life they create is mine.
I have cracked skin,
    cursed by the winter breeze.
Crooked fingers,
    earned straightening my life.
Broken nails,
    from experiences that strengthened.
Rough edges,
    engraved by endless attempts at refining.
But in these imperfections
Unique stories are discovered.
Yes, my hands tell my story.
Each wrinkle has a line.

Emily Goodsell, Grade 11
Bonanza High School, NV

Top Poem Grades 10-11-12

Over a Dry Hill

She danced upon the sandy shores of Africa
With the sky above, an indigo blue.
Her cinnamon red painted toes, covered in sand.
The salty sea splashing upon her ankles.
Into the sky she dreamed, her soul soared,
Like a golden eagle on a summer morning.
Forever did she dance, until the indigo blue sky above her
Hued into a golden safari sunset.

She lay down upon the shore of sands,
With a smile upon her deep red lips,
And with her finger she drew a man, a man in the sand.
Of an unknown love, who, in a small town and over a dry hill, waited.

This man,
Painted a woman with his hands,
With rich colors upon thick paper.
And he waited, looking out his long, glass window
Into the golden safari sunset

Wondering…

If a woman across a town and over a dry hill,
Is waiting for him to dance with her upon the sandy shores of Africa.

Sarah Marie Horton, Grade 12
Alta High School, UT

Top Poem Grades 10-11-12

Hail to Cheese

When texture is called for and flavor needed,
If dishes seem common and bland,
The council of only one food is heeded,
Possibly the greatest category in the land.

With types and forms untold,
From the smooth and meek,
To the strong and bold,
It will grant the taste you seek.

Out of such a humble source,
Frost white milk so plain,
Guided by art and skill it runs its course,
To take true form and then to deign

Across all the world is known,
Hail to cheese upon its throne.

Kevin Housley, Grade 10
Pocatello Sr High School, ID

Top Poem Grades 10-11-12

Chess

Patiently they wait on the board
All of them trying to protect their lord
Silently they wait to attack
Waiting for the enemy to turn its back
Gazing over the land with eager eyes
Always vying for the prize
Seeing a breech in their defense
Not acting on this makes no sense
Without knowing the enemy has opened the gate
The winner smiles and declares checkmate

Joe Kennedy, Grade 10
Pocatello Sr High School, ID

Top Poem Grades 10-11-12

My Mom

With a mom in my life
I receive from the start
A lifetime of pleasure
To hold in my heart…

She's someone to love
And encourage and praise
With a feeling of joy
That enriches my days.

Her values are high,
And she's constantly shown
The will to move forward
With plans of her own…

She's the future unfolding
Before me each day
With the highest of hopes
Every step of the way…

A mom is to love…
Though perhaps very few
Have ever been loved, mom,
More deeply than you…

Timothy Kile, Grade 12
Trask River High School, OR

Top Poem Grades 10-11-12

Dancing

alone
and without cause
I twirl across the empty room
attempting grace
achieving little
falling and flying and swimming and gliding
across the empty floor
I envision myself
beautiful
and free
dancing
in castles
in orchards
in ballets
through rain
I float and swirl from whimsical scenes
back to my empty room
alone
but in my dance
I am beautiful

Kathryn Muhlestein, Grade 11
Woods Cross High School, UT

Top Poem Grades 10-11-12

Puffs of Serenity

Someone played with the clouds today,
They looked like white feathers,
Painted in wisps
Just barely leaving marks,
High above the green rolling hills,
In the cool blue color of the sky.
I'm going to lay here
In the grass for awhile
And enjoy this beautiful day.

Erin Shipka, Grade 11
Stanwood High School, WA

Truth
Here's the truth
What's the truth?
How do you know if it's true?
Why is it true?
Did you see it?
Can you believe it?
The truth behind what?
In front of what?
The truth is…
Nobody knows the truth
It is hidden deep inside the rabbit's fur
Will it ever be retrieved out?
Or will the truth be unseen forever?
Ricki Konnerup, Grade 11
Stanwood High School, WA

Why God?
I hate the way I speak to You
And don't hear Your reply.
I hate the way that you know all
I hate it that *we* die.

I hate that I can't see You
When I'm told You're always there.
I hate when You take the little ones
And leave their teddy bears.

I hate when You take loved ones
I hate it when I cry
I hate to see them leave here
And when I have to say "good bye"

I hate that I can't see them now
And the fact I'll be with them some day
For death marks my soul with sadness
Then offers a sunny ray.
Jennifer Burton, Grade 12
Mountain Crest High School, UT

You and I
I lie awake at night,
looking for your face.
I lie awake at night,
waiting for your sweet embrace.
I love you more than words can say,
I hope we will live to see the day,
when all our pains and fears are gone,
and you and I will write a song.
A song about our past,
and how long our love will last.
I wish with all my heart,
that you will be a part,
of my life, I pray,
each and every day.
Katie Phillips, Grade 10
Scappoose High School, OR

Language
Life is a language
There are many different ones and they all have their own personalities
But languages usually have a longer mortality
They can grow and they can change
To others they may seem very strange
But no matter how strange they may seem to be
They always make sense to somebody
To many there's only one that they know
Some have studied others and there are many places they can go
Some people can understand each other perfectly
To others what another is saying can be a total mystery
They can easily endanger another
There are many secrets that they can cover
They're not always what they seem to be
Some may seem hard when they're actually quite easy
Many are influenced by their culture
Some pick off others like a vulture
Some stand the test of time
Make a mark on the world and forever shine
Life is a language
Stephanie Thurman, Grade 11
Tillamook High School, OR

The Peace of Nature
As I walk down the path,
the leaves and grasses beckon to me.
I reach out and touch their silky stems.
Different colors burst out as I turn each corner.
Leaves are changing, green to gold, orange and red.
Picking them up, I see them sparkle and shimmer in the sunlight.
Wind gently sends my hair swirling around me.
After breaking free of the softly creaking branches,
leaves go soaring to greet the clouds,
then gently sway down towards earth.
As I continue walking down the right-hand path,
I pause and gather leaves into my arms.
With Mother Nature changing behind me,
I turn another corner and the sights disappear from view.
Serena Park, Grade 10
Edmonds Homeschool Resource Center, WA

Forgive
I forgive for all the times
That you have gone wrong
For all the times you said it wasn't done right
And all the nights that have been wasted with Hamm's
For all the times that you weren't there
And said I would fail
For all the times that you didn't say sorry
I forgive for the yelling
I forgive for the whipping
I forgive…for all the times I have said I love you and didn't get a response
For something that is so hard to do, I cannot forgive myself
For forgiving you
Dustin Baggett, Grade 11
Wilson High School, OR

Mom

One time God said to one angel.
You are going to the Earth.
What happens when I feel cold?
The person grabbed you in her arms.
What happens when I am scared?
The person protects you from everything with her life.
What happens when I need love?
The person giving more than you need.
And what is her name?
You would call MOM.

Juan Castro, Grade 10
Buhl High School, ID

Like You and Me

The Jews were people
Like you and me.
They were rejected, scorned, beaten, and flogged
Not only by Hitler, but by the rest of the mob.
"It's off to the concentration camps,
That's where you belong."
"You don't fit in;
You should be gone."
So off they went
Against their free will
To be tormented, wronged,
And eventually killed.
We are all different, that's what makes us unique.
Different beliefs, different lives, and different physique.
All these things
Make us who we are,
Special, loved, and so much more.
The Jews were people
Like you and me,
Worthy of life to forever be.

Amy Fox, Grade 12
Valley Christian Secondary School, WA

Can You Hear Them*

Can you hear them crying in the wind?
Begging for mercy.
Asking what they did wrong.
Barely holding onto every minute of life.

Can you hear them singing a low tune?
Singing a song of death just around a corner.
Humming that long song to sleep.
Crying while singing.

Can you hear them walking in the wind?
Hearing their bones rub against each other.
Falling to the ground day after day
Can you hear them?

Melissa Ming, Grade 10
W F West High School, WA
Dedicated to the Holocaust victims.

Winter's Song

Winter winds
blow with fury
whipping past
like quick shutters.

Trees lean
invisible forces
pushing, pulling
dancing with wet leaves
sticking to the ground
crying out for their last chance at beauty
the color of their youth long trampled out.

Dark dusty skies
moving slowly past
reaching out, grasping
with his twisted fingers.

Rain pouring down
sweeping across pavement
her comforting song
pounding
pressing cold damp hair to my forehead
covering me in her beautiful sorrow.

Jackie Schonbrun, Grade 11
Edmonds Woodway High School, WA

Elegance

Elegance is the thing with branches
That sprouts in the body
It grows taller than those around it
Always becoming greener

And greenest — the Evergreen — is seen
And strong must be the man
That could cut down the brilliant tree
That fed so many hopes

Seen in the darkest places
Or in the stormiest weather
Never will it go extinct
Living to be longed for

Brandon Winwood, Grade 11
Nampa Sr High School, ID

Love

Love
Love is a word
Love is a word that comes straight from the heart
Love is a word that can tear you apart
No matter where no matter when
The word love will be there till the end
Love
Love is a word

Scott Whiting, Grade 10
Emery High School, UT

The Truth

Simple thoughts
With simple meanings,
But none of them seem to be very clear.
Hopes and dreams,
Wanting and longing,
All with thought of love.

Just when you thought you knew
All about what love is and
Keep all the childish hope
Even when you know the truth.

Wanting isn't good enough,
Waiting can be long;
Hoping, scheming,
All that love is gone.
Tomorrow is a brand new start,
All with thoughts of love.

Just when you thought you knew
All about what love is and
Keep all the childish hope
Even when you know the truth.

Lauren Simpson, Grade 11
American Fork High School, UT

Light

Now is redemption
Forward is the light of men
Demons of the dark

Bill Wolkoff, Grade 11
Kodiak High School, AK

Forest

As sunlight in shade
Shimmers and shines
Woods live and die
On the sword of seasons.
High Eden engrossed in particular glory,
The winds whisper
Over foggy bogs and wild leaves
As shadows cast their contour.
Organics, flora and fauna,
Incarnate in this haven,
Keen to balance and rebirth,
Project their mystic mirth.
Spellbound in mist and ancient lore
The mysterious' veil
Projects myriad sensations
Emanating from boughs every pore.
Essence and aroma flux
As skies arcane
Flurry up above,
Returning Elysium.

Derek Smith, Grade 11
Davis High School, UT

Allie Castimore

I was born and raised in Bevans, NJ
The mother of five
A hard working woman I was
In my younger days, I lived on a dairy farm
Every morning, the cows would wait for me,
To relieve the pressure from their heavy udders.
I was a friend to all,
And never hesitated to help a friend in need.
Who was humble, yet very giving, I could not stand to see people suffering.
A mother, a driver for military officers, and a devoted wife,
I loved life, and believed that helping others,
Gave me sheer satisfaction, and joy.
In my spare time I loved to go dancing, or paint things.
I touched many people in my life, lived a good life.
At the age of eighty-eight, I had lived a full enough life,
And decided it was my time to go.
I passed away peacefully,
My ashes are lain to rest on the banks of the Flatbrook.

Allie Bohus, Grade 10
Pocatello Sr High School, ID

Sincerity

Sincerity is an ocean, whose waves wash "junk" to shore like plastic rings of doubt.
It holds all types of fish with colors that blend together as one.
The ocean holds neither "fault" nor "flaw;"
Its mesmerizing beauty lies beneath one's eyes.

It can be gentle and moving or wild and reckless;
Sincerity is your own little ocean in which only you can control.
To use it to your disadvantage is to cause pain with harsh words
Your serene ocean can become a roaring, tropical storm,
And if not stopped, another Katrina will once again be formed.

To lie is to build clouds of self-doubt and worry,
Because once a wind breaks out a bigger one will soon follow after;
Pain again restored; although it may look bleak and the pounding waves seem louder
Keep spirits high and a mind open
Only then…will your ocean's untouchable beauty show.

Jeanette Juarez Gonzalez, Grade 11
Nampa Sr High School, ID

Imagination

I nstilled in the minds of everyone is imagination.
M iraculous lands far, far away come from imagination.
A nimals with hair of gold are the spark of imagination.
G ames played with creatures unknown to man, that's imagination.
I nward dreams of fairies and elves are nothing but imagination.
N aughty ninjas and wonderful wizards are in your imagination.
A pretty pink pig flying in the sky is nothing but imagination.
T he tales of a walking, talking snowman following you around, that's imagination.
I n my bedroom is an underwater world, the spark of imagination.
O utstanding treasures found at the center of the Earth come from imagination.
N othing but the creative part of everyone's mind, imagination.

Shawntelle Walker, Grade 10
Pocatello Sr High School, ID

Jealousy

Jealousy is watching the other team win.
The heart wrenching feeling.
That single tear running down your cheek.
It's that single moment when you realize you've lost.
The utter disappointment.
Jealousy is watching the other team win.
The anger towards everyone but yourself.
Anger turns to sadness.
Wishing you could just start over.
Jealousy is watching the other team win.

Charis Becker, Grade 10
Oak Harbor High School, WA

Love

Love is such a word,
That should only be said with meaning.
Not the kind of word to use,
When you plan on leaving.

Love is such a feeling,
That can make you smile, as well as cry.
It is the kind of feeling,
That makes you still want to try.

Love is something you look forward to,
And sometimes look back upon.
One day everything will be going fine,
And the next you'll wonder what went wrong.

Love is confusing,
Love is blind.
It's usually easy to feel,
But true love, is hard to find.

Ky Lee Schmunk, Grade 11
Lind Jr/Sr High School, WA

A Dark and Empty Place

The road is cold and desolate,
The weariness and drain.
Walking through the world alone,
Though seeing the people go by,
They see me though say nothing,
As if I don't exist,
Sitting there on the bench,
I see someone,
But different,
She stands alone against a tree,
She looks over,
And down towards me,
She walks over and takes a seat,
Maybe this world isn't so cold and desolate,
Maybe it's not weary and drain,
Maybe we can be together,
To the last of our days.

Ammon Grannis, Grade 10
Orem High School, UT

Erom Reven

Nevermore,
That word haunted him forevermore.
Born with nothing,
He sought out for his purpose.
He traveled many miles,
With nothing but a dying dream.
He traveled through war zones,
He traveled through fields of death.
Finally he had found the answer to his long awaited question:
To bring misery and suffering to all.
He looked back at his past,
And smiled for the first time in twenty years,
For his purpose was being served.
Nevermore would he search for anything.
He was Erom Reven,
Nevermore.

Holly Martin, Grade 10
North Bend High School, OR

Good-bye

It's time to say good-bye now,
I'm going far away.
Secrets follow me like a shadow,
There is nothing left to say.

Leave this place of familiar surroundings,
Enter the world of the unknown.
Excited, yet nervous, all kinds of feelings.
And soon, my weaknesses will be shown.

I am not bitter, I hold you dear.
It's been too long since I have felt change.
But now it's time to let go of all my fear.
It might be a bit different; it might feel strange.

So farewell, my old friend,
New world, here I come!
I have nothing to lose, this is not a pretend.
But I'll never forget this home where I'm from.

Christine Bove, Grade 10
Valley Christian Secondary School, WA

Love Is a Rainbow

When its storms, rainbows save the day
They are rare, beautiful
Each color has a meaning

Red is for the love that we share,
Green is for the trust that we have,
Yellow is for our everlasting friendship,
Orange is for the respect we give each other,
and blue is for our future…

…Together, forever.

Maggie Conley, Grade 10
Oak Harbor High School, WA

All You Do
These thoughts inside keep turning
around and around inside my head.
Taking over everything,
all I can hear is what you've said.

I cry into the dead of night,
and I don't know what to do.
I know that what I did was right,
but I can't stop thinking about you.

Please just make me hate you
Do something to make me mad.
I can't continue to live this way;
life just sucks when you're so sad.

I want to scream; I want to shout;
I want to make everything okay.
I want this burden to be gone
and forget all that you did say.

I really want to just give up,
to let out this defeated sigh.
After all, what kind of life can you live
when all you do is cry.
Kali May, Grade 11
Tillamook High School, OR

Mountains
They are tall and steep
Climbing the slope to reach the top
Marvel at the sight.
Aaron J. Seamons, Grade 11
Preston High School, ID

On the Battlefield
Sadness pervades,
Young men collapse to the earth,
In extreme agony.
The steady sound of gunfire,
Ring's in their ears.
It's the only music,
On the battlefield.
A constant rhythm
Playing,
Over and over.
Life,
With love and a warm home,
All in the past.
As lives are taken
On the battlefield,
In sad wonder
I ask: "How many will die?"
"And will they go to heaven?"
That is life on the battlefield.
Amy Gray, Grade 10
Arlington High School, WA

Reptilian Majestic
The wind howls as he flies wings beating soundlessly.
Mountains, lakes, plains all flash past in the blink of an eye.
He twists and turns with grace unparalleled,
crimson scales flash with moonlight.
A tendril of flame escapes his gaping maw.
His eyes open wide a full moon reflects,
his shadow races below wanting to win the race.
Perching on a mountain peak he raises his head
and lets loose a tremendous flaming roar.
His call answered by his mate who waits below, their song echoes in the night.
Then as the song fades Reptilian Majestic takes flight.
Matthew Schuster, Grade 10
Waldport High School, OR

Whole
Vex is fire red like freshly drawn blood
like the red eyes of a tiger
sensing his end with no escape.

It rages through my mind, and gnaws at my soul
like a tiger ripping through a gazelle with teeth and claws.
My true love left me.

It's depressing to know my one love left,
and to know there might not be another true love for me.
It makes me want to crawl in a hole and never come out.

I don't want to hear the sounds of trees or feel the breath of the wind.
Or taste the mist of the ocean,
I want to be whole again.
Tyler G. Calvi, Grade 10
La Center High School, WA

Polished Rock
It's late. The night is dark.
The moon is absent, and the city lights forbid the stars to burn.
I have no destination in mind as my car crawls the streets;
But I know I'll end up where I always do.
I stand on the wet grass with a plaid layer of warmth drawn about my shoulders.
My silhouette stands against the glow of my parking lights
That hover in the December air, searching for my shadow in vain.
I'm surrounded by the soft flicker of secret candles that blur my sight.
Or is it the sorrow rolling down my cheeks that shuts my eyes?
My lips trace the letters on your stone with a whisper.
The night is silent, except for a sad song that plays from my car.
My tears reluctantly desert their shyness and shake hands with the night.
I lay on the ground with shaking shoulders to shorten the distance between us.
It's just like they said it would be in lost literature and forgotten fables.
And I hate it.
The poetry in my chest is locked in a trunk, and I can't think.
I'm in an empty field, trying so hard to brush away branches that aren't there.
I stand and open my eyes, now swollen red, and draw my blanket closer to me.
With my final crumb of vigor, I go to my car to turn off the sad song.
But the radio was never on.
Seth Fraughton, Grade 10
Viewmont High School, UT

Times Unchanged

Starring into the pools of jade watching
Your lips move; hearing the wind of your mouth.
Waiting for the response of a question
More tones of beauty pass my ear, and it's what I want to hear.
Artistry stays unchanged over the years,
Through which I have known and grew close to you
Sitting aside I can express my rapture
New signs of happiness show as I tell you.
So I now sit here pondering about you,
Time is now flying by and I can't stop
Thinking of the times we have had; our friendship
Grows to a better relationship of love
So I tell you now that I love you and
Cannot keep myself away from your beauty.

Robert Wilson, Grade 10
Olympic High School, WA

March Madness

March is a special time of year.
Black and white magpies whistle their shrill song over the trees
Plants explode into life,
The sweet scent of basketball is carried
on the breeze.
The bounce of the ball is echoed in the boom
of a spring thunderstorm.
Wild cheering from the crowd is heard in the
pattering of raindrops.
I hope my bracket can withstand
the upsets which will surely come.

Ryan Barney, Grade 12
Alta High School, UT

Love

Love isn't what it is today,
But still not what it used to be.
They say they love you.
You think it's true.
But in the end they cheat on you.
It's hard to tell,
Who really can care?
In these days with all this hate.
And then there's those who procrastinate.
So what to do what to say?
Maybe there's another way.
You kiss her lips and hold her hand,
Just to show everyone you're the man.
You say she cheats and call her names.
But inside you know you're to blame.
She's truthful to you,
But what do you do?
You hurt her every time something tempts you.
Inside she's hurt, she's dark and she's blue.
But what do you care?
She never told you.

Rikki Lee Robinson, Grade 11
Community College West High School, NV

Phoenix

If I could be any animal,
I shall become the Phoenix.
I would spread wide, my mighty wings
And soar throughout the cosmos.
If at any time that I may be struck down,
Reborn from my ashes, I would come again.
Alas, my immortality would be a curse,
For I would be forced to behold misery and death
Again, again, and again…
I would suffer for all eternity…and even after…

Kevin Frederick, Grade 10
Oak Harbor High School, WA

A Beam of Light

A beam of light that bounced to catch my dream
Intrigued your smile to flee its bonds of fear,
And see the slithering, softly sliding stream
Dissolve the choking acrid smoke so near.

Step through the curtain of stabbing gnarled briar
And find the fog will, pierced, show what's sincere.
Then beautifully accompany the lyre
While stranded, singing truth of strange and queer.

As light licks off the weary wooden pyre
A misting rain has soaked the mourning night
And driven all to gaze toward flickering fire.
True, I compare you to the shimmering light
Of dawn. A joyous light content to cope
With life and teach one's soul to always hope.

Daniel Sinderson, Grade 11
South Medford High School, OR

Your Heart

Tonight will be the night when I take it away from you.
Next week will be the week that I bring it back in two.
Because we were great for a while.
Doesn't mean we should reconcile.
We were the best of friends.
Our hearts are what we lent.
For the time that we loved.
we had masked our smarts with a glove.
We did not know what was going on.
Only that what we had, our friendship, is now gone.
We hadn't a clue what to do.
I am sorry, but I broke it in two.
I loved you.
and still do.
But what we had.
was nothing but a fad.
I want things to go back to the way they used to be.
Friends forever, you and me.
So I turn time backwards from end to start.
I give you mine and give you back your heart.

Hannah Houk, Grade 10
Eastlake High School, WA

You're Not Promised

You're not promised today, tomorrow, forever.
You're not promised to continue to say I'll stay forever.
There's only chance in a lifetime that you'll meet your soul mate.
There's only once in a lifetime you'll learn how to hate.

Life is not as easy as it looks on TV.
Or it's not as easy for you and me.
Reach out today and touch somebody else's heart.
Just don't be like most people, plain stubborn from the start.

It's better to give than to take.
It's better to be true than to be fake.
Take it from me, don't expect to wake up tomorrow.
You could be in a casket, and their hearts filled with sorrow.

That's why I always keep the thought in my mind that you're not always promised tomorrow.

Keoasha Porter, Grade 10
Rancho High School, NV

Misunderstood

The things she did to get here are probably more than any other would
The things she did to get here are commonly misunderstood
Waking me up for school every morning all I say is mom I don't feel so good
She tells me you will thank me when you're older but right now it's misunderstood
No late night's on the street corner she says it can bring no good
You will thank me when you're older but right now it's misunderstood
How come I can't go to the party all the other people would
You just don't want me to have any fun she says son you misunderstood
But now almost as a man I stand I see most of my friends faces in there hands
AIDS and rape on first dates and seems like no one had a plan but I think I'm starting to understand
It's all just fast money no one wants to be decrepit
Just like visa everyone wants to be accepted
Nobody wants to be in bondage but they don't want shackles and chains
But there shackles are drugs and they sell their shackles for watches and chains
And all of the shackles continue to baffle their brain
They've been on it so long they don't realize it's all the same
But if not for my mom's guidance I could have been deep in their game
But she understood that I could and so she put my sights on higher aim
So now all I can do is give thanks and thank her for her plan
After all of the years of misunderstanding finally I understand

Travis Rouse, Grade 10
Bartlett High School, AK

Labels

Don't call me a perfectionist until you've felt the pressure to do everything the right way all of the time.
Don't call me a nerd until you've found your niche and love what you're doing.
Don't call me unpopular until you've met my brother who's in karate.
Don't call me naive until you've had all my epiphanies.
Don't call me stupid until you've seen my ambition and the ways it's paid off.
Don't call me ugly until you look at my inner beauty.
Don't call me insensitive until you've been through all I'm dealing with at the moment.
Don't call me cautious until you know all of the barriers of insecurity I've overcome.
Don't label me until you know the hurt it can cause.
Never mind, if you don't someone else will.

Sara Sanders, Grade 11
Viewmont High School, UT

My Love of Cotton Candy

Oh light and soft mysterious fluff
Divine delight so gently falling
My dreamy cloud of sugary stuff
That to my mouth is always calling
Sweet candy calling all the while
Of which I greatly wish to taste
To munch on such does make me smile
It draws me in with fantastic haste
So easily melted on the tip of my tongue
The cottony fibers parting with ease
Reminds me of days when I was quite young
The sugary fineness my mouth it doth please
Delightfully soft, and ever so dandy
My favorite stuff that is cotton candy

Heather Butler, Grade 10
Pocatello Sr High School, ID

Love on a Razor's Edge

Love is a jewel-encrusted knife
Beautiful, entrancing with
Its bright, shimmering blade
Hypnotizing, mesmerizing with its
Sparkling jewels, those gems so bright
Amusing even, to play with and to toss around
Until you're pricked or even sliced
Slashed, scarred, but still it is enthralling
With the blood still dripping on the blade
And still you are drawn to it, searching,
To find it and amuse yourself with
To brandish even in combat
But be wary for it can equally
Be used against you
In the hands of another
Plunged deep into your heart
Love is a jewel-encrusted knife

Nick Bratt, Grade 10
Oak Harbor High School, WA

Wonder of Wisdom

Fortune, increase your desire.
Grade towards creation,
With a cup of wisdom on the side.
Your mind fills with envy, intelligence, and bliss.
You're comforted for a moment,
Which is told will last forever.
Years of what you think can help
String and loop in and out of mind.
But you crave a certain unattainable.
It's beauty, a marvel,
As cliché as your pity
To those you think less.

"Take all of your expertise,
And trade it in for wonder."

Ashley Friedman, Grade 10
Las Vegas Academy, NV

Father and Son Watched the Sea

Father and Son watched the Sea.
Father told Son about Life,
Father told Son about Love.
Waves crashed into Son and
Father told Son about Death.
Waves crashed into Father and then
Son understood Death,
Son understood Love,
Son understood Life.

Father and Son watched the Sea,
And both Father and Son understood Men,
And both men understood Nature.
And everyone and everything stopped, and breathed.
And for a moment, all Earth was simple and understood.
And the moment was over, and Father and Son watched the Sea.

Elana Lev, Grade 11
Corvallis High School, OR

A Raindrop Falling

A raindrop falling, gravity calling
Wait for the dawning and just disappear
A raindrop dripping, heavens are tripping
Wait for cloudy skies to be all you can
A raindrop holding, don't begin folding
All populace speaks, I stay together
A raindrop alone, waiting to be home
I'm looking for her, stopping at nothing
A raindrop to serve, please teach me to learn
See differently, smiling at the world
A raindrop falling, gravity calling
Just stop the dawning so I can be here.

Jeff Campbell, Grade 12
White Pine High School, NV

Luxury

Luxury
everyone wants to live surrounded by it
we spend hours of a lifetime
trying to reach it
to live it

The luxury of self-love and confidence
the taste of power
The smell of the upper hand

Everything is at its best
All conspires for you to get what you want
Days never seem wasted
And yet, many will consider it is a lie
I'll leave you with a thought
is always nice to live in a feder box
ignoring everything but the reply of the
kiss that Luxury is

Ana Ibarra, Grade 10
Mount Si High School, WA

Deliverance

Escape
From the hostile
Eyes of the darkened world.
Unloving, driving me away,
Lonely.
Whispers,
Assaulting me
From every direction.
Unwanted, yet always flying,
Despised.
Speaking,
But no one hears;
They don't listen to me.
Unneeded, nothing to say now,
Silence.
Alone
In the silence
Of the somber cellars
And freezing chill of the hard world.
Escape

Jessica Clapp, Grade 11
Idaho Falls Sr High School, ID

Ode to My Poems

Poems…
you are everything
that is within me —
all my thoughts,
wishes,
feelings,
and memories.

You are the soft touch
to my pen.
You are what
speaks to me.

You are my life.
Without you,
there would be no words
within my soul.

Francis Weller, Grade 11
Columbia High School, WA

A Kept Secret

Should I tell them
Will they look at me different
Can life go on the same
Am I just being lame
Would it change my life
Could the truth start a fight

I will just keep it to myself
And hope for the best

Sherra Schoborg, Grade 10
Rancho High School, NV

Modesty

"Modesty," is a tree sometimes with leaves and sometimes without.
It is a system of values with fading clout.
It is humility in the face of worldly praise,
It is an unspoken culture that when challenged brings craze.
It is the will of God,
Within the head bangers it is a simple nod.
It is a right winged Republican in politics
It is being rich enough to build a house out of marble but using sticks.
It is the guidelines that we give to a child,
It is the opposite of wild.

Cristian Martinez, Grade 11
Nampa Sr High School, ID

Chocolate Cake

Yummy delicious warm chocolate cake,
Gooey frosting all over my face.
I cannot resist the magical taste
I savor every single bite, until its tragic end,
O I would do anything for just one more taste.
My mother said only one, but I say where is the harm in having two.
O my, even more yummy more delicious than the first,
Even more frosting all over my already smothered face.
I cannot resist the spectacular taste.
But my second piece also came to its end,
I would do anything for just one last taste of yummy, delicious, warm chocolate cake.
I didn't eat one more not even two more because I ate the entire cake.
Now all I got is a chocolate cake stomachache!

Madeline Woodhouse, Grade 10
Pocatello Sr High School, ID

Life's Western Window

Sometimes when the day is ended and its round of duties are done
I watch by the western window the gleam of the setting sun

And when my heart has been unquiet and its longings unequaled
By the days exhaustion burden and cannot be reconciled

I look at the slope of the mountains and over the restless sea
And I think of the heavenly city
That little, not far from me

And my spirit is hushed in a moment as the twilight falls softly and sweet
And in fancy I cross over the river and I kneel at my master's feet

And so when life's labors are ended and the duties he gave me are done
I shall watch at life's western window the glow of the setting sun

I shall fall asleep in the twilight to awaken on Earth no more
There shall fall over my restless spirit
A hush that is wondrous sweet

And I shall cross over the river
To kneel at my Master's feet — to kneel at my Savior's feet.

Ashley Reed, Grade 12
Jordan Valley High School, OR

What's with Being Popular?

The Cool,
The Football Team,
The Cheerleaders.
Why, oh, why are they liked,
Is it because they're big?
Is it because they're pretty?
Is it because they dress in leather?
Oh, they look good and everyone goes with them,
Then why are they jerks,
Mean to the smart, the smaller, or the different?
Why do the Cool hurt or belittle the others?
Is that *Cool* to you?
Why aren't the kind cool,
The ones that help the little people out,
The people who learn your name.
The people who care about their fellows,
Is that *Cool* to you?

Tyler Winward, Grade 10
Orem High School, UT

Safe

Safe is the creature that relies on slow and secure.
Covered in armor instead of the traditional fur
This shell of armor shields him from harm,
This is why he is content, never at alarm.
Risk, too, this armor can conquer
In danger this animal does not stir

This protective backpack, he will confidently carry
However, this makes his pace slow and weary

Slow, seemed strong in the fairy tale race
For his sluggish and stable strides, led him to first place
Risky and dangerous was the hare's plan.
Proved when he lay to rest like a dead man
While reliable and relaxed was his opponent's strategy,
A gambler this animal will not be.

With a strong coat of armor
And a goal oriented mind
The tortoise is one of the safest creatures you will find.

Sarah Hill, Grade 11
Nampa Sr High School, ID

I Don't Understand

I don't understand
Why people say one thing and mean another.
Why people go to great lengths for something
that only lasts for a short period of time.
Why people won't accept the fact
there isn't a right or wrong answer for life's choices.

Most of all, I do not understand
why I am one of those people.

Jaime Loredo, Grade 12
Great Basin High School, UT

Life's Mountain Range

Life is a mountain range
With ups and downs, repetition and change

From bare ground where nothing beautiful grows
To lush ground where water easily flows

I hope for the beauty that waits at the top
The grace and the glamour from each dewdrop

I can look back at the beauty left down the mountain drop
But nothing compares to the scene at the top

Greta L. Stuhlsatz, Grade 10
La Center High School, WA

The Better Man

A man once passing down the road had walked
Until the point where either left or right
Was left to choice, and looking down them both,
He saw it clear the latter shone with light.
When others passed and chose the right-hand path,
The man looked once, his chin protruding high,
And sneered at them, the lesser in his eyes,
And took upon himself the left to try.
His eyes saw only sky as he looked up
And highly held his head, but to the ground,
Where roots and vines entwined to snare his feet,
He never thought to view this danger found.
   In ignorance he fumbled on his way,
   'Till off a ledge his pride had let him stray.

Becky Love, Grade 12
Covenant High School, WA

I'll Be

I'll be
Your strength,
to no length.
Your eyes,
seeing the lies.
Your ears,
as something nears.
Your truth,
to keep your youth.
Your love,
you can fly like a dove.
Your one,
this isn't just fun.
Your only,
so long as you're not lonely.
Your protection,
in the slightest detection.
Just let me know,
understand this won't come slow.
I'll be,
yours.

Tony Jackson, Grade 10
Silverton High School - Schlador Campus, OR

What to Write?

I don't know what to write,
It's such a burdensome blight.
It's hard to think,
My mind does shrink
Before this writing plight.

Should I write about a damsel,
Or perhaps a witch with her spells?
A ghost would be great,
It would compensate
For my lack of creative swells.

My hand is beginning to cramp,
The light's growing dim in my lamp.
It does irritate,
I will abdicate;
Give up this limerick and revamp.

Brooke Luke, Grade 11
Mountain Crest High School, UT

Issa

Issa,
Black, good.
Swims, reads, writes
Enjoying his time on campus.
Learner.

Issa Goddi, Grade 12
Great Basin High School, UT

Life Stream

Live your life
Like a mountain stream.
Start out small
And build up steam.

There are boulders and rocks
To go around,
If you work
A way can be found.

Along the way
You may be tossed and thrown,
Then along the course,
You find you've grown.

The journey is hard,
The path is long,
You make mistakes,
But must stay strong.

And looking back
At the path you took.
A life is made
From a tiny brook.

Nathan Pollaehne, Grade 10
Emery High School, UT

male or female

his hair was black like coffee grounds
many people think that her lips were sweet as peaches but who's to say
her eyes were the shape of almonds but his were not
she looked like a pear and he looked as a string bean
his hands rough with valleys
and hers smoother than a baby's bottom
they see each other so different
but so in love

attraction

Brittany Marshall, Grade 12
Sumner Sr High School, WA

Stormy Perspective

Oh little drifting rain cloud, why is it that you cry?
Why do your scattered teardrops stain the bright blue sky?
Your brilliant pure white color, turned cloudy and so gray
Can you not see your purpose? The vital role you play?
Trapped in your constant mourning, your shadow and your doubt
You are so blind; you cannot see the sunlight you've blocked out.
Your soul is scarred with anger, the rage is tearing through
Your thunder and your lightning; the world is hating you.
Harsh winds are ever blowing, they sway you all around
You never see their danger — you're lost, and never found.
Oh little sobbing rain cloud, how will your story end?
Will you lose all light, all hope, and break before you bend?
Oh please try and remember those days when you were pure
The days you were so happy, so hopeful, and so sure.
Let in the loving sunshine, its ever warming rays
Let it soothe your stormy soul, and then see brighter days.

Angie Petersen, Grade 12
Madison Sr High School, ID

A Price to Pay

Never have you offered up your compassion to his severed heart
Parry not towards his vulnerable state
As is his demeanor of being inept to retain his desire
To reach out and touch you while in your company
Though, instead of assenting to pacify his lust
You chose to prolong this slow torture
Of reeling in his heart by your illicit exegesis talent
Sorceress, have you no lament? He is at your mercy
For this nefarious manner imposed upon his affections
Surrender to your own! In fear of rejection, you are the coward! It is not he!
For the love of God, serve him justice!
Put this sadistic game to a demise
Catching his gaze as if to consent to his intentions
Only to ensnare his heart for an instant
Then withdrawing from his presence
To make him hunger for a second glance
Know this, in time, he will misinterpret your actions, and tire from them
Finding another to salve his despondency
Ironically falling for the spectator
And this is the dearest price you've paid, and still you are paying

Theresa Gonzales, Grade 11
Bellarmine Preparatory School, WA

In Between Dreams

This whirlwind will stop,
It's the eye of the storm.
The clouds will part,
The sun will warm.
No smiles or frowns; your eyes are serene,
As you lie on this cloud, in between dreams.
Wrapped up in laughter, but washed over by tears,
This peace that you carry drives out my fears.
None of it matters or means a thing;
Just living in the moment, floating in your being.

Ali Feroah, Grade 11
Galena High School, NV

Studious

There once was a girl who went to school.
Her name was Sheila and she thought she was cool.
She was good at math and loved to study.
She went to art class and made a sculpture out of putty.

She got on the honor roll and made her parents glad.
From that moment on her mother never was sad.
Now she is trying to pass her exit exams.
And wishes she would of studied like Sam.

Sam is her neighbor who lives down the street.
Sam studies so hard that by the end of the night he is beat.
The moral of the story is to gain lots of knowledge.
So sometime in the future you might go to college.

Kyle Wilson, Grade 11
McLaughlin High School, AK

The People of Power

Many forms and shapes, half of weather,
Bane of drought, smooth liquid power.
Being of passion, hotheaded man,
Foe of winter, Cleanser, Destroyer.
Flighty, difficult to keep,
Mistress of raging winds, giver of life.
Sturdy, stubborn stone,
Slow strength, ruler of the ground.
Clever, mindful hand, Lord of the Clock,
Knower of every thought ever thought and those soon to be.
Powerful brother, fears and nothing,
Explosive to his foes, Master of Matter.
The Sun, protector of all,
The fair judge, the good.
Cheater, Murderer, Hateful Being,
Twister of dark and light, true evil's form.
Stern, just, watcher of the door,
The strong defender, Guardian of the Heart.
The changing moon, the shiny mirror,
And the shadow of them all.
These are the people of power.

Greg Winward, Grade 10
Orem High School, UT

Darkness

It's pitch black outside,
It's so hard to see.
I'm afraid that it will engulf me.
The darkness is so black,
I can't tell what is in front of me.
I'm so scared,
Somebody please come with me.
I fall into the darkness,
Now I can't see.
Will someone come save me,
Or am I going to be trapped here?
I'm scared in this darkness,
I wish someone was here.
I don't know where to go,
Because the darkness engulfed my entire body.
The darkness takes my breath away,
So no one can hear my scream.
I'm stuck here,
So I just sit in the darkness,
Waiting for someone to come.

Joyce Creech, Grade 11
Reno High School, NV

Wealth

I greet this day with lifted chin and eyes
That I might lean upon the strength of gold.
These eyes have seen the wretched streets where lies
The shameful muck of human filth and mold.
I sit above the land on diamond thrones,
And with my perfect eyes I glare with glee
At each new urchin begging for my loans.
With one small word I slash away his plea.
But pity not the filth and grime they wear;
Their place below is ripe with rude ideal.
Society has granted them a care:
When helpless left, they lose the strength to feel.
But when their eyes look into mine I see
The hint of disrespect and hate of me.

Benjamin Lensch, Grade 11
Covenant High School, WA

You're Perfect

All I ever wanted was to be part of your heart,
and for us to be together and never apart.
No one in the world can even compare,
you're perfect and so is the love that we share.
We have so much more than I ever thought we would,
I love you more than I ever thought I could.
I promise to give you all that I have to give,
I'll do anything for you as long as I live.
In our eyes I see our future, present and past.
By the way you look at me, I know that we will last.
I hope that one day you'll come to realize,
how perfect you are when seen through my eyes.

Carla Hinojosa, Grade 10
Rancho High School, NV

Forgotten
Old and creaky
murky and without a friend in the world.
The only sound
is the wind hitting the broken windows
slamming them into an unpainted wall.
Glass shattered into petite pieces
on the rickety wood floor
wanting to be loved,
waiting to be cherished,
forgotten and left behind.
Amanda Matranga, Grade 10
Silver Creek Alternative School, ID

The Day After
How has your day been my love
Did it mean anything to you
Are you ready to start another love
Do you regret me too?

Love is not meant for everybody
I could never confront tomorrow
the day is so long without you
No one ever told me about the sorrow

If I only knew
My heart now torn and broken
Pleas help me mend
By words softly spoken
Han Abbott, Grade 12
Mountain Crest High School, UT

A Light Through Darkness
His heart was broken,
His life was a mess,
Losing the way
Through grief and pain.
There came a light
Took in the dark.
It gave him the strength,
It gave more each day.
How could he pay?
What did it want?
To save a creature…
That hated himself?
Yes, God must have sent her,
An angel from heaven.
To tell him to live,
A heart meant to give.
A true friend indeed,
An angel to him,
If only to thank her,
For the light…she gave,
To me.
Travis Olsen, Grade 11
American Leadership Academy, UT

Some Days…
Some days are hard
Some days are easy
Some days you're tired
Some days you're lazy
Some days just drive you crazy.

Some days are good
Some days are bad
Some days you're happy
Some days you're sad
Some days just make you mad.

Some days are empty
Some days are full
Some days are exciting
Some days are dull
Some days you achieve your goals.

Some days you're selfish
Some days you care
Some days are awful
Some days are fair
And some days you can't even bear.
Lauren Longacre, Grade 10
La Center High School, WA

When the Ground Fails
The ground is crumbling 'neath my feet.
Nothing steady — nothing stable.
Around me swirls uncertainty.
I try to stop; I'm not able.

And yet upon a hand I trust
To break my terrifying fall.
Most eyes can't see it, but I must —
Invisible. But still I call.

That hand of His it reaches out
To place me on His shoulders strong.
I am safe now without a doubt
For He will carry me along.

He kept His promise through those nails,
I'll trust in Him when the ground fails.
Alayna Fong, Grade 10
McKenzie River Christian School, OR

Jealousy
Eavesdropping by the walls
Hearing their flirting and joy
My heart raging mad
Picturing my life without her
I storm out seeking revenge
Kevin Viado, Grade 12
Kodiak High School, AK

My Bronco
It has two doors,
And carpet on the floors.
Four-wheel high and low,
In case you're in the snow.
And when you put the pedal down,
Just hope there are no cops around.
And when it goes VROOOM,
It will make a throaty tune.
The tires are your bud,
When you go through the mud.
If you want to go fast,
This truck will be a blast.
And you will not be bored,
While you drive this Ford.
It is called a Bronco,
And it takes me where I want to go.
Josh Hoskinson, Grade 10
Richard McKenna Charter School, ID

Stranglehold
Did you think you could resist yourself?
Like an apple,
   Ripe at its zenith,
You have been plucked,
   Pulled
By your own hand.

I warned you.
But no ears chose to listen.
They heard,
   But did not listen

I showed you,
   But your eyes would not see.

I saw.

And while you pulled yourself down,
   You pulled the anger from my heart,

Like a sliver.
Chase Brady, Grade 12
Alta High School, UT

Power to the Generation
Out of control children
share life's beauty
to say no
just in time
keeping the world
and every day memories
screaming
…pass it on.
Katie Schilling, Grade 12
Alta High School, UT

Immortal Treasures

Let those with friends, long life, strength, wealth and might
Boast in their worldly gains and pleasures now.
Let them to gaudy jewels their lives devote
And crowns of pride that circle round their brows.
Let them rejoice in temp'ral places
With furnishings of velvet, sumpt'ous gold.
Oh let them boast in ever craved desires
And never satiated lusts grown old.
But those who trust in things unseen, and boast
In never-fading wealth, and seek not crowns
That pass away, eternal joy shall gain,
Where pleasure in its truest form abounds.
   Forgo corrupt and earthly pleasures
   And live to gain immortal treasures.

Leah Weigley, Grade 12
Covenant High School, WA

Courage Is Standing Alone…
Friendship Is Knowing You Don't Have To

You try to stand alone
Against all you fear.
They try to knock you down
But they can't quite get you there.
They start to get you scared
But you think of getting home.
They hit you and bruise you
But you are no longer alone,
Because your friends are there
So you don't have to stand alone.
Just when you need them most
When you are about to hit the floor
Your friends are there to catch you
Because they know that you are there for them
When they need you most.
So when you think
You are standing alone just remember
All who love you even when they're gone.

Tyler Richardson, Grade 10
Oak Harbor High School, WA

The Tranquil Ocean

As the waves come rolling in
And the sun sets lower and lower
Into the sky
All I can think of is
The beauty of the sun's reflection
On the water and the soft,
Cool sand beneath my feet
Sifting in my toes
As I walk down the beach.
The deafening roar as the ocean waves crash on the water,
The salty ocean air fills my nostrils,
Intoxicating me and transporting me to simpler times
With no worries.

Monica McGrew, Grade 12
Nampa Sr High School, ID

Indecision

My mind is a jumbled maze of twisted roads.
One road will bring me happiness,
While another road will bring me indecision.
A third road will bring harm my way.
My conscience tells me one thing,
But my heart and mind say another.
Indecision is my constant companion.
Doubt is always my best friend.
Right and wrong have been instilled in me,
But the desire to fit in is strong.
Being a teen is hard.
In taking the wrong roads we let ourselves down.
We diminish our confidence, destroy trust.
Luckily, each day brings a chance at redemption.
Daily challenges give us the courage to pick a new road.
Knowledge gives us the wisdom to travel the right path.
I try harder to visualize consequences.
My mind is a jumbled maze of twisted roads.
I strive to travel down the right ones.
Please be patient with me.
Being a teen is hard.

Amber L. Hall, Grade 12
Sparks High School, NV

The Night Beast

I jump in the stalling darkness,
Soar through the cool, damp air
Running like the ferocious tigers,
The ones in my sleepy time dreams.

Over the high plaster walls,
Past the sentry towers and guards
Thrown past the market stalls
Under the archways and bridges

Free in the night, alone in forever
The beast is awakened, the feeling emerged
Born from idle curiosity, created by the day
The path is now open, I dash away.

Tim Coulter, Grade 11
Mount Si High School, WA

Time

Time passes by too fast
It doesn't even wait to give me a chance
There's never enough of it
I'm getting tired of trying to catch up with it
This weariness is making me sick
I wanna give up and let go
Grab all the clocks and throw them out the window
Maybe then we'd never grow old
So we can stay young forever
Never get old *never*!

Charmayne Jim, Grade 10
Owyhee High School, NV

She Is My World

My world has changed forever, my smile appears more often.
When I feel I can't go on in this endeavor, I see her sleep and her cheek soft as cotton.

Her hand limp, her fingers slightly curled, my finger in her palm, she tightens her grip.
She holds me and trusts me with her world. Before I leave, I kiss her tiny bottom lip.

She will never know, that with her sweet soft cheeks, she will never know, that with her fingers curl
My life is changed, my days and my weeks, in her short six months, my mind's a whirl.

She is a tiny baby with one big soul, she's sweet, my love, my Madelyn.
She plays, she smiles, she has control, for who can ignore so charming a grin?

When life was dark, and I saw no hope; when I cried and wished for more…
I saw her smile, she touched my tears and it helped me cope. I now have hope, this I know for sure.

She saved my life, my soul, and heart. I love when she "talks" in her gabasorld.
She is in my whole heart, not just a part. I love my baby sister, she IS my world!

Alli Thompson, Grade 10
Orem High School, UT

I Do Not Understand

I do not understand
Why people use ignorance as an excuse.
Why people come to Job Corps when they don't really want to be here.
Why people can't talk to each other with respect.
But most of all I do not understand
Why people put themselves through so much pain, just for love.
(people put up with things from their loved one they would never put up with from other people.)
What I understand most are people's problems.
I help people with many different troubles,
because I have lived through things that relate to their problems.
Yet, I cannot solve my own.

Sara Kirstine, Grade 12
Great Basin High School, UT

Remember…

I remember that day when my horse and I were being taught, I heard a crash overhead and sirens began to shout.
My teacher stopped her lesson, and ran up the hill to see what was the matter.
The sounds filled my ears and my horse began to act up,
I looked up again to see helicopters sounding off.
Later that day when I got home,
Tears from my mother were pouring down. So I asked what was wrong.
Before she could answer the telephone rang, I answered and it was a friend I had seen that day
She told me that you had died that you had passed on
All in one day in that plane crash that I had seen that day.
My eyes started to water and I began to shake
"Why did this happen?" "Why did you leave?"
I looked to the color's flashing across the screen and I shuddered in realization.
It was on the news, and you were taken from me and my class that day.
About a week later, a memorial was held
For both you and your husband who had died after you.
With a sigh, I now had to stand strong. And I stopped my crying,
I was alone now to stand by myself.
I will always hold you dear, in that small section of my heart, I will always remember all that you were.

Megan Stables, Grade 10
Oak Harbor High School, WA

Thought

River, you flow as do thoughts to my mind,
Constantly coming but ever changing.
Thoughts of the past are often left behind,
And they would be lost without your prompting.
Mountain, barrier standing in the way
Of my progression away from the past,
Halting my advance and making me stay
With these memories so endless and vast.
Meadow, with fields of unending flower,
You give my mind peace as it moves freely
One thought to the next, they grow in power.
As sweet fragrance they're welcomed openly.
River, Mountain, and Meadow, you all three
Unfolded my mind and helped me to see.

Mychelle Clawson, Grade 12
Sugar-Salem High School, ID

Untitled

My life was worth nothing more
Than a bird with a broken wing, who cannot soar

I had nothing to do, no where to go
And I lived on the ultimate low

My parents noticed and out of love
Sent me away to raise me above

So here I am, with a new life
The bird was fixed, with a needle and knife

I cannot imagine where I'd end up
If I ran away, and there I was stuck

I am the person I was raised to be
Because of my family's love for me

My family has always been there
And they will always care

Now my life is worth so much more
Than a bird, who still can soar

Sara Toland, Grade 10
Diamond Ranch Academy, UT

Wolf

Silent eyes in the dark.
Lonesome distant howls, somewhere in the night.
Silent echoes of their cries.
A sense of something watching, deep inside.
The cool and quiet breeze that stirs.
The sound you think you heard.
Your heart begins to race.
Then you come face to face.

Hannah Stagner, Grade 10
Priest River Lamanna High School, ID

The Sweet Feeling of Spring

Everything awakes as the sun
slowly rises in the new sky.
The snow pure and white melts as the day begins.
Water runs down the mountain
into the awaiting river.
Tiny plants brave the new weather.
Starved, sleepy animals emerge
from their temporary hideaways.
Little balls of fluff scream greedily for attention.
The gloom of winter has passed.
All is well now.
The world's hero has returned.
Lives will prosper, lives will grow up.
The circle of life continues.
The sweet feeling of spring has come.

Bailey Corbridge, Grade 10
Orem High School, UT

Radio

My station is my sanctuary.
My station is my life.
The music calms my nerves.
The music calms my soul.
Radio is not just a class.
It is an acquired responsibility.
Talking to all the listeners.
Talking to all the people who call.
I cherish every time I am on air.
I hope that it will last.
The music fades, but my memories do not.

Gary Houskeeper, Grade 10
Orem High School, UT

Dressed in Blue

A pretty little girl dressed in blue,
Whose honest stories were very true.
Beaten by her daddy dear,
That left emotional scars and a terrible fear.
A judge and a jury listening in,
A mother praying that her daughter will win.
Scared straight that he will lose,
So telling a lie is what he will choose.
The pretty little girl dressed in blue,
Was told by God what she must do.
Tell what happened but no more,
And justice will be yours forevermore.
She told the story as true as can be,
And told the judge her heavenly plea.
the judge decided what the verdict was,
Guilty of all charges for this cause:
The pretty little girl dressed in blue,
Told her story which was very true.
She did not lie as you did,
The story that you cleverly hid.

Zoe Graham, Grade 11
Diamond Ranch Academy, UT

Laughter

It rings in the air
Symbolizing happiness
Oh how sweet it sounds.
Lauren Cundick, Grade 11
Preston High School, ID

Late Nights

Between our hearts there lies a sea
Time that separates you from me

Though so close and yet so far
I cannot reach to where you are

So I'll touch you in my dreams
And dance with you on gilded beams

You left your heart with me to keep
My only comfort while I sleep
Danielle L. Feldman, Grade 11
Cascade Christian High School, OR

Grow Up Young Man

Grow up young man
You've got responsibilities
Children and your girl to care for
Don't be drowning in bottles
and hiding from adversity
Always running away to far off places
that you've never seen before

Grow up young man
I can't live my life worrying
Never knowing what to say
because I don't want to hurt you
I see you as a little child
Confused and too stubborn

Grow up young man
You're my bodyguard, remember
You have to protect me
from little brothers
and bad boyfriends
Please seek help young man
I love you too much
to watch you slip away
Ashley McMillan, Grade 11
Salt Lake Lutheran High School, UT

Summer Is…

Tank tops and shorts
Camping and fishing
Dutch oven potatoes
Swimming and sunburns
Lawn chairs on the patio.
Nick Coats, Grade 11
Preston High School, ID

In a Child's Mind

Young eyes come alive to things I cannot see,
Clear gaze focused past the ordinary fixtures of life,
Enthralled with a sight beyond the uninspired yard,
As though the hazy autumn air were filled with wonders. Look.
A command, compelling me to perceive, a doorway into his world. I look.

The castle. And there, the court of a mighty ruler.
A glimpse. Pictures gradually forming in my mind,
Like clouds scudding across the sky, parting to show a luminous sun.
I see a palace, weathered boards transformed to gleaming marble, touched with silver,
A river of golden leaves becoming the moat, to enclose our majestic haven.
Draped in satins, heavy with the memory of exotic places,
We reign. Imagination to guide our hands, the spirit of potential soaring
In the shade beneath the willow.

A call, a harsh noise,
The summoning of a mother who awaits her son, who breaks the spell.
I look around, and there, the faded boards, the sagging steps
All as though tired from their long summers' work.
No longer glistening in the brilliant light of possibility.
It's gone, the fleeting mirage of beauty and wonder, back into regular existence.
But in a moment, in a child's face lifted to mine,
Eyes that assert that ordinary is the only illusion.
Anna Szymanski, Grade 10
Haines High School, AK

Waters of Diversity

The Moon, she ascends into the placid sky,
Plunging the Sun into the ripples of the sea.
Greeting a fallen ship into the depths unheard,
Alluring shadows masquerading mischievously.

How the fridgety of my fingers paralyze the soul,
With ribbons of Incandescence tying the waves.
Crepuscular figures attempting to fragment the thread,
Daunting the mesmeric light, none of which it saves.

Such contrast — no, polar opposites! My eyes project,
As Yin and Yang traverse the ever obliterating sea,
From the nefarious wrath of Beelzebub,
To the miraculous Emmanuel of Galilee.

Pirouetting! Pendulating! Gyrating! Image after image,
Insipid! Limniad! Aqueous! Sprinkling golden rain in the sublime iniquity,
Luminescence! Resplendence! Effulgence! — Oh, what a blissful sight!
A carousel of bewitching complexity.

Complexity in simplicity,
Entangling into the massive sea.
How I, not I, passing by and by,
Am nauseous with the waters of diversity!
Lindsey Sprague, Grade 11
North Kitsap High School, WA

Congruency

Sing to me
Sing to me songs of faraway places,
Of untainted waters,
The facade of happily ever after

Serenade me like John Denver does
Don't search for meaning
Just sing

And keep singing until you believe your song,
That it is no longer theory,
But fact
Sing until I accept that everything will be all right
And you do too.

Jenny Oechsle, Grade 12
Layton High School, UT

Laughter

Laughter is the illustration on a paper
Images and memories of days past
Feelings of tears and emotions
Tied to your heart
The many smiles that will not erase
Floating in your life and mind
Some damaged
Some exposed
Some framed beautifully for all to observe
Revealed or hidden always will remain
Some may need help
To find their true happiness
Things in life change
Laughter stays the same.

Sammy Lee, Grade 11
Skyview High School, ID

My Smile

When I met you
You gave me a smile I'll never forget
When I met you
I saw how wonderful life could be
I finally believed someone was there to save me
The pointless days that dragged on were rushed away
You brought the light of day
I was in awe
I wondered where you came from
How God could create someone just like you
Then you stepped away,
Leaving me in the judging rain
To drown in my own doubt and fear
Trying to fight through the merciless ocean of abandonment
I thought I had found someone to rescue me
From this world
But no it's just me
My smile lost in memories.

Bethany Wallace, Grade 10
Hidden Valley High School, OR

Nemo's Song

The sea is my homeland, my heart, and my woe,
At once my mother, my friend, and my foe,
For the command of man will never it stain
But I myself no power attain,
But I will surrender to the sea, the sea,
And I will swear myself to the sea.
Remember your dreams here, your childhood tales:
Tales of the pirate, albatross, whale.
Songs of the mermaid's throne sing,
The ship's bell of bronze, let it ring,
And sail with me upon the sea, the sea,
And I will be at peace upon the sea.
Look to the horizon, the land you sail toward.
Look to that distant world, free from the sword.
Find the arrow of hate that pierced your heart,
Bleed yourself dry of that venomous dart,
And walk with me by the sea, the sea,
And I shall sleep beneath the sea.

Jonathan Draxton, Grade 10
Park City High School, UT

Will You?

Will you stay this night with me?
Will you love me when I get old?
Will you always be by my side?
Will you stay this night with me?
Will you help me when I am sick?
Will you be there when my tears fall thick?
Will you hold me from dusk till dawn?
Will you show me what love is like?
Will you know my every thought?
Will you make my heart whole?
Will you stay this night with me?
Will I always be in your memory?
Will you always tell me you care?
Will I always love you this fair?
Will you always know how I feel?
Will you please say you love me?

Chelcey Maughan, Grade 11
Academy for Math, Engineering, and Science, UT

Trust

Too far to reach
Too deep inside
I yearn for the feeling but it's just a fane memory inside
To tell one another
Our deepest feelings
To have someone catch me before I fall
To depend on one another
To know that they will keep their word
Too far to reach
Too deep inside
This feeling I search for I will never find

Drew Kelley, Grade 10
Idaho Arts Charter School, ID

Untitled

When fall comes silently
Fresh blue leaves
Would fall from the tree.
Will the fresh blue leaves,
Know that when fall comes,
They will be fallen leaves.
When leaves fall,
For some reason,
Why my heart becomes lonely.
Was I lonely because
I missed someone
Fall must have made me like that.
Fall must be like that
It must make everybody in the world
Lonely and depressed
The leaves and my heart
Look up at the sky up above
On a peaceful fall street.

Claire Myung, Grade 10
Idaho Arts Charter School, ID

Steps in the Sand

Walking step by step
Upon the sand, picking up
The shells hidden on the beach
The sun barely peaking on the waters
This is the memory I must leave.
Go far away from waves and ocean
No more spending long days in the sun
Back to where all you see is land
But I will forever remember
My steps in the sand.

Danielle Rodriguez, Grade 10
Alta High School, UT

Over the Moon and Back

No matter what you do,
No matter what you say,
You'll never be able
to keep us apart.
With love so strong,
You'll never understand.
I fly to the highest peak;
Seeing your face keeps me soaring
Strength inside me lights a candle,
Burning, intense, growing.
Ugliness and hatred prevails
Caught in an Edenic setting.
So if you think
That you can spread the distance,
You'll only be lighting my fire.
Over the moon and back
Into your loving arms.
You'll never be able to part us.

Mariesa Cloud, Grade 11
Tahoma Sr High School, WA

T-Mac, Iverson, Jordan and James

Some say chasing a fiery globe is a waste of time,
But without it, I wouldn't exist to write this rhyme.
I declare style, finesse, and delicacy on the hardwood,
A device to make you run faster and jump higher? I bet I could.
Faces of legends rush to my aid; why we often share the same name.
Even the ancient Greeks take part in my fame.
Many pay to see me screech across the paint,
A new pair of me might make you faint.
Concaves, stripes and lines are all part of my design,
If you could but guess what I am, the pleasure would be mine.

Answer: basketball shoes

Marisa McKane, Grade 11
Alta High School, UT

Understand

I do not understand
why I don't have a father;
why I'm in pain from it;
why he did the things he did to my sister and me.
But most of all I do not understand
why he had to have me;
why he hit me when I was a young boy;
why he called all of the other boys in the family his sons, but me.
He had me crying for a dad.
What I understand the most is that having a father
is not a good thing for me
because I did everything by myself — without a father.
All I know is that I will be a better father than he ever was.

Kelvin Thompson, Grade 12
Great Basin High School, UT

Whitman in 2006

What happened to nature?
It used to be so beautiful
Now all I see are tall buildings and cars
Buildings and cars and roads
Beautiful they are not
See that parking complex? See that area where that giant corporation is?
I remember there used to be trees there
There used to be trees, a fountain, a mountain in the back, and big rocks
Now they are gone
People are so greedy
All they care to care about is dollars
Dollars, with cents, but no sense of caring
They drive their cars, unknowingly giving themselves a death sentence
Death by poison
They all know about it
Know that what they do is bad for the world
Do they care? Do they know?
The thought does not sadly ever cross their minds
And what is even sadder is that
Even if they did
If they did, they would never do anything about it.

Harrison Hess, Grade 11
Thomas A Edison High School, OR

Prison

The prison I waste in is not made of steel.
It does not deny me light, drink, or meal.
The prison I waste in is inside of me.
The Prison I waste in no one can see.
Whenever I see her with somebody new,
My Joys, my delights, always seem few.
I try to get over her but it's useless to try.
Whenever I see her I want to break down and cry.
Her eyes are unequaled in deepness and grace.
And the world seems much brighter when I look at her face.
She's always with someone, she'll always be.
Always with someone, but never with me.

Forrest Plaster, Grade 10
Orem High School, UT

Point of View

I want to fly to the moon; all I need is a rocket.
I want to soar through the sky; all I need is a light jacket.
I want to shoot for the stars;
I want to be able to reach out and touch,
But gravity won't let me.
And if one day I get the chance,
I will go to the moon. I will! You just watch.
While I'm there I will look back and say…
"The Earth looks so perfect and peaceful,"
And you wouldn't be able to tell it's not that way,
The world is at war and countries are in famine,
So why don't we say God bless the world, and not just a nation?

Meg Cross, Grade 10
Orem High School, UT

Why Springtime Bugs Me

Springtime is beautiful
When flowers are budding;
But also at this time
The bugs are o'er flooding.
Springtime's a good thing,
Bugs are a don't;
Why can't there be someplace
Where all bugs just won't?
Those bugs, how they bug me,
All kinds and all types;
Their sizes and colors and shapes just aren't right!
I hate how they run, and I hate when they bite.
They creep on my clothes, they land on my nose,
They crawl up my sleeve, at times make me sneeze;
My skin itches and itches long after they leave!
Wherever I go, whatever I do,
They stick with me always, much like strong glue!
I'm sick and I'm tired of all of the bugs
I want to get out and away from those lugs!
But without them all no flowers there'd be
I'll have to deal with them and be grateful for trees!

Anna Melugin, Grade 10
Orem High School, UT

Life Winds

Life is like wind in a tree
Every way the wind blows
You go with it
Unless you are like a rock
That stays where it is put unless
You are picked up and put in a better place
People that are like rocks
Are usually the ones that make it
Really well in life
Well I know what I am
Do you?

Cody Adam, Grade 10
Emery High School, UT

Autumn Secrets

Autumn secrets float across a golden plain
Setting into the auburn sun
To rise once more and be blown across
The emerald sea of eternal mystery
Of long lost time in some place new
To Avalon we venture to roll in grassy knolls
Discover old stories unknown
Changing of the seasons too soon to count
The grains of rice that have been washed away
On cherry blossom tides
New blessings said for New Year's turn
On down dusty roads of despair
That morph into sunny meadows where they wait
Until next autumn when the secrets start again.

Christine Webber, Grade 10
Valdez High School, AK

Appearance of Greatness

Crept out by glaring eyes.
Held with the strength of a hundred men.
Fearing for death.
Keeping friends close.
Knowing acquaintances makes him stronger.
Holding firm for faith, in times of threats.
Not letting anyone, see him fret.
Preaching a belief to help solve problems,
But no one wants to hear.
His mighty burden made bigger by others.
Every day becomes another.
Being accused of unjust things.
Held captive until let free.
Believers are mad, but can't do anything.
Only to see him lost by the cross.
Seeing a man fall from pain.
Noticing the light leave his eyes.
A great man gone.
Close ones quiver, but they know he will be seen again.
Maybe not now, or the next year,
But in some other existence.

Preston Tripp, Grade 12
Alta High School, UT

Mom

You are my angel when I'm in need
You touch my soul
Even when I'm asleep.
When I don't have words
You speak for me.

You know me inside out
And you love me no matter how.
I have problems
And you try to help me out,
I'm crying
And you cheer me up.
Even for little reasons
You hear me out.

When there's a storm
I walk out my dorm
And I sleep in your covers
Like a little girl.

I love you mom,
I really do,
Without you
I wouldn't know what to do.
Claudia Garcia, Grade 11
Diamond Ranch Academy, UT

Sara

Sara,
Cute, intelligent.
Intimidates, counsels, laughs.
Thinking about the now.
Friend.
Hannah Hodapp, Grade 12
Great Basin High School, UT

When I Try

When I try to speak
You shut me up
When I try to reason
You do not listen

I try to hide inside myself
But you tear me open
I have nothing of my own
No cloak of concealment to don

I want to go away
Yet you hold me back
In some hidden way
All I can do is sit and take the hits

Praying that they won't leave
Eternal scars
DeAngela Davis, Grade 11
Culdesac School, ID

Those Days

I never contemplated those days would come, when you'd turn your back on us,
When you'd let somebody get to you, the way they did.
Through time you morphed into them,
But you never realized how strong your words were,
Or how they could pierce through a heart.
That day I'll never forget.

You locked yourself in the bathroom and had said your good-byes,
I remember the pounding on the door and tears streaming down your cheeks.
Confusion gets the best of us, and at that point it had the best of me,
It had twisted my ideas around deep within my head like a pretzel,
I was bewildered that you would attempt such a thing as this.

If only you knew how I felt, what you put me through,
Knowing just fragments of what you were going through,
And me feeling vulnerable all the while, I by no means knew what to utter,
Never knowing what may perhaps set you off into a frenzy.
What led you to such heart wrenching agony?
It's as if every second had led to a new slash in your heart.

I never had a notion those days would come, never thought you'd do such a thing,
As to turn your back on your own family,
And let somebody get to you the way they did,
The way he did.
Kellie Newton, Grade 10
Oak Harbor High School, WA

Secrets

Our secrets still remain.
Your true name kept inside.
Buried deep inside my heart,
unknown to those closest to me.
You showed me the way to paradise.
So many things left UNSAID and kept inside,
hidden from those who know me best.
So many questions left unanswered when we decided to part.
You stole my heart and have yet to give it back. Was I not good enough for you?
Did I not care enough? Did I not show enough of my love and affection?
What happened to separate us to opposite ends of the universe?

I love you. I miss you. I need you.
Time went by so fast when our love was strong. As our love languished,
my heart was finally crushed and gone, time goes by so dreadfully slow now.
Why did we walk away from something so great? You and I were illustrious.
Was I not enough for you?

Just love me. Hug me. Kiss me. Hold me tight and never let me go.
Our love kept secret for years. Why do I drown the memories in tears?
You make me laugh. You make me smile. Make our moments last forever, please.
I dream of the day I will wake up in paradise. I'd go to the end of the world for you.
My love is still true and these secrets will still remain.
Mercedes Mendiola, Grade 10
Oak Harbor High School, WA

My Mystery Person

This person is such a mystery.
She loves me no matter what I do.
She simply says that's history.
She says don't worry I still love you.
This person I love so much
When I am feeling sad and hurt,
Can heal me with a touch.
Why is this person such a mystery?
It's because her love for me I can't fathom.
If there are pills for perfection she must have 'em.
I try to love her like she loves me, but it's impossible
Because a mother's love is untouchable.
No matter what I do no matter what I have done,
She is proud of her son,
That's why I love my mum.

David Burton, Grade 12
McLaughlin High School, AK

Daytona 500, 2004

The day before an exciting event,
The track is full of drivers and their team,
Lined up, around the track is where they went,
Winning the upcoming race is their dream.

At last Sunday is here, so they line up,
Orderly in their lines, waiting for green,
Determined to make the chase for the cup,
Waiting for those words, everybody screams.

Jr. starting in the number three spot,
Around the track, two hundred laps they go,
Dale Jr.'s car is for sure looking hot,
Certainly Dale Jr. will win the show.

The checkered flag has been flown; there's no shame,
And Dale Jr. Pulls into victory lane.

Regina Wike, Grade 12
Union High School, OR

Night Lights

Twinkling, a sprinkling of stars in the sky,
I wish I could touch them, but they're up too high.

Shining so pretty, burning so bright,
Looking like diamonds set in the night.

Glinting like crystals caught in the light,
They keep glowing clearly with all of their might.

Lighting the sky, delighting my mind,
They stay ever-burning and guiding mankind.

Beautifully twinkling and winkling away,
I'll miss them when finally night turns to day.

Cortney Hand, Grade 12
Home School, AK

Wall of Vanity

You've worked so hard to stand where you are now,
With pomp and pow'r you kneel so low and bow,
To pricey things which men have toiled and strived.
You pushed and pulled and through your foes connived,
Those many things you thought would hold the key,
Now leaves you lost and anywhere but free.
The wall of vanity you built so high,
Has made it hard for those to hear you cry;
The one thing that I yearn to say is this,
Such walls can never stand with humbleness.
Deflower such array of pompous lust,
And with your heart take up a brand new trust,
    And soon you'll see the simplest blessings 'round,
    To trust another you had never found.

Lauren Hostetler, Grade 12
Covenant High School, WA

Stop Trying

All alone I'm like a stone
You let me down by promising a sound
Am I a mistake? Just another piece of cake
Well, wipe off your plate; try to clean your slate

Stop trying I feel like I'm dying
You always say so but how do I know
I don't know you I don't want to
I've given up there's no such luck
Go away. Far away
I'm doing just what you do
You're nothing to me; I don't want to see
So stop trying
I wish you were dying
Stop trying.

Jennifer Jorgensen, Grade 10
Emery High School, UT

United We Stand

America was like an unsuspecting bug
That was snatched by a frog
The terror that spread throughout the land
Like an oil spill in the Atlantic
Many heroes exploited their courage
That great and dreadful day
Terrorists planned to confuse and separate
Instead they bound
And tightened our goal
The design to make us weaker
Actually strengthened and united
The towers shook, trembled then collapsed
Heroes rushed in
Victims ran out
No matter what the cost
Freedom demands a price

Ryan Findlay, Grade 12
Mountain Crest High School, UT

Hate Is Striking a Match to a Fire Cracker
Hate is the lighting of the fuse.
It begins with petty arguments that never get resolved.
The tension of it all makes the fuse shorter and shorter.

The fuse gets shorter and shorter as arguments erupt into screaming quarreling fights.
Now sometimes everything gets better and the fuse stops burning,
but we all know that doesn't happen often so the fuse keeps burning getting shorter and shorter.

Until the fuse reaches its end and causes a violent explosion of tears and pain.
Tearing friends, family, and lovers apart.
Hate is the striking of a match to a firecracker.

Brian Silveira, Grade 10
Oak Harbor High School, WA

Life
Life is a never-ending maze, full of twists, turns, and dead ends.
As we start off, most of us have good attitudes, but as we get deeper and deeper into the maze we may get frustrated.
When we hit dead ends or seem to never get out of a twist we might get completely hopeless.
When we reach this hopelessness, it determines our true character and who we really are.

This hopelessness can become a turning point in our life.
It is when we get to choose what type of person we want to become.
It is also a time when we can start making the best of things.
And then we can turn the twists, turns, and dead ends of our maze into challenges, adventures, and achievements.

Holly Hancock, Grade 10
Pocatello Sr High School, ID

Presence*
Your presence liberated me from the oppression of misery. The cogency of your love proves competent to indulge more than a man's moral needs. So satisfied I am with your sophisticated and prestigious ways, that I preserve my profligate life and mark the inception of a pregnant couple. To integrate our bond "Till death shall we part" will be the summit of our relationship, a bond worth speaking and a promise worth keeping. Like an angel, your face entertains the art of Heaven with an endless light that would set the sun in shame. I came to terms with life and found a meaning to live, because you are my life and with you I'm living. Years previous, darkness dominated and corrupted the purity of my heart; deep-seated with hatred I rested with no peace. This jaded my will to live until an angel came along and in her I found peace and now the pain forever ceased.

Phang Thach, Grade 11
McLaughlin High School, AK
*Dedicated to my best friend Kristyn Saephanh

Education = Sky's the Limit
Education is key to any and everything with this key you can do things beyond your wildest dreams,
without this key you'll open the door to useless schemes.
People say education is overrated, but those are the ones who've been baited
baited into the world thinking that street smarts is enough and all you have to do to be successful is be tough.
But tough doesn't get you a job in the White house, tough doesn't get you a mansion down South, tough gets you in prison and
jail while your wife works minimum wage to pay your bail.
Wouldn't you want to be a entrepreneur or scientist, instead of scrubbing floors and washing dishes, wouldn't you rather have
your own office and assistant instead of wondering if he's going to fire you over the smallest thing you did,
Wouldn't you rather be at the top sticking it to the man instead of at the bottom holding out your hand, wouldn't you rather be
a teacher enlightening kids with education instead of bumming for quarters at the train station.
Or maybe you want to work at an accounting firm instead of at the soup kitchen waiting for your turn or wouldn't you love to
explore the stars instead of robbing and stealing cars.
Well whatever role it is you want to fit EDUCATION COMES FIRST THEN SKY'S THE LIMIT!!!

Raissa Lyles, Grade 11
Rancho High School, NV

My Days Are Spent at the Beach

The ocean is where I am most at home,
Here I was born fifteen summers ago,
Since then I have come to let my thoughts roam,
I sit on the beach watching the tide flow,
Guiding the flotsam and the jetsam in,
To live, I need the ocean, this I know,
Because the sea creatures are now my kin,
I have spent so much time here, they know me,
I play with the crabs and collect seashells,
And take long walks in the sand just to see,
Children with sandcastles, shovels, and pails,
I love the ocean with its salty taste.
The sun sets too fast I think with sorrow,
But I'll soon be back again tomorrow.

Nadine Wrye, Grade 10
Capital High School, WA

The Secret of the Summer Skies

The darkness of midsummer's night.
Its bolero is all but light.
For this demon covers all,
The sun cannot neglect its call.
It will come eventually,
You cannot beg, nor could you plea.
Inevitable, but therein lies
The secret of the summer skies.
One small orb shines through the night.
It crashes in and wins the fight.
Its soft glow is just enough
To show darkness it's not so tough.
It serenades a song of love,
A requiem from high above.
To sing the Earth to peaceful sleep
While through darkness its light does creep.

Erica Peterson, Grade 10
Oak Harbor High School, WA

The Time Had Come

The thrill was the greatest ever,
The blood ran through the veins,
The hands were as cold as ice,
The heart was beating like thunder,
The time was now.

Time to show how hard you had worked,
This sport was hard and full of dedication and heart,
Day after day the work was brutal,
The time was here to prove some heart.

The whistle blew and the time had come,
All thoughts were on the match,
When the results were in,
You had won.

Zachary Steele, Grade 10
Orem High School, UT

Graduate

The whole world fits inside of your head,
Wake up because you're brain dead,
Inspiration would give you light,
Maybe you need some insight,
You cannot see the world by the light of a firefly,
Life will soon pass you by,
Conquer your troubles,
Before they multiply and your crisis doubles,
The sun would shine,
And your heart could join mine,
We could take to the air,
To do whatever we dare,
Put on that cap and gown,
Then you can skip town,
Make the grade,
I am here to aide,
Give yourself life,
Or I can never be your wife.

Shayla Dalgliesh, Grade 11
Prairie High School, ID

Mountains

On hot days keep in mind the mountain's ring
An elevation high, respite from heat.
Those towers tall with forests green in spring,
Untamed, so rocky, steep, and high so neat.

The rushing water tumbles over rock,
That provides shade for even fish in lakes.
The deer and moose will roam for miles to dock,
A wolf on track for food will cause the quakes.

Be watching out for falling trees that die
The quiet isolation marks the peace
The camping trips in mountains make one cry,
The healing peace will cause the pain to cease.

The view from overhanging cliffs so dire,
A lovely sight that sets one's soul on fire.

Adeline Lustig, Grade 12
Prairie High School, ID

Lasting*

We haven't known each other very long,
But our relationship is getting strong.
We might do things we both regret,
But that night we said "I love you" we will never forget.
From that night to this day and until I die,
My love for you is as amazing as a summer sunrise.
Our love for each other will last forever,
And no matter what happens we will stay together.
You have healed the hurts from the past,
This is one of many ways I know we will last.

Arthur Harabedoff, Grade 10
River Ridge High School, WA
*Dedicated to Jenny Fyfe

Mirage

In a desert wasteland I once wandered,
Searching for a well,
Imagined drops materialized,
To my parched lips they nearly fell,
An oasis I envisioned,
Within my troubled mind,
With hope I struggled onward,
Relief I did not find,
A pool appeared before me,
It covered the dry land,
As I walked towards it,
The water turned to sand.

Lauren Womack, Grade 11
Preston High School, ID

In Vain

The autumn wind is cold and fresh
I'm sitting down in front of him
Staring at his cold pale flesh

Looking past the black suits pressed
The setting of his tomb is grim
The autumn wind is cold and fresh

They speak as if they knew him best
But I know my memories will never dim
Staring at his cold pale flesh

Watching as he's put to rest
Sobbing, remembering his constant grin
The autumn wind is cold and fresh

Is the bullet still lodged in his chest
Yes, stuck in him like a needle pin
Staring at his cold pale flesh

Preventable? Maybe only with the vest
And that man is still on a win
The autumn wind is cold and fresh
Staring at his cold pale flesh

Sky Harrison, Grade 12
Alta High School, UT

It Can Be Given

It can be given,
It can be returned,
It can crack,
It can be fixed,
It can even be
Thrown away,
But it can never be
Broken
Completely…
Love is a gift

Eric Conner, Grade 10
Oak Harbor High School, WA

As She Drives By

She's grace; she has faces in many ways
You can tell she's going to go somewhere in life
She's dedicated in what she does and she has fun with all the above
She's very unique and full of stage
Things get tired, but she holds on for long
Time passes, time flies
She takes time out of every day to think of what brings her to this day
She has courage for words and ways for her pain
She paints her portrait of black and white
She never fails to fight for what's right
She's a one and only person
A one and only type
She's shamed by things and famed by face
She captures scenes of life
There's no example to figure her out
She is starred and she is untimed
She finds a place where she could cry
Wonders and wanders through every day
Walking the streets knowing she can breathe
There is nothing ruined for this child, she only comes once in a while
Don't forget her or you may forget yourself.

Samantha Coughlin, Grade 11
Clover Park High School, WA

Life's a Video Game

Life's a video game you have chances and you can start over.
You can win and you can lose. There are many obstacles.
Problems to overcome, friends to obtain and enemies to destroy.
Allies to make. But if you lose this game well it's game over.

Kris Fisher, Grade 10
Oak Harbor High School, WA

The Eastern Light

The time he was in the forest
and the woods were green and live
with the feeling of mystery. With the morning sun rising in the east
and the fish jumping in the big lake toward the west,
he cast his line in
and waited.

As he lay in the sun he realized that a cloud had grown
over him and was growing bigger yet.
Looking at the clouds he found entertainment
in the beautiful shapes it made. Watching the swirling movement
he was distracted from his task at hand.
The only thing that could rescue him
from the entrapment was the sun.
It broke the clouds and burnt his sight which made the fisherman look away.

As he cast his line back he sat and waited.
The evening light was retreating
towards the western sky, casting long shadows of the mystery.
The forest was turning gray
as he began his way home, towards the east.

Lance Abbott, Grade 11
Cascade Christian High School, OR

My Life

My future begins today,
Whether it's fast food or Broadway.
Nothing is left in my mother's hands,
No more chores, bedtimes or commands.
What shall I do and where should I go,
Paris, France or Alaska…Barrow?
Is this world ready for me?
I'll take a chance and you will see.

Crystal Jones, Grade 12
Kodiak High School, AK

The Lost Soul

In a corner of a dark room,
Lies a helpless soul.
Her bony hands reach out for help,
Her scratchy voice just wants to be heard.
Her hair as black as spades
Defines her white chalky skin,
Which glows in the moonlit room.
A burning hot tear glides down her cold cheek,
Pain shadows her once again.
She gasps for air,
Grasping the cold brick wall.
She can't hold on, not one second more.
Pain pierces her mind
As scenes of the past burn her eyes.
The strings which once controlled her,
Commanding her right, left, here, there,
Have now withered away.
She falls through the thick crisp air
That slices her lungs, cutting off her last breath of life.
She falls and reaches,
But never finds a place of belonging, a place of love.

Lynette Phillips, Grade 12
Preston High School, ID

Left Behind

With tears in her eyes she came through the door,
Looked at her mom, threw her bag to the ground.
She sat and let her tears fall to the floor,
Her mom looked at her and didn't make a sound.

Her heart was sad because of what was done.
He left them without a warning at all.
She did not know where the place was he'd gone,
When he left she felt like she was quite small.

Why did he leave, what was wrong with this man?
Didn't he care of the feelings she had?
What happened to him, he just left and ran.
Nothing eased the pain, not even a tad.

But one thing could take away all the pain,
He died on a cross, His body was slain.

Mirjum Woods, Grade 10
McKenzie River Christian School, OR

Walking the Halls

Moving through the halls of high school
You see everyone
But
Are they just a person to get past?
Or
Do you know them?
Maybe
But are you turning them into a memory?
Or are they going to be something that happened?
Are you remembering whom you passed?
Or
Are you only getting to class on time?

Kade Pedersen, Grade 10
Orem High School, UT

A Lovely Truth

I sat to write of love not long ago,
But as I sat and pondered what to pen,
A sullen voice accosted me and then
Reminded me that "love" I'd never known.

"Not so!" I cried, and thought of all those loves
To which I daily give my simple heart:
My love for life and for its every part!
Would these then be a lesser form of love?

So sat I sulking in my pensive mood,
Attempting there to somehow then produce
A way to see if truer were the one.

But then with happy sigh I ceased to brood,
And smiled within as thusly I deduced:
A romance is but one of many loves.

Alison Duever, Grade 12
Santiam Christian School, OR

The Minions of Takhisis

Oh the dragons, of my dreams,
Fly by color, fly in teams.
The dark ones come, and now are here,
Roughly taking what was dear.
First the small ones, white and bold,
Live in lands, harsh and cold.
Now the blues, with powers of lightning,
They are loyal, fierce when fighting.
Come now red wyrm, hot like sun,
Handler of fire, the largest one.
See the black's fly, full with power,
Evil kings, their venom sour.
Last of all, the green lizards soar,
Down below, the acids pour.
On the field of battle, they come,
Their darkness flowing, the damage done.

Riley Barrington, Grade 10
Pleasant Grove High School, UT

The River
Gently it cascades
Through the woods
Cutting a moist band
With its flow
  Tossing,
  Turning,
  Rumbling,
Accelerating through the rapids
Tumbling to a halt
In the lake.
Greg G. Russom, Grade 11
Preston High School, ID

Incomplete Game
The days are
Lonely,
I weep under my
Prolonged mask
Of envy.
The same thoughts,
Feelings,
Collide into a
Bundle
Of anxiety.
I can't think,
Can't feel.
My body is lying
In the middle of
Utter silence.
No words are spoken
To my soul.
Just longing for
The puzzle
To be created
Once more.
Bonnie Rosell, Grade 11
Diamond Ranch Academy, UT

You Never Walk Alone
You never walk alone, my friends
Though you may think you do.
For in your sorrow and despair
God always walks with you.

There's no hour, no passing by
He is not by your side
And though unseen He is still there
To be your friend and guide.

Whenever you think you walk alone
Reach out and you will find
The hand of God to show the way
And bring you peace of mind.
Tommy Okpeaha, Grade 12
McLaughlin High School, AK

What Is This Face?
What is this face,
Which holds disgrace?
What is this mouth
That speaks?

Through unturned pages yearned
This soul it cannot see.
Hidden between the lines
The memories unfold.
Unforgotten words;
Stories left untold.
Abby Artig, Grade 10
Salt Lake Lutheran High School, UT

Oh, Look!
I can't write my poem
My pencil lead broke
You don't believe me
You think it's a joke
It's serious as ever
And plus, my paper fell
Come to think of it,
I am not feeling too well
With all this noise around me
I cannot concentrate
Would you accept it
If I turned it in late?
Never mind that,
'Cause it's never getting done
My headache's grown worse
And you said this'd be fun
So I'm not writing my poem
I'll just turn in a blank sheet
I'll never write a poem
Oh, look! It's complete
John Potter, Grade 10
Central Kitsap High School, WA

My Mom
Gave birth to me
takes me to school
helps me with homework
buys me clothes.

Cooks me food
supports me in everything
cares for me when I'm sick
hugs me when I'm sad.

She is an example to me, my hero
I don't know what I'd do without her.
She's my everything
thank you mom, I love you.
Kristin Hunsaker, Grade 10
Orem High School, UT

Sincerity
"Sincerity" is a church
A nun, quiet and peaceful
Waiting in search
Of true honesty

A pastor, just hoping
That one day he can make a difference

A choir, ready to sing
Of what they believe
Knowing they will be heard
Knowing what is right
Madison Gingrich, Grade 11
Nampa Sr High School, ID

Summer Storm
A gentle drop of light
descending from above.
The sun in all its might
is raining down its love.

A stillness in the air;
silence to be heard.
Clouds gather, white and fair.
Peace is not assured.

The wind begins to blow.
The clouds have all turned black.
Deep rumbles start to grow
as lightning breaks in cracks.

Harsh rain tears up the soil.
Dripping leaves cling to life.
Violent noise sings turmoil
while Nature hands out strife.

A stillness in the air;
silence to be heard.
Clouds lighten, white and fair.
Peace is now assured.
Justin Hammer, Grade 10
Orem High School, UT

My Shadowed Eyes
Just another face a reflection
Another person on the street
Lost in thought caught in —
Netted like a fish slowly
Caught in the threads of time
So easily over looked, forgotten
Potential hidden driven away
Driven by others waves
Natalie Howell, Grade 10
Pleasant Grove High School, UT

Romance

You and me, glass and water,
Both a liquid, both are clear.
But one flows swift, while the other takes an age
To find its way from here to there.
Yet even I, a child much like glass,
Can find that destination.
You, my dear, a beautiful flowing river
Can make a course and flow to where you wish to be.
We are akin, and very different
The rain does fall caressing the windowpane.
A kiss of a lover on the face of the lady.
So easy to break, so easy to manipulate
But gentle is the touch from the misted air.
You go places while I stay.
A world full of days, for me, is all the same.
I always will know however far you go,
You will return to me.

Bobbi Gooby, Grade 10
Sandpoint High School, ID

Gary Hiltbrand

My family was my life,
And I worked hard to give them joy.
I was proud of my daughters,
And when Lacy won the beauty pageant it was amazing.
I worked hard at that title agency
To keep it running smoothly.
I had no signs of being sick
When all of a sudden there was a twist,
But no one knew until it was too late.
That night I never thought that it would end this way
When my heart failed and all was lost.
I was only 53 and still young inside,
But in the end I saw the love from my family.
They cared so much
And yet I knew that things were not the same,
In that time I saw that they knew me in their hearts
And even if they didn't know me in life they know me now
Because my family loved me.

Patrick Hiltbrand, Grade 10
Pocatello Sr High School, ID

Life as a Plant

I feel like a plant sometimes,
Being battered by the winds.
My stem is weakening,
as my leaves wilt into the mud.
The cold chills me down to my deepest layer,
and the rain plunders through my outreached roots.
But I know we plants will make do;
though it seems like the end,
we will prevail,
and pop up again soon.

Anna Whipp, Grade 11
Cascade Christian High School, OR

Skiing

Life is a ski resort on a good snow day.
Conditions are cold, smooth, and soft.
Skiers float through drifts effortlessly
while attempting to breathe between face-shots of snow.
You laugh happily on the lift with your friends.

Then the temperature warms;
water droplets form and drip from your skis.
Sharp, jagged rocks emerge at the surface of the snow.
They cut everything in their path,
tearing up your equipment.
Then the next snowstorm comes and covers them up.

Ali Gray, Grade 10
Pocatello Sr High School, ID

The Message

"Blessed be," said the angel to the poor man
Who had nothing but the sad thoughts in his head.
And blessed he was,
For the angel gave the poor man
A message from above.
He said, "God loves all his children,
All you have to do is give;
Give just one simple thing, that someone else might need,
And God will deliver you
If only you do heed."
And although the poor man had nothing
He looked for those who had it bad
To give just one simple thing,
The only thing he had.
The message from the angel traveled to and fro
And reached the ears of others
who had nowhere else to go.
And down came the angel
From Heaven once again
This time to deliver one very special man.

Kendra Bazzano, Grade 12
Diamond Ranch Academy, UT

Head Games

When you broke up with me, that really hurt
But now we always seem to flirt
Why did you dump me if it's not what you wanted
It felt like you tore my heart out and stomped it
The way you flirt with me makes me miss you more
But I still don't get what you broke up with me for
I don't know if you miss me or even want me back
But it seems that way through the way you act
I know, I miss you and I still want to be with you
If I had one wish, it'd be that you'd feel this way too
Would you ever consider giving us another chance
In this little confusing thing of romance
But all I'm really asking you,
Is do you still feel this way, too?

Trista Whited, Grade 11
Buhl High School, ID

Rainbows

Red, orange, yellow
Green, blue, indigo, violet
Beams made only from
A beautiful mixture of
Warm sunshine and gentle rain.
Clover Elizabeth Golightly, Grade 11
Preston High School, ID

My Loss

Where are they, the few I knew
Gone, are the ones I cared for,
We met in school, but I played at home,
Where have they gone, my few friends.
We played
We laughed
We cried
We danced
We sang
We did so much together.
Now down the barren halls I walk.
I never said "Good Bye,"
I never said "I'll miss you,"
I never said anything,
I just left
My life has restarted,
My heart has healed,
Some,
But I still wish I could see you.
Yes, one last time
Tristan Fishman, Grade 10
Idaho Arts Charter School, ID

Thank You

It's been hard.
Moving so many places
Less would have been good.
It's been hard.
Never having close family
More would have been good.
It's been hard.
Going to seven different schools
Less would have been good.
It's been hard.
Until now never having a best friend
More would have been good.
It's been hard.
Having no place to call my home
Less would have been good.
But what can I do.
It's happened.
I've met many people
And done many things
In the end it will have made me stronger!
Thank you.
Joseph Moreno, Grade 10
Windward High School, WA

Beautiful Roses Await

Why do the roses die?
Why are violets always blue?
Why does sugar taste sweet temporarily?
Why does my heart feel this way?

Questions that will always be questioned
Questions that leave scars on my heart
It bleeds as time reaps away at it
Broken, cold and empty; no, I cannot do this alone

Invisible light shines through the darkness somehow
I grasp it; holding on with hopes to find life
Where I cannot stumble, shed tears of emptiness and fear the unknown
I will fall, but you will catch me
I will cry, but you will kiss the tears away
I will fear, but you will comfort me

I wait for the next season
Where roses will never die,
Where violets will never cry,
Where sugar is sweeter than ever
Growing and withering shape me,
As the everlasting ticking of time unfolds its many mysteries
A priceless present of love
Marie O'Neill, Grade 10
Newport Sr High School, WA

Gossip

Gossip is an unbridled horse.
Restrained, he is harmless enough,
grazing quietly and unnoticed.
but the minute someone forgets and leaves the gate open,
all hell breaks loose.

He gallops through town destroying all in his path.
Kicks in a window, stomps through a flower bed,
and nearly tramples a passerby.
Still he charges on, disrupting daily life and knocking everything off balance.

Finally corralled by a brave soul, the town is left to shift through the rubble.
The window is replaced, a new bed of tulips is planted, the passerby receives stitches,
And a higher, thicker fence with a heavy gate and a shiny lock is built around Gossip.

But the new window is drafty in the winter
The flowers aren't as vibrant or healthy as their predecessors,
And the passerby is left with a permanent scar.

And as for Gossip?
He spends his days quietly grazing in his secure new pen.
The lock on the gate is beginning to rust.
Erin Stutesman, Grade 12
Parkrose High School, OR

Death's Candle Lit

The foolish worldlings every day submit,
In letting down their guard, temptations slay
All Christian holdings there, death's candle lit
The Bible's leadings quickly blown away
The star of God within us soon will fade,
If we neglect to fight the devil's snare,
Far from the hand of God we all have strayed
In sinning we now drift to Satan's lair.
That evil tempter's power may surprise
'Tis stronger than a man may ever think
We must prepare to in this struggle rise
For if we are not ready we will sink
    But focusing on Christ will win us through,
    And cleanse our bloodied hearts to make them new.

Ben German, Grade 11
Covenant High School, WA

Being Blinded

The eye of prejudice one's soul consumes,
With every first impression misconstrued.
Believing everything you hear is folly,
And to this new design our old subdued.
We look at others lower than ourselves,
And our own eyes, this fault, we cannot see.
Our pride will make us "partial, blind, absurd;"
And leave us all alone in agony,
The selfishness so bound inside of us,
Needs only recognition as its cure.
To lose all vanity and be content,
Will leave you with the chance to love so pure.
    No worth is found in prejudice and pride;
    No honor when behind some hate you hide.

Sandra Morrow, Grade 12
Covenant High School, WA

When Dreams Begin

There is a time when dreams begin,
When eyes close shut and minds give in,
There all your world becomes abstract,
There your life becomes an act,
There fiction can become a fact,
And all high hopes can win.

Let's leave this world of troubled strife,
And enter the land of fantasy,
Where the sky is green and the grass grows blue,
And three and three can equal two,
You'll find there's nothing you can't do,
In the time when dreams begin.

Yes three and three will equal two,
And you'll find there's nothing you can't do,
For all that's false can now become true,
In the time when dreams begin.

Jennifer Christensen, Grade 12
Mountain Crest High School, UT

Emotions

Emotions are the creator of your body's reactions
That exists in the pit of your stomach
And conducts the flow of feelings
And knows no restrictions

And as air is discreet
Physically it does not exist
But its existence you can feel

Emotions fill the soul
Without them you are empty
It's the essence of life
It's a sensational feeling that comes from within

Marisela Luna, Grade 11
Nampa Sr High School, ID

Despite All Things

Prejudice is a black dog looking for a white fire hydrant
Despite the love
Despite the hate
Despite the friendship
Despite the truce
There's the dog looking for the fire hydrant
Black dog white fire hydrant
White dog black fire hydrant
It doesn't matter both ways we feel like nothing
Despite the love
Despite the hate
Despite the friendship
Despite the truce
The truth is we were all the dog and the fire hydrant
Once

Tosh Welshans, Grade 10
Oak Harbor High School, WA

I'll Remember

Do you remember that time
We laid out on your deck
Looking at the ebony sky?
Do you remember?
We each picked out one of those
Buttercup stars and made it our own.
Every night we would go out
And find our gleaming stars.
Do you remember now?
I still look up at my bright star,
And I think of you.
I see your almond eyes,
Our sandy faces laughing at the sapphire sky.
Though fields of gold separate us now,
You are still my best buddy,
Always, and forever.

Marissa Floodman, Grade 10
Alta High School, UT

My Generation

Influenced by what we see, what we hear, what they do.
Swaying to the rhythm of generations.
Authority hunts us down, freedom blows us away, falling faster through the crowd.
Finding a difference in an army of one and a world of billions.
Who's to say when we should leave or stay.
I'm your daughter and he, your son, marching to a drum of monotones.
Dulling the dreams inside our heads, numbing our minds from growing apart.
Tradition stuck in our skulls, guns glued to our hands.
Right and wrong is duking it out like Mike Tyson and Muhammad Ali:
Too strong for our own good, too fast for our own feet.
We don't know how to quit while we're ahead, we don't know when to just shut our mouths.
We start tumbling down in a fury.
Then the bell rings and we go right back to where we started.
Now, just a little more tired, just a little more bruised.
But now we know when to strike and when to duck.
Don't give up, keep pushing yourself. We're bound to step on a few toes.
Remember, there's nothing wrong with apologies.
Don't let your pride wave too strong.
Keep your flag at half mast, until the day comes,
when we're all grown up enough to understand,
that it's easier to raise a flag with more than one hand.

Fallon Hankins, Grade 11
Mountain View High School, WA

The Sounds of the Creek and the Beauty of the Forest

The forest seems to me to be the best of nature's world.
Everything is green and peaceful.
Trees and plants are everywhere,
I am grateful for the forest.

Flowers are blooming and colorful.
Seems like the spring is coming.
The flowers sense it is time to grow.
The road seems to be nicely patched in dirt, and fences surround the sides.
Trees are covering the road and keeping it shady in areas.

The squirrels, rabbits, butterflies, deer, birds are many!
They are making happy noises and playing in the water from the creek.
It means the summer is coming but first comes the spring.
The creek is making peaceful music-like sounds which babble down along the rocks underneath.

The sky is brilliant blue with little bits of clouds. Such beauty!
This is my favorite time of the year.
This season takes me into relaxed and happy moods.

Anna Henkel, Grade 12
Mount Si High School, WA

Why

As I lay here thinking back on those days when I used to be free. I see that this is a true tragedy.
Many died in that hard fight many cried on that fateful night. Our tears were just our fears in trust. We lost what we love. We
hated who we saw. This man, this figure of power. How can one man be our savior? How can we believe what can't be seen?
Who are we to trust what must be just? I don't see what to believe. I can't tell what to follow or why I have to. Can't I be my own
savior, my own god? Must we cry over lost loves? Must we die to prove our might? Why did it have to be, can you truly not see?

Katie Sanders, Grade 10
Crater High School, OR

The Explosive Seed

A seed of sin is sown within my mind
It probes and digs in search of lust to find.
I know it's wrong with such desires to start,
They cause such damning pain within my heart.
My crafty heart is blinding dim my sight,
To think on lust as lovely, pure, and white.
So thoughts, come now, a further step I'll take,
While sin assaults my soul as did the snake.
Although undone within my heart the sin
Is lurking low and hopes the siege to win.
These thoughts themselves aren't wrong, but tread a path
That leads to death: to my deserving wrath.
    I've failed Him now, the fruit I ate in vain,
    My hopeless state, bears now the sinful stain.

Clark Edwards, Grade 10
Covenant High School, WA

Evil Is Good in Disguise

For all the Goodness in the universe,
    those who know it do not understand it.
But to conceive the knowledge is to corrupt one's wisdom,
    for no Good comes without a counterpart.

To keep balanced the two forces in eternal suspense,
    Evil comes into being.
    The Force that which all despise,
is inevitably the misunderstood thing.
For its ever existence is a gift, bequeathed
    by the desired pureness of Good.

What defines those that are Good,
    defines, in turn, the living Evil,
    and if Evil did not exist,
what would be known as Good?

Zihao Xu, Grade 11
Sunset High School, OR

Pride

Beware blind pride, thou often pierce the heart
To deep unending sadness; tears spring forth
By thy entrenching grasp. 'Tis not an art,
To rip to shreds a soul of untold worth,
Instead, 'tis only selfishness amiss.
Strange, self-condemning god of blasphemy,
Though wilt, along with partner prejudice,
And cousin vanity, be put to death.
Unless, of course, that little, unknown fact
Performs an awesome transformation now;
Through shame and horror, fill the humble lack.
Self-interest sleeps… to ardent love, arouse!
    The crit'cal eye by nature spies a speck
    Before it hauls the plank of timber wreck.

Deanna Strohm, Grade 12
Covenant High School, WA

Secret

A secret is a chameleon changing colors,
Movable eyes looking deep into the soul,
Waiting to hit with its enormous tail,
Swifting, shifting, soundlessly in the wind,
Like a leaf in early autumn.

Stormy clouds starry night,
Lurking predators in shadowy sights,
Jumping out of the soul,
Like a frog leaping out of a hand.

Truly keeping it close,
To the caring heart,
Holding it until it is no more.

Israel Vidales, Grade 11
Nampa Sr High School, ID

Tried

When that lightning in the sky fades
the ground is soft and damp;
more or less than it was before.
Those bright eyes of yours fade as well.
Unlike those stars that creep into the night.
Moon shining so bright…
unlike that sun that failed to make the light.
Some of those whom even breathe upon it.
The living of the day can rest.
No more will there be violence
among the love caressed night.
The cares gone, no longer existent.
The shadows fall later in a hidden time.
Through the beam of the dim light
the moon soon creates those sounds casting eerie sights.
I walk upon the nightly air as it facades into the mist.
Those dark corners,
those lonely thoughts…
though once and always you must resist.

Jasmine Edayan, Grade 10
Arts & Communication High School, OR

Peter

He looked so happy and content with is life,
He always knew just what to say to make you laugh,
But who would know it would all soon end
With a jagged knife or a deep swim.
Just what went wrong to take his own life?
No one knew why but soon they would know,
The last days he spent he wasn't alone.
For we were all there,
Near or far,
Thinking of him and wishing on that star,
That one day we might find out just what went wrong.
That one awful day,
The last time he decided to say goodbye.

Missy Angell, Grade 10
W F West High School, WA

Rose at Midnight
Ruby red petals rustle in the wind.
This exquisite beauty,
Too perfect for words.
Her emerald stem stands tall and proud.
Moonlight pierces through the clouds.
Midnight comes on the back of the wind.
A quiet sigh,
A stolen kiss,
Then all is silent.

Julie McNeely, Grade 11
South Whidbey High School, WA

Easing into Rest
Eyes begin to droop
Drifting into the empty darkness
That surrounds me
I feel my chest rise and fall
Slower and slower with every breath
I hear nothing but the twitch of a finger
And the blink of my eyes
The warmth of my blankets
Is overwhelming
Giving way to relaxed muscles
All I taste is the heat
Rising off of my body
And all I smell is the crisp
Linen pillows I rest my head upon
Just before giving way to sleep

Lindsay Burt, Grade 12
Sumner Sr High School, WA

Dreams
Released as the wind blow
Limitless as the ocean
Uncontrolled as the clouds
Boundless as the rainbow
Without a care in the world
Nothing to be alarmed about
Just free

I will never ever be free
As anything
I will forever be me
For eternity I will always
Have a concern in my heart
I will constantly care about someone

For once I wish
I was unbound of me
I hope I didn't have a care or
A trouble in my soul

Just free
Of the world

Rogina Mojumder, Grade 10
Reno High School, NV

True Love
True love is the soul's sanctity within another;
it comes with the blissful song that is longingly waited to be heard.
It is surrendering your heart to soar with another's.
True love is the sensuous feeling that reaches so deep,
it can never be forgotten, and is always yearning to be embraced.
It feels like the color of the crimson skies at sunset,
passionately surrendering its heavenly light for two people to hold.
It is the beautiful kiss that motionlessly bonds the purity of love for another.
Forever it is felt, captivating the essence of time.
True love never perishes,
it brings forth the moment of truth for two people who are nothing alike,
but at the same time are seen as one.

Jessica Dettmann, Grade 10
Fremont High School, UT

Remembrance of the Moon
The harsh cold moon in October
Pierced my heart over and over
It reminded me of the numerous moons
I once shared with the one I loved
Before he was killed by a drunk driver
I dream of that driver sitting in his chair hitting my love
Without a care not knowing he was there
And with his last breath he whispered to me love me, forget me not
As I walked closer down the aisle to the man I will marry
I remember the words I love you, forget me not
I glance to the man I must marry, he smiles
It tore my heart to think of my love
The one I were to betray through the marriage of this man
I ran, ran from that man who smiled that day
That night I drank trying to numb my feelings away
Got in my car to visit my love in his grave
But on my way I glanced at the piercing moon
And struck a man in my way

Allison Cowan, Grade 10
Oak Harbor High School, WA

Is Life a Dream?
I keep asking myself is life a dream, no answer.
Why I ask myself this kind of question?…
I don't know!
Do you think life is a dream?…
Well I think it is, or maybe not!
My reason why I think it is a dream is because in our lives, we are first born,
grow up, have fun and then we come up to a certain point in which we die.
In our dreams it happens the same thing, but different.
We first go to sleep and then we start dreaming, remembering things.
It's basically letting our spirit travel around the world.
A lot of things could happen in our dreams.
Then you wake up! Your dream ends.
Everything you were and had, has disappeared.
You have nothing left from the dream.
Sometimes I think that life is not a dream,
because if it was then it shouldn't be called life.

Eunice Sotelo, Grade 10
Oak Harbor High School, WA

Serenity

I hear the pitter patter of rain,
The rain that is crisp to taste, smell and feel
It's night and all you see are the droplets falling
And then…Illumination

The rain is gone and there is nothing but silence
Left over the city like it never happened
I see the stars, the moon
And something else I will see soon

It's the blue sky with bright light that I will see later on in life
I do not think or dream it, but it comes
The moon I stare at makes me wonder in delight
What will happen every night

Peace, stillness
Everything I hear, everything I see,
It's night, nothing to do but rest
In the calmness of life

Jackie Gemlich, Grade 10
Spring Valley High School, NV

Dancing

Dancing is the key to my heart,
It helps me when I fall apart.
When I'm having a bad day,
I'm grateful dancing is my way.
Dancing reminds me of the rain,
It helps me through the grief and pain.
I wish that everyone could feel
The way, I feel when I get to dance all day.
So, when you feel grief or pain,
Just go out and dance in the rain.
That way your life won't fall apart,
Because dancing will be the key to your heart.

Brooke Beck, Grade 12
Alta High School, UT

Love

Personality bright as the sun,
You can turn my bad day around,
Every moment with you is a good one,
Even if I'm wishing for my grave,
The sound of you saying my name,
Or even just a smile or a wave,
You make me feel perfect inside,
I hope for you it's the same,
When I'm home and haven't seen you in three hours,
But that's three hours way too long,
So I close my eyes, wish you were here,
Dim the lights, and play our song,
Losing you is my worst fear,
When you're with me is when I feel best,
I love you Lacie, don't think any less.

Wacey Jewkes, Grade 10
Emery High School, UT

Living Life

Living life day to day,
Passing obstacles on the way.
Keeping friends close by your side,
Knowing within them you can confide.
Live your life on the edge,
And remember the country to which you pledge.
I've learned a lot through the years
Through my smiles and sometimes tears
Remember…there will always be someone there
Someone that really does care.

Chelsie Sitterud, Grade 10
Emery High School, UT

Rows of Men

Men in rows, guns in hands
Rows and rows of wild thoughts
Desperate to get home
I march a sergeant's command
Toward death, seeing fear
I look left and slowly right
To see a man one last time
I walk closer to the enemy
Ready as I'll ever be
My little girl dances through my head
Her little princess dress she wore all the time
I wonder: Does this man have a family
As I wonder, I feel a tear of the thought
I just killed a man

Tyler Brklacich, Grade 11
Woods Cross High School, UT

Hero

Everyone thinks they know who I am,
What I'm about,
And what I need in life.
They don't know who I am on the inside,
I'm a hero.
I'm a lifesaver,
I'm a lot of things that nobody will ever know about.
These actions may only be in my head,
Daydreams you may like to call them.
But it's still who I am and what I'm about.
Some people call me sick,
Maybe even think I'm a little insane.
They don't really know,
How could they ever tell what I'm thinking?
My friends want me to see a doctor
They always think they know what's best for me
Well they may know sometimes
But not all the time,
No, they don't know that I'm a hero,
Somebody that everybody looks up to.

Marci Jenkins, Grade 11
Woods Cross High School, UT

Eyes

As I look into my eyes,
I see life.
Life I never knew,
To the world beyond.
I see freedom and inspiration.
I see me the true me,
The flower that blooms in adversity.
But all I can do is wonder,
Or can I do what I see.
It is up to me,
Me and only me.
When I look into my eyes and see.

Alyssa Sperry, Grade 11
River HomeLink Program, WA

December 7, 1941

An attack on America
A day remembered forever
Soldiers of our country died
Our enemy sly and sneaky
They catch us off guard
Knowing we won't have a chance
Some of our soldiers fight back
But there is no use
The enemy has won this battle
And hurt the American family
But we will fight back
And we will overcome this enemy
Because we are America

Sterling Blackham, Grade 10
Orem High School, UT

Mountains

A majestic view
Rising above the skyline
They elevate my soul.

Caitlin Jones, Grade 11
Preston High School, ID

Choices

Victory or defeat
Right or wrong
Conscience contradicting
With the will of the throng

Appease or disappoint
Pain or glory
The difference is
An unfolding story

At last you choose
To fight or play
The consequences begin
Should you have gone another way?

Adam Judd, Grade 10
Orem High School, UT

Summer Breeze

It rustles through the leaves of the trees
And slides down their trunks.
It surfs over the grassy meadows
Spindling golden sunlight into veils of sheer bliss
As it wakes the sleeping creatures, causing them to dance.

It flies over the water, making the particles swing and glide with passion.
Creating crystals of shimmering light, wild beauty.
Untamed, it encompasses everything in its path
And shows the objects its mysterious joy
While pushing them toward breathtaking destinations.

It swims over and under the winged acrobats of the sky
And excites the lazy, loitering fluff.
It speeds along the seashore, tossing salty, stinging spray
And bounds over tsunami-like towers
While diving into calming hills.

It whispers to the sands
Telling them to "Fly!"
While it shouts around the mountains
And moves on with a reckless air.
It billows past my face and rushes on toward the sun
Running home to the distant horizon.

Ashley M. Josi, Grade 11
Tillamook High School, OR

Sidewinder

Deep rumbles please the ear,
while Hondas run in fear.
A rich strong smell drifts by their noses,
coming from its enormous hoses.
Environmentalists cry,
because the emissions are too high.
But to car buffs it's a beautiful sight,
to see this American might.

If you stomp on the gas,
its tires will wear out real fast.
You can even haul your ten point buck,
'cause this tire burner is a Dodge truck.
It drives around like an air force missile,
it looks as clean as a whistle.

The idea for this truck came from Gale Banks.
He wanted to show the world how much speed a diesel could make.
Sidewinder is its name;
World's Fastest Truck its claim to fame.
Two hundred and twenty-two miles an hour
wow this truck has power.

Jacob Simon, Grade 10
Camas County High School, ID

Victory Sings Joy

I manifest a warm summer light,
    the existence parallel to heaven.
Gleaming like an enchanted jewel,
    its laughter satisfies hope.
Dreams caress and embrace the spirit,
    remind us the zeniths of our triumphs.
Resurrected internal fait conjures courage,
    divinely massages our soul.
Feast on the riches of pleasant resolutions.
    Tomorrow, victory sings joy.

Jace Yeager, Grade 12
Columbia High School, WA

Deceiving Eyes

I'm lost within this moment of your eyes
    In a world of deception and defeat.
    But I hold on to every sting of lies
To keep the capture of your stare complete.

A love so lost and shattered 'cross the floor.
    But I will tell myself I'm whole and sane,
    Until the day you open up that door
To break this heart and give me tears that stain.

So what do your eyes tell me underneath?
    Am I an image only used for lust?
    Or did you really mean what I believed?
These secrets locked away will turn to dust.

Give me your eyes once more before you go,
Then leave me here with no real truth to know.

Rebekah Abbott, Grade 12
Alta High School, UT

Head to Toe Love

My heart skips a beat when I see his face.
His icy blue eyes that sparkle with shine.
When he holds me close, my heart starts to race.
    A love so strong, so glad he's mine.

My knees get weak and start to shake.
He treats me well, and he calls me his Queen.
Oh he's so sweet, like icing on a cake.
    He is kind to me, and is not mean.

Whispers in my ear, the words that I love.
He says I love you and gives me a kiss.
A love so pure and white just like a dove.
    A love that I will hope to never miss.

Now that I'm in your arms I love you so.
    I love every inch of you head to toe!

Megan Hatch, Grade 11
Alta High School, UT

Dreams

What would you attempt if you could not fail?
To the dreamer, faraway isn't real.
Would you dare to tread that unexplored trail?
Or brave the world and free your heart to feel?

Have you ever dreamt you flew through the stars?
Or ventured into the depths of the sea?
Wished you could heal broken hearts and old scars?
Or dreamt your true love would come set you free?

Dare to dream dreams that have never been dreamt,
For when you dream, you can do anything.
Dreams are never vainly wasted or spent.
Live life to the fullest and fear nothing.

For the future belongs to those who dream,
And believe in the beauty of their dreams.

Brennen Fong, Grade 11
McKenzie River Christian School, OR

What Is Love?

Love is…
who can say what love is
everyone can only give their opinion.
Love is the never ending smirk,
the grin,
the twinkle in your eyes.
Pounding.
Pounding of every racing beat,
your mind spinning, never ending thoughts
sweating profusely.
Love is whatever your mind
comes up with.

Cassandra Marshall, Grade 10
Oak Harbor High School, WA

Last Goodbye

It's so hard, to say goodbye,
To the ones you've loved.
And it's so hard to just let go,
After they're gone.
There are times, you will see,
You're all alone;
And there are times, you will find,
You're not wanting to carry on.
Just look inside, into your heart,
And you will find all the times from long ago.
As days go by, it'll take time for you to realize,
That the ones you've lost so long ago,
Are always there watching over you.
Just keep in mind that no matter what,
Love will conquer all and memories will last a lifetime.
There is no reason to mourn the ones you said goodbye to,
But to relive the memories you shared while they were still alive.

Kara Howard, Grade 12
Lakeside High School, ID

The Passing of the Unspoken

I walked along
Choosing not to know
You were gone, never to return.

I thought you would be here
forever and a day.
How I regret my past time.

It's funny how you lose
all desire for joy
When joy is exactly what can save you.

I don't want to think.
I don't want to exist.
But I want to live: for your sake.

Sean Hillis, Grade 11
Cascade Christian High School, OR

Greed

Greed is the choice poison
For the sinner inside us all
It is taken without reason,
And forever corrupts the soul.

It is the feeling of self-indulgence,
And the obscurity of existence
That permeates our blood
And filters through our soul.

It is found in the back of minds,
Shadowing human determination
All the while preserving
Mankind's ethical humiliation.

Adam J. Moore, Grade 11
Skyview High School, ID

Honor Is a Lone Warrior

Waging a hand in war
for the warrior to be strong
fearless for regiment
the stench of a blood-pale stain
on a silk white cloth
from battle after battle

Brave for those who fear
the feared to complete a duty
to earn respect of
your own country

Fulfilled by your courageous efforts
to be for the long silver sharp
double-edged sword waiting, longing
to be opened from its sheath
Honor is a lone warrior

Kassondra Dorrenbacher, Grade 10
Oak Harbor High School, WA

Alone

A man alone.
Stands on the shores of a beach.
A beach speckled like pepper,
with water smoothed the bleak black stones
on the yellow-white sand,
of lime stone worn by the many years of erosion
and crashing waves.
Viewing the crystalled blue water on a refreshed sun dried day,
as the man listens to the calling of the wind
through the tall grass that stands strong
at the top of the cliffs.
Cliffs that surround all of the beach to the right;
gently sloping to a prairie filled with sweet smelling grass and flowers
(of many starting to bloom)
with coast gulls flying over head,
the sun laying its head down, for it's the moon's time to come.
All is calm now, yet
the man still stands alone.

Josh Lamb, Grade 10
Oak Harbor High School, WA

Where I Want to Be

In the woods where nature's nectar is sweetest is where I want to be
In the woods where every breath is harmony is where I want to be
In the woods where ever step is ecstasy is where I want to be
In the woods where nature's wonders wander is where I want to be
In the woods where the wild spirit lives is where I want to be
In the woods where every thing is at peace is where I want to be
In the woods
In the woods
In the woods where I find harmony is where I truly want to be.

John R. King, Grade 12
Trask River High School, OR

I Do Not Understand

I do not understand
    why roses have thorns, but yet they are so beautiful
    why it decides to rain on a sunny day
    why I, instead of another dancer, am injured all the time.

But most of all
    I do not understand
    why people say the generations keep getting worse
    but they do not do anything to make it better
    (adults must like to have children and let them roam around,
    they let them back talk and give them everything they want,
    and even when they scold them, the children do it again.)

What I understand most
    is the passion for ballet,
    you're able to let your emotions go and put them into steps,
    it has such a freedom and always relieves your stress,
    you can defy gravity with each grande jete, and when you dance
    you are happy.

Monique Betty, Grade 10
Pocatello Sr High School, ID

The Baboon

On a cold, musty day in June,
was born a fierce and fat baboon.
This baboon was unlike any other,
for he could see in technicolor.
He saw blues, oranges, purples, and reds,
he even saw yellow when he wet his bed.
His powers he kept to himself,
in a diary on top the shelf.
Bobo, his cousin, found the book,
not only that, he took a look.
The secret was out! The baboon was doomed!
"Everyone will think I'm a freak," he assumed.
He decided to stay put and take them all on,
for this baboon was unusually strong.
Before long his mother came in,
with nothing more than a satisfied grin.
She told her son it'll be all right,
for there's going to be a celebration tonight!
"What's the occasion?" asked the baboon,
"Why, you of course, you crazy loon,
we discovered your gift not a moment too soon."

Brody Lund, Grade 11
Stanwood High School, WA

A Special Gift

An angel came to me and said,
Your lover will soon be dead.
But do not fret, and do not fear.
For his life you can save,
With the love in your heart and one special gift.
I stood shocked, to hear such a thing
My love was sweet, gentle and kind.
So why would the good Lord call him to the great divine.
I cherished him so over the next few days,
Helping him dodge all the troubles in his way.
Then the wind stole my hat that he had given me,
With grace it landed in the street.
My night in shining armor went to retrieve it,
Not seeing the car ahead,
Sluggish time passed me by
As the angel's words appeared in my mind,
His life I could save with the love in my heart
And one special gift,
I pushed him aside and out of the way
My love and my life was my gift to him that day.

Samantha Verhei, Grade 12
Freeman High School, WA

Juicy Grapes

Drops of sweet water
Soft, smooth, purple skin
When pierced, waves of flavor come forth
Candy from Mother Nature
An addicting drug, always craving more

Francisca Vasquez, Grade 12
Kodiak High School, AK

Rainbow

Nature's soft paintbrush
Brightly streaks across the sky
Caressing the day
Filtering light through the clouds and rain
Painting a picture for all.

Jamie Lynn Summers, Grade 11
Preston High School, ID

I Thought

I thought about how to achieve my goals
In the long run.
I figured out if I sacrifice one move
Then it will be done.
I thought about how to demonstrate my dreams
To the finishing line.
It takes a lot of effort and time to place
Me in that zone.
Throwing away your faith what you already own,
Isn't the best way to be showing.
Give yourself discipline and good progress
Growing.

Richard Hunt, Grade 12
McLaughlin High School, AK

Grammar

For me grammar's not a strong point
For me grammar's something I don't understand
Teachers nag at you all the time
Even though they don't use proper grammar all the time
Sometimes I wish there was no grammar
But even as I say this
I wonder if it's possible
To communicate without grammar
But now I remember the five senses we have
For we use them every day
Most days we think nothing about them
But we most certainly can't do without them
Now I wonder what it'll be like
If everyone spoke without grammar
Maybe life would be better
Without all the sophisticated
Grammar

Eddie George, Grade 10
McLaughlin High School, AK

Silence

The creeping silence of the violence
That hides underneath all of my tragically untold lies
Yes this is truly where my destination resides
Outside the world seems unchanged
Yet my mind's eye
It has been claimed

Jay Lyman, Grade 10
Black Canyon High School, ID

What Is Greatness?

If you have never sacrificed unto blood, you wouldn't know.
Greatness is falling short every time but never giving up and continuing to climb.
Greatness isn't won on the battlefield.
Greatness is earned in the countless hours spent training.
Yes, greatness isn't earned on the battlefield it's only recognized there.
And those who were not great before the battlefield cannot possibly find it there.
Greatness is part of those who have it
Not an award to be given.
Greatness can be brought not with money or worldly goods
But with blood, sweat, tears, and time.
If you pay with these and earn greatness, it will never leave you.
Greatness isn't how many medals you have won,
But how may battles you have fought
It's the sacrifice made to get there that makes greatness
It's the trials and adversity faced
A man continuing on and not cowering or crying about how unfair life is or how big the trial.
Greatness is being beaten but not broken and always striving to be better
Greatness is never being satisfied with where you are.

Lance Forsgren, Grade 12
Preston High School, ID

Winter Night Presence

The moon hung from the sky on a cold winter night
It appeared as a great shaped crescent
Wandering along the sidewalk, the three girls chatted as if it was a pleasant warm summer night
Little did they care; it was a chilly night for their feet to be pacing
These three young ladies kept on trotting and laughing.
Christmas was just around the corner therefore so many houses were glowing with lights and overwhelmed with decorations.
As the girls kept chatting, they were still careless of the weather and admired the abundant houses with decorations.
Although the girls were cold, their hearts were filled with warmth by gleefulness and extensive laughs.
They were pleased with each other's company, but were not aware of their distant walk in the cold winter night.
The moon still appeared behind some clouds and kept gleaming.
It was a still, hushed night, but with the presence of the girls, the night was disrupted with their liveliness.
The moon stared upon the three young ladies kept wandering and conversing, until they safely reached their destination.
The cold winter night stood serene again as the moon floated in the sky with its brilliance.

Desiree Sanchez, Grade 10
Oak Harbor High School, WA

Dreams

Every day I see all these different people.
Going about their day with floating dreams.
Ones of another place to form an escape, of the future and all the wondrous things they wish to achieve.
As days go by some dreams fade away and new ones begin.
My dreams will never recede.
I grasp them tight within my hand and wrap it around me like my second skin.
So I can walk my path in those dreams and live in them.
A day passes a new beginning is open, and as a new beginning comes and each day passes my dreams never fade.
Every breath that escapes my mouth brings strength to this dream.
Growing weak as I do at times almost like fading, yet still we push on.
All I have are my dreams and they to me.
Everywhere I look all there is to see is more possibilities.
Those that pass either have given up on a dream or never had one to begin with.
It began at birth and sees no end 'til fulfilled.
Through all the demeaning, belittling, and little faith from those, I still see no end to my dreams.

Nichelle Glasgow, Grade 10
Fort Boise Mid High School, ID

Faith

Faith is the speck of dirt being tossed about in the wind
Sometimes you see it
Sometimes you don't
At times it's big
At times it's small
Its strength and power remain constant

It may be invisible
It may be as bright as the sun
Either way you believe it's there

Webster says it's having complete trust
A Walk to Remember compares it to the wind
The Bible says it can move mountains
I believe it's all of these above including one thing
Showing your absolute loyalty to God
Faith is belief without doubt or question

Savannah Ax, Grade 11
Nampa Sr High School, ID

Noblesse Oblige

As I was out walking I saw in the street,
A dark figure was riding whom no one would greet.
His air of impatience was hard not to see,
And he treated his servants as cold as could be.

I watched while he sputtered and swore in their face;
He cared about no one and showed not one trace
Of kind thought or remorse for he lashed them with whips,
And he strutted and smiled with hands on his hips.

For Noblesse Oblige was not rich in that day
And love for his laborers held on him no sway.
No compassion could rouse him from feeling this way
And he sits on his throne with his whip to this day.

Larissa Lovelace, Grade 12
Covenant High School, WA

Fate

Fate is the rain
Teasing you with small drops,
Then soaking you to the bone.

A thunderstorm, unpredictable one moment,
Extravagant the next.
Cold, then warm
A remaining chill;

Wonderful, peaceful, a blessing then
Catastrophic, disturbing, a curse.
Powerful,
Fate is the rain.

Kayleigh Caldwell, Grade 11
Nampa Sr High School, ID

Learning to Let Go

Chest puffed out with head held high in the air,
All the less important there below me.
I put my nose high above to the sky.
There were important things for me to see,
Like what to do for the rest of the day.
The difference between me and these men,
Is that they were not on my same level.
I didn't even want to be with them.
Even if I was above these people,
There were things that even I could derive,
The main thing being, treating people better,
And learning to let go of all my pride.
    Though there are lots of people I'm above,
    The Lord shows us the ways to act through love.

Jesse Stipek, Grade 12
Covenant High School, WA

Fear, Fun, Love in Life

You think this place is all games and fun?
    Well trust me, you're not the only one.
    Everyone wants to play hide and seek,
    But all they're looking for is just a peek.

They search for the truth why love's not found,
    They look in front, but never around.
    It's almost like they forget it's there.
When they whine and complain and say it's not fair.

Ordinary people, in their ordinary ways.
    Same old people living ordinary days.
Wanting and searching for something unclear.
    All they need is to get over their fear.

Don't fear to be crushed, or even heartbroken.
    Get over it now; it's a one time token.
    You live life once — why can't you see.
    Fear, laugh, love; be who you want to be.

Brittany Dabney, Grade 10
Central Kitsap High School, WA

Santa Maria Senza Lustro

In the elusive dark of night I dream,
Sight beyond the reach of human eyes.
Burning eyes, in a soot-stained world
A creature once by glory garnished
Once ruled by thought, logic, and reason,
Her immaculate beauty seared and tarnished
A tattered thing of holy treason.
The smoldering death of hallowed grace
Suffocated by reluctant repentance
As tears streak the ideal face
Unable to escape her regal sentence
Reduced to archaic sculpture cold
She of the eyes, so damnably gold

Daniel Clark, Grade 12
Alta High School, UT

The Eagle

I see the eagle soaring high above
searching for truth, the answers, and the things we all love.
Along the canyon walls, there's something to seek
but it's hard, he's blind, and emotionally weak.

He tries to fly with his broken wings
and he's still willing to take on what fate brings.
It's hard to breathe but he pushes on
through the tears and the pain that he's felt for so long

The Eagle peers down as he floats through the clouds
staring down at the world with its earthen mounds.
So what can this wondrous creature I see be
but of course it is nothing, nobody but me.

Travis Cox, Grade 11
Triumph Youth Center (Yic), UT

In All Things I Do

In all things I do
I love to be with you
In your eyes and smile
I can't stand being away
from you more than a while
you shower me with love
that does not come from above
but brought by the passing of a dove
I love you so very much
and hope that we will again
be returned to that joyful feeling
from one to another the feeling
brought by a dove the feeling
of love as Cupid's arrow
came from above on the wings of a sparrow

Corey Chinn, Grade 11
Rancho High School, NV

The Barrier

Hate is a strong word
the very opposite of love.
Just like there can be no good without evil
so goes it with hate and love right.
Removing all hate from ourselves
would remove what we knew as love with it.
If no one had hate, no one could have love.
So why do people insist on not hating?
When it just makes me love the things I like that much more.
We should not hate everything it's true
but not having some hate will take away that barrier
the barrier of what you like
and what you dislike.
My feelings are just stronger
I either love it or I hate it.

Taylor Harris, Grade 10
Orem High School, UT

Little Caesar's

Oh, What a fitting name,
Cheap quality goods for an affordable price.
Only Caesar himself could have created such an inspired idea.
How unfortunate that he was carved up in much the same way
A pepperoni pizza is.
And let us not forget the Meal Deal,
A true slice of ancient Roman life.
Little Caesar's.
An exceptional name for an exceptional pizza.
God bless 'em.

Brendan Sines, Grade 12
Alta High School, UT

Sisters

Sisters
That's all I've got
Sisters of all ages and sizes
Even though from the same family
We are as different as the colors of the rainbow

Some of us are tame and mellow
Others are wild with enough energy for everyone
We have straight and curly hair
Our eyes come in blue green brown
We come as tall and small

We have our similarities
We have our differences
We have our fun times
And our fights
Yet with all we go through
We still love each other

Bethany Hardman, Grade 10
Orem High School, UT

Tears Fall in Silence

Tears fall in silence
A leaf twirled through my window and landed in my hand
My tears fell in silence when a stranger steals my thoughts
So I cast a glance to where the world is
I let my eyes follow the wind
My tears fall in silence when my stranger steals my thoughts
I remember the night when I knew of a love song of rain
My tears fall in silence and my stranger fills my thoughts
And I wonder…
What would I see when my pain ends?
What would I see when my pain ends?
What would be left of me?
I wonder…
A raindrop kissed me on my forehead
And my tears fell in silence
And my stranger filled my thoughts
My tears fall in silence
And my stranger…steals my thoughts.

Jennifer Batterman, Grade 10
Spring Valley High School, NV

In Response to Romance

All the muses of Romanticists are dead,
Is that not a lovely way to look out upon the world?
In the cold heart the blossom withers and the poet
His natural inspiration.
No emotion, no feeling to evoke, winter
Becomes the Age of Reason
And a microcosm within itself.
Hooray, hurrah, the Regionalists are out of date,
The Thames is a point of contemplation;
Not the river but the bridge that passeth over and
No point to make 'cept this:
Cold freezes the muse,
The man may tax our gas —
But he better not touch our
Coffee.

Kellianne Rumsey, Grade 10
Northwest Christian High School, WA

Airhead

Her soft, black hair is as dark as midnight.
She rarely yells, gets mad or starts a fight.
She has spirit, tenderness, and beauty,
But which is made up for her stupidity.
Her glasses make her look intelligent,
But do not be deceived, they are quite bent.
The one word to describe her is airhead.
At least that is what most people have said.
Her friends see her as a disguised blonde,
'Cause of her questions like, "What makes a pond?"
And, "Does Alaska really have oceans?"
It is unknown where she gets her notions,
Except maybe the *I Love Lucy Show*.
She loves it, go figure, but even so,
There is never a dull moment with her.

Fektista Kuzmin, Grade 12
Nikolaevsk School, AK

Relationship

Disheveled and broken, the dream's been crushed.
Thrown away, whatever was is now flushed.
Crumpled, destroyed, pond'ring what did you see?
You move on, wondering did this have to be?
Convinced that it's through, nothing left to say,
Letting go, the feelings of warmth don't stay.
Wishing I could go back, redo the past.
Option isn't there 'cause time goes too fast.
These things aren't as bad as they used to be.
It's a strong trust that has made me to see
I've changed for better, seen the bright side of things.
What was this love that all of the songs sing?
I will get over it; I'll try to be content.
I'll consider what happened as being heaven sent.
Life's been hard; trials never fail to abound.
I'll have to meet each with feet firm on the ground.

Zach St. John, Grade 11
Covenant High School, WA

Burnt Bridges and Empty Remains

A shredded white cloth flails regardlessly in the wind,
Surrounded by the rubble.
Eventually the war for passion and love lost.
Paralyzed to fight this endless struggle.

Two months somberly flew by without modest hesitation.
Upon your return, no feelings left to spare.
Thoughtlessness accompanies my broken heart.
This symbol of regret and devotion ours to share.

Expiration has reached its inevitable peak,
Forgotten are the dreams of resolution.
Determination so soothing now fades out,
Caressing the sores left by love's pollution

Never again will sweetness be whispered.
Bruises form where once your touch laid.
Erased was the emotional truth.
Emptiness where our powerful memories were contained.

Eyes falling upon the bitter surrender,
Wishing so desperately for an awakening.
You roll up the soiled, torn clothe,
The only salvageable remain left for your taking.

Krystle Ricks, Grade 10
Rigby Sr High School, ID

Numb

As days quickly slip through my numb hands.
I notice myself in an endless night.
My soul is lost among the others on the sand.

Scared and cold, I am alone on this land.
Evil haunts my dreams and scares away the light.
As days quickly slip through my numb hands.

Tears rolled from his eyes, his face that was tan.
Yet I knew it was not love at first sight.
My soul is lost among the others on the sand.

But remember, to fall in love is "grand."
Like a slap in the face, love took a bite.
As days quickly slip through my numb hands.

Love is popular with increasing fans.
But at times there will be scream filled nights.
My soul is lost among the others on the sand.

Life lies helpless at the feet of man.
I walk through the cold holding Death's hand tight.
As days quickly slip through my numb hands.
My soul is lost among the others on the sand.

Mary Henning, Grade 12
Alta High School, UT

Splendor

Splendor is the sun
Crackling and clicking on the surface
That helps to create light for sight

And heats the world's surface
To a beautiful warming glow
Where turtles and toads enjoy

It creates the light bulb
That flickers and flutters on
When an idea is present

And joys within the soul
Like butterflies between genders
It creates a fabulous splendor

Jackie Leen, Grade 11
Nampa Sr High School, ID

Coffee

The musty smell
That makes me crave it
Sweet yet bitter taste
Warmth that pours
Down my throat
Feeling of happiness
Now awake and finally ready
To start the long day
Knowing that tomorrow
I will stop in the shop
And spend what little cash I have
To experience it again
A sweet addiction.

Jennifer Gubbe, Grade 12
Sumner High School, WA

Open Your Winged Eyes

Star dust falls from the pattering wings
As they caress my cheek,
Open your winged eyes, my love!
I pray, your heart to keep.

Unfold their coquettish charm
Do not, their enchantment mask
But unveil the soulful depths
Of abiding adoration obscured
Manifest their eternal splendor
Of untainted sapphire skies

Star dust falls from pattering wings
As they caress my cheek,
Open your winged eyes, my love!
I yearn, your heart to keep.

Talia Sharp, Grade 12
Heritage High School, WA

The Moon

The celestial orb glistens
as the call of nature listens
It's calming light soothes my soul
When the night does its toll
I stop to hear the raven's tale
Of how the night got so pale
The moon's glow gives me peace
So I know the world is at ease

Angela Evans, Grade 10
Oak Harbor High School, WA

Mothers

I wanted to be a butterfly, but
You wouldn't let me spin a cocoon.
I wanted to be a horse, but
You wouldn't let me gallop and whinny.
I wanted to be a bird, but
You wouldn't let me fly
I wanted to be a little girl, and
You helped me become a woman.

Emily Mesenbrink, Grade 10
Idaho Arts Charter School, ID

Promise

You've changed my friend,
From good to bad.
Just like I predicted,
I'm hoping it's just a fad.
I wish I were wrong.
Please God say she's well,
Tell her I'm still keeping the promise,
And make sure she won't burn in hell.
There she goes,
She'll never come back,
Until she realizes,
The good life she'll lack.
I know she misses me,
She tells me all the time,
Although you may not hear her,
It's screamed in her mind to mine.
I'm keeping my promise,
We made in my backyard,
I'll always keep this vow,
Even though it's getting hard.

Jordan Main, Grade 10
Northridge High School, UT

Snowstorm

Freezing, ice and wind
Blistering wind stings the face
Snowflakes falling hard
Total whiteness all around.

Tammy Forsgren, Grade 11
Preston High School, ID

I Do Not Understand

I don't understand
why people need to die
why we need to live
and what it takes to succeed.

But most of all, I do not understand
what happens when I die
(what will others think.
Will I be missed? Will they care?)

What I understand the most is
when people die,
their ashes will be shed
and they will become one with the earth.

Kevin Brewster, Grade 12
Great Basin High School, UT

Glaciers

Beautifully simple
White waterfalls silently fall
Simply beautiful
Water twinkles like diamonds
Smooth white ice gleams and sparkles.

Megan Lynn Haslam, Grade 11
Preston High School, ID

What You Did to Me

You smiled at me
I smiled back
You hugged me
I felt warm
You held my hand
I felt happy
You told me I was beautiful
I believed you
You held me
I felt safe
You kissed me
I loved you

Rebecca Isaacson, Grade 10
Orem High School, UT

Oh

That two-lettered bit
Holds such disappointment!
Sudden saddening,
Understanding,
And reluctant acceptance
Of calamitous emotions.
It is a quietly,
Resounding,
End.

Maria Liang, Grade 12
Alta High School, UT

Why?

I was out to lunch,
when I heard the news,
he wasn't able to go,
he disappointed everyone but he would never really know,
the tears we shed,
the pain we felt,
how sad we all were!
It's easy to think it's not true,
since he wasn't the one to tell,
I had to hear from someone, who didn't really care,
I wanted to scream at him and tell him it wasn't fair!
I didn't know what to say or do,
all I wanted to do was cry.
I never got the chance, to really ask him why?

Lindsay Belnap, Grade 10
Orem High School, UT

Rainy Days

Rainy days
Cold and dreary
Yet beautiful
Every time it rains it's a fresh start
In life we don't get fresh starts
I wish every time it rained
It would wash away things we've done wrong
But unlike the world,
Things can be washed away
And new can't have a fresh start
No matter what,
We will always have things we've done that don't work
And nothing can ever change it.
The only thing we can do is change what we've done
So in the future we don't make the same mistakes.

Telisha Reece, Grade 12
Skyview High School, ID

Upon the Cross

I hear the rain go drip, drip, drip,
The thunder crash and boom.
Then I hear the people screaming,
For fear of the unknown.

I see the rain, pouring down from the sky,
The lightning crashing,
Through the dark black clouds.
I see the building fall before me.

I feel the rain on my face,
As the Earth quakes beneath me.
I feel the wind as things fly by,
But yet I have no fear, for I know He comes to save me.

Alex Johnson, Grade 10
Orem High School, UT

Hate

Hate is like death, it spreads sorrow
hate can bring people to murder
causing loss and more hate
hate can bring revenge
hate can also bring joy to others
knowing the one they hated so, is gone
but by bringing joy to some
it can bring more hate, consuming some in hatred
bringing more murder and hatred
hate can be an everlasting rivalry
or a short lived battle
but whatever the case
hate is like death, it can spread sorrow.

Justin Oakley, Grade 10
Oak Harbor High School, WA

Stranger?

I saw someone that I once knew,
Her time had been stolen, her life was unkind
And her happiness couldn't shine through.

Someone different stood before me, someone new
Slight resemblance brought the memory in my mind
I saw someone that I once knew.

The way she looked gave me a clue
That to being in darkness she was inclined
And her happiness couldn't shine through.

The things she said I wished weren't true
To the pressure of life she had resigned
I saw someone that I once knew.

A soul so troubled doesn't know what to do
She saw how far her life had declined
And her happiness couldn't shine through

Her life didn't turn out like she wanted it to
A life of sorrows just beginning to unwind.
I saw someone that I once knew
And her happiness couldn't shine through.

Billie Kuner, Grade 10
Explorer Academy, WA

Life

Life is but a memory,
of hope and joy,
as life ends,
it feels like,
a piece of us is breaking,
as we wonder what shall happen when we leave,
crazy as it seems,
it all happens within our head,
then why is life but a memory.

Jesse Cullen, Grade 10
Oak Harbor High School, WA

Beauty

Secrets and whispers
Coming from a silvery voice
Soaring above the heads

Silently Beauty stands and waits
But can you find her?

Sand slipping through
The empty air
Its touch as smooth as glass

Silently Beauty stands and waits
Do you see her?

Her fair eternal form
Balances on a high wire
Can you save her?

Tumbling, falling
Where is she now?
Collette Hatch, Grade 12
Mount Si High School, WA

Parrots and Princesses

A joyful bird
With wings of color
A proud beak
And arrogant manner
Yet in its beauty
Withheld from view
Are the harsh words
This bird can speak

This mighty cockatoo

A happy girl
With hair of gold
A gorgeous smile
And stately presence
Yet in her loveliness
Deep inside her
Is the pride and hate
That will one day be unleashed

This haughty woman
Chad Turner, Grade 12
Box Elder High School, UT

Hurricane

Black clouds, eerie sky
Rain first comes in drops then sheets
Gales of wind bend the trees
Giant waves come rushing in
Devastation left behind.
Michele Marie Christensen, Grade 11
Preston High School, ID

This Season's Love

Spring blossoms with a kiss of innocence so pure.
Time lost in moment's bliss
Spring blossoms with a kiss, melting through passion's abyss.
Smiling lips of soft allure
Spring blossoms with a kiss of innocence so pure.

Summer love warmly thrives in naive hearts of youth.
Gazing in each other's eyes, summer love warmly thrives.
Makes both spirits come alive.
Too young to see the darkened truth
Summer love warmly thrives in naive hearts of youth.

Fall sees passion swiftly fading as love seems to fall away.
One's heart is silently debating.
Fall sees passion swiftly fading.
One sits in the darkness waiting, while lonely night morphs into day.
Fall sees passion swiftly fading as love seems to fall away.

Winter breaks a heart in ways so cruel, for the other one is gone.
One left a cold and bitter fool.
Winter breaks a heart in ways so cruel.
Amongst the air despair takes rule, as hate lies down in pawn.
Winter breaks a heart in ways so cruel.
The other is forever gone.
Christina Della Iacono, Grade 10
Spring Valley High School, NV

Double Path

In this world there are demons and there are angels
Then there are us humans with both in our cells
Coexisting flames and water surging throughout the blood of one
The curses we hold, the spells we enchant, the light in the sun

A fallen angel reveals himself to the beauty of darkness
Only then will the shadows and shining light destroy this mess
Dark can control wind, water, earth, and fire
But it may also cause a hidden evil desire

A purified angel shows herself to the horror of light
Only then shall she reborn the true reason for this fight
Light may also use the elements of power
And it may cause purity to forever shower

But unfortunately we do not control the elements
We are but humans that do not have a strong sense
We give into our dark side we pray to the pure
In this empty world there is pain we must endure

We either choose to live forever in the light
Or for all eternity to be in the dark and fight
Robert Pont, Grade 10
Boise Sr High School, ID

In Light of Last Night

My curfew long ignored, I strolled the streets,
When from the fog a twisted form drew near;
Yet when my lamp fell fixed upon his face,
A handsome man emerged, a gifted seer.
He bid me come and praised my wizened wit —
And charmed my heart from home-taught, reasoned doubt;
So that what small debate in mind declined
From righteous choice, to thought of death without.
Yet through the boggish maze a light pierced forth
And shone I'd walked ten strides in mindless daze —
I turned, rememb'ring Light's clear honesty
Then ran straight home to where safe keeping stays.
   He waits for me and knows my wayward will,
    So truth must house my heart and guard it still.

Tyler Wickstrom, Grade 10
Covenant High School, WA

The Storm Inside

Eyes drawn to yours.
What is this display I see?
Close yet far,
Blue eyes like a stormy night.
Empathizing with you I try;
Only you and a higher being can fix this tangled mess.
Please know that in this world you're not alone,
My friend. Forever I will be by your side

Amber Page, Grade 12
Puget Sound Adventist Academy, WA

Too Late

We heard the message
late that night,
telling us that
he was ill.

We thought nothing of it.
We thought it was just the flu.
"He'll get over it
just like me and you."

We didn't go visit,
"We're just too busy."
We still should have known
the right thing to do.

My dad's birthday
was a bright but dark time.
We were told to hurry
in order to say our goodbyes.

My dad rushed as fast as he could,
even though the rest of us had to stay.
I went on through the day not knowing,
that my uncle's only family was just too late.

Alyssa Peters, Grade 10
Camas County High School, ID

Never Give Up*

Dreams
Dreaming big
Never giving up
Reaching higher and higher
The sky is the limit
Reaching for the stars
Never giving up

Looking ahead
Imagining my future as bright as the stars
No task is too hard I can do it
Never giving up

Striving for perfection
Making something of myself
A life of happiness a life of success
Never giving up

Always doing my best
Nothing is impossible when your dreams are big
This is what I've waited for
Watching my dreams come true
I know I can do anything
Because I never gave up

Brittany Brundage, Grade 11
Woods Cross High School, UT
Based on a quote by Ralph Waldo Emerson,
"Hitch your wagon to a star."

Things i love about you*

your eyes, which held me captivated
where i stood.
your smile, to dazzle the sun
and warm every corner of my soul.
your voice, like a sparkling mountain stream
that flows into my heart.
your walk, and the way your gracefulness,
takes my breath away.
your hair, about which i dreamed
running my fingers through as we lay together…
your hands, whose caress i crave,
to hold my face in their tenderness.
your arms, i long to have around my neck
as you pull me close to your warmth.
most of all.
everything you are.
changed the way i feel about my life.
i love you!
forever and always,
'till death do us part.

Nikki Ellsworth, Grade 11
South Albany High School, OR
Dedicated to: Cody Smith

Once Upon a Time…Well 5 Years Ago

Once upon a time…well 5 years ago I was dead
November 3rd 2001
I laid on the couch in my fuzzy puppy pj's feeling more pain than I'd ever want you to know.
Mom came home frequently, making frantic calls, you were at work, you had all but abandoned me

December 21st 2001
You came home with a new Harley-Davidson going on rides was some of the only time I got to spend with you.
But it also got me out of a house dense with worry

December 23rd 2001
I wanted you to sit with me, just to talk, I want you to know what I'm going through at school, all you did was walk away

December 26 2001
I was convinced I would die, the pain was too much. When you'd look at me, your eyes would fill with pain and hurt
Then I'd wonder if maybe, just maybe, dying would be for the best.

December 27 2001
You came with me for the first time we drove for two hours I sat quietly in the back staring out the window
We reached the hospital and realized something, I couldn't walk. About two hours later, we we're told it was Arthritis.
They said x-rays would be needed they never said 92, two hours and one shot later we left

January 12 2006
Do you remember any of that? Still to this day you give me that look. The one that says "you hurt me."
Do you really think I wanted this? You act like you do. I would change it if I could. Don't you understand?

Maddison Rodriguez, Grade 10
Oak Harbor High School, WA

False Friend

It's been 76 days since I last saw you.
That's 1,824 hours, 109,440 minutes, and 6,566,400 seconds.
You can imagine what it was like for me to be left alone.
You might have an idea because you were the one that left me.
However, I think it mattered more to me.

I think I valued our friendship on a higher level.
It was harder for me to say good bye. You've called me all but twice.
And just those two phone calls were awkward. I just don't understand why.

We were as close as sisters, if not closer.
I felt like a part of me died when you went. In a way, it did.
I tried to keep in touch and think that the distance didn't matter.
Before we departed, you were always with him.

I was barely in your life for the past month you were here. Why would you throw away our friendship
Because of distance and a boyfriend? I feel I wasted my time and effort on you.
I was always there when you needed me. All the promises you made are forgotten.

You'll never come back and you'll never be in my life again.
I'm slowly recovering, a victim of atonement.
I'll be all right soon and you'll be a ghost.
I have no more strength left to try to mend what you broke.
Farewell my fallen idol and false friend.

Shawna Andrews, Grade 10
Oak Harbor High School, WA

Part of Me

There is so much I'm going through
It's all from your lies
Everything is tearing me apart
From all the mistakes I've seen in your eyes

Part of me wants to be with you
Even though you'll always be my fear
Part of me wants to make it through
Even though you'll always be right here
Nothing is what it seems

Memories are coming back to me again
From all the wounds you've given me
I don't even know who I am
From all the pain that you have seen

Don't go inside of me
'Cause I know I won't trust you
I can't be with you
'Cause you took a part of me

Tristine Esquela, Grade 10
Oak Harbor High School, WA

Our Freedom

Our freedom shouldn't be taken lightly
because freedom isn't free.
Don't think of it slightly,
oh why can't they see?

All these people complain
because it's not good enough…
They must be insane
because they don't understand this stuff.

The media doesn't help,
all it shows is guns, killing and war.
we don't see anything good,
oh, if only we could.

If they saw the good that is happening,
the people would all sing.

The freedom that is coming
to us and other countries
is worth more than many things.

The sacrifices that have been given
make life worth living.

Our freedom is our greatest gift in this world we have today…
and it's the only way.

Spencer Munyan, Grade 12
Mountain Crest High School, UT

Forgotten Assassin

Among the Egyptian lilies
Their fingers dipped in honeyed aromas
Pale faces peering
At the sleeping palace within
The open window calling
As they nod against the nighttime breeze
That cloaks their tapping rhythm
And rather sings a haunting song
Of longing that poisons the dreamless slumber
And stirs the silence

For he crouches
Among the Egyptian lilies
Fingers cradling a draught of poison
Wild eyes peering
For Anthony sleeps well within
Twill never wake from his widow's touch
Who won't suspect the darkest of nights
That cloaks the sourest of strangers
And rather take the black-oiled asp
Whose poisoned kiss will be her last

As she is silenced

Ashley Ylst, Grade 12
Alta High School, UT

Roadkill

She lies helpless in the middle of the road.
She ran from something not pleasant,
but instead of making it to greener pastures,
she is forever stuck in the middle of her journey.
Roadkill.

She thought she wanted something better,
she thought she could run from her troubles.
Instead of that,
she met her match before her time.
Roadkill.

I wonder if she regrets it now,
running away,
or if she feels better off,
if a sudden end and resolution is all she really wanted anyway.
Roadkill.

Paige Davies, Grade 10
Camas County High School, ID

Hope

It comes from unexpected places,
Bringing courage and lifting faces.
It changes battles and wins all wars.
Brings faith to Faithless, and heals old scars.
It leaves all happy and helps all out.
From all misfortunes, banishing doubt.

Gabriel Sharp, Grade 11
Preston High School, ID

A Love Once True

This is the sound,
of a bleeding heart.
Breaking in pieces,
all torn apart.

These are the dreams,
left out to die.
As the summer sun warms,
morning love has gone dry.

Here is a shell,
of a cold-hearted person.
Alone and angry,
with no feelings in sight.

As we expressed our sorrow,
my feelings started to die.
As they faded away into dust,
nothing was left between us.

Here lies the end,
of a love once true.
This unfinished song
written solely for you.

Carly Wright, Grade 11
Great Basin High School, UT

Thunderstorm

A crash of lightning
Crackling thunder through the sky
Split second color
Black clouds and silent grumbles
The lullaby of my dreams

Brittany Foster, Grade 11
Preston High School, ID

The Bird Across the Street

A bird guilty of a heinous crime.
At times I wished he's swallow a dime.
One year annoying,
The next amusing.
Pestering others with his pastime.

Always singing the same two notes.
His tune across the black road floats.
He starts at first light.
It lasts until night.
To singing the day he devotes.

I'd have sworn his brain was misplaced.
He grew on me despite distaste.
Though I wished him ill,
Sweet I found him still.
Now I know not to judge with haste.

Stacey Wiser, Grade 10
Mountain Crest High School, UT

Love Undone

The streets quietly shuffle as bakers and tailors whistle about their work.
Rich aristocrats and wealthy travelers begin to glide into the Town Square.
At the opera house, beautiful, flowing arias linger in the atmosphere.
The low hum rapidly grows until it is a mass of audible intensity.
A tall, stately gentleman strides along the cobblestone walk.
He grieves his lost lover, recently abandoned.
She said he was negligent, never caring.
In truth he did not know of her many needs.
If only I could turn time around, he thought, then she would see
I was mistaken; she is not as strong as I thought she was.
We would sink back in time and walk along the pier,
Talking and laughing like once we did, in love
His head hung as he slowly strolled quietly home.
His heart sank deeper and deeper as he thought of his love,
Knowing she would never again love him as she once did.
Even if she did not, his love for her would never die.

Hilary Alexander, Grade 10
Idaho Arts Charter School, ID

Happiness

Happiness is a day on the mountain.
Waking up early.
Hitting the first runs of the virgin snow.

Happiness is a day on the mountain.
Stopping in for lunch.
Meeting up with your friends to take a break from the long morning.

Happiness is a day on the mountain.
Last runs appearing.
Almost time to go.

Happiness is a day on the mountain.
Tired yet relieved.

Long drive back, but it's good to say it was a good day on the mountain.

Joshua Hunt, Grade 10
Oak Harbor High School, WA

One Day Soon

I live my life with a devil on my left,
To keep me from the truth.
And an angel on my right,
To show me the way to the light.
Needless to say there is always a fight,
A clash between good and evil to win my might.
Because I have all the strength in the world,
To find my own way no matter how much time I've wasted or sold.
So what?
If today,
Isn't my day.
And so what?
If tomorrow's not my time,
Just remember that one day soon this world will be mine.

Jazmin Gardner, Grade 10
Spring Valley High School, NV

Misplaced Ideals

What is the significance of ideals?
To become something unattainable
We labor night and day through thick and mire
Simply to one day be sustainable

As we grow we change and form these ideals
Hand crafted carve ourselves as if from stone
We build a dream and strive to make it real
In constant search discovering our own

Throughout the years I feel temptation bring
A rise to cherish misplaced affection
A desire to be my own lord and king
We must convene a moral attention

If idolatry be my greatest vice
I will look to my God that paid the price

Asher Jackson, Grade 11
Covenant High School, WA

Frame

I am a picture frame old and dusty,
   holding pictures of fake family smiles
    without their true feelings for each other,
and little babies smiling.

I am a picture frame old and dusty,
   holding pictures of sweethearts,
    best friends forever,
   weddings being held,
and people turning older with each
       blown
         out
           candle.

Danielle Bars, Grade 10
La Center High School, WA

It Helps to Move On

It sucks to be in treatment without your freedom
   but it all pays off
   if you work the program.

I'm a whole new person without my past
   but when I think about it
   I feel I have a whole new task.

When I think of the past and the things I have done
   I think of the future
   and the things I can do.

To help the people with a past like mine
   that would make my day,
you can't change your past but you can move on
and I think that's the best thing you could do.

Krystle Lauree Knight, Grade 10
Pendleton Academies, OR

Every Day We Remember What Happened

Every day we remember what happened
on that fateful day when you stole millions of lives.
We always remember that day when it comes around every year,
and every year we have that same memorial service,
and always we hold the three minutes of silence,
for the memory of the ones that you took from us that day.
We did not know why you did this.
Then we started seeing things with the date of
September 11, we saw 9-11 which is also 911 emergency.
We did not know if it was significant to anything.

Then one day we just stopped asking why,
we just stopped all together.
Now it is just a sad memory in the minds of everyone;
this we will never forget.

Jessica R. Owings, Grade 10
Priest River High School, ID

Depth

Hollow Soul speak your sacred gibberish
Of confused twilight thought and baffled mind.
Orate, empty spirit, eternal pain,
Eternal loss, and lost gain far behind.
Soul, sing sorrow upon the faint mores.
Sing desolation and your cowardice,
Thunder, abomination and your woe;
Revel in broken hearts and marks you've missed
Upon the living stone, now crumbling rock,
Inscribe your diligent vengeance and rage.
On flesh mangled by certain vexing doom,
Simple symbols now carve upon the page.
Instead, soul say I speak I sing I write
Then simply ask a vanity or right?

Aaron C. Willows, Grade 12
Covenant High School, WA

Scarred

Some things mark the outside of us
As plain as a map drawn in dark Chinese ink.
Like God's tattoo they make us exclusive to the outside world
And so we become separated from the others.
Our marks became an exceptional ice breaker
After others ask how we came to be unique.
And then there are the artificial marks that put us into groups.
The numbers along an arm
That put them into lines leading to Auschwitz.
Some scars remain internal
Unknown to even the one's marked.
A scared heart is the worst
The pain never really seems to go away
No Novocain for love or lack of it.

Katrina Zwick, Grade 12
Mount Si High School, WA

Statistics

We all have a weakness:
Alcohol, anxiety,
Drugs and depression.
I'm not like them.
I won't give in.
Please believe in me.

Lauren Beatty, Grade 10
Alta High School, UT

Adventures!

Word by word,
Page by page,
Chapter by chapter.

Being pulled in by unseen forces,
Farther and farther in,
Harder and harder to pull out.

Fighting against pirates or dragons,
Fighting your way across storming seas,
Or through rainy jungles.

More and more,
You don't want to stop.

Adventure after adventure,
Book after book.

Amelia Martinez, Grade 10
Orem High School, UT

Forever Touched By an Angel

Four years old
welcomed with a punch
sneaking out
terrorizing the neighborhood

Halloween on the rooftop
blowing fire at little kids
but best of all
was the long talks of the future

a past of
so
many
memories…

but as I look into the future now
all I see is an image
of you in your son

and your spirit
in each of us all
I am truly
forever touched by an angel!

Tasheena Stephenson, Grade 10
Orem High School, UT

Chaos

Give up your thoughts, give up your pain
On this of all nights, give up your pride
And give in to a chaos of the mind and body
My chaos of the mind and body

Give in to me and look at yourself
Look deep into the mirror because you know what's really going on
Take a glimpse in that mirror, that I share with you

Give in to me…give in to this
The simple and honest truth
This sublime feeling lost in chaos

You want the honest truth?
For just one day I wish I was something I'm not
Something you are…something you were…
and the honest truth is, it's all for you

On this over all nights, I don't ask for much
Just walk with me into the night
On this over all nights, let your mind lose control
Let your body walk away, but always keep your spirit close
for THIS is chaos
this is my chaos
of the mind and body

Zach Hawley, Grade 10
Newport Sr High School, WA

Spring

When all is green and lush and rainbows shine bright.
The rain comes down like tears from heaven above.
Cleaning and washing the Earth,
Creating a new fragrance fresh and sweet.
Majestic flowers appear bright and full of life.
Happiness is never lost,
For the sun's warmth and brightness forbids gloom and despair.
Cheer is spread throughout the valley, overflowing with abundance.
Faces regain their color, lost, from the long winter.
Trees begin to re-grow their leaves, bringing forth color and joy.
All is well and the future shines brighter than the dawn of day.
Days are longer, giving people more time to enjoy the Earth's beauty.
Encouraging them to live life to its fullest.
And love life with a passion stronger than any other passion.
Spring comes after winter,
For if it didn't imagine the gloom and despair
That would fill our souls.
Spring gives something to look forward to
And if there were nothing to look forward to
There would be nothing hoped for
Life would have no reason to exist.

Amanda Moosman, Grade 11
Preston High School, ID

Time

It kills every living thing
But cannot live without life.
It conquers the mightiest of kings
And destroys the hardest mountains.
It gives man a chance to experience life
And has the tallest trees grow.
It is the mystery of all mysteries
But it is also the key to all the answers.
It cannot be seen or heard
Yet it is all around us.
Sometimes this is the best thing a man can have,
But it can also be his biggest enemy.
This is the hungerless monster,
Yet it is still thirsting for more.

Brent Willmore, Grade 10
Orem High School, UT

The Sun

Outside the weather was rainy and cold
It's dreary watching the rain hit the ground
Fed up with the rain I don't make a sound
Rain day after day gets boring and old
I long for when it would be clear and bright
I can't wait for that lovely day to come
When our chance to have sun is slim to none
It would certainly be a sure delight
Hoping and praying for the sun to show
At this point, I was feeling oh so low
Wishing for sun impatient little me
I woke up to the sun what do you know
You have to wait for what you want to see
With the sun shining intense as can be.

Zach Hanna, Grade 10
Prairie High School, WA

Lost Scent of Summer

I gaze at the rolling hills of grass
 Covered in daisies and honeysuckles
  Dip my feet in a cool crisp pool
Jewels of sun bouncing on the surface
 Smell of lavender, olives, and heather
  Taste them on my tongue.

Now

That pool of clear water
 Is leaf covered and dark
  Roads are lined with naked trees
Their clothes on the ground
 I walk these hills of brown
  Longing for the lost scent of summer.

JoDanna Wishon, Grade 12
Columbia High School, WA

For You

When I look in your eyes
It shines like a star
Warming my heart
Like nothing could ever pull us apart
You're like the diamond in the rough,
So pretty and amazing just yet found.
You say it all without a sound,
Just look at the ground.
You're like a chocolate so tough on the outside,
But sweet in the middle,
I don't know why I wrote this in a riddle,
But I would give anything to hear you giggle.

Celeste Knowlton, Grade 10
Camas County High School, ID

Paper Card Castle

Who is she?
My smile just caved in like a
Paper card
Castle,
Devoted but devoid of life;
For shells cannot have feelings,
Even with their eyes drawn out. I am
Temporary. Then
Forgive me; I did mean to intrude —
I know — your castle is strong, worthy,
Noble.
But mine is weak, now, without your support,
And all your glance
Leads me to believe is that: this
Super glue is faulty,
And hope is a sheer excuse
For flight, when love
Collapses
Like a paper card
Castle.

Emily Linroth, Grade 12
Kamiak High School, WA

Why Not?

How far is too extreme? I'll watch sin's flame,
Just have some fun, and slip away from blame.
Removing bricks, just one or two, can't hurt —
Until life's tower tumbles to the dirt.
Alas, my sin! I should have gazed, content,
But chased a fleeting rainbow's end, and bent
Life's gifts to evil, seeking Ruin's lie.
How can I conquer sin? Why should I try?
Though my best deeds are rags, I look above
For help, and though I fall, a wave of love
Rolls yet again across life's pitted sand
And smooths guilt's jagged stones, that I may stand.
 No lure now tempts: with Truth before my eyes,
 I won't look back, but strain to reach the prize.

Rosemary Shelden, Grade 10
Covenant High School, WA

Champions

The one game that will decide
The champions of the world.
The World Cup.
The roar of cheering crowds.
The sun shining brightly on the field.
The wind billowing gleefully.
Setting the mood for this game.
All the long hard trials,
That have come and passed.
All led up to this one game.
The teams warming up,
Nervously.
Each player has a light in his eyes,
A light that gives his excitement away.
The only thing is,
There can only be one champion,
And there has to be one loser.
One team will go home with the trophy,
The other with nothing.

Kenny Crump, Grade 10
Orem High School, UT

Freedom

Freedom isn't free
It costs lives
Men and women have died
For what?
So that we can believe in our dreams
And what do we give in return
Complaining and grumbling
About tragedies of war
Freedom is like money
One can never have enough
It must be earned
Some citizens think freedom is free
They have never known
Or loved those
Who unselfishly
Made the ultimate sacrifice

Trevor Woolstenhulme, Grade 12
Mountain Crest High School, UT

Wanting to Stand on Thin Ice

I know what love is
Since you showed it to me
It's like standing on thin ice
Trying to balance
As you hear the ice below
Shifting, cracking
But still you try to stand
Trying your hardest
Inevitably it will break
You know that
But still you try…hoping against hope

Micah Rees, Grade 10
Utah County Academy of Sciences, UT

Paper Flower

Beautiful; the crepe that crinkles into folds of shapes
created a pattern of attention and love,
As the pose bent it relaxed out into leaves and the gypsy smiled.
The contour line was coursed over with a finger
Full of red dust that glistened to the paper and stuck, the gypsy smiled.

Crevice after crevice looking closely it went on like
its intention was to have you seek Atlantis and its miracles,
yet don't stray afar, for this flower will make you believe
that you're more than you are.
Creation of such hangs on a wall, whiter than the rafts stuck out
so to see the times of old that pass, and the color of imagery.
It is so far away, it was careful and crafted for the fragile and
learning, so to get the jest of such a yearning.

The hands that touch the stem bleed, for the thorns of simple
have pricked the complicated and seep into the cuts finding a blood
to infuse with a view of something new.
It wilt not, for its creator is tranquil, full of the air breathed in by the natural,
as it passes her hair dancing in the air, the gypsy smiles.
Though the crepe is old, and the color fades, the gypsy's smile
Never goes away for the love of a paper flower is simple and pure.

Alicia Benavides, Grade 12
Nampa Sr High School, ID

Moon Shadows

The white moon, lights up the sky, it's looking down on me like God's eye.
I'm dosing off into sleep, the light shining all around me.
I see the moon shadows on the floor, I see them move towards the door.
Out they go to flood my home, such beauty I have never known.

Samantha Shulock, Grade 10
Oak Harbor High School, WA

Silent Love Song

May I join you in this waltz? For time's quartet I faintly hear.
The crescendo, ah, it grows and grows, and the end will soon be near.

Oh waltzes, I do love them so; their rise, their fall, their three clear counts
— My love — reminds me of it all; your call, farewell, my hope for more.

Yes, I know, 'tis obvious — the love I hold for you my dear.
All around already know. My love for you is clear.

I love your ruby gown tonight, it is the best in all the ball.
My dinner jacket's a bit off-white; the tag said ivory, after all.

Now — there's something I must say, in my very special way.
So just before I bid adieu, I must say that I love…

I wish to ask, but do I dare? My words shall leave my motives bare.
The palpitation of my heart shall make it so my lips don't part.

So then, my love, I shall not ask, 'til we're on that cherry blossom avenue.
I shall still just walk alone, singing my silent love song, to you.

John Tanalega, Grade 11
Advanced Technologies Academy, NV

A Walk

As I was walking the other day,
I turned and looked the other way.
As it started to rain
And the light of day dimmed into shadow,
I just stood there in the rain,
Thinking of days that won't come again,
Of days gone by.
For I am weary of this Earth,
Of death and suffering and pain.
And sometimes I think of another place
Where all is whole and all is well,
When thunder cut through my reverie
And I went on down the road.

Trevor Bygland, Grade 10
Kent Meridian High School, WA

Too Late

In city streets, so damp and cold and black,
I sit with punks I ache to call my friends.
But, drinking heartily, they pass me back
Their booze and crack, to do with what I please.
They look so happy; I want what they've got.
The ice cold beer invites me with amber eyes.
It beckons me. They stare, I drink, they laugh.
I sob, disheartened; foolish, I have sunk
Into the depths. Destruction waits for me.
How could my soul despair and sink so low?
And now, too late, false hopes I clearly see.
I longed to be a part of emptiness,
And now it's clear, I've made a wretched mess.

Emma St. John, Grade 10
Covenant High School, WA

Alone

I'm sitting in my room all alone
Where no one can hear my faint moan
With all the lights off
There's not a sound
No one can see me as I frown
I think to myself of the day that's gone by
Even though it almost makes me cry
Then I think of what you said to me
But it just added to my misery
With words so harsh, cruel, and vile
But I just gave you a soft smile
You just cast me aside
But you didn't know how much I hurt inside
I think to myself why did you have to say those things
Those things that make my ears ring
I feel so lost, dazed, and confused
I feel as if I have nothing left to lose
So I'm sitting in my room all alone
Where no one can hear my faint moan
And where I fear I will always be alone

Lacey McKillop, Grade 10
Spring Valley High School, NV

Sweet Home

I hear the sound of music…
The wind calling back my name…
My mind turns back to my childhood, where I was born…
Where the first time in my life I opened my eyes
And saw my mother's face.
She smiled down at me and said,
"Oh, what a beautiful child."

I still remember my home. My home where I grew up.
Where I learned to ride horseback.
Those days followed my path.
I listened to the wind.
It told me to keep going, until I reached the sea.

The water tickled my feet.
The sand was like my bed.
I close my eyes and dream of becoming someone,
Someone who would make my mother happy.
I dream and dream until I feel something touch my face.
I open my eyes and see my beautiful horse, licking my nose.
I hug her neck…
She smiles at me…

Oh, where else can I be than my home…

Rita Svistunova, Grade 10
Heritage High School, WA

Safety

My heart beats as of a thunderstorm
Surrounded by the innocence of white clouds
The soft rain trickles down
The promise of safety
Broken by the unpredictable strikes of lightning

Katie Lowber, Grade 12
Skyview High School, ID

Two Roads to Walk, One Road to Choose

Why didn't I resist when first enticed?
The habits formed will haunt me all my life
And never be completely laid to rest,
But cause regret that stabs me like a knife.
The consequences stare me in the face;
I daily wrestle hoping to o'ercome
Instinctive habits grounded in my soul,
And beg for help each time my sin has won.
Don't be the Foe's defenseless, foolish prey,
Lest you become enslaved to his desires
And dragged along through winded, tangled paths
Until you've sunken too deep in the mire.
Pay heed to truth and endless pleasure gain,
Or yield to lies and suffer endless pain.

Emily Anderson, Grade 10
Covenant High School, WA

Time Tears the Heart

It was the kind of love that came at the wrong time,
He had a pure heart the Greek Gods could not dream of,
A coach would call him prime,
But sometimes you just cannot call it love.

I do not blame him or myself,
Nor those who birth me,
But the logic of time itself,
Because of it our love could not be,

They said we were too young to understand what we were feeling,
Those words pierced me like a sword with acid upon it,
I was left in a black fog of my emotions that were still dwelling,
How could they know my heart and who is in it.

So I lay in my room and watch the clock as each lonely second strikes a further hole in my heart,
And count the days until our love is no longer forced to be apart.

Jessica Scroggins, Grade 11
Cimarron Memorial High School, NV

Beat

Your voice is the symphony with melody and beat, each instrument contributes to the song
The trombone steady and alone, the flute carries the tune
Drums! Beat beat beat feel the heat
Piano solo
The trumpets blow with a steady flow all coming together under the conductor's bow
With the flick of the wrist and the nod of the head
The race is off until the next command
Crescendo to a grand pause, players alert and ready
Down fly the hands and away they go
Beethoven, now Mozart, Chopin and beyond
The melodies of great minds unfold upon the stage tonight
Oboe takes flight — all is silent
Its notes ringing through the air interrupted by the snare
Da da da da da da da da da da da da da da da da da da da da...
Stop!
The audience still hears the music, feels the music
But the conductor stopped. The music from the heart never stops.
It continues to play on and on, no beginning, no end
Just existing, pulsing pulsing
Feel the rumble in your chest
The wind the rain it's all music, do you hear it?

Candace Blas, Grade 12
Chugiak High School, AK

Undeniable Dreams

The haunting voices of unknown poets reach out through the waves of time yearning to be heard.
The whispers tell of struggles to taste the sweet intangible freedom long denied to them.
Unspoken dreams tell of boys and men alike echo through the walls of their prison.
The etchings within the ancient wood cry out with an intense pain that blinds the naked eyes that gaze upon it.
Echoes of lost souls trapped within the walls tell of many things long buried deep within the vault of secrets, never to be heard.
Speaking out through the invisible barrier, trying to grasp the attention of those who glance but never really look.
The yearning for someone to listen to their words becoming greater than ever before.
Do you think they will ever be heard?

Mackenzie Mills, Grade 12
Alta High School, UT

Distracted

Could I be blind from what is really true?
Perhaps infatuation is the clue.
Yet how could this obsession misinform,
My every thought and action and my norm.
It fashions what I love to something more,
Distracting my attention to ignore
What really is important to the soul.
So how did it achieve so much control?
I used it as an idol to admire,
Forgetting who deserves my heart's desire.
For what I saw before can only be,
Affection turned to lust, but now I see
That what I'm longing for is from above,
And it can only come from whom I love.

Bryce Rasmussen, Grade 11
Covenant High School, WA

What Can We Expect

Can we expect feeling a sorrow
after tomorrow?
Do we expect the sun to always be bright
or me being alive?
Do I expect a new television
even if I lose my vision?
We never expect a friend always
being there, or them waking up dead.
Do we expect the sky to always be high
or the next day seeing the light?
Can we expect a baby without an anatomy
or my mama without an ovary?
We never know when things end,
so it's never good to bend.

Zuleima Ramirez, Grade 10
Rancho High School, NV

Sycophantic Whining

Alone I stand but loneliness for me
Holds but a stately, still tranquility.
A rambling voice with foolish prattle fraught
Awakes disgust in me as quick as thought.
A low and grov'ling manner builds distaste
Far quicker than a frowning, silent face.
I cannot stomach silky, golden speech,
Nor bear to hear a wind-bag parson preach.
Such fools as these do naught but build my ire,
Yet never of self-counsel do I tire.
Who knows my heart more closely than I do?
Whose wisdom matches that to which I'm due?
Far better cease the droning, endless bore,
Their sycophantic whining hear no more.

Jordan Hayes, Grade 12
Covenant High School, WA

My Love for Her

Love.
A word sent down from God
To be used with emotion and spirit.
Love can't be touched or taken,
Only felt, through two people.
It's a feeling of ecstasy,
A never ending high that can't be reduced.
No force of nature can stop it.
You shouldn't run from it,
Nor should you hide from it.
Take care of love; you may never feel it again.
Love can only be expressed through the sweetest thing,
One kiss, one breath, one hope.
It is the hope of eternity in happiness.
It will take you where the wind blows,
And she will be waiting there for you,
Greeting you with true love's first kiss.
What is love?
It is one's true feeling of emotion for another.
Keep it floating like a feather, never let it sink;
Love is forever.

Kyle Moll, Grade 12
Banks High School, OR

Miles Away from Home

I thought I could never travel
Black pavement, gravel
Another town, city
A rainbow to this place
Very bright and wide
With brilliance to nature
Town shining bright
Mountainside white
Beauty of the snow
Within the show
Show of snow and ice sculptures
Of Disney characters and such
Stand for some time
Beauty like nature
Nature representing something or someone
Rainbow home is very long
Another hometown, city
Black pavement, gravel
I think I can travel now

Tischa Fox, Grade 12
Nampa Sr High School, ID

Summer's Sun

Summer's fun in the summer sun,
Playing sports with friend, it never ends.
It feels good in the river of pool,
Where you can keep cool and be a fool,
The sun is always out and is a bright orange ball.
Until it gets chilly in the colder season of fall.

Shane Rhea, Grade 10
W F West High School, WA

Frustration

Frustration is a thunderstorm,
a slow and timely event.
Wondering, watching, waiting
for each and every move.

A start so calm,
the wind blowing slowly by.
Tension rises,
clouds start rolling in.

A flash of lightning
gets things started.
Thunder booming,
emotions erupt.

Frustration is the thunderstorm
that lies within us all.
Watching, waiting
for the lightning.
Stephanie Bergland, Grade 11
Nampa Sr High School, ID

Firecracker

The Fourth of July
Ushered in with a bang!
The crowds line the streets
Laughing and celebrating the
Freedoms this country holds dear.
Joshua Benson Steele, Grade 11
Preston High School, ID

My First Pair

When I opened the box,
With a pale pink bow,
I was excited!
My first pair;
"A present for me?" I asked,
I lifted the lid
And to find a pair
Of pale pink slippers
My first pair;
I tried them on,
Just to see how they looked
Mom said to twirl around
To see how they feel
And to find out
That I was a ballerina!
My first pair;
I twirled all night
I even slept in them.
My first pair
Of real ballet slippers
Dioni Wheeler, Grade 10
Idaho Arts Charter School, ID

That's Life

Married to a millionaire,
Mansion on the beach.
Diamonds from Tiffany's,
Porsches racing down the streets.

Gourmet hors d'oeuvres,
With unpronounceable names.
Slamming doors,
Kids are home.

Back to reality,
Children are hungry.
The babysitter arrives,
Off to work.

Mini-mart smells,
Angry customers.
Cleaning all day,
Just want to relax, finally home.

Lying down to sleep,
Cheerios crushing underneath.
Thoughts racing,
Where's my millionaire?
Alicia Chase, Grade 11
Woods Cross High School, UT

Stars

Shining bright at night
Flashing, shooting through the sky
Guides for the outdoors
Big flaming balls of hot fire
Creating a sparkling patch of joy
Randi Drury, Grade 11
Preston High School, ID

Memories

I was filled with anxiety
as I walked onto the plane.
I had never left home alone,
but I would soon return again.
Being in a new country
was like living a new life.
As my hands said "hello" to foreigners,
my heart had jumped with pride.
Everything was different there.
From varieties of food and music,
to new styles of people's hair.
I'll never forget this trip I took,
or the second family I had found.
I'll always have my scrapbook,
all nice and neatly bound.
Ashley Eskelson, Grade 10
Pocatello Sr High School, ID

I Do Not Understand

I do not understand
    Why friends fight
    Why we die
    Why I have little brothers

But most of all
    I do not understand
    Why life is so hard
    (I really don't like
    How confusing everything is)

What I understand the most
    My best friend
    Who's understanding
    Who's always there for me
    Who's always there if I'm scared.
Erika Hanson, Grade 10
Pocatello Sr High School, ID

Little Sissy

Dear little sissy
I love you
With all of my heart
You mean everything to me
So cute, so sweet
Those *big blue eyes*
That *beautiful* brown hair
I miss the sound of *your voice*
I wish I could see you
Giggle once more
To hold you and put you to sleep
Is what I long for
I love you little sister
Always and forever
Forever and always
Dalila Lawler, Grade 12
Diamond Ranch Academy, UT

Hope

Laying in bed
Staring at the ceiling
Eyes are closing
I can't go
on
any
longer
It's tearing me apart
I ask questions
I get no answers
I am terrified of what might happen next
But
There is always hope.
Rylee VanLeuven, Grade 10
Orem High School, UT

Camas Football Team of '06

We play in a hundred degree heat.
We do three hour practices.
We play in the blue and gold.
We work as hard as any team.
We beat you up.
We make sure we mercy rule you.
We have done our job if you want to quit before fourth quarter.
We will fight it out until the very bloody end.
We pound the ball out.
We do that so you can't breathe.
We will try to inflict pain on you.
We play for one coach that will protect us, at any cost.
We might get chewed out by him, but it isn't personal.
We work so hard because of the one dream.
We do it to play on that blue field.
We do it to play for that blue trophy.
We do all that for one thing,
To bring pride back to Camas.

JD Jewett, Grade 10
Camas County High School, ID

Reflection

As I sit in school looking out the windows,
I watch the trees grow and change with time;
I realize I, like the trees, have no choice,
No choice but to also grow and change with time.
Winter, spring, summer, fall, year after year,
A tree never objects to change.
I, though unlike a tree, have a voice and can object.
But in the end change is part of life,
And theoretically no one can object to change.

Chelsea Bates, Grade 12
Skyview High School, ID

I'm Going to Be My Own Hero

I'm going to be my own hero.
I'm going to reach the stars.
Little girls will want to be more than zero,
Because I am going to go far.

I will take the criticism.
I will be the best I can be.
Little kids will look up and say,
"Hey! That's going to be me."

I'm going to make the money.
I'm going to get things done.
I'm going to be the happiest person.
My job is going to be fun.

I'm going to be my own hero.
I'm going to reach the stars.
Little girls will want to be more than zero,
Because I am going to go far.

Ashley Vaughn, Grade 10
Pocatello Sr High School, ID

My Place

I have a place deep inside my head
A place I often go to wipe away all dread
I float on a cloud to get to it
Over the rainbow there it sits
The mountains are high and the trees tall
It is a large open space, not one wall
There is a deep blue lake with smooth gravel shores
Here hanging branches of flowers are the only doors
Inside leaves and flowers fairies hide
Many different creatures here abide
Here everything is perfect and just the way I want it to be
So I keep it deep inside my heart and safely treasure the key

Kaylin Mortensen, Grade 11
Woods Cross High School, UT

Questions

The wind thrashed about her chocolate brown hair,
As the moon fell upon her sun-kissed face.
She gazed deep into the star-studded air
And pondered anew at His wondrous grace.

She watched as the waves gave way to the sand,
Crashing and rolling the shells to no end.
She ran the waves where she could not stand,
Overcome by the power He did send.

She looked into the sea stricken with fear,
Doubting if she should make this suggestion.
The salt on her lips was one single tear,
As her heart filled with this single question.

Where was the One who had saved her from sin?
Was He really there like He'd always been?

Chelsea Redding, Grade 12
McKenzie River Christian School, OR

As She Sits

As she sits there deep in thought,
Thought about the one she loves,
She imagines what her life would be like,
If he hadn't had to move away.
She wonders, "If only I had realized sooner,
The reason why he loved me; would I have loved him sooner.
And if I had loved him sooner, would he still be here, with me.
Would he still be here to save me from a fall,
Or fight my fears away,
And would these walls still be around my heart,
If I hadn't pushed him away?"
This is what she wonders as she sits there,
Deep; deep in thought.

David Finley, Grade 10
Idaho Arts Charter School, ID

The Future Untold

One road in front of me does stand;
A path behind lies dead and done.
To look ahead does life demand
And take a step out of the sun.

The future now lies dark and drear;
What step I take will change my life.
That very step is what I fear —
The diff'rence between peace and strife.

But though my future lay untold,
There it stands a new adventure.
And though the questions come tenfold,
I can find peace in the answer.

And though I sway from side to side,
My firm foundation stands untried.
Emily Reister, Grade 10
McKenzie River Christian School, OR

I'm Excited

I'm excited
Not getting a new job excited.
Not watch a movie excited.
Not take a nap excited.
But excited that I am starting college.
Excited that I passed the test
Excited I can get a better education.
Abdullahe Yusuf, Grade 12
Great Basin High School, UT

The Light of Waking

Sleepy days make
sleepless nights.
in which we find ourselves
buried beneath years of sand
to dream simple dreams
of honor…to challenge our enemies
what grace is shown?
what glory won?
when all is dreamt, nothing's won.
Jordin Turner, Grade 10
Alta High School, UT

The Pencil

A tool of the trade
Protected by the first
For speech for press
The pencil keeps our freedom alive
Without the right to write
Silent opinions cannot be heard
The future is interred
Let the words speak
Without being heard
Micaela Tucker, Grade 10
Valley Christian Secondary School, WA

Freedom Isn't Free

It's more than just a country, it's more than just a flag
It's more than all the people, it's commitment in a bag

Our flag waves high for all to see, it shows our rights and liberty
Our true devotion will always stand, by our heart; pledged to the flag

The people are like building blocks, we build the nation high
Other countries admire us, to be like us they try

The people keep it strong, we will fight for what is right
Our devotion shines for all to see, this country's woven tight

Our unity connects us, to all our fellowmen
You'd give your life a thousand times, to be called a citizen

Our founding fathers started it, a long long time ago
They made a declaration, and we live by it you know

While others give their lives away, for freedom we possess
We'll do our best in any test, we will accept no less

I'm proud to be an American, and I will always brag
This country keeps on fighting, to save our freedom and our flag
Cherie Davis, Grade 12
Mountain Crest High School, UT

Cycling to Fame

F ortune	**F** ate	**F** earless
A nxiety	**A** nticipation	**A** ggravation
M otivation	**M** anagement	**M** agnificence
E xcel	**E** ndure	**E** mulate

Fame is more than a race,
You have to believe to achieve.
To be better than the best,
You need to be recognized above the rest.

To surpass all possible limits,
You need to conquer pain and say you did it.
To surrender one's body to complete devotion,
Sacrifices must be made to set a career in motion.

To devour the competition with no remorse,
Perseverance through blood, sweat, and tears must be given the most.
There is no shame in trying to secure fame,
There is only one person to blame if this goal cannot be attained.

This is something everyone wants and can be so easily acquired,
Only if the chosen few souls have passionate will and desire.
Nick Engerran, Grade 10
La Center High School, WA

The Weight of My Personal Opinion

From you, a sense of myself
The ability to crumple up my "need to please"
And trash it without any remorse

You showed me that having to be told
Who I should be
Never really made me

You freed my ambitions
The ones I held back
The ones that could tell the world of me

Because of you, I no longer fear
The sound of my own voice
Or the weight of my personal opinion

Jennifer Passey, Grade 12
Layton High School, UT

Music

A noise, a sound, a beat, a rhyme,
The speed of the notes exceeding the time.
Some decrescendos, accents, and rests,
Expressing the motion of feel at its best.
Movement creeping into your mind
Of precise moments of an extraordinary kind.
Feel the irony gripping your heart,
And realize the need from this, to not part.
Grace presents itself at your nobility,
Pressing to please, while showing hostility.
You embrace the sounds of mortal beauty,
Opening ears and succeeding its duty.
Yearning to hear this sound all day long,
As a melody bursts through the realm of song.

Chandra Holt, Grade 10
Kentlake High School, WA

Love Is Like a Knife to the Back

It hurts when it happens to you
especially when you least expect it.
The blade is the sharpest part,
which is the part that digs into your back.
The blade of the knife is as sharp as a tigers bite.
A knife in the back is like losing someone's trust.
Love is amazing until it stabs you in the back.
A knife should never be aimed towards people.
Love is like a knife to the back
hurting every step of the way.
Be careful who you choose,
'cause you never know who you can
and can't trust your life with.

Ashley Pintado, Grade 10
Oak Harbor High School, WA

Balance

Like a bird flying within the air
The bird and the wind work as one
The sun and the moon control light and dark
Fire burns and destroys with heat and rage
Water cools with great sensation
Earth supports all life with power
Wind breathes life into all that walk the Earth
A circle of balance surrounds everything
Disrupt it, and the world will end

Chris Chase, Grade 10
Oak Harbor High School, WA

Reflection in My Eyes

With trembling fingers I reach out
My eyes are open, but they see something else.
You ask for the words
I tell you what I saw.
Put a label on it and take away the bliss.
You say there's no meaning or point
I turn the page and hear none of it.
I often wonder why I read,
Why read these words on a page
But I never remember the words
Only images.
People look asleep when they're reading
And I think it's because they're dreaming.
I wonder what I look like engulfed in my book
Can you see the world reflected in my eyes?
Can you feel my heart jump and pound?
Can you see my tears of sympathy?
My heart rises in a world that I make real
Places and emotions all become mine
As I release the grip on reality to be free.

Elizabeth Erickson, Grade 12
Northridge High School, UT

Alone with My Drums

Slowly I take my sticks and sit on my throne.
In a desolate, empty room I am all alone.

The glistening bronze is polished and slick.
I tap off the beat with the butt of my stick.

I close my eyes and start to move,
Every muscle in my body feels the groove.

With fierce excitement I begin to pound.
The thundering noise shakes the ground.

The fact that there is nobody around,
Only drives me to make more sound.

Soon it is over the lights turn on.
In the blink of an eye I am gone.

Tyler Swain, Grade 10
Orem High School, UT

Page 79

Forget
Forget about the times you walked
Forget about the way you talked
Forget about the times he called you
Forget about the way he held you
Forget about the times you cried
Forget about the solutions you tried
Forget about meeting his mom
Forget about him taking you to the prom
Forget about his favorite band
Forget about his nice, soft hands
Forget him already, since it's over
Soon enough, you'll have a new lover
Mercedes Cardenas, Grade 10
Diamond Ranch Academy, UT

Questioning Society
Why is that we feel
That we need to be loved?
That self-worth is determined
By whether another
Reciprocates your emotions?
As a society
We are very insecure.
What's the cause?
It's hard to say.
Perhaps it's because
We had a rotten childhood
And are looking to make sure
We are worth a second thought.
Maybe it is a type of reassurance
In the human race,
That in this desensitized world
We are capable
Of considering others' feelings
And aren't as shallow
As we appear.
Amanda Lowe, Grade 12
Reardan High School, WA

A Second Pair of Shoes
I'm dressed irregular today;
I'm wearing something new.
Instead of just one pair of shoes,
I have precisely two.

Underneath my tennis shoes
Is a second cotton pair.
This style is much more comfortable
Than what I used to wear.

I think I made the perfect deal
When I traded all my socks
For this chic pair of cotton shoes,
Wrapped neatly in a box.
Daniel Veja, Grade 11
Heritage High School, WA

High Stock
There was once a black Horse of high standing in life
At Red Barn. He was proud like a peacock's tail show.
Horse was proud of his skill as a jumper, and he
Made it known to all beasts on the farm. "All you low,

Worthless things, ya'll are nothing to me. I can leap.
And you can't." But the brunt of all taunts and cruel fun,
Were those directed toward the brown Mare. He was teased
For not being a real horse. One day Mare said, "Let's run!"

"We shall race from the barn to the gate and then back."
The proud Horse thought this good, so they started the game.
'Round the grounds and jumping that gate, it was Mare,
Worthless Mare, who beat Horse. High stock doesn't bring fame.
Peter Wilson, Grade 12
Covenant High School, WA

Best Friends
The air of July
Captured our treasures in an old holy chest
Patched with our foolish jokes, exposed lies, secret truths
Seized every belly aching laughter
Holding captive every word, every breath
When we're hunchbacked old ladies with canes and fake hips,
We'll sit and remember all the good times, laughing until our dentures pop out
Embellishing stories of how we saved the world one 'mission impossible' at a time
And even in our old age the chest won't be anywhere close to full
Because we're best friends forever
And forever has no end
Kristeen Briggs, Grade 10
Oak Harbor High School, WA

Fight for Freedom of the Flag
Freedom in America is the best thing you can have.
To stand up to outside forces, to protect our precious flag.
Soldiers of the U.S., they want to keep it that way.
That's why they guard our country, that's why they stand up to say:
We had to fight for all our rights; we had to fight for our freedom.
We had to stand up for ourselves; we had to stand up for this land.
We have to fight with all our heart.
We help and do our part.
Because the U.S.A. needs protecting.
That's why we fight for our country.
Later down the road, somewhere down the line.
We're fighting for freedom: we're fighting for beliefs of mine.
It's in a soldier's heart; it's in our country's name.
We're fighting for our rights; we're not fighting for fame.
I'd rather die fighting, than sit back and watch.
I'd rather defend our country to keep it the same.
10 years down the road, somewhere found in time.
Our defenses were broken through, just to commit a terrible crime.
Two special towers fell, lots of people died.
We're glad to have freedom, but we're sorry for the ones who died.
We fought for all our freedom, we fought and then we cried.
Nick Nelson, Grade 11
Project Surpass (Day Treatment – Yic), UT

Pains of Love

The pains of love are like a storm,
A storm so strong it can take down houses.
In the middle it is calm and beautiful
And you think "maybe it's not so bad."
Then comes the rest
Rain, high winds, flying debris and pain.
All the characteristics of love and a hurricane.

Krystal Edwards, Grade 12
Skyview High School, ID

See Red

My anguish is deep.
I am void of allure.
In my mind, I weep.
And it begins…

Put on a happy face.
My friends ask "What's wrong?"
I pick up the pace.
The urge to hide is overwhelming.
Falling timelessly in a chasm of pain,
I sleep as an answer,
Hoping it will keep me sane.
I sink lower…

Finally, the sun awakens.
Peace is brought back to the world.
A beam shines down, like a beacon,
And I move along…

Calm, like still waters.
My heart is free.
Laughter rings throughout.
I am soaring with glee!
The anger falls dormant…until the next storm begins…

Diandria Alcorn, Grade 10
Benson Polytechnic High School, OR

Darreon

I don't understand
Why I hurt inside.
Why some people suffer.
Why life sometimes brings you heartache.

But most of all I don't understand
Why my son was taken away from me.
When I saw him for the last time,
he glanced up at me to bring a smile upon my face.
I felt joy and happiness that night.

What I understand most is
he's in a better place looking down on me;
watching me from the heavens above,
and he'll always be by my side.

Roshonda Washington, Grade 12
Great Basin High School, UT

Life Will Still Go On

This went down a few weeks ago,
I finally decided to let go.
I needed my space,
And this she couldn't face.
She made a huge mistake,
If only it were fake.
Now my life is tore,
Because she wanted something more.
If only she could see,
How much this hurt me.
Now I'm stuck without my brother,
Worse than that without a mother.
He's my very best friend,
Forever 'til the end.
Graduation, she won't be there,
Junior, Senior Prom, it's just not fair.
Achievements and softball games,
Not there either for my fames.
I guess she didn't care to see,
For drugs and alcohol were better than me.
Yeah…she's gone, but life will still go on.

Alana Marie Fernandez, Grade 11
Lincoln County High School, NV

Life

Life contains different things to try,
So whatever you may do,
Don't let life pass you by,
For you can never accomplish too few.

Life throws us several curves,
With many ups and downs.
Just send back an awesome serve,
And kill those droopy frowns.

Life has no rhythm,
Life has no rhyme.
Life has no reason,
And life has no time.

Life cannot be justly defined,
For it has so many things to describe.
Life has innumerable secrets to unwind,
With several avenues in which to dive.

"Life is like a box of chocolates,"
This is a phrase that can definitely fit,
Because life is unpredictable.
You never know what you're going to get.

Carina Kretschmer, Grade 12
Puget Sound Adventist Academy, WA

You Don't

Do you remember that time when you left?   How you went away and never came back?
And oh, how I mourned for you, I mourned for you one of my closest friends.
Because I found that everything I found great, falls down in the end,
And you never came back.
Our other friend that moved, wish never really to talk any more.
It was as if she was using us, just pretending to like us.
But really all she did was lie and abuse us.

When I found out you were moving, my heart sank.
There's another friendship gone down, and I only have God to thank.
My Shire will never be the same, I wished for sunshine, but God gives only rain.
But I don't see how He could do this to me, then again, maybe it was just meant to be.
Do you ever recall saying that you would keep in touch. But you don't, you don't even call as much.
But do you ever think of me, am I still in your heart?

I can't believe you lied to me,
You deceived me and I believed it, just like all the others.
But don't worry about me now, don't even bother.
Because true friends keep in contact no matter what
And you probably don't remember,
But we were supposed to be best friends forever.
But I want you to be happy, because I'm doing well you see.
Some of my old friends and the new are helping me try to get over you.

Melissa Busig, Grade 10
Oak Harbor High School, WA

For the Sake of Thought

As I sneak out to catch one bit of peace, it begins to rain as I walk down the street.
I couldn't stand staying in one spot tonight, so I knew taking a walk would feel right.
I thought it'd be easier than this to see you everyday…and it's not that I hate you in any way…
It's just that it got really hard to look at you, and to tell you the truth I didn't know what to do.
I didn't let you know though because you should be free to go,

I smiled and put on my mask so no one could see, no one will see how hard this will be.
I am strong — I don't need them there. I don't need to know that they care.
I'll cry in the rain so no one can see, I'll cry all alone so you can be free.
Free to go off and be happy, 'cause that's what I wanted for you — can't you see?
I care about you so I let you go and only the rain and the stars know.

I'll make it through all this pain, it'll clear up just like the rain.
For every tear there is a reason — though every smile feels like treason.
But I know in the end, you'll be my friend,
And that is why I try so hard to hide this from you, 'cause no matter how hard it is I couldn't stand to lose you.

These are the thoughts that run through my mind, I tell myself over and over that I'll be fine.
Walking through the streets of town, as all these drops just keep pouring down.
The beat of my steps, the beat of the drops…all of the memories flood back with my sobs.
Sighing at the realization of being alone, I get in my room and know I'm on my own…
This is my journey, this is my pain. No one can help me, only the rain.

Jenny Kadinger, Grade 10
Tri-Cities Prep School, WA

My Cat Mitzy

With stunning speed and agility
she roars up the stairs
little feet scuttling.

Who is this furry creature
so furious and frightful
running around as a wild beast?

It's Mitzy!

With dim, green eyes
and a shiny coat
she can only resemble terror.

Fleeing from the Big Bad Dad
she weaves and dodges
avoiding the wrath of his foot.

Luckily she escapes
in the compound of a closet
so clean and tidy.

Of course, this happens every day
to the little ball of fire, for she is my cat Mitzy.

Jordan Nuttall, Grade 10
Orem High School, UT

Can't Live Without You

You're always on my mind
Every day I think about you
And my feeling never changes
Why can't I let you go
I still care for you
Just the same
As I last saw you
My feeling just gets stronger…for you

I can't seem to let you go. There's not a day that goes by
That you're not on my mind.
No matter how hard I try, I can't seem to let you go.

I put pictures of you away
As a way to let go
So that I can move on
Still why can't I let you go
I've never felt this way
About someone before
There is something about you that I can't live without
Because…

Nick Allen Schier, Grade 12
Trask River High School, OR

The Thing in Diapers

"Gentle" is the thing in diapers —
That depends on the nurturing care of its mommy —
And says a million things without using any words —
But — cries and giggles instead —

And brings joy into this life
As if it were a million bucks —
Yet — it's better because it loves you back

Over time things revise —
But the looks of the eyes are just as gentle
As if it were the first look — instead of the last

Tae'Lor Salazar, Grade 11
Nampa Sr High School, ID

My Polka-Dotted World*

Voices ring and sing to God for polka-dotted things —
  For blankets, balloons, and balls; the child's way.
For all things different and yet the same;
  The sky and the ocean — two ribbons of blue.
The first, the last, the original, the unchanged;
  Love that is true, wars of faith.
The extra, the unnecessary, the unknown miracles;
  Every hair on one's head, the speck of dirt never seen.
A toast to mysteries; the absence of reason;
  The depths of the sea; the eternal pall.
With a taste of heaven; alive and aglow;
  Hands raised, heart unburdened,
    Alleluia.

Kyle Rock, Grade 12
Coronado High School, NV
*In response to Gerard Manley Hopkins

Tom

Like the Nirvana song,
but you made it hurt more
cause every day you spoke,
it made a dent in me.
In the beginning it sparked
well, at least to me.
Every time I saw you
my heart leapt
and the butterflies emerged.
I thought it was forever
obviously, I was wrong.
Every day I asked Matt what he thought
and he told me I was crazy.
You said you'd tell but you didn't,
how the hell is that supposed to make me feel.
If you wanted to hurt me
you succeeded, day after day.
You broke my heart
and pieces are still missing,
and I don't know how to find them.

Maddi Bell, Grade 10
Logan River Academy, UT

Liberty

Your arm stretches out over crowds
Advertising for a change
It's a clear sign of liberty and prosperity
A sign that never ends
your metal body glistens in the light
Thoughts of vagrants fill your mind
Your name is shouted
at the faintest sight of your torch
You deliver dreams with each
Verse played within your halls
Your voice is strong and firm
Yet your lips never move.

Aaron Wolfley, Grade 12
Madison Sr High School, ID

Fright to Fall

Fame cannot be mine to claim
For contests I've done poor
Nor gone trials took for chore
Or burdened troubles bore

Not because I tried or sought
Or sweat of body sore
Nor best to win the highest score
For treasures of life in store

But because of doors I shut
Before found I've nothing more
Or gave up when saw the shore
For fright to fall, when sought to soar

Krystal Hooper, Grade 12
Davis High School, UT

Peppermint

Page after page soaked with
Blood-red ink only blue
Say not what matters
But write what means nothing
Something only exists nowhere
And that is here
In the sleepless mind
Welcome to a dream
Or maybe a reality
But hold on, it moves fast
Only slowing when it gets too dizzy
Pleasantly dizzy
For a while
Holding hands with blurry outlines
Whispering of faces without names
Pay them no mind
They'll never understand
But then again neither will we

…cue curtain…

Christine Locker, Grade 11
Filer High School, ID

D and D

Founded in the twisted one's mind,
A multiverse packed full with adventure and torment,
Path seldom chosen by the masses,
Improbable path to discover one's self and principle.

Asa Daniels, Grade 12
Kodiak High School, AK

Acoustic Guitar

He plucks at the strings, smoothly but forcefully
Releasing the sound into the air like a tired bird in flight.
Floating with such precision, such accuracy, such elegance.
The strumming and the rhythm of the vibes, mimics a storm at sea,
Strong and dangerous, but yet, inevitably beautiful.
He has unbelievable melodious fingers that work in such harmony
To create such entrancing music.
"Tiene mi amor…" his voice coons, as deep as the depths of his eyes.
"Te doy mi Corazon, Te adoro…" The music softens
Into a silky, white resonance, "Eres solo mio…"
The rain drops, of music from his impressionable instrument.
His words sink deeper into the night; almost as if the luminous stars
Strive, twinkling to hear him.
His last words, which sweetly caress each and every vowel, ever letter;
Rolling off his tongue ever so gently, to bring your heart ablaze,
And melt into your body, "Puedes mi reina…"
He pauses with last notes of love, "Siempre…"
And with his last breath, sweetly whispers softly,
"…Te amo, mi amor…"
As the music falters into the night,
And slowly dies…

Katrina Lim, Grade 10
Valley Catholic School, OR

Remembrance

My heart is heavy with sorrow,
Incapable to fulfill the hole that has left me numb with longing.
My thoughts and dreams take me,
To what once was my homeland.
The wind, carelessly swaying the tall long branches,
Delicately combs my hair,
Bringing me the aromatic scent of the lake
That I so deeply adore.
There I take a boat to swim in the deep waters,
Enjoying the company of my lighthearted friends.
We dive like dolphins,
We swim under the sun.
A refreshing walk to the renowned picnic site,
Where I sit and relax as the midsummer's day slowly comes to an end.
Surrounded by family who make me smile,
Eating the food that tickles my nose.
The children raucously laughing and playing,
Their familiar jocular and lively manners make me laugh.
I long to join them in a good game of hide and seek.
But alas, I have awoken,
My dreams and remembrances only distant memories.

Leonisa Veriga, Grade 11
Shorewood High School, WA

Fled

The spices fled,
leaving her senses bereft of feeling.
The warmth was gone.
It all left, when he left.
Her heartbreak traced its way across the floor,
splintering in the wood,
staining it with memory.
It stuck on the carpet,
where once they had pledged love
and she had given what only she could give.
He had taken that with him as well, when he left.
Her heart still dragged itself after,
by the couch, where they had lain.
Where she had whispered into his ear
definitions of herself.
It carried itself on, out the door,
in a ragged line.
It left her lying there on the floor.

Rhiannon Zemler, Grade 12
Medical Lake High School, WA

War

Hello
Hello
A voice rings out
Souls are set free
Red
Red
The color of blood
An answer to peace?
Rain
Rain
The world weeps
Man is dying
Drop
Drop
A child cries
Ignorance is drowning

Hello red rain drop.

Jaime Gudjonson, Grade 12
John F Kennedy Memorial High School, WA

Life Is a Pair of Shoes

Life is a new pair of shoes.
They start out shiny, and smelling of leather.
They have good cushion and traction.
But then, they get their first scuff mark,
    and the laces begin to fray.
The color is no longer the same as when they were first worn.
The smell continues to worsen each day they are worn.
It is possible to restore them,
    but they never feel the same.
And the only thing to do is to buy a new pair of shoes.

Jordan Steele, Grade 10
Pocatello Sr High School, ID

Mirror

I cannot lie to you
Nor to anyone who passes
If broken, you will fall to pieces
Believe and you will be unlucky
I'll trick and torture your soul if I may
But true beauty lies within
Torture yourself and visit a creator
But I'll be waiting when you unravel
Unravel the cotton that you worked for
For so long you doubted yourself
Lost your confidence according to me
You are pathetic and sad
You are lost and I unfortunately found you
Now I am the last one laughing
For when you see me next
I will have befriended you
Silently you'll cry
Shed a tear because you fell for it
I told you once
Not to turn your back on me
True beauty lies within

Sarah Bugni, Grade 12
Kodiak High School, AK

The Dolphin

The dolphin is free
She swims within the vast ocean
She jumps and spins towards the heavens
Without a care in the sea

The trapped dolphin is imprisoned in a tank
She cannot swim for miles
Just a few feet down
Down, to where her heart sank

The dolphin that's free glides without concern
She smiles with cheerfulness
In her heart she has a fire
A fire that will always burn

The captive dolphin wishes for care
She wants to be loved
The deep-sea is where she belongs
Not here, where joy is rare

The free dolphin lives with adore
She doesn't know what caged is
She just knows free
Free, forevermore

Emily White, Grade 10
Capital High School, WA

The Music

The music in my ear
It sounds familiar
It sounds so close
The time is drawing near
The time to play
Is almost here
The rain outside
Hits the ground
The concert
Has started
It is finally here

Carolyn Jenson, Grade 11
Woods Cross High School, UT

Ode to Eye Wear

O, eyeglasses,
many require thee
to see the world around them.
You are a messiah
from the blurry chaos of life.
A sight giver,
clearing their elderly perception —
making crystal the youthful day.
I love the way
you decorate her face, pretty,
framing her hazel eyes.
Plastic or metal, pink, green, or blue,
I find you universal —
a version of you
for everyone who seeks
a new outlook.
In the bright shining sun,
you're a knight's shield.
Protecting against the harmful rays.
All the while, mysteriously,
hiding the secrets that blink behind you.

Lisa Keith, Grade 12
Kodiak High School, AK

Hiding Away

I'm hiding away from this world.
They shall not find me.
I'm too well hid. I don't like the world
and they don't like me.
I have done too many wrong things.
I don't mean to it's the way I am.
I mean no trouble. But I'll keep hiding
away from this world
I want your help but I can't stand
being with more than one person.
I just want to get away
from everyone except for you.
I'll keep hiding till
just a little while alone with you.

Katie Ireland, Grade 10
Oak Harbor High School, WA

The Hypocrite

I say, "I'm a vegetarian," as I eat my cheeseburger,
I drive a Hummer with an environmentalist bumper sticker on it,
I am homophobic even though I like men,
I'm also a feminist
And think women should stay in the kitchen where they belong,
I don't believe in God when I go to church every Sunday,
I kicked a cat at the protest against animal cruelty last week,
"Don't litter!" I shout as I throw garbage on the ground,
I think we should save the animals,
As well as wear leather boots and coats.

Samuel Garner, Grade 10
Pocatello Sr High School, ID

I Do Not Understand

I do not understand
Why I, instead of all the kids in my family, have the most responsibility
Why I am the oldest
Why I cannot seem to get above an 80% on my math tests.

But most of all
I do not understand
Why I must be home by midnight
Even though the party goes to one
(I can sometimes convince my mom
To let me stay later for dances.)

What I understand most
Are my parents who are just trying to keep me safe
Who want me to come home every night
Who love me.

Dallon Reddish, Grade 10
Pocatello Sr High School, ID

Comparisons

In our senior year at high school our age is 18
In the war at Vietnam the age of many soldiers was 18

We carry bags with things to get us through the day
They carried things that were necessities for their lives

What we want most is to be out on our own
They wanted to return home safely to their families

We worry about grades and plan for the weekend
They worried about snipers and hidden land mines

We think about college and our future careers
They thought about staying alive and hoping to have a future

A wrong choice for us can usually be erased
A bad choice they made could result in death

We can think our lives are tough and unbearable
But nothing comes close to what these kids our age had to endure

Carly Anderson, Grade 12
Emery High School, UT

Teddy Bear

Teddy bear
My matted, rumpled friend
Every night you were in my arms
Keeping me afloat in the sea of dreams
Now you're a comfort, a memory from years ago
When creatures slept under my bed
And monsters hid in the closet
Now I'm fine on my own.
And yet, when the lights are out but I am not
I fear dark faces
Sunken cheeks covered with stubble
A cold shiver shoots down my spine
Pushing up tiny mountains on the back of my neck
I fumble for you with blind fingers
My heart is racing
Suddenly, the touch of your worn fur
Sends a tide of relief washing over me
Filling my veins with soothing warmth.
Teddy bear
My matted, rumpled friend
Hold me tonight.

Abby Burns, Grade 11
Holy Names Academy, WA

I'm Leaving with God

As I lay down to rest my eyes,
I hear a voice, the voice of God
Saying it's time for me to open my eyes
To a new life, the life of God

I didn't know if it was a dream
Or if it was for real
So I opened my eyes to see
I didn't know what to feel, I didn't know if it were real

Until He held out His hand
For me to follow
As we were walking in the sand,
I thought about what was going to happen tomorrow

I didn't want to leave my family
I didn't know why I had to go now
But I guess I have to deal with reality
But why now?

I didn't get the chance to say goodbye
Or to say that I love you all
But I want to ask you not to cry
Because I'm leaving with God and that's not bad at all.

Kayla Gourneau, Grade 11
Lakeside High School, ID

Life

Life is what you make it.
Some people wonder if it's worth it.
I myself find it to be a blessing.
For what it's truly worth.
The possibilities are endless.
Some people take it for granted.

Life is a gift from above.
It's bent by the decisions made.
To waste life is just that,
to live life is just that.
Live, love, and cherish your life
because it will eventually be the death of you.

Kyler Leen, Grade 10
Pocatello Sr High School, ID

Basketball

Basketball is my favorite sport,
I get an adrenaline rush every time I step onto the court,
Whether it is indoor or outdoor,
I can't wait to score,
I can feel the win deep down in my heart,
And count every second until the game starts,
Even though some may think this game is lame,
I will forever feel the same,
Because after all it is only a game.

Reagan Snow, Grade 10
Pocatello Sr High School, ID

The Power of Will

I had the gates open,
A sentence was spoken.
Kingdom Herrou made their attack,
Will covered my back.

Will was a gryphon,
The name from his will power driven.
A dragon attacked my gryphon friend,
Only if I knew he was about to meet his end.

I screamed Will's name,
The gryphon was in physical pain.
With my sword,
I crushed the dragon's spinal cord.

The dragon took his last breath,
With Will approaching death.
I cried on his feathers,
We were surrounded by heathers.

I listened to him say,
"You make me prouder every day."
My father made my heart fill,
That was the power of Will.

Deborah Mitchell, Grade 10
McDermitt High School, NV

Winter

Nights, long and dark.
Snow blankets the ground.
A cold chill in the air.
Diamond snowflakes fall from the sky.
Flocked trees dot the mountains.
Wildlife struggles to survive.
The cold and harshness take its toll.
The sun so seldom can be seen.
One can only dream of spring.
Justin Yardley, Grade 11
Preston High School, ID

American Heroes

Waking to watch the breaking news
That was heard around the world
They crashed planes into the towers
As suddenly as an earthquake
Four 747's plummeted like rocks
One missing its target
One hitting the Pentagon
The other two found their destination
People killed that fateful morn
Then we stepped up
Our soldiers avenged the hate
They fight to protect
Each and every day
Protecting freedom for us all
Shielding us from the evils of the world
Freedoms will remain
Courtney Adams, Grade 12
Mountain Crest High School, UT

Fear What the Dark Does Bring

The shadows thinly veil,
The evil lurks within,
The horrors of the world,
Prickled sweat upon the skin.

The stench of death approaches,
Dark wings outstretched in flight.
Its weapons silver pointed fangs,
Its cover only night.

The things that stalk the dark
Are better left unsaid,
For we are only demons' prey
In the land of living dead.

Do not fear mere Earthly fears,
For they are only things
Fear only fear itself;
Fear what the dark does bring.
Mia Mitchell, Grade 10
Sumner Sr High School, WA

For Them

Eyes spark with supposed wisdom
More than mere superiority,
Not just simple skepticism
Unchangeable denial,
They crave your shattered naivety.

Adamant in their convictions,
Cruel words take the place of their fear
Refusing to believe in diversity,
Throwing out accusations
They convince themselves aren't lies,
Crushing your fragile courage.

For them, you acquiesce
Are lesser to yourself
Pretend to believe their reality
Take the easy way out, for them
For them, you break.
Lauren Greer, Grade 11
Alta High School, UT

Regina

Regina,
Sweet, good
Sleeps, plays, enjoys
Making your day better.
Student.
Regina Marcial, Grade 12
Great Basin High School, UT

The Fight

Spinning, spinning, gripping, slipping
Fumbling, tumbling
See the man in the shadows
The one with the scythe
Hear how he bellows
Calling for me, but I fight
Clouds roll across the sky
He calls out my name
Death beckons me, I'm so scared to die
I cannot lose, not at this game
Take my hand and run
Run with me away
I need only to see the sun
I want to make it one more day
The world is spinning, spinning
The fear is gripping, I start slipping
I keep fumbling, tumbling
Down into the shadows
Towards the man with the scythe
He no longer bellows
He has won the fight
Vanessa Booth-Killian, Grade 12
Leighton Hall, NV

My Confused Heart

I want you,
but at the same time I don't.
My heart will say I miss you,
but at the same time it won't.
I'm getting flashbacks that won't stop.
Every time I get one,
my heart wants to drop.
The feeling is so bad,
it could make me cry.
The pain is so much,
I could die.
My confused heart wants a new start.
I could run away,
because here is one place I cannot stay.
Pain is what just seeing you can do.
You don't know this,
because I haven't given you a single clue.
I've left you in the dark,
and now it's left a big mark on my heart.
Sarah Miller, Grade 10
Knappa High School, OR

Emotion

Emotion is the wall
That has stopped and is stopping
From doing the things you want to

Blocking the open path
Obstructing the road, rowing upstream
Making the way more difficult
For people to see

Then that day will come
When the wall comes crashing down
That day will be as bright as the sun
Victor Beauchamp, Grade 11
Nampa Sr High School, ID

Shadows

The shadows shine in by me,
but I cannot turn to see.
I cannot see what moves around,
I cannot see what has been found.
I'm stuck to this wall.
People think I have no feelings at all.
I've been framed.
It has not been named.
You need to save me,
but you hate me.
I watch the shadows every day.
I wish someone would say hey,
even if it's not every day.
Corissa Handy, Grade 10
Northridge High School, UT

Rumor

News was spreading like the plague.
They were feeling on top and cocky,
Telling everyone that would listen.
"This is great!" They think, "I'm popular now."
All because of the news they made up.
On the other end she is hurting and sad.
Why would they be so cruel, so low?
She feels betrayed by all who heard.
It's high school, everyone listens to the latest scoop.
She tries to say, "It's not true, it didn't happen."
No one believes her, she's all alone.
Why listen to the truth when the gossip's so fun?
Nothing happened to them,
Just her innocent reputation ruined.

Bree Woolstenhulme, Grade 10
Orem High School, UT

Selfish Mistake

I can't believe it's ending
All I see are hospital walls
Things would have been different
If to temptation I did not fall.
That night was so crazy
Pouring drinks and feeling fine
But the mood was going to quickly change
It was just a matter of time.
I took one shot and then another
My throat burning as they went down
My body's floating, my mind is spinning
Everyone's playing around
Midnight came fast, I had to go
For I knew I had curfew
Behind the wheel, I go and there it ends
Through the windshield my body flew
Now I'm dying from my selfish mistake
I'll miss my family, I'll miss my friends
How my heart cries, "This can't be real"
This truly can't be the end…

Laverne Delgado, Grade 12
Desert Pines High School, NV

Best Friend

You looked into my eyes
but only you could see
past the shadow that surrounded me
you saw me for who I was
instead of running away like everyone else does
"I'll never leave you" they always say
but only you stayed with me, even to this day
you believe in me when no one else would
somehow you saw something that no one else could
I can no longer wait for you to be here again
you truly are my
BEST FRIEND

Jeremy Madaus, Grade 10
Spring Valley High School, NV

You and I

I see you from afar,
But I can never get near,
For you live there and I live here.

I know about you, I've looked you up.
But you know nothing of me, and I wish you did.
My wish is to be with you from now until the end,
But that can never happen,
For you live there and I live here.

You live with the stars, way up high.
And I live here, way down below.
I look up to you, hoping you'll come down,
But that will never happen,
For you live there and I live here.

My wish is a dream and nothing more.
I know you will never look down and spot me from the crowd,
But still, I wish you would.
That would be my dream, to be here with you,
But that will never be,
For you live there and I live here.

Oraliz Gomez, Grade 11
Rancho High School, NV

Soldier

Dedicating their lives is what they do.
Spending time away from things that they once knew.

Living their lives in complete chaos,
Dropping to the ground when they hear a shot.

Today another man has gone down.
It's quiet with no sound.

Pain and sorrow have been felt,
With all the things that they've been dealt.

They try so hard to forget,
All the things that they do regret.

The killings and the bombings too.
All of the things that they have to do.

Coming back's so hard to do.
They've been away from the things they once knew.

We may never know what it's like,
To see, to hear and to fight the fight.

Caitlyn Robbins, Grade 10
Pocatello Sr High School, ID

The Assembly Line

Get back to the assembly line the anonymous voice screeches.
Everyone takes their faces back from the walls and trudge across the asphalt
to the never-ending clinks and clunks of the machine.
No matter…just another day…just another sunrise.
There is always the future to look forward to.
Yes, the future is said to have promise; promises of festivity and of historical value.
All I have to do is stay on this assembly line in the grey cold.
As long as the assembly line is moving, the machine continues to run.
The machine will function all the way until catastrophe.
Even then, hope in the next world, and all I have to do is push the buttons and pull the levers.
Who needs fun when you have promises?

Michael Farrell, Grade 10
Pocatello Sr High School, ID

Nature's Love

I came into this world crying, and every day shows why, and I end each day sighing asking myself, "are you ready to die?" The shackles of this world have kept me captive, a prisoner of my own freedom. I cannot see the light or the way; I can no longer hope, for even hope has given in. I long to escape my life of twisted misery.

But in the twinkle of an eye, I am in agonizing pain. I cover my face and let my pupils shrink in to the overwhelming light. I glamour at the beauty that lay before me, I regain the strength to stand in awe. The sun awakes to a new day, stretching its rays of hope to all living things. The still lake with its frigid water and the cool, mist floating above, creating a sfumato effect. The crystal, white capped mountains reflecting light to my cheeks, quickly adding warmth and color. The sinuous springs make their way down and the free-falling water with its hammering pound. The chloral filled leaves and mighty, swaying trees, the gentle warm breeze whistling through the grass.

I look up at the mighty, blue sea with its endless boundaries, and take a breath of the calm, crisp, scented air reviving my soul. I close my eyes and hear the chirping and singing of birds, taking their flight into the air. The low, thunderous hoof tops of wild horses making their entry into my sight. Oh, what beauty, what paradise! The metallic, ring of my rusty chains signal the time of my leave. I long for one more view, knowing that I will never understand it. So simple and so perfect, yet so complex. I return to my world, and the sand in the hourglass still falling. I remember nature's patience, its kindness; nature stands still and will never pass. Time does not exist, I have returned with hope even though I am bound by the shackles of this world knowing that…nature's love is the spark that ignites the flames of hope

Andy Dimbi, Grade 12
Nampa Sr High School, ID

Father's Promise

You said you wanted another shot, to be my father again
You promised you wouldn't leave my side this time
And once again I reacted like a fool, and I believed you
You promised to find the shattered pieces of my heart
And put it back together, like a puzzle with a million pieces
You promised to hold my head high when I'm crawling through the mud
You promised to carry me on your back, when I'm walking through the fiery pits of hell
But instead you threw me into the fire
Instead you shattered my heart more, and you smeared my face in the mud.
I'm sad because every time a petal fell off that wild red rose
You fell deeper into that hole
And to believe
Like a fool, I reacted to your heart tearing soul once again
Now I am done
I will find the shattered pieces of my heart
Put it back together, and be proud to say
That I did it without you.

Tyson Scarborough, Grade 12
Lummi High School, WA

Friends Forever

You said we would always be friends forever,
But why am I so afraid to lose you?
Every day I fight heartaches and tears,
From missing the memories of you two.

You were the sisters I never had.
This is the hardest of years for me,
Mere words can't express how I am feeling.
Right now my life feels utterly gloomy.

A couple of minutes from each other's home,
Yet now so very far away.
I look back at the before and after pictures of us,
And I wish that this year will be like the day.

As I walk the school halls,
I forget you're hundreds of miles away.
I turn around thinking you're right there,
But it's not you, so maybe just another day.

Friends come and they go,
But you're always my best friends,
No one will ever take your place in my heart
I pray this wonderful friendship never ends.

Briana Norris, Grade 10
La Center High School, WA

Graduation

I stand here today to say good-bye,
To my childhood;
To recall the memories of my past,
As I knew someday I would.
To leave behind my innocence,
Say good-bye to all my friends;
Kiss the green fields farewell,
And acknowledge now the end.
But, in each tearful end,
In each of our cries;
We stand here all today,
Where our new futures lie.
We are ready now,
To end our childhood days;
And give way to our new lives,
And things will be ok.
We have learned well for this moment,
And with our heads held high;
We stand here now together,
Ready, and eager,
To bid this last good-bye.

Jessica Cannon, Grade 12
Payson High School, UT

Slow Tapping at My Window

The soft drops of rain are enchanting,
strong winds make leaves seem as if they are dancing.
Standing and watching exuberant light tear the sky.
I could not leave, not even if I wanted to try.
Each drop descends onto me,
exploding on contact engulfing my body.
I am freed with each new drop of sanity.
The only thing that would satisfy me,
is if the rain would consume me completely.
So peaceful are these drops of brilliance.
I wonder if I am the only one that can feel this.
Never have I felt so alive so carefree,
new light shines and I can finally see.
The sky lights up with blue and purple shock.
It is magnificent, loss of speech, with no need to talk.
My drops of joy slowly dissipate,
with each slow stride I contemplate.
I wonder when my night of rain,
will return again.

Misty Dawson, Grade 12
Two Rivers High School, UT

The Dollar Bill

Inside your house you notice something green
It's laying on the floor before your eyes
A twenty dollar bill just waiting there
A glance around, when suddenly more wise,
A grab and Mister Bill is stuffed unseen.
When subsequently, you remember Bill
And start to think about what has been done
Conscience starts to eat away your will
In recognizing folly mixed with greed.
Repentance! Father God still forgives me.
Next comes the hard thing, once more I confess;
My parents must hear my desire to flee
From the sin that entangled, now forsook
My dad rewards me with what I first took.

Michael Migita, Grade 10
Covenant High School, WA

Siblings

Summer, nine years old and 4 foot 8
As if fruits and veggies was all she ate
Her family doesn't understand why she's so tall
Her dad wishes she'd play basketball
But like her eldest sister, she thinks soccer is neat
But unlike her sisters, she's really sweet
She has a heart of gold at only nine
Her mother proudly says, "That one is mine…"
She'll only drink water, not soda pop
Maybe that's why she always comes out on top
She fights with her sister, this is true
But will always love them through and through
And I love her, too.

Chelsea O'Neil, Grade 10
W F West High School, WA

Nothing

You should have been there
You could have
You should have cared
You could have
But you didn't
And now you're gone
And you left me there,
Alone
Sitting on the cold ground
With my heart broken
Sitting on my lap
Trying to survive, to breathe
These empty feelings
Are some things that I fear to face
The pain that you left with me
You just left it
You just left
And you left me there
No light, no sound, no heartbeat, nothing
I was just…there
Without you

Angela Agrusa, Grade 10
Diamond Ranch Academy, UT

For You

I watched a man, shred his hands
To save me from myself

Break down and cry

To bleed for us,
confide in us,
then give his trust

He said
Little baby, don't you worry
When you're afraid,

Just break down and cry

April Barnes, Grade 11
Heritage High School, WA

Step by Step

Step by step
with enjoying the way to dreams
Step by step
with repeating the failure
Step by step
with getting over the difficulties
Step by step
with becoming strong.

If you keep working hard for dreams,
your dreams must come true.

Ayaka Nozue, Grade 11
W F West High School, WA

Priceless Gift

I could give you a necklace,
I could give you a ring,
I could give you a parrot that will dance and sing,
But the one thing I choose is not listed above,
For the one thing I choose is all of my love.

Robert Hartshorn, Grade 12
Trask River High School, OR

I Do Not Understand

I do not understand
Why we show lustful attraction to another by harsh behavior
Why there are so many exceptions to the rules of the English language
Why we can't absorb information in our brains as rapidly as a young child anymore

But most of all
I do not understand
Why Chris Farley had to slowly kill himself
With overuse of fatal drugs
(He was a very talented and funny man,
And his death occurred at so painfully young,
His influence ever so strong on many with a sense of humor.)

What I understand most is the color blue
She appeals to many, and is a simple pleasure to behold
Abuse of her is rarely possible,
For she beautifies anything she lays her touch to
Widely she is adored
She can complement any adjacent color,
Delightedness is locked within her veil of captivating power.

Brittany Corbridge, Grade 10
Pocatello Sr High School, ID

Keep Your Arms and Legs Inside the Ride

Life is a poorly made roller coaster there is so much anticipation going up
You know you're about to go crashing down but you don't know when
All you know is it will be terrifying yet delightful.

Before you know what happened you're hanging upside down and you wonder how
You have ups and downs without a clue to why
Then if the ride breaks down you will need somebody to help you get going again
There may be an unexpected turn, an unforeseen twist
How will you deal with this will you just go with the flow?
Or will you wish you never bothered?
Are you still scared? Are you just sitting around depressed it will soon be over?
Or are you waving your hands in the air enjoying every second of the time?

Now the ride is slowing down, the exit is in sight
Maybe you feel ripped off, maybe it wasn't worth those last tickets.
Did you spend those last moments wondering if you should have picked this ride?
Did you spend the time looking back thinking you missed the fun?
Or were you just glad you had a good run?
The ride is over now did you have fun or did you spend the time in fear?
Afraid of what you missed afraid of what was coming?
Well don't worry you're going on a better ride now.

Cody Sershon, Grade 10
Oak Harbor High School, WA

One Step Two Step

I love you and I'm blinded by this
But who could blame me I couldn't resist
For all the pain and suffering I saw in your eyes
I still can't believe you were ready to die
To end the pain and suffering in your life
To hurt those who didn't provide.
For all the love that you sought so deep
For all the secrets you couldn't keep
You were ready to die and go to the eternal sleep.
The only problem with this plan of yours
Is the pain that goes to those who mourn.
Who mourn to help you to the light
Who mourn to help you fight the fight.
So before you go through with this
Remember that I couldn't resist
Resist to help the girl with the closed fists
To help you see another day
So please stay
And I'll show you a different way.

Austin Howard Grogan, Grade 12
Trask River High School, OR

Aftermath

As a modest child I had no dread,
Only thoughtful and pleased about things at hand.
Never ever knowing what is ahead,
While walking up and down my land.

Once foresaw everything innocently,
Of people's goodness, morals and kindness.
A beloved friendship intimately,
Forever vanished throughout my blindness.

Was a child, I did ache for the past,
Of the people I once loved and adored.
Overwhelmed of "why" that never did last
From silence and detest of the abhorred.

Now older and mature I now know "why"
It was all from a hushed little white lie.

Hannah Gresham, Grade 10
McKenzie River Christian School, OR

American Soldier

Honor is a American soldier.
The American flag a soldier full of pride.
Strong will the soul of a U.S. soldier.
Heart full of honor gives the will to survive.
Mind and body is the spirit of the American soldier.
Honorable if the country we live in.
Motivated is our leader for many he must protect.
Dedication is the men and women for the U.S. military.
An American soldier the heart and soul of the U.S.
Will to fight the dream of the U.S. citizen.

Kasey Kenworthy, Grade 10
Oak Harbor High School, WA

Father

Father, you are the one who brought me to planet Earth.
Father, you are the one who held Mom's hand during my birth.
Father, you are the one who taught me how to mind.
Father, you are the one who taught me how to rope and ride.
Father, you are the one who can get so mad.
Father, you are the one who can get so sad.
Father, you are the one who gives me all your time.
Father, you are the one who chews that icky, icky grime.
Father, you are the one who puts up with me.
Father, you are the one who deals with me.
Father, you are the one who can still put me in a bind.
Father, you are the one who is so very, very kind.
Father, you are the one who is number one.

Zack Peterson, Grade 10
Camas County High School, ID

Spring

When the very first signs of spring are here,
The crocuses bloom and the sun shines bright.
The trees get their leaves and the streams are clear,
The grass turns green and the birds take flight
Gathering twigs to build their nests.
Baby birds and mammals will soon be seen.
The newness of life to me is the best.
The valleys and mountains have all turned green,
Wildflowers add their colors
Puffy white clouds dot the big blue sky,
The fish are swimming in the deep clear waters.
The frogs and crickets sing their lullaby.
Spring is refreshing, a time of new birth
When gladness and color cover the Earth.

Matthew Douglas Porter, Grade 11
Preston High School, ID

Self-Love

I tried to be more and rule my own self,
There was no way out, I was losing my health.
I left what was common and sought for more,
I walked o'er my past and closed my heart door.
My friends had now left me to think alone,
To prove that my actions had made me prone,
To all of the hate and struggles within,
That made me a prisoner to my own sin.
But when I realized what happened to me,
I began to gain help and dignity.
I regained the love and support I lacked,
Which helped me discard the baggage I packed.
I thanked God for his mercy, love, and grace,
For my past sins he will always erase.

Christina Gray, Grade 10
Covenant High School, WA

And So I Write

Pity —
Could have been so lovely —
But I write —
Dreaming —
If only we'd been —
No, just write —
Innocent —
It could have been so —
Childlike that night —
Surely you understand —
How can't you feel? —
I know that it's there —
Still I wait —
Hold my breath —
Pray out loud —
And write —
Pen in hand —
Feet toward the sky —
Blood rushing down —
Tear in my eye —

Emily Marriott, Grade 11
Stanwood High School, WA

Grandpa

There he laid, still as stone
Only memories flooded his mind
As he reflected on the ages
That so quickly passed him by.
He had no time to in which to fight
I could not help but cry
I could not play with him anymore
His friendship was so priceless in my life
Now his days were nearly done
His family gathered 'round
The cancer had clearly won
He passed gradually, without a sound.

Sterling Jones, Grade 10
Orem High School, UT

The Test

True courage is hard to find,
In one's self and in one's mind
True courage is hard to see,
By anyone, even me
True courage is a test
Whom passes those that do their best
A test of strength, a test of fear,
A test of those whom we hold dear
A test of Affection, a test of desire,
A test with those who bring us higher
A test of hope, and of reassurance,
A test to be sure of our endurance
True courage is a test for me
How do I find what I can't see?

Stephanie Haralson, Grade 11
Holy Names Academy, WA

The World in Which We Live

The sky is getting light again, the days becoming longer
The children are all out to play, on the streets paved with gravel
The humming birds will soon to fly back from the winters sleep
The bees will buzz once more, while children still play on the street
Though beware little ones, not of the bees, for their sting will go away
But keep your eyes on everyone, we want all the children coming back today
The world is big, and full of things, we want not to corrupt little minds
But where are we heading when we say "all children come inside"
All children come inside, there is a rapist in the street
We do not want for him to come, beware little children of everyone
The children are inside, they follow the words of the wise
But then they turn on the TV, and their minds become full of lies
They soon learn to fear, their love and innocence grows cold
For this is the world in which we live, sad as it may seem
So these little children grow up, and are blamed for things they can't control
"Teens these days" is what they hear, as they search for their identity
The pressure of this world, the things we're faced with daily
There is heartache among the people, of this American nation.

Kaylee Van Gelder, Grade 10
Valley Christian Secondary School, WA

Dreams

What do dreams mean?
Some dreams are superior or dreadful.
Are they showing us what's going to occur in the future or the past?
Are they here to haunt us? Entertain us?
What is their purpose of being in our conscience?
Do our surroundings create them for us and why are they so vivid?
Why do we embrace dreams close to our hearts or disregard them?
Are we able to make them go away or take us slightly further?
We may never know why some are colored and decorated, black or white.
We're puzzled with the question that in no way could be answered...
What do dreams mean?

Amanda Gabbard, Grade 10
Glide Middle School, OR

Fish Don't Have Feelings

Happy? No. If the fish says he is, it is only a lie,
It is selfish of him to think, but he can't feel any other way,
Confused, hurt, and alone, he just wants to say good bye.
Seeing you there, what do you expect him to say?

He wanted to die off *your* hook, out of any in the sea,
Not to old age, cancer or at the mouth of a shark.
Don't say he didn't try: he bit five times, he called twenty.
Then you said you were out of bait, but off your hook dangled an aardvark.

Swimming away, the ocean turned even bluer.
His food became stale, and seaweed just wasn't the same,
The flippers stopped, and he wondered why he ever tried to woo her,
Honestly wishing he could just forget her name.

Please, leave this fish alone. Set up your mast
Sail far, far away from me: "count no man happy till he dies, free of pain at last."

Alan Ho, Grade 12
Parkrose High School, OR

What Dreams Become

Every night I go to sleep,
my dreams become very deep.
I can't awake,
I'm stuck not able to run away.
I don't know where to go.
I don't know what to do.
Strangers come to my dreams
making me give the loudest screams.
When I get to the point
when I know I'm awake
I don't know why I can't think straight.
Maybe because late at night,
my mind stops reflecting light.
And the dark that is left,
called the defect,
is proud because now, he can frighten me.
I don't know what I have just said,
The only thing is that I'll have to stay awake.
That way the dark that stands inside of me
won't stop the light to reflect my dreams.
And what dreams come won't intimidate me.

Isamar Medina, Grade 10
Rancho High School, NV

Nightmare

Sleeping peacefully in your protected room
nothing to cause you harm
but nothing ever stays peaceful.
Soon thoughts of torment enter your mind
will these thoughts ever leave
no they will never leave.

Spinning through your head
suffocating the thoughts in your mind
the once peaceful thoughts now cold and dark.
Sweat pouring down your face
the taste of blood in your mouth
you twist and turn, hope and pray.

A shadow of death overcomes you
choking you with the darkness
feeding off your thoughts.
Getting sucked into its eternal pain
like a knife stabbing your heart repeatedly
and nothing to stop it.

You wish you could somehow change it
do something to stop this misery
and you can, just wake up.

Daniel Green, Grade 10
Orem High School, UT

The Lone Echo

you scream at the top of your lungs
but it screams back at you
you're walking through life
without a soul to help you on your way
you realize you just want to die

then comes into your life an angle…
she gracefully walks in…
into the dark and painful world of yours
and you feel the pain leave you

but she stab you in the back with a knife
and leaves it there…
you give up all hope…
and you're left alone again, to walk your way alone again…
to face life and the pain again

walking life without someone
is like an
ECHO!

Brian Rominski, Grade 10
Oak Harbor High School, WA

Secrets

Secrets are whispers,
Soft and sweet,
Thoughts that are hidden
In the street.

They start on the tongue
Of the ones who dare
To share the truth
To anyone there.

Twisting, turning, tormenting.
The meaning, mutilating each time it is heard.
The fantastic fulfillment
Of spreading the word.

Jade Greene, Grade 11
Nampa Sr High School, ID

The Miracle of Life

Life is a miracle
and the right to live is a gift.
It's wrapped up tight in a ribbon,
woven with dreams.
whether you are very young or very old,
life is filled with wonder and surprises.
The winter moon smiles in the heavens
and quietly hides tomorrow like a secret.
Like life, Christmas too is hidden,
and is not just about presents and a tree.
It's about the fact that Jesus was born 2000 years
to a virgin named Mary, and gave us life.

Marquea Johnson, Grade 10
Life Christian School, WA

Spring Awakes

Awake! Alive!
With opened eyes
Shadows away
And green will sway
In windy bright
Or starry night
Keeping the time
In whispered rhyme
Secrets untold
With breeze unfold
Coloring breaks
O'er silent wake
Frozen moon's shine
Will melt behind
A warmer wind
That's come again
Stretched over peaks
No longer bleak
With opened eyes
Awake! Alive!

Kayla Johnson, Grade 12
Rigby Sr High School, ID

Without a Doubt

I know I love you,
Without a doubt.
I can't think of anything else,
I can't do without.

When you're not with me,
I don't know what to do.
You show me the way,
That's why I love you.

If you want to see me smile,
Then let me tell you how.
You can say you love me,
Without a doubt.

Randall Normandin, Grade 10
W F West High School, WA

Friendship

Outgoing, entertaining and friendly,
Trustful to a T.
Caring and understanding,
Happy to be with me.
Lazy, wild, and crazy,
Grumpy when she is mad,
If I'm having a bad day,
She will always make you glad.
This is my best friend,
Forever and beyond
Always be my best friend,
As the years go on.

Lyndsey Pollard, Grade 10
La Center High School, WA

Miss

Growing up in California
The city urban and full of noise
screams at me and tells me it's just their voice.
San Bernardino is where I was raised
and that's the thing I have to say
California is in my heart
born and raised.

Raymond Saldana, Grade 10
Rancho High School, NV

In Remembrance of Autumn Sublime

The last breath of summer shines through my window tonight;
I never knew something could end so beautifully, so dramatic.
I am falling through rays of light,
Soon touching the beginning of some new kind of beautiful; autumn
The turbulence of a falling leaf cooperates with my mellow mind,
Rustling leaves dance with so many amazing colors;
Reds, oranges, yellows light up the streets, the towns, the mountains
The smell of an ancient forest fulfills my greatest destinies
I race through pines trying to catch every humid breath, every prismatic color,
Every leaf and pine needle laughing at my feet, laughing as I fly.
I feel a chaotic rhythm of my heartbeat,
I'm dancing as the rain starts to fall, soon awakening a new world to discover
Every singing finch, robin and blue jay;
Every falling leaf sweetly kissing the earth welcoming its rest bed.
But wait…what is this white cloudiness falling all around me?
Silent as it reaches Mother Earth, nestling on saplings and leaves,
Smoothly disappearing into the now peaceful river,
Winter has come upon me sneaking around the corner,
As I fall into despair in wait for beautiful spring to blossom.
In remembrance of autumn sublime.

Roxy Diaz, Grade 10
Orem High School, UT

Conformity

I am alone, an independent thinker, a non conformist.
I have my own thoughts, my own mind…
I am me and I rebel against society…
It is me, myself, and I against the world. No one else.
I stand firm by my own opinion and what I believe is right.
But deep down, I must face the reality of being alone.
The reality of having no one.
OH! The things I'd do to be a somebody, not a nobody.
Just dying to make it some place in this world.
A chance to change it…
Anticipating the day…my hopes would soon turn into fulfilled dreams.
Through these fulfilled dreams comes conformity.
Through conformity…comes the communication and interaction of society.
It is evident that our society has relied upon others
the uniqueness the individual seeks…does not exist,
But merely ruins their image…defining who they are.
Conformity has become our source of life
Without conformity, there is no life. But chaos.
Leaving America with a sense of quiet desperation.

Kristine Penalosa, Grade 10
Rancho High School, NV

Help Me
My stomach feels funny,
I don't want to eat.
It's like a nervous, exited feeling,
but I'm sad.
Yesterday I had a crush,
today I'm not so sure.

His hair to his ears,
a nice dark blonde.
He has a kind smile
and a nice gentle voice.
He is kind, funny,
and cool.

But I don't know
if I should like him,
he is two grades above me
and doesn't always acknowledge I'm there.
Should I like him, should I not?
Someone help me
Jessica Black, Grade 10
Orem High School, UT

Don't Understand
I do not understand
Why my brain does not work some days.
Why poems are important,
Why poems will help me in my trade.
But most of all, I do not understand
Why the world turns, or if I should even finish this poem.
Is writing poems supposed to make me wealthy?
(I know my trade will make me that — working on cars.)
What I understand most
Is my brain is on vacation, and it isn't helping me one bit
In my teacher's writing skills class.
Michael Greenlea, Grade 12
Great Basin High School, UT

Ghost on the Highway
The air was cold and black as night
A strange mist strangled the car's light
As I drove down the silent narrow street
A young man strangely popped into sight
With saddened eyes he asked for a ride
Silences grew like a mouse in the grass
When I arrived at the humble house
He had disappeared.
Gray hair and weary face
He met me at the door
"His name was Michael"
He spoke in shallow breaths
"He never makes it home
After his fatal hit and run
Twenty years ago."
Markus Meldrum, Grade 12
Mountain Crest High School, UT

Truths
Remember the time it was made right.
Has it been too long, is it out of sight?
Written in pages of novels short and long,
Only when read by me have the truths become wrong.

Get off the stage open your mind
Walk away this is not your time.
The numbness will flood faster and hard,
Unable to tell but this dream has gone too far.

Why am I wrong, what did I do?
I try my hardest just to please you!
Kneeling in a room staring at splintered mirrors,
Finding a peace, dreaming of my biggest fears.

I know I'm not yours and you are not mine
Love is waiting to inhale the white line.
Sick of this game, sick of your lip
No room for my soul in your heart to fit.

You've got what you wanted, does it make you happy?
Or should I stay, show what not to be
You have forgotten, it is out of sight.
Questions will be answered you are always right.
Miles Sherman, Grade 12
Emery High School, UT

Shattered Bottles Are Shattered Lives
Contaminate your outside bark.
Let the venom displace your mind.
Let it blacken your beat and blank your eyes,
Those eyes which probe for justification.
I will not cry for you.
Let the poison captivate control of your laugh.
Turn the well known chuckle to a scream.
Deteriorate your imagination, abandon those thoughts,
Once worth thinking, now preoccupied with this addictive sin.
Indulge in drink until it's empty, both life and bottle.
Suck that abysmal stink until taste denies to come to tongue.
Let acid blaze your heart right through.
Let time cease its rhythm, the orchestra of life.
I will not cry for you.
Cut, then scar your blood, your once pride and joy;
The apples of their daddy's eye.
For you have found something new.
Neglect the precious times you once knew.
Bury your happy thoughts along with your sallow body.
You have made a choice you can never erase.
I now cry for you.
Rachel Luthy, Grade 11
Madison Sr High School, ID

My Three Saviors

Brother Rudd brought me closer to the Holy Ghost.
Brother Esplin came and took my hand.
Together they're taking me out of my desert toward the distant Son.
No longer in my comfort zone. Past the trials of my own.
I trust in them to lead me on. Guiding me in the footsteps of the Son.
Teaching me about him and the plan.
Using scriptures as the guide. To help us soar and find his side.
Guiding me to the Savior.
Who'll direct me back to my home.
Because he really did atone for our sins, and called them His own.
Now we need to do our part. Teaching what we know in our heart.
Brothers you found me and led me to the Savior.
Now here on Earth I am with my two saviors.
One in each hand leading me to my promised land.
There I will find God the Father and the Son.
Waiting for me with arms open wide, and to thank you for being my guides.
Welcome you into our group hug.
The next thing he would have to say, "Congratulations, you've made it to Heaven."
The gates would open and light appear.
As I walk in I will remember who it was that guided me here.
Finding me when I was lost. To become my earthly saviors.

Jocelynne Hayward, Grade 11
Emery High School, UT

Media Play

Perfect smiles, perfect eyes, perfect bodies, perfect lies.
Perfect skin, perfect hair, perfect clothes, the vanity fair.
Behind the mask what's really there? Spending hours in front of the mirror,
making oneself perfect so the world will stop and stare.
Not showing truth or reality, not showing the realization of what could truly be
Fascination with outer beauty has taken over.
What ever happened to the inner soul, the light from within?
Beauty that has been hidden and yet to have been?
The beauty that a laugh shows, beauty that no one truly sees or knows.
Why do we have to comply with all of these stereotypes?
Why do we hide who we are just to please the others?
Why do we surrender to media images?
Making ourselves sick to achieve the video view of beauty.
Not me, no way, I want to live my life the way I am,
without acting different than who I am for someone else every day.
I am me untainted, unfiltered, unchanged. Who are you?
I am me. Who are you?

Brittainy Baker, Grade 12
Northridge High School, UT

Job Corps and You

As I came to Job Corps, I never thought I would find someone to spend my time with...
When I see you down I just want to hold you close and never let you go...
As the days go by and by I wonder how each day is going to go...
When I sit in class watching the clock tick hoping time will go by quicker...
When I hear the bell ring I walk to find you just to see how you are doing...
Then after class time comes, we make every effort to spend our precious time together before we depart to our dorms...
As I sit in my dorm, I think of you all the time, waiting for the morning to roll around to see you again...

Kendra Swiger, Grade 12
Great Basin High School, UT

Shedding Feathers

Hidden under feathers, secret truth deep within,
Soft cries beneath the surface, below the precious skin.
Outside appearing satisfied, inside there's too much pain,
No one knows the secret, about to go insane.

Inside is an endless pit, will never be truly full,
Tugging the rope of freedom, must continuously pull.
Shadowing the mind, feelings won't go away,
Bad dreams never stop, keep haunting every day.

Memories so harsh, unbearable to see,
The mind still remembers, pictures will not flee.
Distant from those close, thoughts safely concealed,
Alone and frightened, hidden truths must be revealed.

The feathers are now shedding, truth must be told,
Can't hide beneath the layers, emotions turning cold.
Bursting with truth, feelings up in the air,
Faces filled with shock, showing love and care.

Secret is revealed, no hidden truths inside,
Loved ones show concern, no longer have to hide.
Old feathers have now shed, secrets all shown,
New beginnings are awaiting, never have to be alone.

Savannah McBride, Grade 12
Foothill High School, NV

weary

wrinkled, drooping, slouched
the man sits small and sleepy
ridges in his nails
the ones on his brow are weeping
remaining in the past, now

moving his feet slow
across the wooden flooring
all grey colors show
resting, reading, rocking chair
from violins to snoring

relaxed with a book
his old dog begins to yawn
dusty window frames
capturing an untamed lawn

a veteran man
still tired living in war
the battle of life and the love he sees no more
the man is weary, still young

Jennifer Zomchek, Grade 12
Kodiak High School, AK

Painting Adventures

Grabbing the tool, which one will do?
Soaring over the canvas and into my imagination,
Mixing colors and thoughts.
Creating a picture, possibly worth
A thousand and one words.
I paint.
A bright and sunny day, no clouds around
Just the birds singing with the sweetest sound.
Its time for me to finish the ground.
Many different shades of greens
Filling the bottom of the canvas scene.
Rolling hills, hitting the blue acrylic waves,
While the old man stays with his grandchild
And plays.
The wrinkles I so gently place on his face
Tell a story, but that's for
Another time and place.

Karla Bilden, Grade 12
Heritage High School, WA

Bud in Question

Saplings puffed in periwinkle pride
blossoms having yawned and multiplied
parachute, confetti, down to land
pleasantly upon my wrinkled hand.

"Blossoms, if you treasure me, I wish,
wisdom of the mystery betwixt
sprouting bulb and lavender release,
Tell me of the buds from which you leap.

Light to me the way, I pray, how flow'r
locked in layered heads, explodes with pow'r?
Entertain the conscience of a prune,
Conscience to be taken from me soon,"

"Friend, whom we have known through rain and years,
how can you so eagerly inquire
wisdom which enfolds about your breast;
the bud is not the answer, but a test."

Conner McKinnon, Grade 11
Alta High School, UT

Gentle

Gentle is the bubbling water trickling down the rocks.
The fluffy white clouds flowing across the sky.
The wind that makes the trees sway back and forth.
It's the fish swimming upstream.

Gentle is the loving parents watching their children.
The children playing by the bank of the river.
It's the baby that's sleeping in the grass.

Gentle is the sun shining down on everyone.

Kibbee Piper, Grade 11
Nampa Sr High School, ID

Life's Cycle
Life is a cycle of being born and reborn,
Reborn is the afterlife,
Afterlife is never growing old,
old is aging by your figure,
figure is the body,
body is the way of changing,
changing is the world with movement,
movement is the liquids stuck inside.
inside is the cycle of you.
Jeanna Sorg, Grade 10
Oak Harbor High School, WA

Best Friends
When I look in your eyes
I knew that you were right
we're two friends so much alike.
When I look in your eyes
I see the pain you try to hide
as do you see mine
There's nothing we can hide.
though how much we've tried
to make this friendship true
Do I mean this much to you?
I promise you can tell me anything
no matter what this hard life brings
Your problems do mean something
we'll get through this together
then the letters will be right
Best friends forever.
Alisha Thompson, Grade 10
Rancho High School, NV

Barefooted Rivers
Summer.
Summer brings days of sun.
It brings cool wind
with a hint of spice.
Running
down to the river,
tearing off our shoes,
my friends and I
are prepared to bask
in summer's goodness.
Feeling our feet,
on the soft mud, runs shivers
up our spines.
Looking down the sun drenched river
reminds us
that these days are meant
for freedom.
Our days couldn't be spent better,
except it be,
in the
barefooted rivers.
Caitlin Webb, Grade 10
Orem High School, UT

Face of Inner Beauty
I watch you from a far
And I can't help but hate what I see
The face of pain and suffering looking for help
The pain and suffering needs to vanish
I watch with such helplessness
Wanting to help end the suffering
The person next to you
The person causing such suffering
Blacks, blues, reds, and purples covering beauty
This is not what I like seeing
Torment, pain, and suffering building as the time passes
Every day it increases and the pain grows
Blacks, blues, reds, and purples darken and grow
Today you awaken to the face of a friend
Your pain and suffering is over
I came to save you and you are getting better
Blacks, blues, reds, and purples lighten and your true beauty emerges
Once again we see the bright and perky person that is my friend
Nicholas Peterson, Grade 11
North Salem High School, OR

A Letter to My Family
Although our time on Earth has ended way too fast
I'm leaving so much love…more than enough to last

Cherish all our memories, and keep me in your heart
Until that special day comes, when we'll never have to part

The life we built together, has meant so much to me
My beautiful wife and children…my wonderful family

Can you feel my arms around you…I'm holding you so tight
Always remember that feeling, it will help you while I'm not in sight

You know I will be here waiting…making things right for you
Please try to make a new life…that's what I want you to do

Always know my love for you, will never ever end
I know it will be hard…but someday your hearts will mend

God be with you 'till we meet again

Love,
Dad
Alyssa Hunsaker, Grade 10
Orem High School, UT

Pride in Our Nation
P atriotism
R ed stripes waving valiantly in the breeze on a cold winter's night
I ntelligence that our country has
D edication to our country and what it stands for
E xtraordinary men and women that give their lives freely every day
Shaila Carman, Grade 10
Pocatello Sr High School, ID

Fighting for Life

All his energy was slipping away
He slowly closed his mystic eyes of blue
Upon the cold cool floor, very still he lay
What might have happened, he had no clue

Sweat glistened upon his brow like morning dew
His sister's fingers closed around his own
His throat went dry, his piercing headache grew
Her voice comes through in a worried tone

From his throat escapes a deep moan
Hoping this wasn't his last breath
He opened his eyes, releasing a groan
Knowing he had just missed the kiss of death

He looked up into her reassuring smile
Knowing he'd be on Earth for a while

Heather Kitto, Grade 12
Alta High School, UT

Ode to the Schwans Man

He comes to my house every once in a while
    he waits in the hall, on the cold tile.
I tell him we're good and to come next week
    he whispers, under his breath, what a geek.
But that's okay because he's cool
    that's why I'm writing about him for school.
His chicken strips are so nice
    When he brings them in they're as cold as ice.
I love his ice cream and his pie
    he is just such a cool guy.
And even though I don't know his name
    I admire him all the same.
Schwans man if you were here
    You would probably be thinking that I was a queer.

Kyle Synsteby, Grade 11
Lincoln County High School, NV

Sunset, Sunrise, and Life

Sunset and sunrise which here is present?
Sunset contains beauty and bids farewell;
Sunrise brings hope, joy, and brightness as well
But what this sun is the sea must be bent,
Upon the 'wakening of beauty heaven-sent.
Perhaps this sun will rise, and preacher tell,
    All the minstrels of all that has befell
Their city where dance, joy, and precious time spent.

"So which is this?" the minstrels ask the priest,
The priest who walks the coast with sand 'tween toes
    "This my sons is life," Preacher calmly says
    "Neither sunset nor sunrise to the East
'Tis the sun rising for many tomorrows
As you too live every day," and the sun fades.

Kysen Palmer, Grade 11
Union High School, OR

Sting of Battle

The smell of blood and the feel of steel on steel
Red permeates the sight
The feeling of strife rages from hill to hill
As fire provides night's light.
The taste of fear feeds your frenzy.
Will the battle be won?
Loyalty holds you.
Cuts and wounds give misery.
The enemy folds to you.
The battle is won.
Sorrow lends a grieving moment
Your brothers-in-arms are gone.
Who has really won?

Mark Altman II, Grade 10
Coeur d'Alene High School, ID

Darkness and Light

A single spark can light the way
And help us see again,
But it's a dark and deadly place
That thinks all light in vain.

Not a spark is ever lost
In the battle of dark and light.
We should never once give in
And let darkness win the fight.

Evil would never be victorious
If only we let the light in.
Goodness would triumph no matter what,
Darkness would never win.

Adrienne Schoenbachler, Grade 10
Home School, WA

Portrait of Pride

When I went for a walk in the park yesterday,
I was watching the people pass by on their way.
My attention was caught by an int'resting pair:
Arm-in-arm was a man of great girth, with an air
Of superior breeding and lofty conceit,
And a girl, tall and slender from head to her feet,
Who, with nose in the air and her eyes peering down,
You would think she should sit on a throne with a crown!
As I passed by them closer I heard what they said
Of a man they disliked who was recently dead;
Though they knew nothing of him except his low rank,
Their opinion of him still increasingly sank.
Then I thought to myself, *I hope I would not show
Such disdain for a dead man who I did not know*.

Carrie Orr, Grade 12
Covenant High School, WA

Soldier
I am young and physically fit
Determined for success
I am a Soldier
I have overcome many mental barriers
Accepting nothing but perfection
I am a Soldier

I have struggled coping with sacrifice
Performing my duties
I am a Soldier
I am one with the terrain
The nightmare of a dream
I am a Soldier

Silent and still
Repressing emotions
I am a Soldier
Fighting hunger, fighting stress
Fighting fatigue and depravation
I am a Soldier

I am the toughest of the tough
The best of the best
I am a Soldier
TeJay Espe, Grade 11
Stanwood High School, WA

Smile
Everything's so wrong
And your life is falling apart.
You feel burdened and heavy
As you carry your broken heart.

Then one day
A stranger passing by
Smiles at you
And somehow freezes time.

You stop all your mourning
And all your crying.
You focus on that tiny gesture
That finds your heart so dying.

Such a small thing
Yet monumental in its way.
It's brought you small joy
To carry on through the day.

Time suddenly resumes,
The world continues its pace.
But you treasure close a stranger's smile
And the comfort that it gave.
Melanie Lapham, Grade 11
Home School, WA

Love's Essence
Deception is the thorn on a rose,
and that rose is the essence of love.
Love is a cluster of happiness,
honesty and kindness but it will
always be full of pain.
Pain is always near no matter
what you might hear.
This painful state will engulf you
and you will lose your way.
Lost in a world of hurt.
Hurtfulness is deceptions right hand
and in that hand is a rose,
which is the bitter sweet smell of love,
who lives in the bed of deception.

Deception is the rose of lies.
Kasey White, Grade 10
Oak Harbor High School, WA

Summons
A man sits on a doorstep
the guitar
his only companion.
In the silence of
a new moon
melodies dance
with Spanish flair.
They glisten
growing stronger
calling to those
inside homes
behind shut doors
will you come
to listen?
Erin McManamon, Grade 12
Highline High School, WA

Spring
Kites and sailing high
On the strong March breeze,
Daffodils are dancing
To the buzz of the bees.

Raindrops are falling
Pussy willows sprout,
Children with umbrellas
Splash puddles with a shout.

"Spring is here at last!"
Chicks peep to the hen.
Flower buds are popping
And life begins again.
Melissa Vargas, Grade 10
Central Valley High School, WA

The Only One
You're still the one,
I'll love forever,
You're still the one
I want to wake up with every morning
and snuggle with every night,
The one I want to share
all my dreams with,

The one whose hand
I want to hold
Whose shoulders I want to lean on,

You're still the one I want to encourage
to make your own dreams come true,

You're still the one,
the only one.
Emilee Westenskow, Grade 11
Alta High School, UT

Wit
Wit is a thing with a smile
That comes and goes
Like a flash
Brief but bright
Imbedded in cleverness
Waiting for the next move

Wit keeps coming
And going
And speaks on accord
It shows only through a smile
David Dambi, Grade 11
Nampa Sr High School, ID

Freedom Isn't Free
Astonishment hit
Fear running through our veins
7-47 hit and we shook with shock
Perishing because of another's actions
Traumatized for now
But not for long
They brought it here
And we thrust it back
Rage kindled like fire within
United we stand
Fighting to sustain our freedom
And helping the innocent gain theirs
On their ground we now stand
Taking our lives some still prefer
But until it ends
We stay
Samantha Kirby, Grade 12
Mountain Crest High School, UT

An Ode to a Bell

Often like the sound of the ocean spraying
sharp black rocks along the shore.
Similar to the rancid buzzing of an alarm clock
introducing the morning's sun.
Bringing joy to anxious feet
wanting to scatter.
A favorite sound to many young ears
bringing independence closer
each and every time.
It's a short-lived dance
bringing together summer and winter.
Students live by it.
Parents dread it.
Teachers love it.
The roads are flocked with anxiety
as the last one releases us.
Never again will we think so kindly
of such a simple, subtle sound.
Soon it will let us free.
Embarking on what's to come
anticipating every last breath.

Alex Geer, Grade 12
Kodiak High School, AK

Best Friends

Two that miss each other when in opposite rooms,
they never want to be apart,
they seem to live with each other.

Fight over stupid little things,
but then can hug and make up the next second.
Would jump in front of a bullet for each other,
willing to lose their life for them.

After high school still talking, seeing, and being
with each other all the time,
move to be around the other,
and are there for the other whenever they can.

Even then you still don't know their connection
because they can finish one another's sentences
and speak for the other.

That is why they lay in the ground side by side
for the rest of their other life.

Brooke Gaston, Grade 10
La Center High School, WA

Sunday Boating Parties: Or, Two Weeks from Wednesday

When I walked away today
The laughing lobsters followed me
Expressing with the fondest brays
Their thoughts on courtly harmony.

On the road, a peacock panicked
(Burning toast perturbs the wise
And those who grow up unromantic
Find their tonsils in their eyes.)

Soliloquizing photographs
Thought class distinction vulgar stuff
And paddled wildly from rafts
With candlesticks and parchment muffs.

The animadversion of the moment
Found a home in lost headlines
Patronizing its opponents
With orange jam and covert sighs.

When adieus to you we bid
Look into our poems and socks
Under layers of shoe-polish
You may find your missing clocks.

Lila O'Brien, Grade 10
Family Link/Studentlink, WA

Young Poets
Grades 7-8-9

Note: The Top Ten poems were finalized through an online voting system. Creative Communication's judges first picked out the top poems. These poems were then posted online. The final step involved thousands of students and teachers who registered as online judges and voted for the Top Ten poems. We hope you enjoy these selections.

Top Poem Grades 7-8-9

Magic

Magic is like the flowers in spring
Popping up where you least expect
Blooming in mysterious beauty
Magic is like the harsh summer sun
Cracking the parched earth
Destroying with its harsh elegance
Magic is like the leaves in autumn
Playful, giddy, unpredictable
Flowing like a river through the world
Magic is like the winter snow
Submissive unto the wind
Blowing here and there
Magic is like a bluebird
Flying free
Enchanting us with sweet song
Magic is like a wolf
Stealth and beauty
Slinking through the trees
Magic is like a diamond
Shining in the dark
Revealing Destiny

Jessica Carter, Grade 9
Oak Canyon Jr High School, UT

Top Poem Grades 7-8-9

The End of the World

The ocean waves have lapped upon the shore,
The wind has beat the sand into my eyes,
The earth has power beyond a tiger's roar,
And magic wills the huge bright sun to rise.

The eyes of man are full of mystic awe,
As elements take over common life,
We must be breaking earth's stern sturdy law
We cut our world to pieces bringing strife.

Soon our home will disappear forever,
Our great privileges taken back from us:
Punishment for planting hate and never
Dealing with hostile actions as we must.

Every day mankind ignores the crying,
Of every tree and flower, sea and stream,
Creatures flee from forests that are dying,
Nothing's safe from destruction's vile scream.

Clear water, clean air, healthy creatures soon
Will all be gone, no bird will sing a tune.

Carmella Dunn-Hartman, Grade 7
Corvallis Waldorf School, OR

Top Poem Grades 7-8-9

Untold Story

A rare sunny day in early spring
To the leaves of fake flowers wet dewdrops did cling
A groundskeeper wandered pulling weeds with dread
Unfazed by stone rows marking the dead
Glancing at one as he strolled
The unadorned record of a girl nine years old
More than cold silence and earth lay beneath him
A sad story pleading for someone to listen
A mother drunk and a father deceased
On the child cold anger and hatred released
Bruises and cuts blamed on clumsy falls
Forced to endure strange looks in the halls
Constant feelings of embarrassment and shame
A young child crushed under murderous blame
Like rising tide upon castles of sand
Spirit worn away, no longer could stand
Of blame and fear she slowly died
At an abandoned ceremony no one cried
A few years later as the groundskeeper passed
A weight was lifted, someone had listened at last

Mallory Jennings, Grade 8
St Michael School, WA

Top Poem Grades 7-8-9

Memories of a Mountain

A mountain is a ripple
In a vast sea of land,
Yet what it does experience
Cannot be treasured in a hand.

When you read a book of history
It will tell you all the facts
A mountain is a memory
It holds the feelings of the past.

Animals keep the mountain alive
While trees hold it together
The Native Americans gave it love,
But we torture it like a dog that's tethered.

We blew it up for gold,
Bombed it during war,
Suffocate it with car gas
And still we will do more.

We abuse the mountain and kill it
Till all that's left is dust,
Pretty soon, if we're not careful,
That's all that'll be left of us.

Sabine Lefkowitz, Grade 8
McLoughlin Middle School, OR

Top Poem Grades 7-8-9

Appearances

Celebrities pinch, pull, and poke,
Twisting their faces like it's a joke,
Coloring their hair,
Like they just don't care,
About the unrealistic lifestyle they provoke.
They send thousands of dollars to waste,
Covering their faces with powder and paste,
Whether buying a gown,
Or fixing a frown,
They make sure they have impeccable fashion taste.
In my mind, they're throwing money to crooks,
When they could spend it on charity, traveling, or books,
If only I could,
I'd change society for good,
And help the world to stop dwelling on their looks.

Madison Leonard, Grade 8
Canfield Middle School, ID

Top Poem Grades 7-8-9

A Friend to Me Is...

A friend to me is someone who'll be
Giving with love and loyalty
They make you laugh and sometimes cry
They're always there when you've got tears to dry
A friend to me is someone who'll show
Compassion and truth and they'll never go
They'll help you in your times of need
You won't need to beg and you won't need to plead
A friend to me is someone who'll give
The courage, strength, and will to live
They're friendly, smart, and funny too
They'll always stick around with you
A friend to me is someone who's true
And always knows what's right to do
They're never two-faced, or make lies
Good friends are angels from the skies

Kayla Rowbal, Grade 7
Adna Middle-High School, WA

Top Poem Grades 7-8-9

Think of the Others

The road will be rough and you think your life is tough
But consider the others who are less fortunate
Think of the others who lead harder lives than you
Think of the people who must fight for the smallest crumb
Think of the Others

Think of the persecuted, tortured, and tormented
Think of the orphans, widows, the sightless and the unhearing
Think of the third world countries with their disease, death, and danger
Think of the people forced to live there as forever a stranger
Think of the Others

Think of the depressed, distressed, and discouraged
Think of the scared, scarred, and forsaken
For once just think of the others and maybe
Just maybe you may finally realize
That yours isn't so tough and the road is not nearly as rough
Think of the Others

David Shaw, Grade 9
Arbor Middle School, WA

Top Poem Grades 7-8-9

Changing Weather

You left like a hurricane.
The tears came down like rain.
Anger thundered through the house,
With sad lightning shortly after.
The words hurt like hail.
A good bye melted away quickly like snow.
The earthquake was short.
The house left a disaster.
The twisting tornado never seemed to end.

Kate Stewart, Grade 7
Union High School, OR

Top Poem Grades 7-8-9

Willow

A tree, whose branches hang to the ground,
As if to kiss it, and protect the people she shelters,
To keep them safe, to not be found
Three children, two sisters, one friend,
To take the time, which time would lend
To them the tree becomes, a ship with sails that billow,
Even though it's just a willow,
Three pirates duck beneath a vine,
Three maidens, with faces kind,
Take refuge beneath the weeping willow
Later, six years to be exact,
These girls come, they come back
To their childhood playground, of friend and foe
With faces changed, by mirth and woe
With broken hearts, whose wounds do heal
To see the shadows of the girls they used to be
We've changed these years, the six gone past
But in our hearts, these memories last
We see these girls standing there,
With branch and leaf 'a braided hair
And remember the time that we did spend beneath the weeping willow.

Anna Ulmer, Grade 7
Naches Valley Middle School, WA

Top Poem Grades 7-8-9

Description of a Deserted Scottish Abbey

Alone in the heather the abbey stands.
Tenacious weeds have long kept mass here.
No bells, with their curvacious voices,
    call to prayer the pious supplicants
    whose chants once filled the corridors
    with sweet hymns.
Overgrown flowers paint wild impressionistic
    paintings with the wind,
While dusk throws shadows, like aged monks,
    against the crumbling walls.
The sun sets, gilding the sanctuary
    a warm gold.
An evening mist enfolds the abbey
    in its maternity,
Offering the bones of this decrepit
    church, a sweet, final rest.

Robin Bonneau Yokel, Grade 9
Home School, AK

Shocking

There once was a fish called eel
And a boy who wanted to feel
So he had a touch
That hurt very much
And the eel made the boy squeal

Scott Moake, Grade 9
Spanish Fork Jr High School, UT

Grandmother's Voice

I hear it every day
I want to see
Hold and kiss her
Tears dropping
Loving and missing
I want her to be here

Marlen Gutierrez-Vargas, Grade 8
Culver Middle School, OR

Closed Window

Staring out this closed window
Watching the rain fall down
Reminds me of the tears
I've seen fall from her face
She's been hurt by so many
She is so full of disgrace
Not proud of what she's done
Things of the past
You can see it in her eyes
Whenever she comes to pass
She tries to be happy
She isn't very good
You can tell she is hiding under a hood
She covers her heart
Won't let anyone in
It's just like this window
Keeping the rain from touching my skin

Eva Hart, Grade 9
Idaho Arts Charter School, ID

Expressions of Blossoms

Flowers that fly frightfully free,
in a wind that won't let them be,
swing and sway and bend away
to tickle the tall tilted turf.

Roses that romp ruthlessly 'round,
in the rays that cover the ground,
jolt and jump and petals that dump
to the floor are found fair and fulvous.

Lilies that lie lazy and loud,
more bright than the remnant crowd,
pitch and pull, and with the wind roll
deeply downhill like a dream.

Raquel Clifton, Grade 9
McKay High School, OR

Life Goes On...

When you're grounded and you can't do anything but sit at home,
When you're mad after a fight with your best friend,
When you're crying because you feel sad,
When you feel like screaming all your lungs out.
Don't worry because life goes on...
It's not perfect,
It can go anyway,
The way you don't expect it to.
There's a time for different things in life.
There's a time to cry and a time to laugh.
A time to be bored and a time to have fun.
A time to cherish and a time to forget.
Yes life goes on and on and on and on...
So don't expect it to be always perfect.

Dar'ya Sirosh, Grade 8
Floyd Light Middle School, OR

What Is This Earth Coming To?

The world was filled with emerald lush forests
But humankind has destroyed that by setting it ablaze or cutting it
The earth used to have fresh air you could inhale
But the human race has shattered it
The rivers and streams used to be dark cobalt and uncontaminated
But the humankind has also crushed it
The pristine diamond glaciers, which were as great as Texas
But now they lay in muddy puddles
The intense jade-covered prairies that the buffalo used to roam
But now is coated with bitter unbreakable concrete and pavement
The earth was overflowing with cheerful people but now...
Mankind is obliterating each other and themselves

Braz Penfield, Grade 9
Soap Lake Jr-Sr High School, WA

God

God is my best friend,
He will be with me until the bitter end.
I tell him all my secrets and even though he can't respond,
I know he's listening to my every word.
I can feel him praising me when I do good,
And hear him tell me if I should.
If someone held a gun to my head,
And told me they would pull the trigger if I said that I believed in God.
I would tell them I did,
I would die a martyr to God.
But then eventually be saved,
Saved by God.
Yes, God himself,
He would come and take me.
And surely make me,
An angel in his kingdom.
If that is what shall be done,
then surely an angel I shall become.
An angel in Heaven wandering free,
For that is what shall become of me.

Breanna Swars, Grade 9
Diamond Ranch Academy, UT

Snow

Playing in the snow.
Sledding down the hills.
Building snow forts.
Shoveling others driveways.

Going to Snow Basin.
Having a blast all day skiing.
Going to ski school.
Not learning and falling on your butt.
Bombing down the mountain out of control.
Falling and losing everything in the powder.

Parker Bryner, Grade 7
Central Davis Jr High School, UT

The City

The City is always full of cars
It has bumps and really straight roads sometimes
It's as tinny as a little worm
Seen from the sky
And it's as big as a mountain
When you are in it.

I like the City
The City likes me
What would I want more
Since it's the biggest town made just for me.

The cars make pollution
That's kind of an illusion
For who doesn't know the bad
That it's going to do.

Overall, everyone is happy
In their own way
As they walk
In the streets of Lisbon

André Salvada, Grade 8
Central Davis Jr High School, UT

Starlight Stallion

Galloping in the moonlight,
Hooves thudding on the path.
Silver mane is flowing,
No rider on his back.

No halter to restrain him,
No lead rope dangling down.
No barriers to stop him,
Nothing he can't overcome.

Wind flowing through his body,
His freedom he can taste.
Almost like a ghost,
He's vanished into the mist.

Sierra Holcomb, Grade 7
Salmon Seventh-day Adventist School, ID

Fear

Adrenaline   pumping,
                Heart   thumping,
                        Distorts   vision,
        Decreases   precision,
Impairs   brain,
        Feel   no   pain,
            Legs   mush,
    Head   rush,
                Body   tense,
        Sixth   sense.

Taylor Hoj, Grade 8
Wasatch Jr High School, UT

One Tear

One tear can show your pain, your joy
One tear can show just how happy you are
One tear may help someone you love
One tear for you as you cry in your bed.
A tear for your friends to help them through
A tear for your parents and all that they do
A tear for a blessing you received this day
A tear of regret as you shied away.
Remember this as you lie in your bed
How many tears did your Savior shed
One for your joy and one for your pain
A tear for your happiness and the people you love.
A tear for your friends, your parents too
One tear for a blessing He gave you
And one tear for you as you lay here tonight
Trying to sleep on this stormy night.

Tessa Schilling, Grade 9
Elk Ridge Middle School, UT

I Am

I am a blue eyed bit of bubbly joy
I care most about my family
I don't care to be left alone
I wish I could ride a raindrop
I give my humor to anyone who will listen
I want to be a champion in life
I cry STOP! When my daddy tickles me
I can't accept dishonesty and disloyalty
I'll always remember the love people show me
I say what I feel to be true
I feel happy when I'm with my family
I pretend I'm a hero
I see the good in other people
I try to love everyone
I worry about choosing foolishly
I dream of victory
I wonder why a rose smells so pretty
I hope I make my parents happy
I understand there is much still to be learned

Tiffany Jolley, Grade 8
Wasatch Jr High School, UT

Friends and Family

When I was lost
They were there
When I was scared
They were there
When I was hurt
They were there
So
Thanks to all those who care

Ethan C. Roe, Grade 8
Culver Middle School, OR

Speechless

Body shaking
Mind in a blur
Cold
and
Sweaty
Waiting
For my name
To be
Called to speak
I suddenly forget
My speech
It'll be me next
Oh no, here I go!
What should I do?

Kate McWilliams, Grade 8
Culver Middle School, OR

Labrador Retriever

Labrador
Happy, hyper
Running, catching, swimming
Some could play forever
Labrador

Molly Moore, Grade 7
Ogden Middle School, OR

My Dad's Cabin

Under the moonlight
peeking barely through the clouds
thunder starts to strike.

At my dad's cabin
the bright yellow harvest moon
is shining through the night.

At my dad's cabin
phosphorescence is so bright
in the calm water.

The very next day
the boat ride back to our house
missing my dad's cabin.

Anthony Thingvall, Grade 7
Juneau SDA School, AK

Heroes

Somebody to look up to
Somebody to talk to
Sets you on the right path
There for you
Heroes are EVERYWHERE
Big or small
MR. YOUNG'S
My hero

Bailey Anglen, Grade 8
Culver Middle School, OR

My Bike

Feel the cold handle bars
See the people in their cars
Hear the wind rushing past
Smell the dust when you go fast
Taste the dirt when you fall

Dalton Baker,
Best of All

Dalton Baker, Grade 7
Ogden Middle School, OR

Lonely School

A lonely school
On a rainy cold day
In the morning
The bell rings
Teachers teaching
Students talking
Students sitting in their desks
Teachers in front of the class
Lockers closing and opening
Laying around in class
talking to friends
Play around outside
When I have any time
I feel glad to be with my friends

Joel Vega, Grade 8
Culver Middle School, OR

No One Would See Me Cry

If I could stop time
And get over all my pain
No one would see me cry,
Me cry all out in vain
I could make the people look away
I could hide my scream
They wouldn't feel any pity
And I'd never have to be seen
I always feel like dying
I always feel insane
I wish I could stop trying
And fall out in the rain.

Katie Powers, Grade 7
Naches Valley Middle School, WA

The Tiara

A lovely tiara,
Set on a pillow.
Awaiting a princess,
Bound to be queen.

The words are spoken,
Gently it's laid.
Ready to soar,
Like a star up above.

A wave, a sparkle,
That's gracefully hers.
The Queen of England,
Her majesty, Elizabeth.

Ryan Hardy, Grade 8
South Jordan Middle School, UT

Cold Ember Sky

The most radiant sight
Is at dusk, before night
When the sky is set aflame

A Fire Ballet
The clouds, so dolce
Like a dying ember inside the blaze

As the sun sinks low
The sky-fire dies down to a slight glow
One glowing ember is left

That glowing ember
That one glowing ember
Reflects on a cold ember sky

Alysa Jo Fratto, Grade 8
Mountain Ridge Jr High School, UT

A Tribute to the Wanderers*

The cacophony
Of the melancholy melody
Is intriguing to
Even the greatest of performers
To the extent in which
They are confused.
Even the most
Brilliant of minds
Are embezzled by
The sounds and notes
Of the music
If you would call it that.
Some call it nothing,
But some call it
The most beautiful symphony
They have ever heard.

Carsten Floor, Grade 8
Lewis and Clark Middle School, ID
*Inspired by "Interlude."

The Life of a Writer

All is quiet but for the sound of his pen,
As it goes "scratch, scratch, scratch."

The paper slowly filling with thoughts
As they glide from his mind to the parchment,

Like ice on a boiling summer day,
The words melt together into poems and stories.

Written by a man like no other,
With the name of Sir Arthur Conan Doyle.

Wonderful writings from jumbled up words,
Put onto paper and placed into books.

The darkest of mysteries full of suspense,
Filling readers with excitement and fear.

Though now he is buried in a stony grave,
His words are still with us today.

Miranda Reoch, Grade 8
South Jordan Middle School, UT

Water Polo Isn't for Me

Water polo I am not good.
But coach and mom say I should
Learn to play because I'm tall.
To catch, pass and shoot the ball.
I should not choose a sport that fits the size of me.
I should choose a sport that fits my personality.

Robert Miner, Grade 8
Wasatch Jr High School, UT

For Someone Who in Some Place or Time

Defended their friends and
What they thought right.
Who befriended the child that no one else would,
Not for pity or credit, but because they could.
Who gave up the last piece of pie,
To the wistful child with a tear in her eye.

For someone who in some place or time
Helped with a project
Not accepting a dime
For all the work they contributed to.
Always ready to help, anywhere, anytime.

For someone who in some place or time
Loved the person of opposite sex,
Overlooking the flaws that others detect.
Showing their love through kindness each day,
And encouragement given through a single word,
A word no one else had the heart to say.

Makiah Salinas, Grade 8
Horizon Middle School, WA

Rejection

Rejection is a knife
It leaves you thinking there must be more to life
You cry
And you sigh
Wishing you could fly
Away from the ones who hurt you

Every now and then someone comes along
And they sing you a song
About being a friend
And love you to the very end
They are an answer to your prayer
But you don't dare
To say it aloud
For fear that they will disappear into a cloud

Once you find a friend rejection's no longer a knife
It's a learning experience that will better your life

Sierra Sivertson, Grade 9
Elk Ridge Middle School, UT

Little Brother

Around me laughing and playing
Until I grow wrinkles
Among my sweetest childhood memories
Past the candy shops, playgrounds, and games
Since the day he and I were infants

Clare Quitoriano, Grade 7
Rogich Middle School, NV

Ocean Green

The delightful color of ocean green,
Filled the blue-green water beneath my feet.

Its icy, cool touch like pearlescent-blue rain,
Was everywhere, splashing, squishing, and sifting with joy.

The crystal-blue sky was surrounding the air,
With grey-green pelicans fluttering over head.

The emerald ocean was reaching for the moon,
Trying to grasp it and call the globe for her own.

Its waves were growing as high as mountains,
This was indeed a glorious sight.

I looked out to the sea and what I would find,
Was it seemed to be grabbing,
For anyone who dared to be taken by her hand.

I moved closer and closer to the glassy, turquoise water,
Waiting for the waves to carry me away.
I waded out into the water hoping for the best,
And felt the warm, comfy touch of ocean green.

Ryan Smith, Grade 8
Mountain Ridge Jr High School, UT

Curious

I'm curious
Tree climbing
People questioning
Crime scene investigating
Case inspecting
Friend sneaking
Secret plan eavesdropping
Brother spying
Bad guy stalking
Problem solving
Eye sparkling
Interested

Jamie Reynolds, Grade 8
Wasatch Jr High School, UT

Monotone

Same thing day after day
No rest or respite
Will this ever end or
Am I doomed to never ending
Mediocrity?
I grow weary with time
This jumble of events
That is life
Everything's better in color
But nothing's better in monotone

Hanna Hutcheson, Grade 9
Winston Churchill High School, OR

Is Life About Love?

A high school crush,
Friday night date,
I thought I found
My life's good fate.

That rose you brought
To my front door,
It stabbed my heart
Left on the floor.

I thought life's all
Was all 'bout love.
But found that wrong;
My heart got a shove.

It's not about you
Together with me
Forever my heart
With the Lord shall be.

My life has purpose
Beyond just with you.
It shall be fulfilled,
And maybe love too.

Tiffany Hylkema, Grade 9
W F West High School, WA

Book of Life

Life is like a book,
The pages turning,
The suspense growing, you not knowing what's going to happen next.
The book gets dramatic
You don't want to stop reading
Then it gets dark
Terrible things happen
Then all gets better
And the book ends.
Proud, powerful, and meaningful.
The book is remembered by all,
And is told as the greatest book ever.

Elizabeth Brooks, Grade 7
St Anne School, WA

Fear

As each day passes by, I look back with a heavy sigh
and watch myself as if in, a dream that will never end

Is life merely a thought like a long dream and is not
what it seems to be at all? at the end is there a wall
where people learn their fate? is there a heaven gate?

All of this I do not know, I do not know where we will go
I know faith is all you need, to fulfill this very deed.

There must be something real, because in my heart I feel
that this all didn't just appear

There might not be a heaven here, and no hell for us to fear
don't you ever try to fathom then, that eternity is too long to comprehend?

The answer to this is that no one knows until they have to go,
so you can wait until you're told what your future will unfold

Before you go, say goodbye to the ones you love, before you die
because they may never see you again, ever

Thomas Miller, Grade 7
Corvallis Waldorf School, OR

Bubble Gum

Bubble gum
It comes in different flavors it's sticky and it's sweet
it's chewy and it's flavorful and always such a treat
You can blow ten foot bubbles or make loud popping sounds
stretch it clear to China or smack it really loud
Twirl it on your finger put a million pieces in your mouth
stick into someone's hair then sit and watch them shout
There are lots of different flavors like watermelon and strawberry
you have blue raspberry and original or green apple and sour cherry
It comes in kinds of suckers and lots of kinds of candy
you can get it in a 1 pound bucket or you can have just one piece handy
It's been around forever this treat called bubble gum
it's the funnest exercise for your mouth and it's always tons of fun!

Jessica Sizemore, Grade 8
Central Davis Jr High School, UT

May He Rest in Peace

Richest son in Falls City,
Gambling, investing, oh what a pity.
Always switching from private to public schools,
Why did you have to act like one of those fools?
Relatives having to go to jail,
I just can't imagine you lying there dead and pale.
At age 13, the last you lived,
You stole your dad's car, we all know you did.
You wanted to see how fast it went,
What you didn't know, was that your life would be spent.

Christi Kopetzky, Grade 8
St Michael School, WA

The Champ

A champ is a boy with heart.
A boy who thinks he can.
A boy who tries from the start.
A boy ready to become a man.

A champ doesn't care about what people think,
no matter what he's a star.
A champ will never sink,
because he takes the chance to go far.

A champ is not cocky he's humble,
he talks not with his mouth, but by being the best.
A champ doesn't stumble,
he simply stands above the rest.

A champ's mind like Albert Einstein,
knows what's going to happen,
his choice to give up or shine,
will determine if he's a true champion.

Devereaux Filipe, Grade 8
Wasatch Jr High School, UT

A Father Comes Home Drunk

Hi Daddy, how are you today?
Why do you always push me when you get home?
Can't we be a family again?
Can't it be like it was before you started to drink?

Am I such a bad little girl?
Is that why you drink?
Please stop, that is hurting me.
Why do you hurt me?
Why?

No, don't hurt Mommy.
I'm the bad girl.
Please don't hurt Mommy.
Daddy I love you, stop hurting me and Mommy.
Please, I beg of you, Stop!

Kayla Admire, Grade 9
Buhl High School, ID

Love

Love is a warm pink color
It sounds like a breeze blowing through you.
It tastes like chocolate melting on your tongue.
It smells like roses and warm vanilla and brown sugar.
Love looks like a sparkle in your eyes,
A smile on your lips that just won't go away.
It makes you feel wanted, warm and happy.

Jenna Hutchinson, Grade 9
Buhl High School, ID

Christmas Eve

It happened on one Christmas Eve
At least that's what I do believe
When my father killed a mouse
As my mother was to leave

The little mouse was in our house
Climbing over my new blouse
I yelled for help, I screamed, I cried
"Please rid me of this little louse!"

It was a horrible yuletide
As that little mousy died
Although it sounds a bit insane
I felt as if I was freeze dried

Thoughts were running through my brain
My bravery I tried to feign
But parents must have heard me scream
I now fear I have much pain

I really didn't want to scream
I now have almost no esteem
Because of that little dream
Which was just a little too extreme

Katie Baker, Grade 8
River HomeLink Program, WA

Nature's Voices

Whispering through the tall trees
Telling little secrets to all who will listen
What wonderful things it tells and just on a breeze
And those things will make the person's life glisten

Murmuring to the plants
Chattering with the creatures
Even to the smallest of the ants
Nature's teachers

Whispering sometimes thunderous sometimes soft
Never stopping it's wisdom sharing
Sharing its wisdom to all who won't scoff
Always open to anyone who will are caring

J.C. Anderson, Grade 7
St Mary's Elementary School, AK

America

Freedom, liberty, justice, independence, I get a feeling as it trickles down my spine.
It means I can stand strong, but can also fear, and still I'm happy for the way I can live in this country.
As our flag flies high beating against the wind as it lights up the sky on a foggy night.
I'm glad to live and breathe here, and to be an American to know that I can stand strong, and free.
We've crossed the open sea, and fought for our country and rights,
13 stripes and 50 stars stand for the 13 original colonies and fifty states
America! America! America! America!

Brandon Robinson, Grade 9
Bonneville High School, ID

Blue Like Jazz

Blue like the dream of what you wanted that went away in a cloud of mysteries and sorrows
A dream that never would have come to you if you hadn't been hearing that blue
That blue, that sounded like jazz

Blue like at night when all you can hear is a soft insistent song that cannot be explained
It's like loss and tears and smiles all at the same time
On the sidewalk, be-bopping with a hat on the ground, to collect any coins that might be tossed in
Dark and indigo with flashes of diamond sparkle
The occasional wide dark smile, soft and wise and friendly and luring
The smile of a survivor who's thankful for everything, all surrounded by blue
That blue, that sounded like jazz

Blue like a girl with no other why to survive but for her music that flows from her lips
A dream of diamonds and gold, that one day everyone will know her name
But for now she sings so that her soul can rise up and fly
So that for a few moments she can be free and nothing matters except for that music that sounded like blue
That blue, that sounded like jazz

Blue like the color of all you can see when you're looking around you
A rescue helicopter ready to take you to safety, but all you want to do is cling to that blue
Ocean-blue, salty-tear blue, instead of what it used to be: jazz blue, dark blue, rich blue
That once-upon-a-time, now shrouded in sorrow that used to be
That blue, that sounded like jazz

Sarah Hansell, Grade 8
Hansell Home School, OR

The Moment I Saw You

The moment I saw you, walk through those double doors,
I felt a strong connection, from my heart to yours.
It was as if time had stopped, when my eyes came upon you.
Everything but you and I stood still, and our relationship had become anew.
I've never felt the way I did, when you came into my sight.
I've never looked at you the way I had, on that love-stricken night.
So many thoughts and feelings ran through my mind.
While I frantically searched for a way, to overcome that nervous time.
Sweat builds on my hands, and also on my face.
My heart was beating faster, than its ordinary pace.
Butterflies flew in my stomach, excitement circulated through my veins.
Ecstatic yet so shy on that night, my love for you stood and still remains.
The best day of my life, so far as I've been living.
You've no idea of what I've received from you, and to this day you keep on giving.
You're by far the most wonderful girl I've ever met. Too many qualities and great things about you to name.
I hope we stay together forever, because life without you would never be the same.

Chris Roberts, Grade 9
Buhl High School, ID

I Am from Plums and White Elephants

I am from plum picking
And raspberry freezing
From lots of computers
And skiing every Sunday

I am from Christmas parties
And weird ones too
From salty gravy
And mad cows

I am from big remodels
And living downstairs
From remote controlled cars
And model airplanes

I am from 11 dead frogs
And 2 dead goldfish
From Monopoly
And Chutes and Ladders

I am from myself
Fiona Bestwick
From believing
And experiencing

Fiona Bestwick, Grade 7
Lake Washington Girls Middle School, WA

Beautifulness

Swift things are beautiful,
The lightning striking through the sky,
Chasing friends on a grassy lawn,
The last day of school trying to say bye to everyone,
Playing games on the computer.

Slow things are beautiful, too.
Slug sliding on our back steps,
Rainstorms with hot chocolate flowing down your throat,
Reading a book in the corner,
Watching fireworks on the Fourth of July.

Katie LaRue, Grade 7
Ogden Middle School, OR

I Think I Love You

I think I love you and here is why,
When you're not with me I want to cry.
It's such a privilege to hear your voice,
You and only is my final choice.
Imagine the reaper singing lovers song,
You and me my darling, we sing along.
We have rejoiced and we have suffered pain
But now the sunlight's swallowed up the rain.
I know I love you, now you know why;
I only ask you this, just don't make me cry.

Kelly Reeder, Grade 7
Morgan Middle School, WA

Canyon Ranch

Deep down in the comfortable canyon,
Sizzling sun and warm winds blow,
Noontime heat of day,
Snakes hiss,
And birds sing,
Coyotes chase squirrels,
The creek flowing by rapidly,
Horses galloping,
As the dogs chase them,
They kick as they seemingly fly away,
We feed the animals,
Before taking a long awaited ride on the quad,
And heading to dinner,
can't wait to visit next summer,
And feel at home again

Laryssa Yoder, Grade 8
Culver Middle School, OR

On the Never Moor

Faster than a willow the wisp
Gliding on the breezes kiss
The faintest flicker of a bright orange fire
Freed at last from the muddy mire
In the heart of the Never Moor

Ground sped ever so quickly near
Reflecting the world in a shifting mirror
Shades of ever changing green
Each one different with a bright new sheen
Inside the Never Moor

A long deep breath, the memory's over
No more am I in a gray green field filled with clover
I stand upon a darkened shore
The memories gone forever more
Resting in the Never Moor

But now and forever I'll try and recall
My first bareback jaunt and I didn't fall
Though time will pass and memories fade
This one will stay unscathed by shade
Deep inside the Never Moor

Alisa Lee, Grade 8
Sequim Middle School, WA

November

November flies by like a bee.
You hardly realize what you see.
The leaves are so pretty and bright,
that they're almost out of sight.
When the month is almost over,
it starts to get colder.
November zooms by like a fly,
that you hardly have time to say hi.

Kysa Finley, Grade 8
Sunnyside Christian Elementary School, WA

The Pearl Inside

There once was an oyster,
As plain as could be.
He would clam up his shell,
So that no one could see.

He was so shy,
Not sure how to open up,
He needed to pry apart
His shell, shut up.

One day he awoke
A new shellfish.
"Make me determined."
Was his wish.

Now outgoing,
He let his shell part,
Letting all the other oysters see
That he had a heart.

Never thought well of himself,
But that thought had died.
For he opened up,
And discovered the pearl inside.

Melissa Dailey, Grade 8
Komachin Middle School, WA

Sorry

I'm sorry for disobeying you
I'm sorry for being mean to you
But why
Why did you have to go and die
Why
I should have paid attention
I should have looked for the signs
I should have been there
Before you died
I pray for you each night
I cry for you each day
I just wish I could have said
Goodbye
And I love you

Miranda Reed, Grade 7
Walker Middle School, OR

My Big Boy Bike

When I was seven I got a new bike
My mom said, "is it to your like?"
I rode it every day after school
When I fell I felt like a fool.
I got a new dad his name was Mike.
He taught me how to ride my bike
Now I'm thirteen and have a new bike
But I still have my dad Mike

Chris T. Lemley, Grade 8
Mt Olive Lutheran School, NV

The Wanted Friendship

If you're my friend, I really need to know,
sometimes I think you are but other times it does not show.
You try to prove yourself to me by doing stupid stuff,
sometimes I just scream and say I think I have had enough!
But I do not and I hope you respect that,
I really want to be your friend, that truly is a fact.
You should know it really hurts when you brag to kids at school,
I guess you have never realized what it is like to be uncool.
I know I can be jealous, rude, and obnoxious just as well,
but you do not have to ignore, just open up and tell.
Do not bottle up your anger but do not spill it out on me,
I just want to be your friend and be your company!

Mary Webb, Grade 7
Nikolaevsk School, AK

All Wrong

I think there's something wrong with her eyes;
she looks in a mirror and a look of disgust creeps onto her face.

I think there's something wrong with her ears;
every time she gets a compliment she spits it out as if it were hotter than a pepper.

I think there's something wrong with her mouth;
every word that falls out is dripping with toxic negativity towards herself.

I think there's something wrong with *my* mind;
I know what she's doing to herself could eventually go too far.

Yet I still haven't told anyone
    Anyone.

Becca Pelham, Grade 7
Walker Middle School, OR

We All Know…

Nearly every middle school kid across the nation knows that feeling…

During the slide show on fungi spores,
And at the school assembly with the monotone speaker.

It creeps.

It comes during math,
Or when you're supposed to be studying.

It's stealthy.

It comes unexpectedly.
It grips your brain.
It fogs your thinking.
It drowns out the teacher.
And before you know it,
You're in its clutches…

La La Land.

Stephanie McEntee, Grade 7
St Mary's Elementary School, AK

Trees

reaching into the sky
pulling down pieces of sunlight
and wind
and rain
watching time pass
sometimes lazily
other times much too fast
soft and worn
rustling in the breeze
waving in the wind
always there
when you need them
Trees

Madeline Lee, Grade 7
Lake Washington Girls Middle School, WA

Desire to Grow Up

Sometimes I wish I could stay as a kid
Not so many responsibilities
Always praised for the job-well-done I did
Possessing youth and great ability

I want parents to go home to at night
Want to play every day without a care
I'm trying to fill my childhood with light
So that I'll have precious memories to share

These years are something that I'll look back on
Remembering the wonderful time I had
And I'll think to myself, "Where have they gone?"
Those memorable years of good and of bad

Our childhood is something that we let go
Desire to grow up, something I don't know

Sage Bicchieri, Grade 7
Morgan Middle School, WA

Rhythmic Soul

A rhythm of feet and hands working together as one to
create a harmonious melody that defies reality,
A song that the soul creates,
Something unique created by madness or out of feeling,
I get lost in its true majesty,
It feels like my destiny to bring such peace onto the Earth,
It tastes like the fresh fruit created by nature that is the
sweetness in everyone,
My heart beats parallel to the freedom that flows
through my veins.
The sound of it creates a shield that you cannot
pierce and no one wants to,
It sounds like the roughness and smoothness of a heart
that is loved and one that is broken,
When hand-eye coordination is broken, so is the melody
which everyone so desperately needs.

Jordan Reisher, Grade 8
Komachin Middle School, WA

Sleepless Night

"Time for bed." Your mom cries
You agree rubbing your eyes
But when you lay down to go to sleep
You hear a sound that the walls won't keep
You fluff up your pillow pull your blanket to your chin
You know no sleep will make your kindness thin
And yet you know no sleep will come
You hear your heart beat like a drum
The next thing you know it's 3 am
Sheep! Now your ready to scream at them
And as you begin to yell and yell
Waiting, waiting you suddenly fell
Asleep, asleep finally asleep
You're so tired your sleep is knee deep
The next thing you know beep, beep your alarm has sound
You're ready to slam your clock to the ground
You press the snooze to make it stop
You're still so tired you're ready to drop
But on and on it drones
The room is filled with the sound from your groans
No sleep, no sleep, no sleep will come

Lydia McCorkindale, Grade 7
North Layton Jr High School, UT

The Beginning of Fall

I stare at the mountains standing so tall,
And noticed the signs of beginning of fall.
Lot's of rain and cold, cold snow,
And obviously not much to mow.
The birds are all flying south,
Toward the tallest mountain's mouth.
All the trees' leaves have already fell,
And I notice the draining well.
Fall is here and that's all to say,
For it's almost the end of the day.

Cjaristy Lane, Grade 7
Joel P Jensen Middle School, UT

Secret in Cerulean

A dark wisp rides the steady cobalt horizon,
Brusquely disturbing the ubiquitous sea.
The stark black rock is crowned with sultry verdure.
Remarkably, the sprawl thrives.
A foreign breeze rustles those palms.
With great leisure, the tide creeps,
Cooling the blistering white shores.
Cerulean waters gently lap those sands.
From above, the sun beats without relent.
Harsh radiance swallows the slight bit of land.
A scarlet flower opens in that heat.
Surf thunders in the distance.
From the eyes of a triumphant civilization,
This lonely place remains a secret.

Ingrid Beattie, Grade 9
Mount Si High School, WA

Spearmint Forest

Spearmint forest
Green on the top
Refreshing, haunting
As sweet as sugar
Perfect

Kori Jeffries, Grade 7
Rogich Middle School, NV

Divorce

I remembered last night,
the morning of the fight,
the terrible morning
that didn't end right.

It broke up my heart
right from the start
that horrible morning
that tore our family apart

I know it sounds dramatic,
but this is how I feel
I wish it was all a dream
that wasn't at all real.

Maybe you should have waited
'till I was actually ready,
maybe a few more years,
'till I was emotionally steady.

So this is my life now,
there's nothing I can do,
but no matter how apart we are,
I will always love you.

Rachael Gudewicz, Grade 8
Molasky Middle School, NV

Life Goes On

Love:
Butterflies in stomach, head is light
Heart beats quickly, legs grow weak
Eyes meet, hold the glance
Face turns red, floating on air

Hate:
The fake smile, high hollow laugh
The shifty eyes and careless look
Hear the rumors, start your own
Head feels hot, heart is cold

Life:
Want to cry, want to scream
To hold someone, to be held
Feeling lonely, part of the team
Life goes on, life goes on.

Kelsey Kunde, Grade 9
Bonneville High School, ID

Changing the Car's Oil

As I ratcheted open the oil pan,
I could hear the drip of the rain outside.
I reached the end of the threads,
And oil dripped onto my hand.
I jerked my hand out of the way quickly.
My elbow clanged off the driveshaft.
The oil plopped into the collector.
I jumped with joy,
And crashed back down.
I popped the hood latch,
And threw up the hood.
My truck gulped the new oil down.
My job was done.

Kurran Kelly, Grade 9
Buhl High School, ID

Friends

My friends are the best
They are caring
They don't care if I cry
Or if I am laughing
They always call me
They help me whenever I need help
When we hang out we laugh together
We tell stories
Having fun

Alea Wilson, Grade 7
Ogden Middle School, OR

Falling Friendship

She has tried so hard
to stay strong,
but she cannot keep it up.
Soon she will just fall down.

She seems so strong outside,
but it is so obvious
that she is breaking down inside.
She is falling too fast.

If she keeps it up
too much longer,
she is just going
to fall much harder.

The laughing and teasing
haunt her night and day.
She wants to give up,
no matter what others say.

Her friends try to help,
but she pushes them away.
She never tells them
but they keep her going.

Kielley Bade, Grade 8
Molasky Middle School, NV

Dogs

Loyal
Always by you side
Listening to your commands
Dogs

Soft fur
Colored fur
Black fur, gold fur, white fur
Dogs

Running, playing
Catching, swimming
Dogs

Tired, angry, playful
Sad, anxious, bored
Dogs

The best pet in the world,
Dogs

Jason Librande, Grade 8
Meadowdale Middle School, WA

The Fog

The bell tolls for the midnight hour
All is dark and silent.
It rolls in without warning.
Nothing is visible,
Yet nothing is invisible.
It is impenetrable
Yet is is weak.
Many fear it
Yet it draws away.
It changes everything,
Yet nothing is changed.

Isaac Becker, Grade 7
Sylvester Middle School, WA

Upstairs

sometimes
I race up
the stairs

thudding, tumbling, racing
there is
something
that I must do

but once I have
thudded, tumbled, raced
I forgot
that something

so I sit

Keeley Tillotson, Grade 9
Tualatin High School, OR

Horror of the Holocaust

Born in a time of horror
With terrors happening before my eyes
But happy that I'm alive.

My life is like unto the ocean
Changing, changing,
Swirling in all directions, confused
Wondering what will happen next
And never knowing.

Searching for something greater, better
Yet knowing you'll never find it
Until after four and a half years, finally seeing a light
And going to it is like running to Father in England.

Happiness, joy,
Something greater, somewhere else
I am Hannah Hajek.

Kaitlin Wamsley, Grade 8
South Jordan Middle School, UT

Love Is

Love is the essence of life, the relief of sorrow;
love is the light in the darkening shadow.
Love is a game and you are her pawn,
in a game that lasts O too long.
Love can be as soothing as a violin
or as tragic as the death of men.
Love is the treasure that we all seek,
but the finding of this fortune is O so bleak.
Love is every man's jewel
but if you don't take it you are a fool.

Sean G. Jones, Grade 9
Silverton High School - Schlador Campus, OR

Myself

I am a soldier of the Continental Army.
I wonder if I will live through the war.
I hear gunshots all around me.
I see my friends killed in action.
I am a soldier of the Continental Army.
I pretend I am a hero that survives.
I feel ill, dirty, and tired.
I touch my cold gun, waiting to shoot.
I worry that we will lose the war.
I cry when I think of my family at home.
I am a soldier of the Continental Army.
I understand that I am risking my life.
I say that we should have confidence.
I dream of the British laughing haughtily after winning the war.
I try to not think pessimistically.
I hope I will return home alive.
I am a soldier of the Continental Army.

Marty Horn, Grade 7
River HomeLink Program, WA

Candy

Candy, candy isn't it sweet
It tingles your taste buds
And rots your teeth
We all love it
And like to eat lots of it
All the flavors of the world
Jelly filled, sprinkle toppings, creamy swirled,
Gummy, chewy, chocolate coated,
Fruity, rich, sugar loaded,
Sweet and sour
These are the kinds we do devour
Candy, candy isn't it sweet
It tingles your taste buds
And rots your teeth

Alyssa Nuss, Grade 7
Ogden Middle School, OR

The Bridge

That big old bridge that's just south of town,
it's big, bulk, and scary,
you can go across it, just don't look down.

That bridge just might do its job,
but every time I cross it I just want to sob.
It's high off the ground and not too fun,
if I go across it should I walk or should I run?

I wipe off my tears of fear,
after being scared for all those years,
while suddenly approaching that ugly, black, bridge.

I take my first step, I didn't jump or hop,
and went all the way to the end, I didn't even stop.

Rooting out loud, then hiding in embarrassment,
I saw a whole bunch of people looking at me,
but I didn't know what that meant.

After settling down in that little old town,
once again I put my foot on the black,
and suddenly I had realized I was on my way back,
without a lack across the big black bridge.

Nichole Milano, Grade 7
Helper Jr High School, UT

The Painting

The painting looks at me
It brings memories and feelings I never felt before
I see beautiful, majestic mountains
I almost feel the fresh air again
The fragrance of flowers almost fills my lungs
The sound of water can almost be heard again
It reveals past
The painting

Yuliya Kononova, Grade 7
Ogden Middle School, OR

Mem'ry

I remember
A childhood memory
I was riding a bike
My parents urging me to keep trying,
So I kept peddling,
They still motivate me
to keep on keeping on

Kyler Byington, Grade 9
Elk Ridge Middle School, UT

New Book

When I first saw you,
new, shiny, perfect.
I couldn't believe
that you were mine.

Open the cover,
the spine crackles.
Smells of a new book,
crisp, clean, so new.

I turn the first page,
so smooth and crisp.
I know I'm the first
to have that joy.

When I first saw you
behind the glass,
I knew you were mine.
My own new book.

Jessica deJong, Grade 8
Central Davis Jr High School, UT

The Magic of Muffins

There was a time —
My house was gloomy and cold,
My friends were all gone
And I was alone
The day was too long
The clock seemed to stop

And there was a time —
My house was cheerful and warm,
My friends were all laughing
While we baked muffins
With time speeding by,
Until the muffins were done

And there was a time —
That all of us sat,
And smiled together
As we all remembered
And talked with each other
Of the magic of muffins

Caitlyn O'Mealy, Grade 9
Parkrose High School, OR

Fog

I have no family, I have no friends
and I feel like everything in my life is coming to an end
I'm depressed and kind of mad
you can't even tell the difference if I'm happy or if I'm sad.

You always try to change me and control me
but how can you when you don't even know me?
I really do love you I thought you loved me too
but I guess you don't even like me so you know what? FORGET YOU!

Everything I ever say or do is wrong
and it feels like we can never even get along
I don't understand why you have to be like that
always putting me down just so you don't feel like crap.

If I don't acknowledge these feelings soon it's gonna get worse
I need someplace quiet to think someplace I can call my own
I'm lost deep in the forest of my emotions
and I can't seem to find my way home.

Brittanie Asmussen, Grade 7
Ritzville Grade School, WA

Let Me Show You the World

Let me show you the Milky Way up in the bright, starry sky.
Let me show you the beautiful sunset setting over the huge mountains full of color.
Let me show you the harsh blizzards which you've never seen before.
Let me show you the amazing Northern Lights which are shown very rarely in time.
Let me show you the wildlife that live through the trees of the mountains.
Let me show you the flowers that bloom in spring up in the long canyons.
Let me show you a shooting star and have you make a wish.
Let me show you Mt. Everest, the tallest and biggest mountain in the world.
Let me show you the whole world of nature.

Tyler Brimley, Grade 8
Wasatch Jr High School, UT

Friend to Friend*

Well Friend, I'll tell ya
Life for me ain't been no pair of leather boots;
It's had scuffs on it,
And broken heels,
And the shine has faded away,
And the places I've been in these boots haven't been the best places,
But all the I time keep steppin',
And keep movin' along,
And put shoe shine over them scuffs.
And sometimes the zipper breaks so you can't zip 'em back up,
But where there's a store go in an' fix it,
So don't pass that store by,
Don't let that zipper stay broken.
Don't let them scuffs stay there.
For ya can keep on steppin'
And life for me ain't been no pair of black leather boots.

Krista Toussant, Grade 7
Mears Middle School, AK
*Inspired by Langston Hughes

The Taskmaster of Life

Pain the Taskmaster of Life
Filled with ways to motivate
Driving life forward with its clash
Responsible for all advancement.

Pain lashing out when something's wrong
Content when all is right
Ever vigilant to strike again
Whenever needed.

Nobody likes pain
All try to avoid it
But we all need pain,
To keep improving life.

Tauras Vilgalys, Grade 8
Leota Jr High School, WA

My Road

I walked this road which you won't follow,
Bathing in my endless sorrow,
I hoped to see you here tomorrow
But you would never, ever follow.
I stand here in my pool of sorrow

I ask again
I ask you why?
You turn away, you take a step
I try my hardest not to cry.

I walk my road, I walk it now, and some dare to ask me 'How?'
All I say for my reply is 'Determination.'
You see me then, but now you bow.
"I wouldn't follow then, but I will now."
I walk past you, I leave you now.

Read these words, so you will see, freedom is not really free.

Michaela Barrett, Grade 8
Trinity Catholic School, WA

Darkness

Darkness is whole,
Darkness is definitive,
Darkness is everything,
It gives us fear,
It fills our hearts and minds,
It is inevitable that we shall fade into it,
As we came from it,
Most fear to go back,
Of course there are some who wish to return,
They revel in the darkness within themselves,
And embrace its power,
It is their strength,
Their only constant,
As they scream themselves to sleep.

Troy Gayer, Grade 8
Carson Middle School, NV

Personification of Nature

Nature is a beautiful and wonderful thing.
We all take advantage of it without even knowing.
We always tune out natures' pride and dignity.
This is why…
When the wind screams and the trees roar,
All we hear is silence.
Silence as pure as gold.
If we just take a moment and listen.
The ocean sings as the wind sweeps above it.

Listen carefully to the skies above us.
The sun shouting with joy in the bright afternoon.
The rain weeping within the clouds.
It just takes a moment…
Close your eyes and grab onto nature.
Let it take you…
Let it destroy all your problems in life.
The problems that beat you with worries.
The problems that shield your eyes and ears.
Shielding you from the true beauty of nature.

The beauty and personification of nature.

Thao Ha, Grade 8
Lewis and Clark Middle School, ID

Happy

I met this one, the other day.
It made me happy, some weird way.
It came to my doorstep, and knocked on the door.
I fed it, and kept it, but it wanted more.
I gave it my love, and gave it my thought.
I gave it some color, but it still lay caught.
Finally I decided, to let it go free.
Maybe that's what it wanted, all I know is it made me happy.

Stephanie Letourneau, Grade 7
Martin Middle School, NV

Living a Lie

I know now that I was living a lie,
And, that you were just a complete waste of time.
I also realize now, why everything I used to do
Was never good enough for you.
So now I'll go again,
On my journey to find who I really am.
I finally know why it was so hard for me,
To be the way you wanted me to be.
So just leave me alone, go away
Because I don't need another bad day.
I'm tired of all the abuse.
You're not worth my time,
And without you I'll be fine.
I've said it once and I never want to say it again,
Just leave, get away from me!

Lizzy Bijelic, Grade 9
Diamond Ranch Academy, UT

Sapphire Blue

Back forth went the tide of the ocean,
Calling me to her,
The sapphire blue water foaming a creamy white foam,
I ran to the water its gentle touch was like ice,
I dived into it; its deep sapphire blue color enveloped me,
Gently it cradled me and rhythmically massaged me to a slumber,
Waking from the slumber on the beach warm and cool heated by the flaming gold sun above,
The sapphire sky was the stage for the clouds as they danced across the sky changing their shape,
Rising from the ground I looked to the ocean her blue dancing with the red orange light of the sun,
I walked away from the sapphire blue lady of the tides with a heart of awe and wonder.

Donavan Terranova, Grade 8
Mountain Ridge Jr High School, UT

The Place Where Black Belts Are Born

It is merely a large empty room
It has bright lights and cool air as if you are on stage
Around the edge there are punching bags to take out anger, wooden benches for relaxation,
And in the front there is one large mirror to see yourself relaxing
The room is full of trophies, some big, some small,
Each with a different person who guards the room from all your worries
Pictures line the walls as if you are in a photo album; they show the past of this room
And all of the people who have walked through its doors
Walking through the door you would think it is just an ordinary room with no special value
But to me it feels like a place of relaxation
A place where I leave all of my worries about school and home outside the door
The sounds are loud; people are screaming; there are loud thuds
The empty room smells like dust that is trapped in the heater
It smells like hard work
It tastes like winning first place at a tournament
I don't think of anything inside of that room; I just concentrate.

Melissa Powers, Grade 7
Komachin Middle School, WA

Marine

I'll never forget the day we met our endless high school love
Being together watching the sunset I was your whole world way up above

All the memories we had being together, never letting go
I was fortunate and glad and knew I'll never be in a state of woe

The day we both said "*I do*" you were the one for me
And that I will always love you this is how it was meant to be

I was thinking of us the laughs, the smiles
But ever since the day you got on that bus I knew we'll be apart thousands of miles

You left me alone feeling empty and depressed
Spending hours talking on the phone I couldn't put everything to rest

You were overseas while I was back home
You were in another country while I was in California alone

It's been a little over 2 months since you left now that I know you are doing well in Iraq
things have been a lot better even though not a day goes by that I wish you were back

Brittany Jake, Grade 9
Elk Ridge Middle School, UT

I Am Sick and Tired of Being Made Fun Of!!

I am praying to be strong to
stand up for myself and for
my family and for others.
I am capable of all that I put my
mind to.
I hate people that make fun of
me and family and others.
I wish that I was rich.
I wish I was semi-cool.
I wish I had lots of friends.
There is a little story to this.
Try to figure it out!

Jacob Bewley, Grade 7
Ogden Middle School, OR

First Day of School

Papa, is this the place?
It is Papa?
Is it here where I'll stay alone?
Surrounded by millions of eyes staring at me?
Couldn't you go to school too?
I don't like it Papa.
There is no one here to care for me.
I don't want to learn.
I want to go home with you and Mama.
Oh, Papa come back!

Briana Castillo, Grade 9
Buhl High School, ID

Mystery Girl

She is, She is

She is the most beautiful girl I have ever seen
She is the most beautiful girl I have ever met
She is the most beautiful girl in the world

Her eyes are as beautiful as a red red rose
Her hair flows through the air like tree branches in the breeze
Her skin is as smooth as silk

She is the nicest girl I have ever seen
She is the nicest girl I have ever met
She is the nicest girl in the world

I think about her every day

Her laugh makes me happy every time I hear it

Her smile is the most beautiful I have ever seen
Her smile is the most beautiful smile on anyone I have ever met
Her smile is the most beautiful in the world

She means everything to me

Devin Holdiman, Grade 8
Horse Heaven Hills Middle School, WA

One Day

One day when I was two,
Even before he taught me to tie a shoe.
From heavens above,
To down below,
God knew he had to go.
Even though I did not know,
Who he was or what to do,
I knew he was in a place of peace and no hurt.
It's been twelve years now,
And I can finally see how.
My daddy's with me each and every day.
He's there when I play,
Even when I pray.
If you drink and drive,
You too could take someone's life.
So make your actions wise,
Because it's not fun when someone dies.

Kaylee Meek, Grade 9
Diamond Ranch Academy, UT

I Love You, Goodbye

How come they never realized?
How come they couldn't see?
That every time they hurt each other
They were hurting me
The words that they said and the tone of their voice
I didn't want to hear but it wasn't my choice
It's just not fair to always live in fear
So I said "This needs to stop or I'm out of here"
For days and days they just kept going
So I snuck out of the house without them knowing
Every day I walked by and they were still there
I came to the conclusion that they didn't care
So I sat down and wrote them a note
"I love you goodbye" and that's all I wrote

Jacqueline DeRosso, Grade 7
Sylvester Middle School, WA

Soccer Suspense

Around you hear the crowd
Off in the distance different sorts of sounds
Until the whistle is finally blown
Past the opponents you run with hope
Between the players you swerve by
Down the field you travel and fly
Atop the goal box
Near the net
Below the ball your foot strikes
Across the sky it travels like the speed of light
Down back to Earth travels the ball
Through the goal's arms
Into the net
Underneath it all, the crowd is cheering
Inside I feel the victory and win

Sarah Jordan, Grade 8
Canfield Middle School, ID

Differences

Difference in appearance,
Makes no difference in the end.
Because what matters most
is the heart and soul of a friend.

Black or white,
Dark or light,

Makes no difference to me.
When we all work together,
and live in harmony.

Kate Lowen, Grade 7
Walker Middle School, OR

Life

Life: too short
To live it
Life: too fast
To see it
Life: too scary
For some
Life: too dull
For others
Life: not worth it
To them
Life: they miss it
For her
Life: to love
For all

Dana Carlson, Grade 9
W F West High School, WA

How Complicated Could It Get

How complicated could it get
When a daughter's father
Just leaves?
No communication,
No love shining her way.
She has an empty hole
That can never be filled.

Oh how much more complicated
Could it get?

She walks through a cold, deep
Cave of darkness
Without her daddy's hand.
Is the love from him still there,
Or did he forget?
Is he hurting too,
Or does he also have a hole?

How much more complicated
Could it get?

Alisha Lewis, Grade 8
McLoughlin Middle School, OR

Soaring

While I sit over the world and think about the ones I love,
My life sits below me as I soar like a dove.

Looking down on clouds of white fluff,
Wondering why life is always so tough.

Across the world I go with nothing but me,
The ones I love I can't wait to get back and see.

Land in front, land in back, nothing underneath but ocean,
A perfect place to sort through thoughts, close your eyes and feel the motion.

No looking up from here I'm as high as one goes,
What's next no one yet knows.

What is our next word or thought on this trip worthwhile?
Not something one can know but one can seek with a smile.

Felecia Sapienza, Grade 8
McLoughlin Middle School, OR

The Endless Dream

Something is changing, you feel it in your soul,
You hear an awful clanging, and you hear it to the full.
You sit in front of the fire, your thoughts going deep,
Wondering a long while, if you should take the leap.
There are two paths that you could take, one left, one right,
You're pondering which choice to make, when you're suddenly gifted with sight.
You take the left and all you see, is darkness for miles around,
You hear something and try to flee, when you realize it's you making the sound.
You take the right, and you feel a sensation,
Everything is filled with beautiful light, and darkness is not a temptation.
You wake up and take the right, only to realize you took the left,
Your soul cannot see the light, as you witness your own death.

Meghan Watkins, Grade 9
Elk Ridge Middle School, UT

Dreams

I know someone who had a dream,
And now, today, he is placed on a beam.

At first no one listened while he poured his heart out
So to be heard he began to shout.

After long, people began to hear,
For now there was nothing to fear.

Never ending did he fight
All he wanted was the right.

The right to be free just like you and I,
But tragically, he had to die.

He died for his people, for the chance they could live
And will always be remembered because he gave all he could give.

Heather McMaster, Grade 9
Elk Ridge Middle School, UT

The Cold Blue Wave

There is a cold blue wave
That flows inside me,

That cold blue wave
Is my feeling that flows inside me when I'm angry.
It is red when I'm sad,
It's gray but when I'm shy it's blue,

That cold blue wave
Flows inside me when I'm by you.

Billy Wolf, Grade 7
Komachin Middle School, WA

Imagination

My imagination is running wild,
Into a world of smiles.
With purple bubbles, pink duckies,
Green elephants, and blue puppies.
A journey to the dream world has just begun,
As I jump into a pool of fun.

Filled with joy,
And creating toys,
Making my imagination soar,
With the birds, dragons and more.
Prancing through the fields at top speed,
Crossing the finish line with great applause to greet me.

Anything can happen,
When you use your imagination.

Matisse Lehman-Carter, Grade 7
CLASS Academy, OR

Unintentional Masks

Under all the unintentional masks she wears
is a girl who really cares
She'll hide behind an invisible wall
and act all big when she feels so small
but under all the masks she unintentionally wears
yes under all her skin deep layers
is a girl who just wants someone to care
to notice her beyond how she does her hair
she wants someone to reach out and grab her hand
to take her home back to her once happy land
but each time someone reaches out in love
she flies away like a frightened dove
for she's tried to love but failed before
so now she's shut that once open door
she goes around with her masks making everyone believe
she doesn't need anyone; but they're deceived
she's got everything together, or so she thinks
but really there's some missing links,
one day she'll find it, and she'll see
how happy life can really be

Jennifer Hill, Grade 8
Hill Family Home School, WA

An Image

There is an image I must now uphold.
A look, a life, a way that I must choose.
I forge a path, my story must be told.
For I am strong, and that I must not lose.

The pressure of my life bears heavy weight.
A journey ahead, a place I must go.
Remain true to yourself for your own sake.
With love in my heart, I shall let it glow.

It's up to you, but a choice must be made.
I made a choice, my cards have been played.

Jody Buck, Grade 9
Holy Names Academy, WA

Shy

Her lips curve downward,
Forever locked in a fearful frown,
She tries to speak,
Her mouth runs dry,
You never hear a sound,

Her eyes dart from side to side,
She looks down at her feet,
She looks up at the sky,
She mumbles a few words and runs away,
Yet she has nothing to hide.

She knows everyone can see it,
She doesn't try to refrain,
She finds bliss in the silence,
That drives most people insane.

At last she has come to terms with the weakness,
And embraces it as a strength,
In not speaking to others,
She has found a way to escape.

Lydia Johnston, Grade 7
Sylvester Middle School, WA

In Ancient Rome

Once we started the long journey home,
We saw the ancient city of Rome.
The capitol, the architect,
Where the buildings all once stood erect.
As we look at the ancient ruins,
We see the ancient Romans doings.
And now this poor, this completely doomed place,
All its traces aren't erased.
Shall be built back from the cloud,
And all the Romans will shout out loud.
And this is how the Roman's home,
Became the modern place called Rome.

Dominic Deacon, Grade 7
Pioneer Intermediate/Middle School, WA

I Wonder Why Life Isn't Fair
Many things happen in life
We can't go back and change
You can't remove or rewind
Or even rearrange

Your sister goes to the movies
You're left at home
She's out with friends
You're all alone

You focus on the small things
Your head's up in the sky
When suddenly you realize
All your time's slipped by

So maybe life isn't fair
But in the end you'll know
In the long run
It all helped you grow
Marina Davies, Grade 7
Sylvester Middle School, WA

Eagles
In the sky above
Above the fluffs of clouds
Amongst the heavens above the earth
Beside the fighter jets
Soaring along
Ryan Doble, Grade 7
Rogich Middle School, NV

Friendship
Friendship to me,
Is like two cherries,
On a tree.
Sticking together,
Hand in hand,
Until the end of time.
Holding on to the,
Friendship that was made.
Never letting go,
Until it is time to go.

Love,
Amanda Kay Freeman.
Amanda Kay Freeman, Grade 7
Marsing Middle School, ID

My Pet
Puppy
Small, furry
Jumping, running, barking
He bites my finger
Animal
David Pacheco, Grade 8
Culver Middle School, OR

Emotions Fly
Over the flower-covered country,
Across the salty seas,
Around the earsplitting world,
Like a soaring bird.

Through the overwhelming woods,
Toward him,
To her
Past me.

Outside down by the old rickety bridge,
Beneath the heavenly lit stars,
Down by the murky river,
Above the rocky, dusty road,

Within our hearts,
Since the dawn of time,
Without restrain,
May emotions fly.
Morgan Clements, Grade 7
Robert Stuart Jr High School, ID

My Very Best Friend
Someone who doesn't believe in an end
Someone who would never pretend
Someone who has a hand to lend
Someone who I would recommend
Someone who I could always depend
And that someone is my very best friend
Lena Giang, Grade 7
Sylvester Middle School, WA

Heart
I am something inside you
I keep you being swell
Some see me as scientific,
And some religious as well.

But most of us see it,
As none of those at all,
But still it's all the same,
And still we all it call,

A heart — the center of us all.

It warms us when we're nice,
And kind and loving too.
But when we're mean, it turns all cold,
A lump of mushy goo.

So if you love your heart,
You'll be good and nice and sweet,
And eat lots and lots of protein,
Because your heart is meat!
Paul Cardoza, Grade 8
American Leadership Academy, UT

To Be a Champ!!!
One more round
Palms slipping on the mat
Sweat dripping
Mouths yelling
Two for takedown
Ten seconds left
Score 5-2
Thinking what else to do
I shoot, grab his leg…
Whistle blows…
Nervous to walk to the ref
The ref grabs our wrists…
Lifts up the arm…
Crowd goes wild
I am the champ!!!
Evangeline Hood, Grade 8
Culver Middle School, OR

A Book
The library card is your own special key,
The door is your own special book.
Your key can unlock any door,
And open any adventure.
Try battling against a dragon,
Or joining a fairy for tea.

The only thing you have to do,
To get this special privilege,
Is just decide which door,
That you want to open.
Emily Klopfer, Grade 7
Mears Middle School, AK

Alex
His temper is
like a rising storm
on a cold winter day.
His touch is
like a soft breeze
on a warm summer night.
His soul is tainted,
but his heart is pure.
She's his sister,
but I make her jealous.
I understand,
he's hot as lava.
I wish I was more than…
His baby sister's little best friend…
Or…
One of the guys…
How much difference
is two years?
Surely not
enough to hear about.
Jacqueline Estes, Grade 9
R A Long High School, WA

Happiness

Happiness is like the sunshine,
It sounds like the playful giggle of children,
It tastes like sweet chocolate,
And smells like fresh baked cookies,
Looks as if nothing could go wrong,
Feels like a hug after a bad day!

Aleigh A. Hunsaker, Grade 9
Buhl High School, ID

Just Don't Go Away

"So what's going on?" I hear my mom say.
"Nothing," I reply, and then look away.
"Okay," she says, and starts to cry.
I feel sudden guilt, like I just want to die.
"Hey mom?" I say, as she walks away.
"I love you and hope you have a good day."
She nods and leaves through the front door.
I see her climb into her car as rain starts to pour.

At six o'clock, I turn on NBC,
And literally scream from the sight that I see.
There is my mom, lying dead on the ground
With so many people there to surround.
Her car had crashed and landed on its side
And I can't help wondering if it's suicide.

I kick and I scream 'til I'm shaken awake.
I hug my mom close and begin to quake.
"What's going on?" I hear my mom say.
"I'll tell you. I promise. Just don't go away."

Alice Wong, Grade 9
East Anchorage High School, AK

Obstreperous

It was an ordinary, normal, boring day,
When Mom told me to get cleaning away.
I dusted and mopped, scrubbed and polished
And cleaned out the garage until the dirt was demolished.

Though the worst chore was yet to come,
Oh how I hated it, how it was bothersome.
I turned on the vacuum, it roared and then purred,
The hose flew up at me like a chirping blue bird.

I pulled and I pulled with all of my might,
But that vacuum had sucked up my hair, so very tight.
I yanked at that hose until my poor head was sore,
Why did I even bother to do this stupid chore?

The dust around me was rising; I coughed and coughed,
Oh wait, there it is! The button labeled off!
I lurched for the switch, finally at last,
This terrible chore was over. It was gone and past.

Whitney Lewis, Grade 8
South Jordan Middle School, UT

Friendship Is Like the Great Big Golden Key

Friendship is like the great big golden key
It's close to our hearts for eternity
The golden key can open many doors
Also close them for others to explore
People with a ringlet of many keys
Will sort those certain keys as they do please
Others with only just a few big keys
Know what is really truly meant to be
You know what special keys will always stay true
And never turn their back away from you
Losing your keys is like losing your friends
You know they're there but never see them again
This is to thank all my very special keys
And let them know how much they mean to me

Allison Ashmore, Grade 8
Horizon Middle School, WA

Reflection

Mirror, mirror hung with care.
Staring at the empty air.
Show what you see inside.
From you my true-self I cannot hide.
Tell me what you truly see.
When you're staring straight back at me.
Tell me why I feel this way.
Tell me something I'll never say.
Why is my life going this way?
What can I do to change myself?
First one must be true to thyself.
Then one must let others see.
How they wish to truly be.
Last one must look deep inside thyself.
And that's all I must do to change myself.
Mirror, mirror sitting there.
It seems like you're the only one who truly cares.

Meghan O'Donnell, Grade 9
Galena High School, NV

Friends!

There and here,
When lost, help is there
When lonely, someone is there to boost you up
When falling, there is a shadow
When depressed, tugging of a rope is there
When needed to talk, there was someone to listen
When needed to study, there was a buddy
When death, there was bliss
When there was harm, there was anguish
When needed a shoulder, there was bolder
When in trouble beyond belief, there was guilt
Now and here
We stand together, as we watch each other's backs
Through thick and thin we'll always be known as
FRIENDS!

Lacey Washburn, Grade 9
Soap Lake Jr-Sr High School, WA

Divorce

Divorce!
No way,
This can't be
Can Mom and Dad do that?
No, no, they can't
They can't do this
to me.
Divorce.
What a horrible thing.
Divorce.
Kiera Williams, Grade 7
Molasky Middle School, NV

Night

Night hides out all day
Until it's her turn to play,
She plays with the stars
As she dances on Mars,
She flies through the sky
As her time passes by,
Soon her time is up
It's her sister Day's turn,
To light up the world
In her own special way.
Chelsea Huffman, Grade 7
Mears Middle School, AK

Rainy Days

Rain Rain Rain
You hate it you love it
but it never goes away
it has its ups and downs
playing in ponds
sitting by the fire
but you can't play baseball
or ride dirt bikes
rainy days you hate them you love them
Nick Williams, Grade 7
Ogden Middle School, OR

Softball

A calm pitching mound
On a cold rainy day
In the evening
The crowd cheering
Bats swinging
The ball hitting the catcher's mitt
The ball soaring over the plate
The batter swings
I scream out the play
I throw the ball to first
I relax after the play is complete
On a cool April evening
Determination for the third out.
Sarah O'Gorman, Grade 8
Culver Middle School, OR

Daughter in the Graveyard

Hi, Dad, it's me again
We are all doing fine
Mom is all excited about the new house
Brooke is doing well in school
And I am doing fine
Mom is all excited I will be driving soon
Dad, you don't have to worry Mom is doing good
Dad you don't have to worry Uncle Jay is watching too
He is making sure I am not dating or we are not driving Mom crazy
Well, Dad, I will talk to you soon.
Just think now you don't have to worry
We love you so you don't have to worry
Erika!

Erika Hoover, Grade 9
Buhl High School, ID

Children of the Holocaust

I am Agnes Ringwald
My life was like an amusement park ride
At first, it was great, but it wouldn't last for long
I was unaware of the inhumanity around me
When I was eight, they took me from Pestszenterzsebet
They forced my family into ghettoes
I still wouldn't believe we would be outright murdered
As apathetically as ants
In 1944, they took us to Auschwitz
They took my mother and me to the gas chambers
I was one of the 1.5 million Jewish children who were murdered
Carl Prince, Grade 8
South Jordan Middle School, UT

My Life Is a Fantasy

When I ride in a truck with peeled paint and low gas
Almost ready to leave me in the streets of traffic,
I ride in a delicate gold carriage,
Flown by white horses with angel wings
As soft as velvet.

When I walk through the doors of my house with hinges loose and squeaky
Yelling to be repaired,
I walk through doors of cold crystal draped with Egyptian cotton,
Every thread soft and smooth,
Glistening and sparkling under the moons light.

In our world of laws, and politics, and religion,
There is reality.
But there is also our make believe hidden in the corners,
Only peeking out during some of the darkest times of the reality we created.

I don't want to always have to worry about being left in traffic.
I don't want to worry about repairing things as simple or complicated as a door.
So my life…
Is a fantasy.

Kathryn Morin, Grade 7
Mears Middle School, AK

Forest Walk

Went forward, went backward,
Through the forest onward,
Marched to the left and right,
Went I and my pride,
Watching for ways to escape its grasp,
Suddenly a light appears,
In the midst of the branches,
Shone a white light of hope,
I approached and discovered a flashlight,
My hopes fell apart,
Until another light appeared on my face,
My brother walks toward me in shock,
Asking if I am okay,
I reply with a silent yes,
And we walk back home safely.

Mark Fefelov, Grade 7
Nikolaevsk School, AK

Perspective

You're feeling down, and in despair.
This issue is over, regret will soon appear.
You crawl inside your petty thoughts,
reviewing moments you wish you forgot.
Over and over, your mind disappears.

Although, it doesn't have to be this way.
It's the way that you view it,
that will determine your fate.
Optimism can be the key,
to figuring out the upset.
An altered perspective,
will allow you to see,
the better side of the bad.

You're feeling down, and in despair.
There is a time to fret, and some time to fear.
Then you look back and contemplate,
it happened to better your life in a way.
Over and over, your mind will soon be clear.

Your altered perspective,
allowed you to see,
the beauty within the beast.

Lyla Rowen, Grade 9
Reno High School, NV

Nightmare

Nightmare
Why do you scare when people know you are never there?
Show thyself to me
And show me you are not a withering tree
Show me you are not scared and hiding in the darkness
Show me you are all you can be
And not my imagination fooling me

Becca Prengel, Grade 7
Cedar Heights Jr High School, WA

If Only

If only I could be beautiful,
Then everyone would see me.
If only I could be smart,
Then everyone would be my friend.
If only I could be talented,
Then everyone would love me.
If only I would see that image doesn't matter,
Then I could love myself.

Hannah Chesley, Grade 9
North Cache 8-9 Center, UT

Mysteries

Have you ever wondered why?
Why the grass is green and the sky is blue.
Why after the effortless number one,
follows the expected number two?
Or maybe it's the simple things,
like the way someone's smile can light up a room.
Or when a car speeds by,
and you hear the tires go, zoom!
And have you ever met those people,
who don't care about anyone but themselves?
And then the others,
who put their pain and anger up on high shelves.
Why? The question you always ask.
I guess we all just seem to be,
living in a world,
that's one big mystery!

Keelie Proulx, Grade 7
Lincoln Middle School, OR

Vision of the Night

Underneath the brilliant starlight
I can see the moon on the water
The grass feels like a featherbed
In a cold barn
The wind is wrapping its gentle frigid arms
Around my ice cold body
Water is building in my eyes from the winds steady blow
All around me are sounds
The willow tree flexing its ancient fronds
The tiny silver fish mashing in the sea
What happens to a vision of the night
When a rainstorm hits
When the bulbous purple and gray clouds
Roll in on the horizon
And soon they break into a million pieces
A shattering of moisture
A perplexing gesture of sadness
Water everywhere
And afterwards
The muggy air, thick with moisture
And the scent of forgiveness

Sam Viklund, Grade 7
Sylvester Middle School, WA

The Day I Broke My Arm

The day is still fresh in my mind
It was on Wednesday, January 18th

The sun was not shining on the Rogue Valley that day
It all happened at wrestling practice
At McLoughlin Middle School in the good old U.S.A.
Coach Kregal was demonstrating his favorite move on a student
Young Jonathan Parker was selected as the victim
I hit the mat and you would have thought an earthquake occurred on the West Coast Fault Line
And I heard my bones crack and pain rushed through my arm like a Duraflame Log

Mother and Father rushed to my side
And they did not use any inappropriate English words

My arm was repaired with plates of steel
Which are as strong as the sides of the Titanic
So the next time I go swimming, let us hope it is not a repeat of the sinking of the Titanic

Jonathan Parker, Grade 7
McLoughlin Middle School, OR

Saying Good Bye

With each breath the pain of the past day decreases like the sun on the horizon as the morning turns to night.
The day gets farther and farther away but it will not leave me fast enough.
I try to push it out of my head but memory floods back like the giant wave that ruined my village.
The anguish of the day will never leave me.
It will be branded on me like my name.
Every time I let my mind wander,
Let my conscience drift away,
it will rush to me faster than the river that carried me away from my love.
I was a fool not to hold tighter to it.
My body feels like it is missing a part.
I know I have to say good-bye.
I say it to the world and to my friends.
I have to rejoin the missing part of my life.
I don't know where it is but I will find it when I say good-bye

Talia Shulman, Grade 8
Lake Washington Girls Middle School, WA

Imaginary Light

I close my eyes, I drift away to a place where I always wish to stay.
Far away from all worldly things, in this place I can spread my wings.
Far away from the sensible, the ordinary, I retreat to my own world of the imaginary.
Where I can escape from the chaos and vulnerability, of the place — or state of mind — of which you call reality.
To the one true place I can be myself, and where creativity is the greatest wealth.
Late at night or in the day, I take the familiar path to a place so full of light and so very far…far away.
This is the land I call my home, where the spirits of my imagination are free to roam.
They need me here, I am their guide, I'm with them on their life's journey — merely along for the ride.
These souls live and breathe inside my head, they are with me even as I lie asleep in my own bed.
They are always here — their hopes and dreams, their darkest fears.
They are always with me and will never leave, and that, in itself, is the greatest gift I will ever receive.
I must leave now — for it is getting late, another time I must decide their fate.
I must now return to the paleness of reality, and make the choices that will take part in my own destiny.
They will wait for me until I return, out of sight, until I can make the journey once again —
To my secret sanctuary of Imaginary Light.

Victoria Osborne, Grade 9
Dufur School, OR

Ice Hockey
Call the ice a battlefield, where the battle begins.
Call the stick your weapon to use against the enemy.
Call the gear your armor, to help protect yourself.
Call the skates your speed, to retreat just in case.
Call the puck a cannonball that can destroy a stronghold.
Call the goal a stronghold, to keep enemies at bay.
Vance Mattila, Grade 7
Mears Middle School, AK

The Ride
When I climbed into the chute
The bull turned around and bit my boot
I sat there startled, in a daze
Then the bull started jumping around in a craze

As I rosined up my rope
I was thinking, what a joke
The bull I had was a weak one
And I had no chance of winning this one

I crawled up and nodded my head
The bull felt like a metric ton of lead
As we fired out of the box
The bull cleared the back of the chute with his hind hocks

As the buzzer rang and I bailed out
I couldn't believe we had won without a doubt
When I reached the fence the crowd came alive
I had reset the arena record, a score of 99.5
Beau Lewis, Grade 9
Dufur School, OR

Red, Red Rose
I'm like a red, red rose
Because all you see is red
Red represents all the bad
Things I did and said
The stem is green
Green represents all the bad
I was taught and seen
And from that green stem the red flower grows
And sadly to say
I'm like that red, red rose

In the middle of the forest
Is a red, red rose
Lonely and lost the red flower grows.
Planted in dry dirt
And without the proper comfort
The flower was hurt
And so fragile when the wind blows
Sadly to way
I'm like that red, red rose
Rocky Raymond, Grade 9
McLaughlin High School, AK

I Am
I am a rose, I am lonely
I am Annie Vineyard

I'll always remember when my cousin got hit by a car
I give love and laughs
I pretend to be a normal person
I worry about my friends and family
I feel lonely
I can't get money!
I wish my friends would notice me more
I wonder why this girl pretends to like me
I hear laughs, but not mine
I see stars in the night sky
I care about my friends, my family, and my dog
I cry when something bad happens to my friends or family
I dream what was last on my mind
I hope I will get an A in every class
I say "Hi, how are you?"
I try to make new friends
I want the movie *Chronicles of Narnia*
I understand my friends

I am Annie Vineyard
Annie Vineyard, Grade 8
Wasatch Jr High School, UT

My Tree
This is my tree,
A tree that I made a fort in,
A tree that I hung a swing,
A tree that I broke my arm falling out of.
A tree I've climbed so many times,
A tree that I loved and could hardly let go of,
A tree that I had to part with
and can only see every so often,
My tree and best friend.
Nate Hughes, Grade 7
Ogden Middle School, OR

A River's Journey
Rushing with set determination,
One destination with the earth as its road block.
The small stream creeps over rocks,
Washing a trail across the dirt.
Streams from all ways come into one,
But still have one destination.
Growing into a river,
Determination stands strong,
Pushing through every obstacle in its way,
Its destination coming closer.
The river speeds its pace,
Finally pushing through the last bit of earth.
The river emerges into the tranquil ocean,
Finally ready to rest.
Kirstin Klippel, Grade 8
Wasatch Jr High School, UT

Secrets and Illusions
Awaking every night
To the horror of his dreams
Yet finding out it's real
And is surely what it seems.

Desperate in his fright
He shouts out in the dark
To the spectral demon awaiting him
That places upon him, its mark.

It appears gruesome and grotesque
Deadly claws and horrid face
It chills the spine and the air
And speeds up the heart's pace.

Send it to the Abyss
Anywhere but here
Imprison it in the Brazen Vessel
To the Gates of Hell, it should adhere.

The lies it tells
The mask it wears
It shrouds my mind
It fulfills my dares.
Andrew Pegram, Grade 8
Thurman White Middle School, NV

Brother
Around me he walks
Within my heart he lies
Among my family he's loved
Toward the world he walks
Past high school he leaves
Mercedes Scarbrough, Grade 7
Rogich Middle School, NV

Breathtaking Beauty
A gentle breeze swept over me
While I was walking on the shore;
Eye looking far as eye could see,
Taking it all in, wanting more.

Soft white sand covering the beach,
Wet by small rolling waves it was.
Some tiny shells within my reach,
Placed only as the ocean does.

High in the sky the sun had been,
Though now the light slowly faded.
Why I was there, I knew just then —
To see all that He created.

The vast ocean — what a grand sight,
And there I stood, throughout the night.
Lauren Keller, Grade 9
McKenzie River Christian School, OR

Our World
People in this world are starving.
And here we are acting like we're kings.
Why don't we pitch in a little?
We can get back to loving our world instead of hating it.
While some of us are trying to do our part
Others are making it worse by throwing away food
That people in China would die to have.
What I don't get is why people in the world are starving
And here in the US we're having problems with being anorexic and bulimic.
I say that we're thinking too much about ourselves and not enough about others.
So let's try to make not only us happy but others too.
Kaylee Larson, Grade 7
Hood River Middle School, OR

My Place
Reading a book I can be whoever I want to be

Lost in a story of heroes saving the trapped princess
And stories of happily ever after

But in the end you save yourself
From the person you are running from

While reading that one single book, your life can change in the biggest way
And many a friend you will make from all over the world

The second you're sucked into the powerful plot of a great writer
The world starts to fade away and you lose yourself in the words

I am content and comforted in reading the story of others
And it makes me happy to know that the truth will come to the surface

As the book comes to an end and reality starts to sink in
My life will be another chapter that will soon start again

In the end I will eventually find who I am destined to become
Brianne Ramos, Grade 8
Komachin Middle School, WA

I Love You
Have you ever loved somebody and never wanted to let them know
And when you're with them your feelings always show
How happy and excited you are inside
That you picture your life as a fantastic ride
On a deep roller coaster of adventure to pursue
And about one month later you're saying "I love you"
To that person that will always understand how you feel
Even if you tell that person that you use to steal
Candy and love cards to bring them to school
And when you talk you accidentally drool
Together you guys will laugh through thick and thin
And no matter how much you guys argue your love will never end
So there's 8 letters, 3 words and 1 true meaning you see
And that's what "I love you" means completely!
Sarah Canul, Grade 7
Sylvester Middle School, WA

"It All Began with a Mouse"

A well-known man walks down Main Street,
With children running after.
"But wait, it's you we want to meet,"
And soon their cries turn to laughter.

Little black mouse with big ears and red pants
Has appeared and is singing a song.
It also appears he has made up a dance,
And is doing it to go along.

All at once a princess comes out of the dust,
Already complete with a crown.
And by the look of her she must
Have had a fairy to make her gown.

The magical world of Walt Disney has come,
His amazing talents have spread.
Blow a trumpet, beat a drum,
For where his imagination has led.

Kary Clemons, Grade 8
South Jordan Middle School, UT

Knowing You

Before I knew you, I was alone and confused
I knew I was missing something
I knew I was missing you.
I knew what I was missing but I still didn't believe
I wanted to see you and touch you
before I gave my life to eternity.
I was waiting for the day that you would finally come
I could see and touch you
and then you would lead me home.
One night you came but not physically
you came and spoke
only in my dream.
When I woke up from the dream in which you came
I found myself in a hospital bed
thinking my life is not a game.
I knew my time had come and I was going to die soon
but I'm not going to Hell
because I know you.
Even though I was facing death
I didn't fear I knew I could rest
I was going home.

Brigitta Fader, Grade 7
Sylvester Middle School, WA

My Hero

B eing like Lance,
I mpossible accomplished,
K icking the sprint to the finish line,
I see him as a hero, my role model, a survivor
N ever give up is what he teaches me
G o, LIVESTRONG.

Cassie Bean, Grade 8
Culver Middle School, OR

Parents

I don't understand parents
Why they have to be so mean
Why they are always so tired
Why the make us do chores
I don't understand parents
Why they are so grumpy
Why they drink that icky black stuff
Why they go to work
Why they are in a rush
Why they do too much stuff
Why they have to travel
Why they wake up super early
Why they send us to school
Why they need a massage every day
And why they can't play.
But I do understand
That they love us
That they play with us
That they give us gifts
That they tuck us in at night
And that they want to be with us every moment of the day.

Cory Van Arnum, Grade 8
St Mary's Elementary School, AK

Touched by the War

I am a woman who is touched by the war
I wonder how long it'll be
I hear the drums of the enemy
I see the soldiers falling down
I am a woman who is touched by the war
I pretend all the fighting will be done
I feel the pain the soldiers endure
I touch the tears of my little girl's face
I worry we won't wake to see our flag
I cry when the British raise their guns
I am a woman who is touched by the war
I understand that he went to serve
I say liberty will be ours
I dream of that day that we will be free
I try to help all that need
I hope the war won't be long
I am a woman who is touched by the war

Marissa Harris, Grade 7
River HomeLink Program, WA

What Happens When a Loved One Dies?

What happens when a loved one dies?
Do you still have a life worth living?
Do you hate them for leaving you?
Do you still feel the sweet things in life?
Do you wonder what will happen when your time comes?
What happens when a loved one dies?

Morgan Curriden, Grade 7
Rogich Middle School, NV

Tornadoes

As the sun beams through the sky,
I start out, oh so high.
Hasting through my strengthening gain,
I had just begun to rain.
Like an eagle striking prey,
I come down, day by day.
Driving down, much more foul,
I proceed my rumbling howl.
As I hit destruction's near,
People scatter, filled with fear.
Stumbling through the rumpled streets
These beings float up from their feet.
After windy seconds pass,
Homely items seen for last.
As I leave this horrid site,
Dreams sail off, through the night.

Corinne Zander, Grade 9
Elk Ridge Middle School, UT

Why?

Why did my mother leave me?
Why didn't my father stay?
Why can't I ever be free?
Why have I lost my way?
Why did my peers all taint me?
Why must I cry all day?
Why can't myself I be?
Why can't I? If I may
Why did my love condemn me?
Why didn't he just stay?
Why did he do this, how could he?
Why did he go away?
Why to live you pay a fee?
Why can't I be okay?
Why can't the population see?
Why don't they hear what I say?
Why must I always scream and plea?
Why is life the saddest play?
Why can't there always be a key?
Why can't we all be gay?
Why?

Ashley Gren, Grade 7
East Valley Middle School, WA

Take a Chance

You can't ever be
someone who wants
to discriminate,

It's always good
to not discriminate.
Take a chance and free away.
To not ever discriminate.

Amal Zayed, Grade 7
Walker Middle School, OR

Caramel Sky

Amber through the clouds
Golden, cascading
As free as a flag in the wind
Sweet

Corey Soderberg, Grade 7
Rogich Middle School, NV

Friends

They stick to your side
Friends are so nice
They know what to say
You share your secrets
You can trust them with anything
They share your life
You get in fights but you get over it
Friends laugh and play
You're friends to the end
You never leave each other's side
Friends have similarities
You sleep at each other's houses
Friends are like family to you

Paige Carlston, Grade 7
Kearns Jr High School, UT

Life Is Life

Life is life
That's all I can say
Life is life
It takes away
You don't know where you're going
You don't know when it stops
Life is life
Live it well
Don't end up thinking,
I
Shoulda'
Coulda'
Oh well

Elliott Wilson, Grade 7
Sylvester Middle School, WA

The Same Sun

I gaze into the horizon,
A heap of fire lies against the ocean,
The sky reflects the fire's color,
Permeated with a glowing orange,
The ocean hums a sweet song,
Putting sea life to rest,
Slowly the fire distinguishes,
And all is lost in a black canvas,
Stars begin to be painted,
Life is not lost,
For the sun will rise again.

Rebecca Cubitt, Grade 9
McNary High School, OR

My Pet

Dog
Friendly, hairy
Running, playing, sleeping
They are very soft.
Animal

Chris Crouse, Grade 8
Culver Middle School, OR

Camping Fright

I lay at night and listen,
To the loud nightly storm,
I hear the rooftop leaking,
Through the ceiling of my dorm.

Of course I am so terrified,
I lay here, I'm in fright,
I'm trying to not be so afraid,
I'm trying with all my might.

I hear the others snoring,
I am the only one awake,
I try to think about tomorrow,
I'm going swimming in the lake.

I'd like to go canoeing,
And maybe make a pretty craft,
Or maybe write an exciting story,
I think I'll write the draft.

And now as I still lay here,
I am not so freaked out,
I think that I am falling asleep,
Thanks to my thought, no doubt.

Vicka Perekurenko, Grade 7
McLoughlin Middle School, WA

A Good Friend

A good friend sees past
The way you look.
A good friend is there
When you need a
Shoulder to cry on.
A good friend can make
You laugh more than
Anyone else can.
A good friend will
Stand by you no
Matter the situation.
A good friend is
Someone you can
Love who will be
There for you whenever
And love you just as much.

Myriah Gould, Grade 8
Meadowdale Middle School, WA

The Rose

Red and beautiful
Love it sings
Yellow and radiant
Brilliantly pink

Bringing care and hope
Stunningly white
Means peace
With no reason to mope

All of them mean wonderful things
Pleasant to look at
Smiles they bring

Except the final one
For it isn't so happy and fun

Dark black and twisted with thorns
Brings screaming and crying with reason to mourn

And yet it is this
The dark angel loves most of all
For with one tiny flower
Death does fall.

Kasey Tupper, Grade 9
Soap Lake Jr-Sr High School, WA

January

A new year is here
For all to hear
The birds are gone
The winds are wild
They chill and bite
From morning 'till night
The ground is thick with slush and sleet
And I barely feel my snow covered feet

Kollin Shinn, Grade 8
Sunnyside Christian Elementary School, WA

Color

Today I'm pale and muscular sky —
    tired and soggy
    careless and loose
    dull and sleepy while sitting in class
Now I'm a dotted and checkered crimson —
    sturdy and wild
    tidy and fiery
    bold and flashy while concentrating at home
Today I'm a freckled and spotted lime —
    globular and flat
    curved and loose
    glassy and glowing while eating chocolate cake

Olivia Zabka, Grade 8
Wasatch Jr High School, UT

Skiing

When I ski I feel the cold air
Sometimes the cold freezes my hair.
I speed through the snow
Then the run ends before you know.

The lines are long but are fun
You're glad you waited when it's done.
Then you go to the park to hit a jump
And hope you don't end up in a snow lump.

The ride home is fun
Especially when it's done.
When you wake up the next day
You don't want to do a thing except lay.

Spencer Brueske, Grade 8
Leota Jr High School, WA

anticyclonic emotions

when tears fall from the sky,
a rainbow always appears,
but when tears fall from my eyes,
I've nothing but my fears.

When a candle burns, it shines its light
for all around to see,
but when my heart burns, it's filled with fright,
there is only darkness inside of me.

When a rose blushes, its new spring bloom
love and romance fill the air,
but when I blush, embarrassment fills the room,
flooded feelings of despair.

when a star falls, granted is the wish of a child
youthful dreams coming true,
but when I fall, my dreams are exiled
and my hopes come crashing through.

when mother nature works her magic,
miracles take place
and when it one day works for me
there'll be a smile on my face.

Ashlee Copling, Grade 9
Spanish Fork Jr High School, UT

Natures Music

When I am down and feeling low
I listen to music to help me cope
because the sound of music's flow
reminds me of the ocean and gives me hope
to over come my problems
not matter what it may be
I can always count on the sea
to help me solve them.

Brittany Gordon, Grade 9
Elk Ridge Middle School, UT

Neighborhood

To the first house
A beautiful home
Flowers blooming, birds singing
Grass is growing fine.
To the second house
No one is at home
The smell of rotting flowers
No one is coming.
To the third house
A party is there
Music here, people dancing
The house is moving.
To the last house
Cars passing by
Children playing with their bikes
Bees coming to sting me.
An interesting place, my neighborhood!

Kim Laboca, Grade 7
Juneau SDA School, AK

Snowy Days

Winter has come,
It's finally here!
Now is the time,
To laugh and cheer.
First we'll go sledding,
Until the night.
Then we will have
A snowball fight.
My cheeks are now stinging,
Because of the cold.
Then my parents,
Will come out with the old.
They give me hot chocolate
And now it's OK.
And that is the end,
Of my perfect day.

Eric England, Grade 7
North Layton Jr High School, UT

My Backyard

In the peaceful breeze of my backyard
In a tender and sunny day
In the mid afternoon
Birds chirping
Roasters crowing
Siblings yelling
A pig bathing in the mud
Bunnies bouncing in the sun
Chickens pecking on the ground
I read on the bench
I sit and think
On a cold and warm day
It'll cheer me up

Veronica Lopez, Grade 8
Culver Middle School, OR

"Crack" Goes the Bat!

The ball is thrown.
"Strike one," the ump yells, "Strike two!"
I put the bat down, point to left field.
The crowd silent, wide eyed, and amazed.
Here comes the pitch,
"Crack" goes the bat.
It's hit, I hit the ball,
To left field!
The ball is out of there!
Touch the base, and make my 314th home run!
Never in the history of baseball has this been done.
But now, after all my hard work, my name goes in the Hall of Fame!
There it is…
BABE RUTH.

Dana Sullivan, Grade 8
South Jordan Middle School, UT

A Silent Promise

As of today a silent promise was made
A silent promise made unto myself
A silent promise that will take some work
And I'll have to strive to make it happen
But I know it is what's best for me
And if I stick to this silent promise I know things will work out
A silent promise that I will someday make my dreams come true
I won't give up on my goals both big and small
And as the years go by, I get older
And time is even more limited than before
And this silent promise increases in size
As time withdraws
Don't turn your back you're almost there
Don't look away keep your eye on the prize
Don't lose this now you've come too far
Those are the words that will be running through my mind
When I feel depressed and feel like giving up
I've seen it happen to many others
And I won't let it happen to me
As of today a silent promise was made
A silent promise made unto myself

Kylie Maughan, Grade 7
Central Davis Jr High School, UT

Literature

Around a drafty library the books breathe life.
Inside the bindings lurks imagination beyond compare.
Upon musty shelves dwell unknown foreign lands.
Behind smooth pages and ink you see things unforgettable.
Outside the cover is silence and gloom.
Within is a powerhouse of sound and action.
Within the molded book, taste adventure, horror, and fantasy
From stories that will endure through the ages.
Inside the walls of these hallowed halls you will never want to leave.

Allen George, Grade 7
Robert Stuart Jr High School, ID

Daddy

Somethings will always be in style
Good solid things like honesty,
and trust and caring about people.

It's qualities like these
that keep us aware of who we are
And what we can give to life.

It's qualities like these, Daddy,
that you've taught me to value,
Through your influence, your example, and your love.

It has made me love you very much,
And has made me very proud to have you for my daddy!

Kimberleigh Payne, Grade 7
Nikolaevsk School, AK

Concrete and Paint

If the walls could talk
I wonder what they'd say.
They really have seen it all.
Every drama,
Caught first hand.
The walls saw it all.
Every he said she said scenario
All the gossip, the rumors,
The truths, the lies.
High school dialogue
In all its glory.
The walls saw it all.
I guess if you wanted an informer
You would know exactly where to go
Because the walls saw it all.
But the walls remain mute
So you'll have to rely on another source.
Because the walls can't talk. They only watch.

Megan Hestir, Grade 9
Decatur High School, WA

Don't

Don't plan to say the things of your heart,
And then just back away.
Take the chances as they come,
And your confidence won't sway.

Don't bury all your feelings
Deep inside your heart.
I know it's hard to take great leaps
Not knowing where to start.

Don't worry about the right words to say
Just follow your heart and you'll know.
Don't let your fears overcome you
Because then you'll be forced to let go.

Kenzie Bertram, Grade 9
Cole Valley Christian School, ID

Liar

I can't believe what you say anymore
I just don't believe you anymore
'Cause you've lied too many times before
So your family has shut and locked the door

I never heard you say that you had
A good relationship with your dad
And you say it makes you sad
But that's a lie
And you keep kickin' your mom in the teeth
And you wonder why they called the police

It seems sometimes you've even got a list of lies
Already made up in your mind and which ones you're gonna try
So I think it's best if I decide
To turn and leave you behind
Then maybe you'll do what's right

Sometimes your family needs a little relief
'Cause they're sick of being kicked in the teeth
They just can't take it anymore
So your family has shut and locked the door
They don't want to see you anymore
Anymore

Travis Hales, Grade 9
Project Surpass (Day Treatment – Yic), UT

Night Light

Do you see a great big light?
When you go to sleep at night?
Shining through your window's glass?
Reflecting on your lawn's green grass?

This light, so bright, cannot shine through
The daylight as it becomes anew.
But if you wait, you will see
The light you heard about from me.

Just wait until the clock strikes eight
And look outside, but keep your eyes straight
If you look up by the stars
It shines somewhere right next to Mars.

And as it fades right with the day
Watch again and you just may
See the light once more from space
And watch the comets perform a race

This light, some say, is ancient old.
Much older than silver or gold
And if you look around, then soon
You will find that it is the moon.

Matt Paauw, Grade 9
Mount Si High School, WA

Perfect Feeling

Everyone has something, someone, or someplace that they cherish
Where they feel secure, and safe from everywhere else
Where you know you fit in, and your heart knows you belong
My place is the most beautiful structure man has ever built, a baseball field
It surrounds me to a point where I am so secure, I feel indestructible.
The feelings you get when you are one strike away from a complete game is unstoppable
It smells like pine tar, and nerves rubbing together to create friction that no one sees
One day of hard work on a baseball field, leads to a lifetime of accomplishments
Nothing could ever compare to the feelings and moments you experience on that field
You can't get the tastes of seeds, Gatorade, and defeat out of your mouth after it is all over
It hangs around like the sky does to the Earth
The freshly raked dirt slides layer after layer on top of each other, to create that evenly uneven infield
It all comes down to that moment, that moment when you strike that last batter out
with strike one, two, and then three.

Cody White, Grade 8
Komachin Middle School, WA

Daddy's Little Girl

I am not a little girl but I am a little girl to you and I always will be,
I want to have fun and spend time with you but I just can't
Some say I look like you I say yeah I do and I am proud,
Some say I act like you I say yeah I do but that's ok.
I love you with all my heart even though you can't see it I do,
Sometimes we argue but only because I act just like you,
Some say really that's your dad I say yup that's him and he's the best,
Sometimes I just want to hug you and when I do I can't let you go,
You say things I don't want to hear but it's ok because it just makes me stronger,
I wouldn't be the person I am today if it wasn't for you,
I have learned it's ok to be mad and sad and even happy and never let go of the past because it makes you a stronger person,
So don't give up now we're halfway out and I need someone to the end,
And I hope it's you my dear dad because there's always a brighter future ahead of you and I want you in mine,
I want you to be there to give me away to my future husband,
I want you to be there when I give birth to my first child
I want you there when I am in trouble
So don't you see I need a guiding star and you're that star my dear dad
I love you with all my heart
Your little girl
Crystal Lynne Chavez

Crystal Lynne Chavez, Grade 9
Southridge High School, WA

Spring

In spring the rain melts away leaving the living creatures, flowers, and plants nourished for the seasons to come.
As I look out my window in the middle of nowhere I can see a frog jumping with energy from one lily pad to the next.
As I gaze out my other window the eyes of a fox and mine meet making a magical connection that only we feel.
As I finally get the energy to get out of my bed I feel the surprisingly warm heat of my room.
For the first time in many moons I greet my shorts and T-shirt's that I have been so excited to see.
I walk down the steps and the usual fire that takes me from the cold state of Oregon
and transports me to the warm beach of Florida is gone, replaced with the scent of hot berry pie.
I walk outside to see the amazing colors of the flowers, which are just starting to open up.
I take the wheelbarrow out of the tool shed, which reminds me of the best wheelbarrow rides in the past.
I see the birds coming to the bird feeder again finally after many months.
I look down the alley and see the horses trotting in the distance; they walk with pride because they too know spring is here.
Already with only taking a few steps outside I know this is going to be the best spring of my life.

Emma Levy, Grade 7
Lake Washington Girls Middle School, WA

Dreaming

My emotions fly through the air,
Like the wind carries snow.
Tell the world
My feelings that surround me.
Dreaming of you night, morning and day.
The thoughts I see of you and me,
Caress my mind rapidly.
Together always, never apart.
But only in my dreams, I see you and me.

Allison Jones, Grade 8
Lied Middle School, NV

Different

Encountering this.
Seeing this.
Enduring this.
Being treated differently
for your personality,
for your skin color,
for your belief.
We never seem to be treated the same in this world.
Some, like dirt.
While others, as prized possessions
Some are made fun of
or teased.
When they hate and don't deserve it.
Others are favorites
when they love it but don't deserve it.
I hate prejudice.
It's unreasonable and unfair.
Everyone is made equal.
Is that what you think?

Ivy Chen, Grade 8
Willamette Christian School, OR

What's Really Happening; A Note from a Hidden Heart

When I cry I hide it
When I laugh, I laugh out loud
When I want to talk I will, when I don't I won't
When I have to go, I leave
And don't show my regrets
Wherever I go I try to be happy
Even if those I love are far away

This might be sad
This might be bad
I don't care anymore

Who I am is everything
Me, not you
Not you, me
This is how it is.

Charlotte Sawyer, Grade 8
Leota Jr High School, WA

Light Bulb

Bright, blinding, yellow; the light bulb.
Inventor of the light bulb
Having over 1,000 patents,
Also creating the phonograph.
Living for an incredible 84 years,
A total of two wives.
The laboratory is his home,
Like the sea is a fish's home.
How the world went on before his inventions,
I'll never know.
His mother taught him school at his home.
Some people call him the Wizard of Menlo Park,
But that's not the only place he left his mark.

Kyle Crowther, Grade 8
South Jordan Middle School, UT

Unnoticed Beauty

To most people it's very dirty.
But I look deeper than that.
The pebbles, the dirt, and the water.
Strange, beautiful, and mysterious it may be.
It shines and it glistens.
You may think it's dull.
But I look deeper than that.
Feel free to think whatever.
Or feel free to look deep inside.
You will see something you've never noticed: beauty.
Don't be one who carelessly passes.
Be one to see the real beauty.

Noelia Imani, Grade 8
Wasatch Jr High School, UT

My Fantasy

Stress, tears, rumors, life.
There's no way to escape.
No place in the world.
Except one.
When I'm there,
Everyone else seems to just, disappear.
This place is sacred.
A sanctuary, a fantasy.
When I'm there, I'm free.
Nothing else in the world seems to exist.
Our world, just doesn't realize
The greatness that lies within its thickly bound pages.
Nor does it realize
The joy
That is buried under the large knoll of words.
It's a place of magic and mystery
Love and adventure.
A place that's all mine and at the same time, the whole world's.
This place is my escape, my holy world,
This place,
Is my refuge.

Kayla Hutnik, Grade 8
Komachin Middle School, WA

Pouty Kyle

Kenny Kyle is a baby.
He whines, crawls, and shouts;
He breaks everything in the house,
And the worst of all is, he pouts.

Matt Sides, Grade 8
Mt Olive Lutheran School, NV

Riding a Bike

As I grip his seat
I hear his first cry
I can see him falling
I don't want to let go
Watching the blood trickle down his face
His eyes squinting
Tears roll down his cheeks
I put him back on
As I let go, he topples
Screaming to the ground
My heart breaks again and again
As I let go
Watching him slide off
He kicks the wheel
And tells me to put him back on
He grows with his frustration
And makes it further
As I grip his seat
I see his first ride
As I let go he cries with delight
He made it

Katie Jahnsen, Grade 9
W F West High School, WA

Feelings

I am angry today at so many things
What will tomorrow bring?
More anger, more hate
I will just never know
I feel it so strongly
But does it all show
It boils inside me
It wants to get out
I try to hold back
I try not to pout
I want to break things
But then want to break down
In big tears of feeling that I can't sort out
When will it be over?
When will it stop?
I wish someone could tell me
I feel I could pop
In due time it will end
But not soon enough
This feeling of hatred
On me is too rough

Sofie Vermilyea, Grade 9
Delphian School, OR

Inside

Everyone has a special place that is filled with love inside.
When you open up and feel it, then you know you're safe inside.
Inside of my special place you will see wonders that can't be explained.
You will see colors that blend and make happiness, love, and joy.
You find gifts that contain peace and friendships without ends
So just have fun and enjoy it, you will never feel the same.
It doesn't matter if you taste it and smell it, just open up and feel it.
It sounds like love at first sight.
Just when you're about to leave it your heart just won't believe it.
So remember that love is a very special gift that should be loved, treasured,
and kept in your special place.

Anson Winsor, Grade 8
Komachin Middle School, WA

Friends*

I have been one acquainted with friends
The laughter
The smiles
Being yourself and knowing yourself
The lies
The hate
The times getting away feels so great
Boring days they turn exciting
The times you care
The times you share
The secrets
The happiness
Talking about each other
Talking to each other
Covering your feelings not letting them show
The forgiveness
The rejection
The hard and scary parts of life that are forgotten with your friends
The times that the only thing that gets you through the day
Are your friends
I have been acquainted with friends

Marie Thoma, Grade 7
Sylvester Middle School, WA
*Dedicated to my best friends

Sword and Wing

Thy satin wings, thy emerald scales, of fire, of ash, of steam;
The dragon flies into the sun with a magnificent gleam.

His silver sword, his golden arrows, his pride, his lust for blood;
A knight soon follows to grind the dragon into the dark mud.

Thy mash of teeth, his gleam of sword, thy flap of wing where eagles soar.
The battle ranged on;
His arrow, thy tail, locked in combat, lost without an oar in a sea of hatred.

A misjudged move, a misplaced wing, a cry of pain, and then silence.
A melancholy feeling, a feeling of peace, as the two enemies leave their hatred
and fly together into the wind

Preston Altree and John Nice, Grade 8
Whitford Middle School, OR

The Magical Song

Feel the strums of the acoustic;
time to fold into the music.
Let it unlock the chains from your feet;
now we'll feel free and feel the beat.
The moonlight lights up the lawn;
goes so well, let it rhyme with the song.
My feet become one with the ground;
my ears are filled with the magical sound.
The music is nice, not a dangerous noose.
Let your hair down; let it all loose.
No longer tight; now you're undone.
The music has started; it has now begun.
Your body and soul don't want it to stop;
it's all you hear and you feel on top.
I told you you'd feel it; isn't it strong?
Now everyone please share the magical song.

Jessica Banks, Grade 8
Gordon Russell Middle School, OR

My Writing Willow

Rain softly falls as tears of joy,
They gently trickle down the leaves,
Leaves of a willow, a symbol of silent beauty.
Under such silent beauty sits a girl.
Her long brown hair flows down her back,
As if a waterfall in fullest splendor.
She sits under her silent beauty…
Writing…writing…writing her thoughts,
As they blossom into elegant roses.
The sweet smell of rain makes it all so real,
Though it is a dream.

Amanda Ellen Olsen, Grade 8
American Leadership Academy, UT

Missing

A grocery store or a mall
A gas station or a bathroom stall
If it's pumping or shopping
You find yourself stopping.
Right no left, no what's the best bet
Up no, down or should you just
Give up and fall to the ground?
Should you start looking for a pay phone?
Or stand waiting here all alone
Are people starting to stare?
No, why would they care?
Just go sit on that bench
And think about how to get out of this trench
Then around the corner comes the group
You almost get up and give a hoot
No, you just go stand with the crowd
For nothing uncool is even allowed
Put on a smile and go back to normal
For everyone around here is nothing but formal

Braly Whisler, Grade 7
Sylvester Middle School, WA

Dreams

The dream could never satisfy the want,
He thought there must be more to life than this;
Then grabbing his inheritance he left
In desperate search for life of perfect bliss.
When stepping out into the great unknown,
A worldly darkness lurked about in him;
True happiness he reached for, but then found
The goal has been a merely shallow whim.
Just like a conquered soldier did he fall,
Wealth squandered on the pleasures of the earth;
His dream, his life had swiftly been destroyed,
Wrong actions did not equal his soul's worth.
    For birth to death affects one's destined fate,
    But changing course of life is never late.

Callie Doremus, Grade 9
Covenant High School, WA

Lawn Mower

Yesterday I saw a monster in my yard.
    It was attacking my dad!
He had sharp fangs that race toward you,
    And eat little children's feet.
    He growled a real loud roar.
It ran toward me and opened his mouth,
    Turning around, barely missing me.
He runs up and down the yard eating everything in his path.
    Then, when I think all hope is lost,
    He stops to empty his enormous belly.
    But when I think the horror is over,
        He comes back!
        AHH!

Alexandra Cromar and Michael Kaelin, Grade 8
Wasatch Jr High School, UT

My Mom*

My mom is the greatest,
She's loving, caring, and not the least bit frailest.
In a family of four, she used to run and play,
She used to hardly pray.
She never had any holdbacks,
She probably could have been a fullback.
But, now she not what she used to be.
A careless doctor caused a heavy fee.
With nerves severed,
Her life is now endeavored.
She holds onto what she has left,
But she also has pain and agony to heft.
I would give anything
For her to have everything
The way it used to be.

Robert Ferguson, Grade 9
McLaughlin High School, AK
*Dedicated to my mom who has lived a hard life.
I love you always and forever.

Black

Black is a solemn bird
Unnoticed
Black is a fruit
Left for the poor
Black smells of a
Sleek cologne
Black is a quiet spy
Moving through the shadows
Watching through the window
Gazing, gaining
Useful information
To keep secret
Black is not a fashion statement
Or a dress code at your school
Black can be a death wish
But don't think that
Is cool
Willis Schafer, Grade 8
Reid School, UT

The Darkness Within

Blackness is all that's left of me
See my soul crumble to pieces
My heart is dark, from light I flee
Blackness is all that's left of me
These eyes, they hide in misery
Fade away, my last hope ceases
Blackness is all that's left of me
See my soul crumble to pieces
Phar West, Grade 8
Central Kitsap Jr High School, WA

Star Sailor

I earned my education,
But it had no relation.
I saw a request,
For NASA's best.
I went to apply,
And knew I could fly.
I shortly got a letter,
That said I couldn't be better.
I was sent away,
In the dawn of day.
But unexpectedly soon,
'Twas as black as the back of the moon.
First American woman I was,
Moving in space, creating a buzz.
I told it like a preacher,
And a young woman's teacher.
I altered the humanity,
For woman's vanity.
I am Sally Ride,
And I had great pride.
Jessica Haslip, Grade 8
South Jordan Middle School, UT

Boys and Girls

Boy
Strong, protective
Playing, climbing, loving
Guy, stubborn, miss, queen
Singing, dancing, brushing
Pretty, beautiful
Girl
Greg Knefel, Grade 9
Buhl High School, ID

Babe's Race

She crouches down
Her knees bent low
She listens for
The sign to go.

She looks to the left
She look to the right
She concentrates
With all her might.

She hears a BANG!
And off they go.
They ran like lions
After a doe.

She's almost there
She's near the end
It's only just
Around the bend.

She breaks the tape
Her hands held high.
She's won the race.
She starts to cry.
Brian Larsen, Grade 8
South Jordan Middle School, UT

Together Forever

Thank you for being there,
for showing that you care,
for always putting in your time,
and never giving out a whine.

And when the hard times came to a start
there was no pulling us apart
and in those times there was no doubt,
there was no place where you were out.

And as a friend it's clear to say,
you're here with me for every day,
and on those days you need me too,
I can only hope I'll be there for you.
Klarissa Wren, Grade 9
W F West High School, WA

Students Are Sponges

Students are sponges,
soaking up ideas,
absorbing new information,
with pores that are very clear.

Students are sponges,
sitting in class,
waiting to be called upon,
others, wanting out of there fast!

Students are sponges,
engaging in schools,
floating in shiny pails,
sheltered from jokers and fools,
trying not to fail.

Students are sponges,
ringing out knowledge,
with dripping ignorance,
branded by diplomas or college,
changing one's innocence.
Tina Phanmanivong, Grade 7
Mears Middle School, AK

Sea-Shaped Stones

She pushes, and spins,
Like a washing machine.
She reaches in, and out,
Shoving them on her way.

She is a giant to them,
A huge roaring giant.
They are little, and clean,
Some bright, and some dull.

They are small, but precious,
Sea-shaped stones.
Kristin Gollofon, Grade 8
Leota Jr High School, WA

The Track

The place I go just for fun
that takes away my fears
The place I go just to run
and hide away my tears.
The quiet sound of stepping feet
on a warm summer day
The quiet sound of my heartbeat
my worries slip away.
I don't know what it is about it
why it comforts me so
Something about me circling around it
especially when I feel low.
Natalie Bliss, Grade 8
Wasatch Jr High School, UT

Segregation

As I looked at all of the other folks,
eating and drinking peacefully,
I wondered if they'd be so kind,
to make a space for me.
I made my way around the line,
that barred me off a tad,
and hollered if they wouldn't mind
to scoot over for a lad.
They looked at me and stared,
down at my big oval face,
and said that if I've come to stay,
this really is not the place.
I didn't understand,
why couldn't I come to sit,
because all I wanted to do
was eat and drink a bit.
I quietly walked back to my seat,
across the dividing line,
and I wondered if they'd ever let me
have a space of mine.

Hannah Kotzen, Grade 8
Lake Washington Girls Middle School, WA

He Was a Bright Jolly Man

He was a bright jolly man
I deeply respected him I was his biggest fan
We did fun things like go to the water park
We had parties that started in light and went until dark
For he was a bright jolly man
One day a sickness swept over him.
He was real sick and he grew very thin.
He had cancer for there was no cure no answer.
I only visited him once I could not bare to see him.
I don't understand why he got sick for no apparent reason.
One day I heard he was gone
He was a bright jolly man

Luke Wilson, Grade 7
St Anne School, WA

Winter Days

Hot chocolate, snow, and cloudy days
That is what makes winter days
You can drink a glass or two
Of hot chocolate with a few
Marshmallows to top it off.

If you don't like cloudy days
Just curl up by the fire
With a book
Then you will see a look
Of delight on your face
Just because you love winter days!

Cheryl Thonney, Grade 7
Sunnyside Christian Elementary School, WA

Early Morning

Morning brightness shining throughout
Roosters calling out
Hungry chirping birds calling for their mother
Yellow buses picking up children to start school
Eating breakfast before school
Kids standing waiting for the school bus
Kids riding the school bus to school
Teachers driving to school to teach
Kids being taught

Brittany Myer, Grade 7
Ogden Middle School, OR

Fallacy

What causes men to want and think of might?
The inside-out small mind that lacks foresight;
To make a man to see himself the best
And raise him highest above all the rest.
This lie, so twisted, wrong, sickly, evil,
Has had the human's good become so chill.
He wants to have the title of a god,
And yet he thinks that now this is not odd.
Did they respect the laws that hold in place?
What is man's striving for the highest grace?
To be the maker while they are made
As servants that pleasures of life evade.
    Such is man's life unchecked that's soaring high;
    He falls to earth and caged he sits and lies.

Joe Savage, Grade 9
Covenant High School, WA

The Ford Team

When the ball is out, the Fords are nearby
So let's start the game in five.

Go Jenna, go Jenna, go, go, go
Never stop, always go for the gold.

Their number one supporter
Is of course Mrs. Ford.

Up to the court, down the court there Katie goes.
Her back step is all she needs to make it gold.

Andrew assistant coach again,
He always says, "Good job, do it again."

When it's all over, Coach Ford always says
"Tomorrow, ball practice again."

Then I realize.
Great coaches.
Great supporters.
And great players.
Make great friends.

Jackie Sparks, Grade 8
Wasilla Lake Christian School, AK

That Car

I like to ride in the back of the car,
but I know driving lessons are not far.
Why can't I stay in the back-seat,
where I have room to rest my feet?
Where I don't have to look at any road,
where I don't have to carry any load.
Yet I know, driving lessons aren't far,
then later I'll be out of that car.
I'll finally be at that final rest zone,
back with my friends, no longer alone.
In the front of that car.

Emma Jennings, Grade 7
Wy'east Middle School, WA

The One Love

The one I want the one I need
I can't wait and can't breathe
Your lingering arms around my waist
Your caressing touch upon
My face.
I feel your lips upon my
lips.
That warm sensation as they call a kiss.
My body in your arms
Makes a shiver down my spine.
The words that you whisper stay inside
Of my mind.
those three small words that make my
Life sane.
I gave you my all
So baby I'm not playin' a
Game.
When that kiss touches my face
My heart starts to beat
So just know I love you boy
And that will never change.

Lauren Evans, Grade 9
Diamond Ranch Academy, UT

My Friend

I never had a friend
That was so true
That never looked at me so blue,
Thank God I had you
Cause my life would never be true
Until the day I lost you.

Taylor Covington, Grade 9
Elk Ridge Middle School, UT

Life

Imagine life is like a road
you just don't know when it will end
other times imagine life is like an eagle
free and no worries

Phian Nitiprawoto, Grade 7
Mears Middle School, AK

Insecurity

People laughed…
They said she wasn't normal
They said things that broke her heart
And as she watched the days float by, she tried hard not to cry

People told her she was beautiful, but she knew they were wrong
Because when she looked into a mirror she just started to cry
She hadn't seen herself like this before it was a whole other side
She was scared and wanted to run and hide

It took her awhile to face it again but when she did she was beautiful
She stared for awhile she didn't know why
And then she started to cry

Maybe people were right, maybe I am beautiful
But before the next thought came to her head her inner voice said something instead
He said "I'm glad you have seen what you haven't been seeing
You should have listened to me a while ago"

As she waited for him to talk again she saw a light from within
It was powerful and full of energy
Somehow she knew this was her voice inside her
So she just smiled and said thank you!

Hailee Nisbet, Grade 7
Sunset Ridge Middle School, UT

Two Languages

The guitar is an intimate instrument
The mood of the song changes depending on the vigor of your stroke
The pitch of the note changes depending on the stretch of the string
The song sung by the guitar is the song sung by your fingers, dancing around the frets
The song sung by your wrist, strongly yet elegantly pulling the pick across the strings
The song sung by your body, swaying with the music

The guitar is the interpreter
The translator
Between man and song
Two different languages
That are brought together through it

So the next time you feel like speaking music once again
Pick up a guitar, sit it in your lap, and speak

Speak with your body
Speak with your meticulous picking
Speak with your fingers pushing and pulling strings
Speak with your guitar
And it will translate your movements seamlessly
Into the intricate language that it sings

Josh Voss, Grade 7
Seattle Hebrew Academy, WA

Time Capsule
Who I am
I am a kid who doesn't
Want to fail the 8th grade
but that is my decision
Not anyone else's.
I am a kid who plays hockey
and wants to play hockey in the future
And if I can't I will find another profession.
I am a kid who wants to
Have a good job to support my future family
I am a kid who wants to get
A degree in something like a
Mechanic, an engineer or a job that pays
Good money.
I am a kid who
Used to play baseball but stopped
And I don't know why.
I am a kid turning into
A man.

David Fleck, Grade 8
Komachin Middle School, WA

Only When Brothers Help!!!
My brother tries so hard to help me out,
He puts me in a bind.
But, when he tries so hard to tell me what math's about,
It's the blind leading the blind!

Alyssa Serrata, Grade 7
Mt Olive Lutheran School, NV

I Can't Let Them Down
I stepped up to the plate
Kicked the dirt around to stall
My bat is in my hand
I am ready for the ball

The pitch is off
This time I could be great
Then I took the bait and swung
I hold the team's fate

I swung and missed
Oh no, I can't let them down
I took a deep breath
A practice swing to bring the bat around

I look at the pitcher, then the scoreboard
The next thing I knew the count was 2-2
The next pitch was off
Without thinking I swung and the ball flew
We scored 2 runs before I knew

The game was won
Boy was that fun

Maxwell DePina, Grade 7
St Anne School, WA

Ocean Blue
As I longingly gaze at the ocean blue sky
My thoughts drift away with the clouds floating by
The ocean blue memories of summer has past
The crystal clear moments I knew couldn't last
Ocean blue water creeps into the bay
Ocean blue skies were creating the day
Icees you buy for a dollar a cup
Ocean blue syrup will flavor it up
Ocean blue tears fall from ocean blue eyes
With ocean blue words as we say our goodbyes
Feelings of ocean blue sorrow recede
The thought of next summer is one that I need
Ocean blue kisses lining the shore
I'm counting the seconds, I'll return once more

Stephanie Carlisle, Grade 8
Mountain Ridge Jr High School, UT

Afternoon Math Class
Sitting here in class like a lazy bump on a log.
Thinking like a wise old man.
Turning over memories of days gone by like wheels and a cog.
Sitting here with my attention span eroding like an old tin can.
'Til the smack of the ruler on my desk.
Brings me back to attention like a soldier that was at rest.
Bringing me back to my test.

Darren Butler, Grade 9
Buhl High School, ID

My Shoes
Throughout my life
I have tried on many a pair of shoes.
Shoes that glitter and sparkle, but lack a sole.
Shoes that were too big.
Shoes that were too small.
Shoes that felt uncomfortable and weren't meant for me.
I've tried on shoes that were heavy
weighing me down.
There have been shoes with poor balance that only create pain.

But like Cinderella, there's just one pair that fits me.
It may not be in style.
It may not be sparkly or glamorous.
But they are tough and lightweight,
Comfortable and balanced.

They are simple, yet reliable
and durable
and strong.
Not flimsy or thin, or will cause me to fall.
My shoes tread a bumpy road,
but I know this trail can take me far.
My shoes follow the Savior's footprints.

Sierra Hoffman, Grade 9
West Albany High School, OR

My Dreams

I dream about being on the Oprah Winfrey show, winning a prize, or meeting someone famous, like Robert DeNiro or a college principal there to give me a scholarship to his school.

I dream about my friends and family, will they be here in the near future, or will we all be gathered around a hole mourning over the loss.

I dream about visiting Africa, seeing the wild animals, like the giraffe, or visiting one of the tribes, maybe I will stay for a month or maybe only for a week.

I dream about ordinary dreams, maybe I will be climbing a tree or falling off a cliff. Maybe I'm even buying a cat or meeting a monster and becoming good friends.

I dream about my brother in my clothes, he bugs me and locks himself in my room; he comes out in my shirt and jeans.
I SCREAM!!!!

Kaleey Sorensen, Grade 8
Central Davis Jr High School, UT

Loneliness

She sits in her room so lonely and sad, as she dimly remembers her long gone dad.
She doesn't seem to remember his face, all she has of him is in a little case.
A baseball mitt, a picture, a bottle of cologne, he was the greatest person she had ever known.
When she closes her eyes she can see his face, so happy and unknowing of his unlucky fate.
As she stares out her window, as she stares at her wall, the phone rings and she has a call.
From her mother, her brother, her uncle, or her aunt. She knows when she gets up she can't
Tell them how much she misses him so, and how much she wishes she could go,
Up in the sky, up in the stars, and leave her heart behind with all its scars.
She'd leap for joy at the sight of his face, the face she last saw in a long brown case.
Her tears would turn from sorrow to bliss, and her dad would bend down to give her a kiss.
But Death only came for her father alone, and she reaches down to pick up the phone.
To tell them that she doesn't care, what they're doing or playing out there.
Then she went back to her disheveled bed, and laid down without a word said.

Olivia Shapley, Grade 7
Morgan Middle School, WA

Roach Approach

How many bugs have you killed?
Poor defenseless bugs that didn't do you any harm.
Well I'll tell you mister; us bugs are getting tired of being stepped on, squished,
squashed, and flushed down the toilet.

Hey man! I've got kids to feed.
How would you like it if you were walking home from a hard day's work BAM! Out of
the blue a huge foot comes crashing down and there's the end!

All I'm asking is that before you make that fatal blow, you think about the ramifications
of your actions,

Well have your views changed?
Any deep guilt?

Hey big fella! Have you heard anything I've said?
Wait! What are you doing?
Watch where you're going!
You're going to step…

Kirsten March, Grade 9
Buhl High School, ID

Family

When the sky is dark with just the moon for a light,
Think of your loved ones who's smiles are bright.
As long as the wind blows,
And as long as the river flows,
Remember who you love the most,
Your family.

Kaylee Kolin, Grade 7
Ogden Middle School, OR

Mirror

What is that
staring back at me?
Some sort of creature,
is that what I see?
Something strange,
is it real or just my imagination?
Is it a strange world
on the other side
or just a reflection?
In that world there is a person
moving with me
at the exact time I do.
What is the strange place?
Let me see
I stick my hand out and try to go through.
The person does the same
and stops me.
I guess I'll never see that other realm,
that mystical place,
that I'll never see.

Amy Miller, Grade 8
Wasatch Jr High School, UT

A Life Deprived

I lived in Rome for two short years of my life,
My family and I endured much trial and strife.
Before I was born my fate was decided,
But through terrible times my family stood undivided.
My parents worked hard to support us all,
But their efforts proved worthless at Italy's fall.
Then on one rainy October Saturday,
The Nazis came and took us away.
We were pushed into trains like animals going to slaughter,
All during the journey we were deprived of food and water.
We arrived at the death camp five days later,
And that situation was far from greater.
Men were sent to work, no better than slaves,
To take care of dead bodies and dig mass graves.
My mother and I were sent off to shower,
It was a trick; we were dead in an hour.
I'm Mario Sonnino; I was two when I died,
I was one of the millions of whose life was deprived.

Katie Rose, Grade 8
South Jordan Middle School, UT

Rain

A soft pitter patter on the windowsill
calls to you softly away to the hill
and though you don't want to, you instantly obey
you fling open the doors and you walk away.
You won't be heard of I am sad to say.
That is what you get for
listening to the rain on a stormy day.

Tabitha Watson, Grade 7
Reid School, UT

A Box of Chocolates

Tickle my fancy, oh sweetheart of mine
The feeling you give me is wholly sublime
Wrapped in gold you look like a king
Choose you I would o'er any diamond ring
Did you know, I once knew a Duke?
Russian he was and named Bartuke
He told me once, "With you I am pleased
Up to half the kingdom I'll give you he teased
From titles to treasure to jewels or a cruise
The prize is open for you to choose!
So ask away, my pretty young lass"
"Duke," I said, "I know at last
I want nothing more than one simple box
Filled with the richest chocolates"
So sweetheart you see of all things divine
You're the one I chose to be mine
I love the way you melt in my mouth
I love the way you travel south
To my tummy where you lay
My box of chocolates every day

Grace Morrissette, Grade 8
Canfield Middle School, ID

Just Because of My Religion

What happened to this world?
I was still yet only five.
The world was like a ferris wheel,
Sooner or later it would stop.

Although I was of a different religion,
I did not deserve this segregated treatment.
It was like being squished like a bug.
If only you could understand this pain.

I hated that yellow star,
More than you could imagine.
I despised not being able to go to school,
Everyone deserves an education.

Although I am not here anymore,
I wish I could tell the tale.
For I am and will always be that little boy.
I am Abraham Beem.

Aleksndr Arteaga, Grade 8
South Jordan Middle School, UT

The Road

The road crumbles
Beneath my feet
I walk on
Dazed and confused
I don't know where I'm going
But I have hope
In my sad heart
Gladness too
And I'll get there
You'll be there too
Welcoming
With smiles and hugs
As I crumble
In your arms
Katelyn Rawson, Grade 7
Central Davis Jr High School, UT

Failure

Failure is never an option,
because then you never succeed.

Failure is never an option,
because then you never can lead.

Failure is never an option,
because then you never fly high.

Failure is only the outcome,
if you never attempted to try.
Karli Boman, Grade 9
Elk Ridge Middle School, UT

There Is Hope

The Earth is a place of pity and woe.
Violence, hatred, and death are part.
Racism and pessimism,
When Did It All Start?
Religion shouldn't be used for power,
But It Is.
Money turns good to evil,
bad to worse,
and what's more,
people judge by looks.
They Don't Stop And Look,
at what they have lost,
but there is hope,
where few see it,
there are people who see
what humanity has become,
and what it will be.
Those People Are Heroes.
They are needed hated or not,
the impact they make is not forgot,
even if their death is silent.
Trevor Larson, Grade 7
Sylvester Middle School, WA

The Light

All humans stray from the light, but only the noble step into it once more
Don't try to deny your faults for we all have them
There is no good, there is no evil, just hate
Why must it take a man with a gun to make people stay in the light
Believe in the goodness because it lives in you
In everything, in everyone there is the light
The everlasting energy that can overwhelm any evil
It's in all stories that we create because that's what we believe
The ranks of darkness swell
The rings are there and they consume everything
They wait for the ones who cast themselves into shadow
They themselves stray from the light
For they know that with a light the human is invincible
There is a soul and it seeks truth
And for that we are doomed
There is no truth in the world
Only belief
Do not stray far from the light
One more light to be put out from the bonfire
They're waiting
Geoff Fitzpatrick, Grade 9
Leota Jr High School, WA

Writer's Block

My blank paper stares back up at me.
Students writing furiously, competing with the time.
A thin pencil wedged between my fingers.
The faint, rhythmic beat of the clock.
Subdued tapping pencils of hurried students echo through the room.
Squeaky, rubber erasers remove unwanted words with phenomenal speed.
I wonder if I too, will ever be able to start writing.
Katie Dashiell, Grade 9
Bellarmine Preparatory School, WA

Who Am I

Maybe I am not found
I am looking every day
Trying new things, making good and bad choices
I learn from the past and try to hold on
Sometimes I fall apart
But someone always seems to put me back together
Maybe it's me trying to help
Maybe I am two people
The girl inside of me, who doesn't want to grow up
Who lives in the moment, with friends, love and family
The other who is found, who hides in obvious places
But the girl tries not to find her
One who falls apart
She is not sure of herself
She is confused and sad
She has chances of becoming somebody
But always fails because of others
She has hope and hangs on
She never lets go of the things that could help her find her new and true self
Trisha Hostetler, Grade 9
North Marion High School, OR

Our Soldier

We hope the day will never come,
When our own soldier
Will leave home with his gun.

We try to be strong,
We hold back the tears,
But inside we tremble with fear.

We love to see his grinning face,
And know, no one will ever take his place.

Throughout this day forward,
I will never forget,
The fun and joy our family has spent.

He's an American soldier
He's America's pride,
But to me he's my loving cousin,
On my father's side.

At West Point is he,
With American flags flyin'.
I wish the best,
To my cousin Ryan.

Megan Skiles, Grade 9
Dufur School, OR

Racing

Feel the bike jerk forward as you take off.
See the dust soar up as you race up the straight stretch
Hear the loud annoying buzz of the 2-stroke engines.
Smell the fumes from all the different exhaust pipes.
Taste the dirt when you get roasted.

Tyler Crites, Grade 7
Ogden Middle School, OR

I Am a Slave in the Revolutionary War

I am a slave fighting for my freedom in the Revolutionary War.
I wonder if I will make it home alive.
I hear the sounds of battle all around me.
I see death and destruction everywhere I look.
I am a slave fighting for my freedom in the Revolutionary War.
I pretend I am fearless but inside I am terrified.
I feel tired and cold.
I touch my wound to see if it is healing.
I worry I will not see my wife and children ever again.
I cry when I'm alone at night.
I am a slave fighting for my freedom in the Revolutionary War.
I understand this is something I must do.
I say this will be over soon.
I dream of a country where we will be free.
I try to be positive.
I hope to be a free man some day.
I am a slave fighting for my freedom in the Revolutionary War.

Spencer Moody, Grade 7
River HomeLink Program, WA

My Love Song

When you walk into the room,
I regret every blink,
Because that means I miss a second beside you,
I love every little thing you do,
I could write pages and pages,
My feelings can't be summed up in quick phases,
I pray for you daily,
As well as perspective,
Dealing with pride and thoughts of being rejected,
When I'm next to you everything is fine,
When your eyes connect with mine,
I want to be your one and only,
Your smile fills my lungs and brightens my day,
You turn it from grey to blue,
I guess what I'm trying to say is:
I love you.

Jeremy Redkey, Grade 9
River HomeLink Program, WA

Untitled

At night I lay and think of you
Hoping my wishes and dreams come true;
Wondering what kind of guy
If you would ever give me a try.
I tell all my secrets to the skies
Just one look into those eyes;
Long and deep into the night
Way too far to stop my fright.
This thought of true love
I can never be rid of;
Inside I'm nothing but screams
I need to sew up the seams.
Your smile sends me to the heavens
On a scale of one to ten you're an eleven;
The way I feel isn't fair
All and all do you really care?
You could make me really shine
Someday I hope you could be mine;
Will you soon take my heart
Or will it simply be torn apart?

Hayley Kindell, Grade 8
Adna Middle-High School, WA

Boots

If you have ever seen a pair of boots,
Don't be too careful, they could be brutes,
You should ignore the fact that they are tall,
Search for a spot to hide near the wall,
They can be mean, dirty, or old,
But they won't harm you, they can't do it on their own,
So when you meet a pair of boots,
They could be mean, old brutes.

Michael Schmitz, Grade 7
Ogden Middle School, OR

Rhythmic Dreams

Flying, falling, rising up,
To a world of unending pleasure.
Grasp it and feel, take a hold,
Euphoria without measure.

See a picture in your mind,
A personal, genuine masterpiece,
Let it unravel onto the paper,
Your hand a graceful dancer.

The time is imminent,
You aspire for praiseful plaudits,
Success is gratifying,
But is it really vital?

My life is like a symphony,
Each note played an emotion.
Christian Ruske, Grade 8
South Jordan Middle School, UT

You Left Us

You left us with knots in our throat
You left us with tears in our eyes
You left us with broken hearts
You left us crying like little children
You left us with unforgettable memories
You left us praying for you
You left us without saying a word
You left without saying goodbye
I ask "Oh Lord why did she have to go?"
I ask God why you have to go
But that question is not to know.
Maria Landa, Grade 9
Mead High School, WA

Spring

Spring is in the air
Bears waking in their lair
Flowers are blooming
Birds are cooing
Spring is in the air
Mitchell Myrick, Grade 7
Sylvester Middle School, WA

Imagination

Blazing tons of thought
nothing that is not

A dream of fairy tales
things that never fail

Wild field of determination
nothing but imagination
Tori Diederich, Grade 9
Elk Ridge Middle School, UT

The 4th of July

The explosions of color, of light,
Of sound.
Old Glory flying, so high,
So Proud.
The soldiers who fought, and died,
For me,
Did not go in vain, our land
Is free.
To commemorate this US,
Custom,
We send up fire to celebrate,
Freedom.
Kalli Klein, Grade 8
Hilda Lahti Elementary School, OR

Professional Bull Riding

Hanging off your seat
Everyone is on their feet
He is a bull rider
Who is not an outsider
He jumps on a bull for some fun
Out in the hot beating sun
After the eight second buzzer rings
He gives his hat a fling
The next day he is off to Arizona
And his fans are left in Oklahoma
His ride goes smoothly along
As he hums his favorite song
He is my favorite
I can't hide it
He is so hot
all the others are not
He is definitely a desperado
Who's name is Adriano
Lindsay Meeks, Grade 8
Culver Middle School, OR

Blooming Daisy

In my front yard stood a bloomin' daisy,
When I saw her I
Knew spring was here.

Blooming daisy stand strong
All summer long,
She grows healthy and tall.

Everything else begins to wilt
Blooming daisy
Is dying, fall is arriving.

Winter comes and her
Hope is gone
Remember daisy, spring will come.
Sarah Moran, Grade 9
Mount Si High School, WA

Where Is the Sun

Cloud of grey,
With raindrops too
But where is the sun?
They say the sun comes up every day
Then where is it today?
Dark and dreary
With sad hearts and faces
Where is the sun?
No playing outside
Just have to stay inside
And wish for the sun.
Fog mixed with the clouds,
And rain drizzling down.
But where is the sun?
Puddles of mud
Made from the rain
No sun to dry it up
Just rain, fog, and clouds
Where is the sun?
Erin Blott, Grade 8
St Mary's Elementary School, AK

My Twin

My twin has the same eye color
the same hair color
and we look so much alike
that my friends get us confused

I have no twin I'm myself
today going into outer space
spinning until I'm split into two pieces
making us twins
but then I'm back like the speed of light

I'm myself again with my twin again
Nicol Dodd, Grade 7
Chehalis Middle School, WA

Can I Sit Here?

A shaky smile crosses her face
Unwelcome stares make her heart race
Her ragged nails dig into her palms
This is not where she belongs
Appraising eyes look over her clothes
Her shoulders slump like a wilted rose
Smirks and sly grins exchanged
The grin on her lips begins to fade
She's the new girl, that's for sure
It's the ailment that has no cure
The cafeteria is an endless maze
She takes a step back in a daze
This isn't chance; this must be fate
She's just made her first mistake.
Tian Kisch, Grade 7
Redmond Jr High School, WA

It's Just Me There

I walk up to the starting line
Stopwatch in my hand
The crowd is roaring now
As the starting gun goes up
And my foot goes to the line
Then everything goes silent
The gun goes off and there I go
Rounding the fourth lap on the last turn
I cross the finish line and realize
There's no one else there
The stands are empty and the stopwatch is still in my hand
It's just me there

Desiree Hepworth, Grade 9
Buhl High School, ID

Lost

Lost
Why do I feel so lost?
Is it because of what he did?
Or because of what he does?
Lost
He acts like nothing's different
He talks like he's still in love
This feeling, it's tingling and it's numb
Lost
Someone's here to take his place
In this long and painful race
Should I go back?
Back to where I began?
Or should I stay with the one who fills his space?
Lost
This is all one big question
Left unanswered
For this broken heart of mine
That is left so shattered

Emmy Yacapin, Grade 8
Gordon Russell Middle School, OR

A Color Filled Person

Part of me is light blue —
sleepy and worn
shy and drab
wishing I were home
in my snug bed
But deep inside there's another part
butter yellow, like a glass of lemonade
lively and wild
perky and energetic
wanting to just burst out
laughing at anything said opposite but possible
because that's what I am

McKenzie Yates, Grade 8
Wasatch Jr High School, UT

The Grave and the Wise of Fate

Two parents of a baby want knowledge,
In horror they tied their son up to die.
A kindly shepherd showed his loving care.
A child raised in today not aware what lie,
To leave better days of old upon range,
He sought to know the right while seeking truth,
Anger that is the driver to the rash,
An answer to a riddle takes a sleuth.
I say the grave and wise gave knowing tries.
To praise the good, withdrawing in the bad.
When finding greater knowledge can't be beat,
Discovery of a crime makes a town glad.
    The disciplined one though mighty and great,
    Lost his life trying to find out his fate.

Will Firch, Grade 9
Covenant High School, WA

Storm

Down the dry path I walk
As the tall trees talk,
The farther I walk the louder they howl
The rains start to get me wet, I need a towel.

The sun jumps behind a cloud, as if playing hide and seek
No matter what from behind the clouds it won't peek,
I look down; there is no more path under my feet
A violent ocean my eyes meet.

The waves run up the muddy sea shore
I cannot run away anymore,
The trees are stripped of their leaves
Wind blowing through my sleeves.

Rain turns to big hard falling chunks of hail
Under a tree I go, hoping my cover won't fail,
Back to the path I return
Trees laying down every way I turn,

I look up at a redwood tree
It lunges at me,
I can't move from the tree on which I lean
Now I'm back in my room, my bed, it was only a dream.

Ben Springli, Grade 8
Canfield Middle School, ID

Winter

Winter is a dreadful season
Liking it, I see no reason
It's cold, dark, damp, and wet
I don't like it, neither does my pet
The trees are bare, the ground is white
The rain keeps me awake all through the night
But the holidays are like God's greatest gift
I hope we're not snowed in by the drift

Kevin DeJong, Grade 7
Sunnyside Christian Elementary School, WA

What Anger Is to Me

Angry
School hating
Face breaking
Paper ripping
Clothes tearing
Door crushing
Locker slamming
Detention giving
Cell phone battering
Furious

Christian Jackson, Grade 8
Wasatch Jr High School, UT

Waiting

I'm waiting
watching the clock
watching the minutes go by
hours, days
will it be weeks, months, years
until you realize
I'm waiting
until you realize
what I'm waiting for
is you

Jennifer Irene Clarke, Grade 9
Mount Si High School, WA

A Yellow Flower

in a meadow so cold
all covered in snow
a yellow flower
peeps through the snow
saying, spring is here

Christine Poulsen, Grade 8
American Leadership Academy, UT

The Putt

Hands were shaking,
Heart pounding with rate rising.
Breeze blowing,
Ball rolling.
Putter dropped with a thud.
I'm standing there as if in mud.
Ping!
Eagle!
A sigh of relief.
Victory was finally mine.

Ryan Alba, Grade 8
Wasatch Jr High School, UT

Peace

Cold, winter, morning
Silent, solitude, alone
Mind, body, and soul

Ian Anderson, Grade 8
Wasatch Jr High School, UT

Utah

Utah is a wondrous place
where magic is everywhere.
Plants are blooming, animals frolicking,
and we grow and learn new things.

If you say you hate this place,
that you'd rather be in California or New York;
Take the time to look around,
I promise you'll find something good.

Our beautiful snow-covered mountains,
that protect us from storms and destruction.
The Great Salt Lake, a water feature few others have.
Our gorgeous valleys and all the foliage and animals that inhabit them.

The thing that makes Utah the greatest of all is the people:
Caring, loving, cheerful, and someone always has your back.
Neighbors that truly care, and are there to listen.

How can you hate Utah,
when there is so much more to love?

Kellie Clawson, Grade 8
Central Davis Jr High School, UT

Me

The sweet smell of flowers in the country air brushes past me.
It fills my lungs with the sweet mood of Great Russia.
Then I breathe out.
Next, I smell the cold hard breath of the green forest I see.

My mind fills over with thoughts of turning back.
I choose to stay.
The dozen candles I was once so happy to see now overwhelm me.

The sun that shines on me makes me want to scream!
I dislike the burning rays, yet I love the rain.

The long braids I once used to wear are now gone.
I start over like a bud that's about to open.
My eyes are sparks of fire.
My hair glistens like the burning wood.

The mood is set.
I am here now.
Once I wake up from this dream, nothing will change.

The world will still be shooting cannons.
I wish I could change the rhythm of life.
Why is it too late?

Lena Palladina, Grade 7
Arbor Elementary School, WA

Math

Numbers, symbols, a quiet, peaceful time,
Where you can think hard,
Or just let ideas flow through your mind.
Writing down numbers, then adding them up,
Trying not to forget steps,
But, even then, sometimes getting stuck.

Math, math I love math,
A mixture of tools, yet a very clear path,
Not like grammar where things don't add up,
Where rules change and you can't just say, "Wuzz up."

You can sit there and listen to the pens clicking,
The pencils scratching,
And the teacher sitting there thinking to herself.
Problem after problem you work on through,
You're almost done,
But tomorrow you will start anew.

Math, math I love math,
A mixture of tools, yet a very clear path,
Not like grammar where things don't add up,
Where rules change and you can't just say, "Wuzz up."

September O'Crowley, Grade 8
Diamond Elementary School, OR

You

You are the one I have loved long ago
In this time I still love you so
You have hurt me long before
That it almost made me open that door
That which would set me free
Free from the point of view you could not see
I love you now and as forever
I will live like this 'till you break that lever
Then you will come and fulfill my heart
Then I will promise that we'll never depart
Because you are the only one I have ever loved

Tong Cha, Grade 9
Shorecrest High School, WA

Hard Life

Everyone knows that life is hard
And sometimes our life is barely barred
We just need to learn to get over it
We just need to progress bit by bit
I know it's something we all can do
It is something that you always knew
Just search real deep and see what you find
Some things you see will just blow your mind
If you don't think that you can make it through
Just remember that life is like a mad zoo
And if you look at life in the long run
You'll actually see that life can be fun

Kody Lundell, Grade 9
Elk Ridge Middle School, UT

Black Water

Black water,
water during the night so black,
during the day so light,
from the water of the night,
the water so black,
black night.

Ty Shepherd, Grade 8
Onalaska Elementary/Middle School, WA

Read a Book

To float away
across the world
to seize the day
with banner unfurled
to journey onward with some friends
to make a feast fit for a king
to fight with a sword that has no bends
to fly with giant wings
to invent amazing, huge machines
to meet creatures none have known
to play a part in a fantastic scheme
to show more courage than ever shown
to wear clothes with bright colors
to experience the miracle of spring
to live in a house with eight brothers
to dry your own clothes with a brisk wring
to hide away in a nook
to play a tune with a fife
to read a wonderful book
that is what's great about life!

Maya Riser-Kositsky, Grade 8
Lake Washington Girls Middle School, WA

Everyone's Different

Everyone's different, no one's the same
There's the strong and the weak, there's the whole and the lame

My grandpa was strong, he'd always take a stand
He loved and cared always, taking all by the hand

The day of his funeral, there was such a sight
Of people who knew him, whose hands he'd held tight

There were hundreds of people, that sad autumn morn
And though they were different, their hearts had all torn

For the man who had helped them, who had taken a stand
Who loved and cared always, taking all by the hand

Goodbye my dear grandpa, thanks for taking a stand
Thanks for loving and caring, thanks for taking my hand

Austianna Quick, Grade 8
Oroville High School, WA

Moving On

It's hard to swallow, it's hard to breathe, I'm gasping for air, I need to leave.
My heart is breaking with the words I'm saying.
You shouldn't have left the world you were too special to die, I'm shaking and I'm going to cry!
I love you with all my heart…please tell me that this is a dream, inside I feel like I'm about to scream.
The next day I awake, I go to see you, I start to quake.
I was so happy but then…I remember, all last night when I cried myself to sleep…
I dreamt of you so soft and sound, I felt like I was in the water about to drown.
The days go by, I'm moving on…I miss you and I'm so sad, if I had another moment with you I would be glad!
I'm thinking of the memories that we used to share, this is the hardest thing I have to bare.
I miss you…

Brandy Day, Grade 7
Thomas Jefferson Jr High School, UT

Why?

Through a dark night when everyone sleeps,
The mind begins to dream, some are nice, some are scary,
But mine are more different than they seem,
As I lie down on a warm bed, my mind begins to wonder,
About strange majestic beasts of the air,
I find myself flying with others of my kind and my whole body is scaly
I find my friends in a small group, as we fly, I ask them for clues,
Why must we fly from the humans we love?
Why must we hide in suits of flesh?
Why must we fight each other for our lives?
Why can't we live in peace and be ourselves?
The others answer with solemn voices,
As long as people lie and cheat, as long as people kill and hate, we dragons are never safe.
I realize what they say is true but still I wish I could walk as myself.
Why did knights attack us? What did they have to prove?
We didn't attack first and why fight when we all know that the great Creator made us both?
As I wonder these great things, we see the sun begin to rise.
Sighing, the flight lands on the ground and looking back at the stars
We begin to slip back into the physical world.
Once again we wonder…
Why?

Richard Scott, Grade 9
Idaho Arts Charter School, ID

Knights of the Round Table

We are knights of the round table, sitting in a circle dressed in armor.
"We shall be in love forever!" Rosemarry yelled out.
"No, no you must be more clever.
Oh don't you see unless we find true love we shall never be!" exclaimed Fairamay from far away.
"Oh but Fairamay can you really believe?
I mean one day you're in love, and the next it just up and leaves." Chimala replied thinking of the thieves.
"Why of course you must believe! It's the way the world must be!
Making you, me, and all of us happy. Oh can't you see?" Brenneka said in agree.
"Of course Chimala's right there is not one for true love in sight!" Charicah said not so bright.
"Now who are we to just give up so easily? Aren't we the knights of the round table?
Giving up on nothing, even true love that we so really want to seek!
So come let us speak!" Rosemarry exclaimed not so weak.
So we raised our glasses and made big passes because we are the great and famous knights of the round table.
We are no fable!

Kya Brown, Grade 9
Centennial High School, NV

Ode to the Sea

Rollicking waves pulsing onto the shore
Gazing at waters too hard to ignore
Losing myself in the steady uproar
Seemingly stretching into ever more.

Setting sun reflects off the sea
Bringing out the wonder in me
Playful movement shows immense glee
Watching alone can set the soul free.

Air smells of salt, fresh and pure
For the sick at heart, here is the cure
To those ever-wandering, the sea is the lure
Shimmering, sparkling, endless azure.

How its soft voice whispers and flows
Accompanied when the gentle wind blows
No telling where it is destined to go
Forever in my memory's glow.

The sea is my haven, my only place
Where the sun shines its glorious rays
And the stars will never stop to blaze
Here, I shall spend the rest of my days.

Sabrina Pol, Grade 9
South Medford High School, OR

Life

What is life?
Life is a flower smell it
Life is like a song so sing it
Life is like a bird so fly
Life is being brave
Life is peace spread it
Life is what you believe is right

What do you think life is?
I think that life is love to share with others
I think life is a challenge that we have to pursue
I think life is personality for us to show and share with others
I think life is a risk so take it
I think life is being yourself
I think life is having dreams so dream forever
I think life is like speaking your opinions so speak up

What is life?
Life is caring for other people
Life is a sacrifice offer it
Life is short spend your time well
Life is what you want it to be
It's your choice

Baylee Butzer, Grade 7
St Cecilia School, OR

The Pause Before the Battle

The men go marching forward
Towards a certain death
Peering through the eerie fog
Silently holding their breath
Prayers are said to God
Pleas for safe deliverance
Continuing to trod
Into fog that's ever so dense
The drum and fife are heard
"Company halt!" they say
"The enemy is coming 'round, so pass along the word"
The column stops, the guns are drawn
And fear pollutes the air
The shots ring out, the blood is spilt
Brave souls forevermore.

Josh Pierson, Grade 9
W F West High School, WA

Beauty of a Woman

The beauty of a woman is not the clothes she wears,
The figure she carries, or the way she combs her hair.
The beauty of a woman must be seen from her eyes,
Because that is the doorway to her heart,
The place where love resides.
The beauty of a woman is not in a facial mole,
But true beauty in a woman is reflected in her soul.
It is the caring that she lovingly gives,
The passion that she shows.
The beauty of a woman
With time, only grows…

Beth Graham, Grade 7
Ogden Middle School, OR

Molly Pitcher

Molly Pitcher was quite a gal,
She helped the soldiers and their morale.

Carried water here and there,
For the soldiers — she did care.

Molly Pitcher stood by her man until the very end,
And for her country, she did defend.

When her husband started to die,
She did not stop and start to cry.

She took his spot
And bravely fought.

For her country she did fight
And her enemies she did spite.

A heroine she was later named,
And through her actions, did gain fame.

Jaime Fowler, Grade 7
River HomeLink Program, WA

Slipped Away

As I sit by the Oak tree
I can't help but think of you.
How you made me feel so lively
but you slipped away,
slipped through my fingers.
Now I'm looking at the
plaster on these walls,
the walls so empty,
like how I feel now,
empty.
I want to burn these walls
because they remind me of you.

Christina Renninger, Grade 8
Eagle Point Middle School, OR

Strawberry Moon

Strawberry moon
Red in the center
Glistening, glowing
As big as the world
Luscious

Raman Veerappan, Grade 7
Rogich Middle School, NV

When I'm by Myself

When I'm by myself
And I close my eyes
I'm an unbeatable gamer
I'm a lion tamer
I'm a world leader
I'm a college level reader
I'm a military strategist
I'm a peace making pacifist
I'm a sizzling pie
I'm a drop of blue dye
I'm a flower that's about to bloom
I'm a bomb that's about to go boom
When I close my eyes
I'm anything I want to be
I'm anything I can be
I'm anything I could be

Lloyd Major, Grade 9
Puget Sound Adventist Academy, WA

On the Field

It starts off dribble, dribble
Back and forth from one foot to another
Dodge the girls as they run towards you
Pass it and run to get open
The ball comes back to you
You are wide open
You heart's racing
The second of truth
And there's the goal

Autumn Yturbe, Grade 9
Buhl High School, ID

Baseball

America's pastime
Some of the greatest athletes
All brought together
It's a sport of strength, power, coordination and skill
When I'm up to bat
I feel my heart thump, thump, thumping
I step in the box
The pitcher winds up and pitches the roaring red laced ball
Runs right past me into the catcher's glove
Stteeerrriiikkkee oonnneee the umpire unmistakably utters
I step out of the box and get the signs as clear as mud
I step back in the box and the ball whizzes by with dizzying speed
Stteeerrriiikkkee ttwwoo
Two strikes my heart skips a beat thump, thump, thumping
I step out of the box
The signs about as clear as a crow flying in a pitch black night
I step back in the box, the windup and the pitch, it's a fast ball
I swing and boom the ball soars off the bat like an eagle soaring in the sky
It keeps going and going like the Energizer bunny
It's a home run, I run around the bases astounded at my might
Then everything gets blurry and I wake up

Devon Swofford, Grade 8
Sunnyside Christian Elementary School, WA

Sorry

Not always thinking of what I say or do.
Feelings getting hurt.
Not meaning to talk behind your back.
Making you look bad and sad wasn't what I was going for.
But when you did it to me first, all my feelings got to me.
I was sad and mad, too.
But doing the same thing to you as you did to me made me feel guilty and even worse.
So here I am today standing right before you to say, I'm sorry.

Lexi Kontgis, Grade 8
Wasatch Jr High School, UT

Why?

Why go to war when you could have peace?
Why shoot another person with a family when you could make friends?
Why plant a car bomb when you could give a hug?
Why be scared of another person
When they are just as scared as you are?
Why try to hurt or be hurt?
Why go spend your time off fighting in another country
When you really want to be safe at home with your friends and family?
Why fight another person when you both would
Rather not fight at all?
Why join the army when you could join the Peace Corps?
Why join the navy when you could help you the homeless?
Why join the marines when you could feed
A starving child for a month with $30?
Why join the military at all when it doesn't take
Much to help out?
Why go to war when you could have peace?

Patrick Ufkes, Grade 7
Sylvester Middle School, WA

Sisters

I am lucky I have three,
I am even luckier because they all love me.
Sometimes they make me really mad,
But because of them I am truly glad.
I get all of their old clothes,
What they've been through truly shows.
Sometimes we stay up really late,
And in the morning we are in an awful state.
Sometimes we are really crazy,
But most of the time we are just lazy.
Over Christmas we had lots of fun,
So that made the good bye weigh a ton.
We are all different but mostly the same,
But the brains we all try to claim.
All three are trying to get a mister,
But I don't think I can let go of even one sister.
Two of them are gone to get a better education,
And now I really can't wait until summer vacation.

Hillary Loveless, Grade 7
Kearns Jr High School, UT

Vertigo

My thoughts,
at ease.
The space around me disagrees.
Falling down, upon my knees,
I sense the sickness
coming over me.

Vertigo,
I lack the ability to pay my respects,
pay then as a whole; final.
I bend my perception
of this harsh reality.
I make it spin
to no longer be aware of the empty air around me.

Adam Coday, Grade 9
Decatur High School, WA

Never Gone

Stains and marks may go away,
Pictures might grow old,
Hist'ry lost or times forgotten,
Stories are left untold.

Ones who died for ones once loved
May fade right out of lore,
When ones once loved join ones who died
In death fore'er more.

But things forgotten are not lost,
Their presence lingers on,
In life we breathe, but in death we see
That things are never gone.

Justin McGee, Grade 8
Leota Jr High School, WA

Book

Read a book then fall and plunder,
Down into a world of wonder.

Like *Robin Hood* and Dr. Seuss,
Read rhymes and tales like *Mother Goose*.

Do wondrous jobs and crazy things,
Catch a blue animal with wings.

Fly way up in a big balloon,
Way up past the big sun and moon.

Fly past comets and through the stars,
See Pluto, Jupiter, and Mars.

Join detectives see what they'll do,
Then you'll go solve a crime or two.

See fairies, ogres, and big trolls,
Climb up mountains, ladders, and poles.

When the story comes to an end,
Go and get a brand new best friend.

Margo Crane, Grade 7
St Mary's Elementary School, AK

Whole

One day I turned on the TV,
And turned to my favorite show.
Then they got around to trash talking,
And into the room refuse did flow.

I ran to the doorway, but it was now jammed!
All sticky and stuck up it was
I couldn't pull it down from the ceiling,
Because of the peach peelings fuzz!

The garbage began to threaten,
The remotes were running low
I tried but I couldn't catch 'em,
As over the trash they did go.

Finally I found what I needed
(inside an old sock)
The answer to all of wishes,
A broken bit of old chalk.

I broke it in half very quickly,
Making two halves, you know.
I then stuck both ends together,
And quickly escaped through the whole.

Christopher Giles, Grade 8
South Jordan Middle School, UT

The Rockslide

Everything's quiet, not a sound.
It takes just a shake, a rumble, a pound.

It starts a slide, a fall.
They all look and bounce like a ball.

Then away all the sound locks.
As I look up at the new pile of rocks.
                Jordan Jepperson, Grade 9
                Elk Ridge Middle School, UT

The Day Everything Changed

The day everything changed
Was the day my dad left
The day everything changed
Was the day we lost our house
The day everything changed
Was the day my parents got divorced
The day everything changed
Was the day my dad got remarried
The day everything changed
Was the day we moved into a new house
The day everything changed
Was the day my sister moved home
The day everything changed
Was the day my dad left
                Ally Brudevold, Grade 9
                Union High School, OR

Waste It

I wasted my breath for
Inebriated memories,
And shattered words,
Tearing at my ears,
I wasted my breath for
Horrified sorrow
And deadbeat no shows,
Laughing at my pain

I wasted my breath for
My mother's love,
And times we shared,
Subtle memories passed,
I wasted my breath for
The dead man whispering,
From insanity's brink,
The apple falling so far from the tree,

I wasted my breath for
My family, hope and ones who died,
The wolf's cry to the moon,
And I wasted my breath
Because I spoke my mind way too soon
                Alyx DeLaCruz, Grade 7
                Komachin Middle School, WA

Faith

Do you have faith?
Close your eyes.
Hold your breath.
The consequences you'll not regret.
Keeping time.
Saving grace.
Hold my hand.
We'll take our place.
Follow me,
Don't fall behind.
Just keep the faith.
And our love will shine.
Stay with me,
And never go.
Our love will blossom.
And our faith will grow!
                Richael Paxson, Grade 8
                Canfield Middle School, ID

Sweet Confessions

I do apologize
I've gone and snatched
the only remaining sweets.
The pastry went nicely,
the light spongy culinary art
tickled my pallet
with intricate tastes of berry,
sweet frosting, and cake.
Sorry, it was a culinary experience,
painless and sweet.
                Drew Abby, Grade 8
                Wasatch Jr High School, UT

Try

Try to love somebody
when you love somebody else.
Try to care about someone
when you care about someone else.
It's hard to visualize someone
when there's someone else standing
in front of you.
It's hard to think about
the person you love
when the person you like
is talking to you!
                Amanda Smith, Grade 8
                Beatty Elementary School, NV

The Fish

The fish swam as fast as a torpedo.
Zipping through the colorful reef.
Across the sand and pokey-edged coral.
Into the darkness of the ice cold sea.
                Alex Peckham, Grade 9
                Buhl High School, ID

Air Raid

Pitch black smoke fills the air,
The air raid siren starts to blare.
People running here and there,
Running for their shelters.

Someone yells, pointing to the sky,
Crying, "I'm going to die!"
Even though we all have to go,
Most would rather save it for later.

Deep in the ground,
With no light around,
I silently start to pray,
Keep the bombs away!
                Luke Koester, Grade 8
                Eugene Christian School, OR

Hurt

I can feel my heart break
I can feel it tear
I can feel it bleed
Runnin' down everywhere
I feel so empty
I feel hurt
By all the lies you told me
It's like I was nothing but dirt
Thanks for your "kindness"
Thanks for your "care"
You thought it would be painless
All of a sudden they all stare
Now you're my enemy
Now you don't care
It hurts deep down inside of me
As if nothing was really there
                Ashley Brevak, Grade 9
                Nome Beltz Jr/Sr High School, AK

The Brook

A brook is like a poet
both going endlessly on,
both meeting obstacles along the way,
both being slowed down,
but always working,
striving.
Then hurry,
rushing only to be quieted at a bend.
Both continuing,
despite everything
only to end in the same way.
Yes a brook is like a poet
constantly changing direction
both have different thoughts
both ending as if they never started.
                Cristian Robert, Grade 9
                West Valley Jr High School, WA

I Am From

I am from a big family
Eleven on my mom's side
Nine on my dad's side
Aunts and uncles
Cousins and grandparents
Great big families, great big memories
I am from family cookouts
From all the parks and yards
All those roomy houses
To all those not so roomy houses

I am from understanding why you're not the center of attention
And what is going on around me
From opening up to everyone then hiding from it all
I am from all the goody two shoes
To all the bums
From hating it all
To not thinking there's anyone that has it better than me

I am from being scared
To feeling like nothing can hurt me
From everyone that loves me
I am from all of these things
Trisha Frazier, Grade 7
Komachin Middle School, WA

Rain

Rain comes in drops and lands in great plops.
Some rain is dreadfully cold.
It comes in many sizes,
and the floodwater rises when rain takes its toll.
Some rain is a threat when you're caught in its net.
And it just won't let you go.
You can run and hide,
And go inside, but the rain will not slow…
The rain will take its toll.

James McMonagle, Grade 7
Ogden Middle School, OR

Holding Hands

Love had made us together,
But it has also taken it away.
I thought that love was here to stay,
But it just brushed away.
As the color of the leaves fades,
As I watch you walk away.
Remember when we were holding hands,
Doing everything.
Love might bring us back together,
But my only memory is us,
Holding Hands.
Sherry Zhang, Grade 7
Lake Oswego Jr High School, OR

Spring from the Four Seasons

The wind is like a fairy dancing everywhere
Nature is swaying and gliding here and there
The fairies are more playful in the spring
Because they're faster with a glistening wing

Laughing and giggling
Having so much fun wiggling
Gazing and resting up in a tree
Browsing at their Spring land fantasy.

Looking over the hills and far away
Nothing seemed to go astray
Everything was the way they wanted
Not a single thing was haunted

Knowing that this was soon going
They wanted this to keep on growing
Since everything was how it seemed
They soon drifted into a fantasy soon to be dreamed.
Geoclyn Aquino, Grade 7
St Mary's Elementary School, AK

Two Paths

As the future flashes in front of me,
Two paths to choose from.
One that I long for, one that is frightening with excitement.
I know everyone. I don't know anyone.

As the future flashes in front of me
I know which one to choose.
I'll be scared, feeling like a bug in an empty jar,
Leaving my best friends,
But I know in my heart, I'll be best here.
Sasha Gorecki, Grade 8
St Anne School, WA

Tower of Reason

High on the hill impaling the clouds
Looms the Tower of Reason never wavering, always still

On you run through bush and crag
Where only hate greets you until your journey is done

Jamming your fingers between the abscesses
You desperately climb desperately now, but only hate lingers

You hang aloft nearing the end
When hate finds you and throws you off

You fall and fall passing stones you've seen
Suddenly realizing why the tower is tall

As you fall and fall like slow death, it seems
Your turmoil and pain was for nothing at all
Kolten Anderson, Grade 9
Rainier High School, WA

In My Life

Every day, I wake up,
I look for a sign to get going.
Maybe today will be the day,
When everyone will enjoy my life.
Always laughing, always working,
Keeping ahead, dropping behind.
Just trying to balance all the things,
Just trying to balance my life.
Looking for hope, looking for joy,
Hoping for ease, laugh with me,
Having fun, but doing work,
Hoping for joy in my life.
Running away, saving the day,
Everything will be okay.
Coming home at night, thinking all right,
Seeing a light in my life.
Seeing the sun, loving someone,
Keeping the joy alive.
Seeing the years, no shallow tears,
Everything's good in my life.

Patrick Meyer, Grade 8
St Michael School, WA

Fall

Fall is wonderful
Leaves are falling everywhere
It all brings great fun

Fall is exquisite
A warm feeling inside me
It's hot cocoa time

Nadya Scott, Grade 8
Olympic Range Carden Academy, WA

Please Listen to Me

Please listen to me,
I've got something to tell you.
It's very important.
Just be quiet,
And don't interrupt me.
Be patient with me,
I'm not done yet.
Don't roll your eyes,
Don't be rude, crude, or curt.
Let me finish this sentence.
Let me finish my story.
Don't make dumb comments,
Just hear me out.
It's my story, not yours.
Don't walk away,
Just sit here and listen.
I've got something to tell you.
It's very important,
Please listen to me.

Roslyn Erlewine, Grade 7
West Valley Middle School, WA

I Am…

I am a wolf with glowing eyes watching over the world in the dark, starry night.
I am the bear atop the mountain roaring, shattering the silence of the land.
I am the brittle old oak tree, standing tall and proud of its roots.
I am the moon in the dark sky, reflecting light on the shadows of my land.
I am the dirt and soil, my ancestor's footsteps having made their mark.
I am the rain's pitter pattering sounds, like the beating drums of my people.
I am the cry of a deer shot in the woods; mourning for the loss of my kind.
I am the wild horse running free, with only the sound of the wind beside me.
I am the deep canyon eroding slowly; sifting away with time as the inhabitants.
I am a star in the clear winter sky; becoming more wise as I grow older.
I am a sunset fading into the sky, the colors of my tribe blend together as one.
I am a fierce howling wind, a force from our ancestors surrounding my people.
I am the white man's rifle killing my people; I know I have let down my tribe.
But I am the hopes and dreams of my people; faith still exists in our hearts.
I am a mountain standing still, for my people will not move from their land.
I am the call of the night owl, inspecting the land upon which my people roam.
I am a warrior ready to fight for the land which is rightfully ours.
I am only just an Indian, watching over my tribe.
But I am the air, a traveling wind, always to linger on our sacred terrain.
I am a spirit forever to dwell within my tribe and to always remain
Across our sacred, desert plains.

Channing Jones, Grade 8
North Jr High School, ID

The War on Junk Food

Food is but a simple necessity of life.
Without it, we would cease to exist.
Then why is our diet a continuous strife?
Healthy food? Oh, why do parents persist?

This is a war where they cannot prevail.
They are fighting in a land where
Burger King reigns supreme, where a child would sell
His soul for a solitary morsel of sugar at the county fair.

In a land where Pizza Hut will deliver.
Where children cram down the creamy Crisco.
As their parents stare in disgusted splendor,
As if being shipped to Alcatraz in San Francisco.

Yet still, in vain, they fight
Against the Twinkies and the s'more.
Even with their artery clogging goodness, they fight,
Against the preservatives galore.

When will the parents give up this battle?
The vegetables their children "accidentally" misplace
Are lacking the desired effect, just like a broken paddle.
They can't win, for junk food has truly made the world a better place.

Ryan Hemsley, Grade 9
Bonneville High School, ID

Nature

Big things are beautiful —
the mighty mountains, regal and commanding,
intimidating, but full of color.
The sky, with all it's grandeur and mystery;
endless with its mind-blowing logic.
The ocean, stretching from shore to shore,
filled with all sorts of life, yet the life is masked
beneath the shimmering waters.

Small things are beautiful —
the single blade of grass pointing upward,
straight and tall and emerald green.
A pebble, sitting at the bottom of a pond,
being eroded into a perfect oval.
And the tiny dew drop, the pearls of nature,
reflecting everything it sees,
sliding down to soak softly into the ground.

Catherine Felt, Grade 8
Wasatch Jr High School, UT

Grief

It clinches you like a writer's hand to a pen,
So dark, like the coat of a black cat,
So motionless, like time itself has stopped,
It pulls the tears out of your eyes
And squeezes the screams out of your lungs,
It will pick you up and drop you in a pit of sorrow
So unbearable you want death to take you and pull you in,
And it will never stop.

Evan Diskin, Grade 8
St Anne School, WA

Lost in the Woods

Lost in the woods on a snowy day,
Don't know if I will ever find my way.
I look all around at the snowcapped trees,
And realize my toes are starting to freeze.
It's starting to get dark out,
And then I start to pray.
I ask the Lord Jesus if He will help me find my way.
It's getting even colder now, and my hands start to shiver,
Hey look! That's where I crossed that frozen river!
I make a mad dash for it, like a frantic little bunny,
But then I remember I've forgotten my route.
This is the river but this isn't where I crossed!
And once again I realized, that I really am lost!
Just then out of nowhere, comes my dad's white Jeep;
Like a monstrous polar bear, grunting beep, beep, beep.
My dad sees me, and starts to wave,
And I think to myself, "Oh goodie, I'm saved!"
As we drive home tonight,
I am filled with delight,
Because when God heard me pray,
He answered without delay.

Cody Jordan, Grade 8
Eugene Christian School, OR

It's Our Choice

The beloved rule of our people is at its end.
The rise of a tyrant is beginning.
To the gallows he would send,
any man he deems unworthy of living.
The world around lived about.
A society in oblivion.
No man would stand to say
to the tyrant, "To the devil with him."

Fear strikes in every heart,
yet all who lived, lived in the shadows.
One by one they slowly part.
No voices sound at the gallows.
The town diminished to nothing but ruin.
Only the life of one man remains.
"To the gallows" declared the tyrant,
"for you are the one to blame."

"Whatever crimes did I commit?"
"Whatever did I do?"
The tyrant spoke, "you've done nothing
so you've murdered, my friend.
You let each fall to their end."

Jeffrey Ha, Grade 8
Lewis and Clark Middle School, ID

Heaven

A blinding light and all my dreams unfold.
The sound of shattered soul and breaking bone.
Away into the light I go as told.

Never had there been a time I was bold,
And never have I tried to set the tone.
A blinding light and all my dreams unfold.

Forever I want my life to hold.
Fear to go, for I fear to be alone.
Away into the light I go as told.

Today I go from the causes of old.
Stopped on the stairways to weep and moan.
A blinding light and all my dreams unfold.

Now my body is just useless and cold.
The truth has come to me and now I know.
Away into the light I go as told.

That's it my life is gone, my soul is sold.
I leave and travel into the unknown.
A blinding light and all my dreams unfold.
Away into the light I went as told.

Elizabeth Pickens, Grade 8
Arts & Communication Middle School, OR

Earth Spirals

Pages of our life turn fast each day seeming shorter and shorter,
until hitting that day of most darkness.
But slowly, Earth continues to shift.
Frost begins to fade and green grass is revealed,
wind turns soft and flowers begin to bloom.
Cherry trees begin their harvest, growing white flowers,
turning my street into a white wonderland.
Clouds fade, becoming more transparent until they become invisible.
Sun becomes more radiant and burns even brighter.
Earth begins to ripple, showing off sun's heat waves,
you wishing they were water ones.
Pages of our life moving forward, get longer and longer until touching peek of daylight.
But slowly, Earth continues to shift.
Frost blankets return, dulling vivid green grass,
light calming breezes turn into strong gusts of wind,
and leaves fall from trees, showing thick brown branches.
Sun fades with each day until there is only an occasional break between clouds.
Air turns so crisp that you could slice through it.
Fog becomes routine until we hit that day of most darkness, and then,
Earth continues to shift.

Lena Cardoso, Grade 8
Lake Washington Girls Middle School, WA

Without a Sound

Is love really what it is said to be, I wonder and ponder this openly. As the day ticks by my heart grows heavy. My heart breaks as I look upon her. I do not care as long as she's happy. It may kill my spirit but I'll stand in the background. Every day I wake up and wonder how will I make through the day's sorrow. Then I see her and my heart fills with joy if only for a second. The pain that comes next is enough to make me cry in despair as I realize I can never have her. This is what it is like on one day being in love with someone you can never have. Even as the pain cripples me I will stand in the background without a sound.

Grant McMurray, Grade 8
Helix Middle School, OR

Blue-Lined Paper

Sitting here; like an object and not a person.
In my desk; with a seat, hard beyond compare, staring at this blank page of blue-lined paper.
I think and think but the words won't come,
The sitting and the thinking and the staring so familiar: have I been here before?
With my pen in hand, poised over the blue-lined paper, thinking, trying to focus my thoughts
Is there any way that I can form the fleeting thoughts across my mind into actual ideas and thoughts;
Trying to create a story, a poem, a play, a something.
Vague images are coming back to me now,
Images of blue-lined paper, my pen in hand poised above; the desk of hardness…but now with compare.
In my mind's eye I see this.
The scenery of the classroom around me changes in my peripheral vision.
The English class from ninth grade…then eighth…then seventh…then sixth…
All with images of the blue-lined paper, my pen in hand poised above; the desk of hardness,
And the fleeting, random, messy thoughts across my mind.
The feeling of drowning in the thoughts that make no sense.
How am I ever to finish the assignment?
Suddenly there's one thought that makes sense, it sparks an idea, and creates an avalanche.
I'm no longer just sitting there, staring.
The desk is no longer hard, in fact, I hardly feel it.
My pen in hand, no longer poised over the blue-lined paper,
It is now writing away, inking up the blue-lined paper.

Deanna Demitropoulos, Grade 9
Bonneville High School, ID

Exercise Can Bring Demise
I love to hike
And I love to bike.
Hiking is fun
You can camp under the sun
But for the more fast-paced
Maybe a bicycle race.
The last time I rode my bike I got into a bit of trouble.
I went over a bridge and all of a sudden
Like little needles piercing my skin
I was being attacked by foreign kin.
These little bees
Came from under the trees,
I ran from them,
Hopefully never to see them again.
Over a hundred yards more
Making me sore.
So if you're up for exercise
You might just meet your demise.
If you disrupt these little yellow bullets,
It will ruin your day.
And so I say stay away.
Alex Pendell, Grade 8
Eugene Christian School, OR

Man's Dying Dream
To be more than man, has been mankind's dream,
To rule high above every earthly thing.
Man strives to rule the cosmos for himself,
But only winds up troubling oneself.
With the lack of gravitas in our world,
The thought of right and wrong has been twirled.
With lack of guidance we lose our morals,
That leads to further death and funerals.
To guidance is where we need to be led
Along to someone from whom we have read.
In what can we trust that He will provide?
The book of answers, it will be our guide.
Belief in someone that loves us deeply,
Is where I will put my trust completely.
Abel Jackson, Grade 9
Covenant High School, WA

Hilltop Memories
I remember that lovely day,
When we went into the hills to play.
The sky was so bright and blue,
I hope you remember it too.
As we watched the clouds go by,
I saw that old eagle fly.
He stood on the hill looking at me,
Telling me how wonderful it is to be free.
Joseph Richardson, Grade 8
Snowcrest Jr High School, UT

I Am
I am not a cloud in the day,
I am a shooting star in the night sky.
I am not a bitter banana,
I am a zingy pineapple.
I am not a daisy on a hill,
I am a red rose on top of a mountain.
I am not a deer that scampers from everything,
I am a cheetah that runs after what I want.
Megan Woolsey, Grade 9
Elk Ridge Middle School, UT

My Imagination Is Free
My special place is inside of me,
But I wish it was free, you see
I want my imagination to be free,
So my special home can truly be.

It's a small one story home,
That is around a watery ground,
Where my dog and I can roam,
And the beach will be in front of my home and all around.

The woods will be around as well,
And so will the stars at night,
Everything will be real swell,
And if anyone tries to buy it from me I will put up a good fight.

I don't know where I'll find this place,
But I will find it, yes I will,
I'll find the place and decorate it with lace,
No matter what the bill!
Kalsin Clark, Grade 7
St Mary's Elementary School, AK

Storytellers
Snatching his notebook, a man left the room,
to his brother who soon did the same.
Splitting their paths, the first heard a loud "Boom!"
Turning 'round he saw who was to blame.

"Quiet!" they hissed when he questioned the crowd,
so he quickly sat down for to hear.
Up in the air hung suspense like a cloud,
though the story's end wasn't yet near.

Listening closely he wrote all he heard,
"To be published quite soon" stated he.
Painting bright pictures with every last word,
You could see the green leaves on his tree.

Dancing and flashing his pen wrote the lines,
whilst the old man kept spinning his tale.
Jakob Grimm's talent in books clearly shines,
While his works help more people prevail.
Jannalee Rosner, Grade 8
South Jordan Middle School, UT

Nobody

As if I'm not there,
As if you don't see,
The person down here,
That is actually me.

Like I wasn't talking,
Or I didn't speak,
Keeping to myself,
Not saying a peep.

Like I am nobody,
Or invisible,
Like the air in the sky,
I am nobody that is why.

But I can reach out,
I can love I can cry,
I can get hurt,
I can even die.

Do remember,
My final words,
To those who have
Hearts of gold…

I am somebody.
Alicia Chase, Grade 8
Estacada Jr High School, OR

A Gentle Breeze

A gentle breeze flows through the air
Seeming to be going nowhere
Not knowing how to behave
Mimicking the movement of a wave

It slows, and gusts
As it blows the dust
Such a peaceful breeze
Flows through the trees.
Kory Pimper, Grade 9
Elk Ridge Middle School, UT

Seven Patty Burger

I have a dream,
To eat a burger with seven patties.

It's like a mountain made of meat,
Even the words make me want to eat.

To fill my stomach to overflow,
I think my stomach will have to grow.

I'll seek a job at a burger place,
And there I'll be stuffing my face.
Tanner Sorensen, Grade 9
Elk Ridge Middle School, UT

My Grandma

My grandma was always kind never had a bad bone in her body
she cared for those around and never thought of herself

Even though she was a little stubborn she was also humble, kind, and independent
but most of all she was spiritual

This past week she passed on and though I can't see her now
I know that I can see her again in the world that is to come

I know that she still watches over me in my day-to-day life
and I will never forget her smile that could make the whole world smile

She was great in the sight of all that knew her but she was the most great to me
I will never forget her and I know she will never forget me

There is hope in all things don't ever doubt
don't take things for granted 'cuz you know what they say
you don't know how great they are until they are gone
Amanda Uptain, Grade 9
Elk Ridge Middle School, UT

The Flight of Another

I see her standing
Tentatively, not wanting to, but knowing she must
She looks at me and gives me a wobbly smile
I smile back and nod. She turns
Her wings shake with apprehension and excitement
But she takes a deep breath to calm her nerves
I can't believe my best friend, my sister, is spreading her wings
And leaving for a while
But I know she'll come back

She leaps and the summer wind caresses her soft golden wings that
Sharply contrast from brilliant sapphire skies
She rides the rolling, tumbling, swaying breezes
I smile as her joyous laughter whispers from above
My bittersweet tears run down my cheeks
I wave as she leaves, diving among the clouds

My best friend, my sister, is spreading her wings
And leaving for a while
But I know she'll come back
Brenna Wasser, Grade 8
Lewis and Clark Middle School, ID

I Broke My Leg!

I broke my leg on a football play.
It hurt really bad with lots of pain.
The bone in my leg hurt, it was not fake.
I was rolled in a wheelchair in the hospital doors.
I went in a scary room with lots of shots and beakers.
A scary doctor walked in the room drooling like a great baboon.
He came in touching my leg where it had lots of pain.
I left with crutches and a cast on my leg.
Matthew Saylor, Grade 8
Eugene Christian School, OR

No Suspected Healings

No healings,
Just sealings
Of mistakes, printed on peelings
Of life
That have been wasted away,
Left with no feelings.
No suspected healings.
No detections
Just expectations
Of what people
Want me to be.
It's like I'm blind
I can't see
What the world
Is trying to bring me.
There's no knowing
What tomorrow brings.

No suspected healings.

Kyle Campbell, Grade 8
Project Surpass (Day Treatment – Yic), UT

The Girl and the Ocean Waves

The ocean waves at me as though we were friends;
But what the ocean doesn't know is that I am not here for it
I am here for her; she is like a sister to me
She is so grown up but yet she is so like a child
She is my friend, my sister in life and death;
I love her and she will soon love me
The ocean waves at me as though we were friends;
But what the ocean doesn't realize is that I am not here for it
I am here for her

Jenae Crooke, Grade 9
Idaho Arts Charter School, ID

It's OK…

It's OK to cry,
When you have been through a tough time.
It's OK to scream,
When the thought won't leave your head.
It's OK to beg,
When you beg for peace in your life.
But it's not OK to let the fear take over you,
Let it go through every part of your body.
Until there is no other place to store it.
Let it sink in your body and head like water on a sponge.
That is not OK.
But if you don't let that happen…
Joy will bring shine to your eyes,
Bring softness to your days,
Take every part of your body to fill it with joy,
Until you finally realize…
That it's OK to offbeat the fear inside of you,
And let the joy be the one inside of you.

Darcey Escamilla, Grade 8
Sylvester Middle School, WA

Springtime

In the springtime air,
when flowers bloom,
with their colors fair,
toward the brightening moon.

Little ones playing in the grass
running under budding trees
near the river clear as glass,
they chase after bumblebees.

Emily Reese, Grade 8
Salmon Seventh-day Adventist School, ID

Moonlight

During the time before a new moon,
During the time before midnight,
During the time after twilight,
During the time with no worries at all,
During the time of silence,
During the time when creatures are fast asleep,
During the time when the moon is full,

The time is now when a miraculous feeling approaches,
The time is now, of a glistening *crescent moon sliver*,
The time is now, stopped,

Then the time was…

Chris Coleman, Grade 9
Mountain Ridge Jr High School, UT

Alaska

Alaska, Alaska, my beautiful Alaska
No other state has better people than Alaska.
Glad to be native!
People come from all the world
To find the life of Alaska.
It may not have big shops
But the people and place is what matters.
Hunting birds…
This is how Alaska is.
The population may be few,
But it's good to be like brothers.
The snow may come in any moment.
The climate may not be the best,
But we are used to it.
There are wild animals…bears, wolves, and eagles.
The lakes are like the blood of Alaska,
The restaurants, the food of the sea,
The mountains full of snow,
The ocean full of salmon.
There is no other place better than
My beautiful Alaska.

Eduardo Granados, Grade 8
King Cove School, AK

Mr. D.

From his line backing spot,
He growls and grinds before the play
When the whistle clatters
He flies from position
Buzzing by blockers
Smashing crashing thumping
Every man in the way,
Until he clomps the quarterback.
Gabe Jacobson, Grade 9
Buhl High School, ID

Flies

They fly all around
they bit you so hard,
they land upon your pie.

They mess your cars,
they drive you mad,
they have two great big eyes.

They always seem
to dodge your swat
no matter how you aim.

They know to stay hidden
'till your swatter is gone
and then they come back again.

They come in all sizes
and carrying germs,
they don't know that they are a pest.

They always show up
Tho never invited.
I wish they would give me a rest.
Joe Fitzgerald, Grade 8
Canfield Middle School, ID

Beauty

Once I heard the choruses,
Of music in the air.
Once I smelled the forests,
Without a single care.

Once I knew the beauty,
Of sunsets warm and bright.
Once I knew the duty,
Of rabbits in the night.

Once I knew all things,
Of beauty, love, and care.
But now I think of all these things,
And from my mind they tear.
Emily Petersen, Grade 8
South Jordan Middle School, UT

Hello Tomorrow

Hello tomorrow,
Forever in passing,
Until the end,
There is no last thing.
A repeating cycle
Of birth, life, and death,
As the cycle repeats,
Value every breath.
Today affects tomorrow
As yesterday today,
So do and speak intended meaning,
For words of idle do not stay.
Your word is who you are,
And you become what is your word,
Do not speak for none to hear,
Because it will be heard.
Words affect tomorrow,
As yesterday today,
So do and speak intended meaning,
For words of idle do not stay.
Chuck Gidley, Grade 9
Santiam Christian School, OR

Dreams

I can fly to a place
I knew as a child
you can see it in my face
it's simply clear and mild
it's like my second home
it's a dream I almost own
Palmis Lopez, Grade 9
Elk Ridge Middle School, UT

Piece of My Heart

Piece of my heart,
  you've wandered away,
To another one's soul,
  to wonder and play.

Piece of my heart,
  you fill me inside,
Of what you have left me,
  to swallow my pride.

To a lovers hand,
  oh, piece of my heart,
The melodic band,
  you play lead part.

Oh, piece of my heart,
  spare me today,
'Til another piece parts,
  I cannot say.
Scout Smith, Grade 7
Mears Middle School, AK

Rock and Roll

Rock and Roll, R&B, and Soul
Rocking out is our goal
We stay up long and late
There's nothing we don't like or hate
We'll stay here until everyone's gone
Just to listen to the song
We could scream until we all go deaf
We could scream until the band has left
We jump, we dance, we sing
Our ears will ring
The sound of guitars drums and the beat
Will be running through our feet
This is how it is
This is how it will be
Why don't you listen to me?
Brad Verbon, Grade 7
Sylvester Middle School, WA

Fire

Burning brightly in the night
Looks like no harm can come from it
Roasting marshmallows
Making s'mores
Y
u
m
m
y
!
Dusty Griffin, Grade 8
Culver Middle School, OR

Scared!!!

A boring park,
Late and scary.
It was very dark.
There were crickets crying,
Owls hooting,
Mice scurrying,
I just sat there waiting.
Started to walk around in circles,
Just staying there waiting.
It was in the cold of winter.
Never again!
Robbie C. Hachenberg, Grade 8
Culver Middle School, OR

Lacrosse

Lacrosse
Bloody, brutal
Running, jumping, checking
It's fun to play
Lacrosse
Trevor Muehlheim, Grade 7
Ogden Middle School, OR

Summer Vacation

It comes once a year
Kids break free from their chains and cheer
No more books
No more essays
and none of those teachers' dirty looks
We all have our plans and different things to do
but I really don't want to get rid of your hopes,
trust me I really don't want to
but have you checked the date?
It is only 10 dash 2

Ali Salvino, Grade 7
St Anne School, WA

Who Knows

While waking in the early morning dawn,
Man wants to know the future with such thirst,
He soon forgets that he is only man.
For this poor man a change of heart comes first.
Or otherwise he takes the road to death,
Where he is caged and mastered for his pay.
Our lives seem hard in all our stress and toil,
But knowledge of the future paves the way.
All people of this world must know that we,
Are not allowed to see what is our fate.
There's only one who knows the path ahead,
And ours is but to labor and to wait.
When we are frantic to know all our life,
We need to recall that sin is a knife.

Hannah McComas, Grade 9
Covenant High School, WA

The Ultimate Tube War

First I'm floating,
  Then I'm boating,
    Next I'm dashing,
      While the tube is splashing,
        Now we're screaming,
          Because we're beaming,
            Now we're laughing,
              Because our hands are weakening,
                Now I'm looking for my sister…
                  I turn my head and "BOOM!"
                    Now I am in the air,
                      Wishing that I didn't care,
                        While flipping, and twisting,
                          In all sorts of directions.

Now I've landed,
  The pain rushing through my back,
    And under my arm,
      But, "HEY" it does no harm!

Annie Branca, Grade 8
Wasatch Jr High School, UT

Bullies

Middle, high and even elementary
Have bullies everywhere I really guarantee.
They pick on you with no apparent reasons,
Every day in all four seasons.
You're just something for them to play,
You have to stop them and say:
Stop! Stop! I've had enough,
You hurt me so and are plain too rough.
When they fight, they have friends to back up
Because I'm sure they know they'll get beat up.
Sometimes they trip people in the halls,
But when they reach the real world,
They'll be another brick in the wall.
I swear, I swear they're all so mean,
The most disgusting things I've ever seen.

Nicholas Mead, Grade 7
Sylvester Middle School, WA

The Junior High Classroom

Never quiet,
Always loud,
Never clean,
Always messy.

Kids yelling,
Kids screaming,
Teachers always talking,
Teachers sometimes yelling,
I am lucky if the kids are quiet.

Two days off a week,
Those two days are the best days of my life.
Sometimes get three days off a week,
If I am lucky.

Cassie Fefelov, Grade 8
Nikolaevsk School, AK

Imagination

There is no limit, outside of reality
The options are endless, outside of reality.
Colors, actions, twirls, and swirls.
Yellow, gold, jewelry, and pearls.
Kings, queens, princesses, too.
Gowns, fancy clothes, and high-heeled shoes.

There is no limit, outside of reality
The options are endless, outside of reality.
People, hobbies, animals, and figs
Costumes, makeup, hats, and wigs.
Monsters, angels, car racers too,
Astronauts, cooks, cows that go MOO.

There is no limit, outside of reality
Lets go to imagination land you and me!

Marika Theofelis, Grade 8
St Anne School, WA

Nightmare!!!

Red sand
Small but plenty
Quick sand swallows you down
Then your life flashes before you
Nightmare!!!
Kha Nguyen, Grade 7
Lewis and Clark Middle School, ID

Dancing Outdoors

Feel the beat beneath your feet.
See the audience grab a seat.
Hear the music everywhere.
Smell the flowers in the air.
Taste the wind that's in your hair.
Alisha Coffey, Grade 7
Ogden Middle School, OR

The Sun*

The sun is joyful,
She is very playful.
She jumps the clouds,
In just a few big bounds.

She is every day,
Extremely bright in May.
She watches when you stray,
Always helping you to find your way.

As the horses pull her across the sky,
Your dreams fly low then soar high.
Her hair is a light, streaming, golden,
Cheeks a bright red molten.

Her dive into the blue,
Makes her feel so cool.
At night when she hides away,
The moon takes her place, in a way.

We will all miss her so,
But now, I too, must go!
Kelcie Hahn, Grade 7
Lake Stevens Middle School, WA
*Dedicated to my best friends Jason Oh,
Savannah Peterson, and Skyler Suedel.

San Diego

I see the grass flowing
for the wind is ever blowing.

Sand particles sting my face
and dandelions dance like lace.

Sounds of rustling leaves call to me
like the rolling waves of the sea.
Boston Gardner, Grade 7
Reid School, UT

Brotherly Love

He beats me up
He plays with my head
He takes my money
Those are probably the only bad things he actually does to me
Compared to what I do, that is nothing
He says he's going to beat me up, but most of the time he doesn't
Sometimes he even says he's going to tell mom of something that I've done
But I would do everything in my power to get him in trouble
Most of the time I am successful
One of my best pranks is the one where I would act like he is hitting me
But really he's not
My mom would yell at him
And spank him
And pretty much rough him up.
You know the things that moms do
But always at the end of the day the war is over
He always says good night and waves goodbye
Until,
The new day arrives and the war at home is again
The brothers' war
An everlasting battle of a brother's love.
Jonah Yakunin, Grade 8
Nikolaevsk School, AK

Shedding Bloody Tears

As the soldier lays dying on the cold wet ground
He sheds bloody tears and listens to the sounds

Bombs are bursting
Bullets are flying
Women are crying
Children are screaming
And men are fighting

He touches his chest, his heart beating slower.
Bloody tears are flowing faster, as he reaches for his picture.
His wife, his kids, and what he's leaving behind.
He says this, "Lord take care of what I hold."

As he sheds another bloody tear. He turns his head and looks across the plain.
He tries to see past the dismantled bodies and gazes to the sunset.
He's going numb. He's starting to grow cold.
A slight warmness is surrounding him.
He knows it's the blood he bleeds.

He whispers, "It's time for me to sleep."
He looks at the picture in his hand.
His wife, his kids, and what he's leaving behind.
As he sheds his last bloody tear.
Kailey Webb, Grade 8
Amboy Middle School, WA

Sorrow

Running around in circles to escape my thoughts.
Trying not to listen but yet they overpower my strength.
My sinful past coming back to me once again.
The lifeless figure existing only in spirit,
Lays upon the ground as if angelic.
This choice now full of regret and terror,
has come crashing back down to reality.
Fearful for what I have done,
start running around in circles once again.

Jessica Catucci, Grade 8
Sacajawea Middle School, WA

Good vs Evil

What makes a bad? What makes a good?
Does anyone know? Is it everyone should?
If it hurts another, if it's called a sin.
When you live your life, unlike it should have been.

What makes a negative? What makes a plus?
Is it something reliable? Everyone can trust?
When everyone's happy, and everyone's pleased.
When all doubt and worry is released.

I can tell you right now, this isn't all true.
For a lot of things are a mix of the two.
Doesn't God have some evil? Doesn't the Devil have some good?
If one didn't exist, are we sure the other one could?

It can't yet be told, what is right and what is wrong.
But when it is our time, we will have known all along.
One can't be without the other, in my line of thought.
When one was made, the other was brought.

But! See for yourself, what you can find.
And never let anyone change your mind.

Savannah Freeman, Grade 9
W F West High School, WA

Shimmering Crystals

The ground and trees were white
After they had been glazed with
The newly fallen snow

The snow flakes slowly fell down
As I stuck out my tongue to catch them

The only sound was the cool clear crisp stream
Slowly making its way down the mountain

A place with no fear, worry or care

The sun peak over the clouds
Making the field look like a sea of
Shimmering white crystals

Jason Brown, Grade 8
Mountain Ridge Jr High School, UT

The Way It Used to Be

When I would get there,
The smell of fresh grass
Would flow through the air.
Everyone was happy,
Getting ready for what was coming.
The teams warming up,
Around the bases running.
Now I arrive at this foreign sandlot,
My passion and love
For the game is gone.
You can see in their eyes,
They are filled with ignorance.
With all of these jokers,
I feel like I'm playing poker.
I used to blend in, being mediocre.
Now I stick out, like a team savior.
I wish things were the way they used to be,
Filled with so much joy and glee.
But that is the past, and so is my passion,
And in one quick flitter,
I am labeled a quitter.

Collin Price, Grade 7
St Patrick's Catholic School, WA

One Crazy Friendship

What was I thinking?
I met you and everything changed.
Suddenly, there was no warning light blinking.
My actions ran free as a dog with no chain.

Toilet papering cops, staying up all night,
I never used to do that.
Usually from fright,
That came from "all powerful" Mom and Dad.

Sledding behind cars,
Has become one big blast.
We don't go very far,
And not very fast.

What was I thinking?
Going rafting with them.
The only reason I went,
Was because I'm your friend.

Half of this stuff,
Was only done to impress.
But only each other,
And none of the rest.

Now when we do things, I think, "Let's go have fun!"

Marilee Egan, Grade 9
Bonneville High School, ID

The Wild I See Around Me

As I walk along the trail of mystery, I see my shadow, round and large like a balloon.
I see two giant barns that could be twins.
Around me I see the cold, lifeless forest around me.
I look at the water reminding me of stained glass set calmly on the river like a church window.
I smell fresh, salty rainwater as I move through the woods of adventure.
Smelling the air is like smelling the deep blue ocean.
I hear a raging waterfall around me because of the wind dancing in the trees.
I hear the crashing waves of the ocean in a rage of fury.
Inside it feels like home embracing me, like a new beginning from the last ending.
When I reach out and touch, I feel rough bark like feeling rough skin.
A new world of bumps and edges.
It tastes like the sourness from something bitter.
I taste the cold, harsh, bitter ice that stings my skin.
At the end of the journey I feel that I have the solution to the trails of mystery.

Austin Henderson, Grade 7
Komachin Middle School, WA

Life

If only we shared something that words could not explain.
Would it matter, would there be a connection with the world and yourself?
Maybe you don't care what is becoming of the future with every step you take.
With every wrinkle in your face comes a year, a year that you can never take back, because that is the past.
Today is the present, tomorrow is the future.
The next step is up to you, the road with many footsteps or a road with none.
You can go where the wind takes you.
Or step out and be an individual, working your way against the wind.

Rochelle Puffe, Grade 9
Idaho Arts Charter School, ID

What's Your Problem?

You've changed so much. I feel like I don't know you.
Tell me! Tell me! Tell me! What's your problem?

What happened to you? You fell in with those friends of yours.
Your problem is you're so-called friends. That's what I say, but you say differently.
You need help. You run from all your problems.
You say your friends help you, but are they really your friends?
Let me, your true friend, help you. Let me help you.

You say you don't need help, but I see right through you.
Even people you don't know can tell something's wrong.
Tell me what your problem is.
You are meaner and meaner to me. You say, "Stay away and leave me alone."
So I do, but I want to help you. Let me help you solve your problem.

You are gone now, running for your life. For the bad things you did to your family and me.
For the bad things, I can't mention to people. You need help, let someone help you.

They caught you; they put you in a bad place. Now you sit there thinking over the things you did.
The memories haunt you. Now you wish you had let me help you.
But now I can't. You did this to yourself.
I wish you had let me help you, but your problem is still there to haunt you.
You never let me help you. "Sigh."

Alyssa Deaton, Grade 7
West Valley Middle School, WA

I Belonged

I belonged,
I was loved,
I was accepted,
So why was I not able to go?
Had I done something?
How could I change for them?
Hadn't I been getting along?
So why was I not able to go?
I asked around,
Where could I go?
My parents cared,
So why did they not care that I wasn't there?
I had learned,
I had been befriended,
I was getting along,
So why was I not accepted again,
After all the questions and them with no answers?

Evangeline Murray, Grade 7
Sylvester Middle School, WA

Realizing

After a beautiful sunset with amazing colors
like crimson red, and a crazy orange
and a light peach
        you realize…

After a starry, moonlight night,
filled with shooting stars
and incredible planets,
        you realize…

After a relaxing, sunny day at the beach,
when the water is just right,
and the palm trees seem like they are singing to you,
        you realize what you have been missing

Landon Henriksen, Grade 8
Wasatch Jr High School, UT

My Sweet Little Kitty

My sweet little kitty with his orange nose
With his long wild tail and cute little toes

My sweet little kitty so little and cute
My little kitty is not very mute

My sweet little kitty doesn't go be fluffy or Kevin
His sweet little name is 007

My sweet little kitty a ball of fluff
I don't know what I would do without you
I love you so much

Talicia Miller, Grade 7
Pateros Jr-Sr High School, WA

For Once in My Life

For once in my life, I belonged.
For once in my life, I was loved.
For once in my life, I was trying to be someone
I did not know myself.

For once in my life, my world broke,
And it fell to the ground with a
Crash of broken hearts.

For once in my life, I was defied.
I was back to my normal self.
However sad, however lonely, but my normal self.

Kathryn Shaw, Grade 7
Sylvester Middle School, WA

Crimson and Gray

Crimson and gray
The tough and the brave
The one thing we will always say
How majestic they are
When it's time to play
Football, basketball, and much more

They act like it's just another day
Even when it's the Apple Cup
But that doesn't make a difference
The joy of winning will pay
For all the expenses to get to the game
To cheer on the Crimson and Gray

Abby Ingvalson, Grade 8
Sunnyside Christian Elementary School, WA

Fishing

Our love is like a fisherman on a fishing trip
I am the fish
You are the fisherman
You sit there for a few minutes
Dangling your love
Waiting for me
Teasing
I try to resist
I try to swim away from your sharp hook
But I can't
I don't know why but I just give in
For a second I feel the sweetness of your love
But as I bit the hook, I get pierced
Pierced with pain
Then I wonder to myself:
Is it worth it?
Is it worth the pain to feel a few moments of your love
Then be rejected for someone else?
I don't know but one day
I won't give in
I will no longer be the foolish fish on your hook

Annie Gaines, Grade 9
Franklin Pierce High School, WA

Will You Accept My Love?

A heart on your locker,
A flower on your chair.
No matter what I do,
She doesn't even care.

I've sent her an e-mail,
Probably more than two,
The only thing I remember,
Is my love for her is true.

I walk up beside her,
It's slow-dance number four.
I stand there rejected,
Loving her no more.

But something brings me back to her,
Like a small tug on my rope.
It makes me look at her again,
And I realize there is hope.

Rylan Montgomery, Grade 8
St Josephs Catholic School, WA

The Fishing Hole

I am the fishing hole.
I hold water all year long.
There is sea life all around me.
I also hold fish inside me.

Every year people come to see me.
from Ohio,
from California, and
from everywhere,
people come to see me.
They fish inside me,
and get their food,
while I sit here all year long.

David Ivanov, Grade 8
Nikolaevsk School, AK

Darkness

Sun is setting, the day complete
Sweetness of the day is beat.
No longer are the birdies singing
Everything is sleeping.

Moonlight makes an eerie glow
As the deep, dark river overflows,
Trees are making strange shadows
I do not know a friend from foe.

Wishing for the sun to rise
Yearning for those butterflies.
But the darkness is still here
The night is full of fear.

Chenin Howe, Grade 9
Idaho Arts Charter School, ID

Sun Comes Up

The light has life,
birds are singing out as loud as possible
children are laughing as excited as a puppy chasing a ball
bicycles ringing without a care.
The sun is shining, covering the world in a buttery warm blanket
and clouds are slowly moving across the sky,
adding entertainment to a lazy summer afternoon.
The dark has life,
lullabies softly ringing out to add noise to a vast silence,
rocking chairs are creaking to lull babies
into a tiny dream world that's all their own.
The stars are finally peaking out to add light to the dark.
Finally all is at peace
until the sun comes up and it all begins again.

Lauren Mason, Grade 8
Wasatch Jr High School, UT

Ice and Fire

Last night it had snowed; today I looked out on an ethereal scene
Halcyon beauty frozen by the timeless magic of snow
Whiteness surrounded me in all directions, blurring and softening shapes
So that all melded into one rolling landscape
The sun tore through the black storm clouds, and rays of gold and silver
Set the snow — crystals aflame, coruscating with a brilliant light
That pulsed through each one, turning each filigreed flake
Into a priceless diamond
Sound was muted and far-off
No grinding machines, no shouts and derisive laughter; nothing
Only nature, in the birds' songs and in the stillness
And all around could be felt the deep, gentle hum of winter
An ageless creature of benevolent power
Speaking of majestic beauty and terror at the same time
Vibrating not the eardrum, but the soul
And I felt it envelop me; I felt myself part of it all
One with the birds and the snow and the world
As I stood that morning in a land of ice and fire

With careful feet, I took the first hesitating step
And broke its crispy softness.

Raluca Ifrim, Grade 7
Redmond Jr High School, WA

We Are Ripples

We are like ripples. Each one unique and different.
Different shapes and sizes, flowing in different directions,
each with a different destination.
We make our river flow, giving it life and motion,
giving it personality and making it our own.
Without the ripples, our river wouldn't flow,
it would be still, like a pane of glass,
and it would always look the same, never changing, never moving,
never trying to accomplish anything.
Without the ripples, there wouldn't be a river.
We are the ripples that make the river, a river.

Ali Kamenz, Grade 8
Komachin Middle School, WA

War

Soaring over the quilted plains,
the pilot tenses as he closes on the point,
ready to bomb the German city,
he nears the front and he tenses more,
ready for the sound of guns,
he imagines the screams and cries,
that will come when the bombs hit the Earth.
The anti-air pound up at the fleet,
of bombers, hornets; an amazing feat!
The sound of bombs soaring to the ground,
the sound of people screaming in despair,
for the inevitable explosion sure to come.
The many innocent in their homes,
are dying for the war that comes,
when one person makes the mistakes,
to annihilate or the world take,
if it weren't for the good in the world,
these wicked people would surely make,
the world into a horrid place,
to live and die in worthless haste.

Ricky Larsen, Grade 9
Elk Ridge Middle School, UT

My Master

My Master's name is carved on the door,
His impassioned rays shower from the sun,
With every breath, I praise Him more,
My Master is the immutable one.

Sasha Pashakhan, Grade 7
Rogich Middle School, NV

A Suicidal Death

A woman whose life changed so many others,
Ruthless, intelligent and extremely vain.
A leader, "Queen of Kings," and somebody's mother,
A giver of life, wealth, destruction and pain.

Captured and shamed,
A usurper on her throne.
Her once respected reputation was maimed.
The last days of her life spent all alone.

A death unfit for a woman like her,
Sentenced to slavery, a ruined name.
A death of poison, of that we are sure,
Murderer and victim one and the same.

Cleopatra VII, immortal forever,
Pharaoh of Egypt, a first and a last.
Determined to reign, Roman rule she would sever.
She is a tribute to glory that lies in the past.

A suicidal death,
"Hiss," she heard at her very last breath.

Jillian Bryant, Grade 8
South Jordan Middle School, UT

The Silver Moon

The silver moon divides the night from day
Flinging its wispy-silver strands to earth
Falling upon the dancing winter snow
The silver light streams down to earth below
Until the earth is filled with iridescent light
Cleansing the earth's long forgotten shadow

Thomas Barlow, Grade 7
Reid School, UT

My Home, My Refuge

My home my refuge
On every wall there is a picture
In every picture there is a memory
In every room there is a pile of clothes
Through every yearbook there are pictures of friends
To remind me of all the good times I had
Through the cold dark door
I walk into a hard wood floor
I hear the swish of a net
A soft rhythm of the leather ball against the court
From running past defenders
The 30, 20, 10, touchdown
Scoring the game winners
A soft clank of the bat
A deep line drive
The sweet crunch of dirt under me
As I slide into third
This is my home my refuge

Austin Kleinhans, Grade 7
Komachin Middle School, WA

My Mother

When I woke up
She opened her eyes
And me, sitting there,
And my soul floating,
Levitating in front of her white face.

"What is that?"
She asked. Am I dead,
Is she blind
And in her imagination
She sees my soul?

Millions of question,
Lots of imagination,
A short life.
She just stares
At nothing, at something,
She just knows
Who I am.

Maria Cordova, Grade 8
Mario C. Jo Anne Monaco Middle School, NV

Umbrella Dark

At night we see a sheet of black.
Dots are pierced out here and there.
Through which we see a light beyond
That fights to spill out from these tears.

Beneath this blanket floats an orb.
It bathes the ground with silver light.
Shadows sprawl along the grass
Hiding crickets from our sight.

The dark umbrella rises up.
The light beyond slips underneath.
It races over trees and rocks
To light the grass around our feet.

Julien Malard, Grade 7
Enterprise Middle School, WA

My Race

Diving into the pool
The water feels so cool
I start to swim my laps
The crowd cheers and claps
In the middle of the race
I set a steady pace
Towards the end of my swim
I can hardly feel my limbs
When my race stops
I look up at the clock
I got first place
I finally won a race

Ashton Dayhuff, Grade 9
Elk Ridge Middle School, UT

My Grandma, My Grandma

My grandma, my grandma
I loved you with no end
It was so hard to say goodbye
You were my best friend

I remember that day
It was not so long ago
When your final hour passed
And I was filled with woe

It was hard to see you leave
I wanted you to stay
But life isn't like that
And you had to go away

My grandma, I miss you
I'll always hold you dear
As every day passes by
It's like you're still here

Kassey Castro, Grade 7
Sylvester Middle School, WA

Memories

Lost forever,
Far, far, away,
Back in the darkness
Of your mind.

Blurry and whited out,
Never thought of,
Fading farther away
Every second.

Childhood forgotten,
Sent back to the past,
Memories gone,
Never to be heard of again.

Sadly but surely,
Our memories,
Disappear.

Chelsea Noonan, Grade 8
Fairview Christian School, WA

Fall

Watch the leaves fall down
They don't even make a sound
As they touch the ground

Wesley Wilson, Grade 8
Culver Middle School, OR

It's All Piracy!

Pirates, pirates, pirates.
Mischief, trouble, no-sympathy.
Yo-Ho yelling.
It's all piracy.

No respect.
They take what they can.
An' give nothing back!
It's all piracy.

Vile, gross, disgusting!
Never take a bath.
No Robin Hoods among them!
It's all piracy.

Running from the law,
Is what they do best.
Their ships are always fast.
It's all piracy.

Pirates, pirates, pirates.
They stink, they sweat,
They sometimes swim.
It's all piracy to me!

Zoe Marzluff, Grade 7
Hidden River Middle School, WA

Training

Up and down the stairs I run,
Just to beat the starting gun.
Harder, harder, I try, I must,
To leave the other in a cloud of dust.

When I wake I often say,
Today is just another day.
When I dress, I stop to stare,
At those sneakers I must wear.

All the day I'm tuckered out,
And in my mind I have that doubt
All in all, I have this fun,
Just to beat the starting gun.

Dillon Hansen, Grade 9
Bonneville High School, ID

Believe

When I wish upon a star
I wonder why you are so far
O you elusive scholarship
I hope you get here before I slip

My goal you see
I want to be
Like an occupational therapist
And not a common terrorist

So help me elusive scholarship
To make my dreams come true
And together we'll ensure I not be blue

Amy Whitelock, Grade 9
Elk Ridge Middle School, UT

Norman and Bess

On a farm in the East of Wyoming,
Two cows were known for performing.
They picked up bluegrass,
Sang very fast
And played 'till one in the morning.

Soon they were rolling in dough.
Their fans came to each show.
They would start with guitar,
Not get very far,
Then switch to the spoons and cello.

It's strange, but I must confess,
This arrangement was quite a success.
Fans could not get enough
Of this fabulous stuff
From the two cows: Norman and Bess.

Betsy Smith, Grade 7
Sylvester Middle School, WA

Rainforest

Man and machine roll in,
to these scorching hot, humid forests.
Gigantic trees look like tiny emeralds,
in a sea of dark green.
Suddenly sounds of motors and falling trees,
break the relaxing music of birds and insects.
Panic and terror strike the hearts,
of the creatures living in paradise.
They hear the sound move closer,
every falling tree makes their hearts beat faster.
The lush forest is dying away,
and no one knows it,
until it is too late.

Matt Anderson, Grade 8
Wasatch Jr High School, UT

Ballet

Ballet is so smooth, fluent and free,
Although the steps are not easy.
It's hard, complicated but a lot of fun.
And when you learn a new step you feel like the best one.
While you dance you can just shove your worries out the door.
There's no need to think about anything anymore.

In slow songs, you dance like a swan, full of grace.
But in fast songs you try to keep up with the pace.
Poised and pretty you are confident and ready.
Humming along to the tune you stay steady.
Ballet is so smooth, fluent, and free,
Although the steps are not easy.

Ariana Nicole Moini, Grade 8
St Anne School, WA

Imagine

Imagine a storm is a dance recital,
    many images occupying your mind.
Imagine the wind is the lyrical dancers,
    flowing peacefully and with rhythm.
Imagine thunder is the audience,
    roaring after every number.
Imagine lightning is the tap dancers,
    entrancing you with every fast step.
Imagine rain is the ballet dancers,
    lightly coming to the floor.
Imagine stars are the seats, all the same,
    empty during every rehearsal.
Imagine the sun is the big open stage,
    waiting to be the base of the entertainment.
Imagine the sky is the big red curtain,
    ready to display a show.

Josephine Castle, Grade 7
Mears Middle School, AK

Basketball

Dribbling, passing, and shooting too,
    That's what I truly love to do.
The best is working with your team,
    Even better is making your coach gleam.
I practice and work the skill,
    Big shoes it is that I have to fill.
One, two, and three are the points you get,
    All you have to do is get yourself set.
        When I swoosh a three,
    My body is not adrenaline free.
Dribbling, passing, and shooting too,
    That's what I truly love to do.

Brenda Otley, Grade 7
Diamond Elementary School, OR

Thunder Storms

Thunderstorms are big and scary.
In the night they wait until you're asleep
To wake you with their big "boom" and flash of light.
They come up at unknown times,
    Just to surprise you.
Thunderstorms are big and scary.

Thunderstorms are large and treacherous.
They yell, scream, and shout,
And even if you're unlucky they throw light.
Thunderstorms have big arms and hands.
They stretch out and grab trees, shrubs, and twigs,
    And start a lively rhythm.
Thunderstorms are large and treacherous
That is true, without a doubt.

Arlene Belicina, Grade 8
St Anne School, WA

My Brother

Why did he go when he knows what' waiting for him?
When he knows the enemies could be so near.
When he knows what could happen in the end.
He went without any fear.

Why did he go without a thought
of what would happen without him here?
He said it would be OK and that I ought
just give him a little prayer.

He went with pride into the war.
For that I am so proud.
But when I think of him so hurt and sore,
I cry like a raining cloud.

I can't wait for him
to be back here with me.
I don't mean to be selfish
but this is his place to be.

Josh Miller, Grade 9
W F West High School, WA

Uh-Chu

Holy's sneeze is like a lion's roar:
Windy, wet, and loud
You can hear from everywhere
It truly is a horrific sound.

Jessica Gardner, Grade 7
Mt Olive Lutheran School, NV

Nothing Lasts Forever

Twirly, Twirly,
Little girly…
Pinwheel colors in your eyes.

Your kaleidoscope is broken,
beads on the floor.

What a nasty deception!
You always believed its pretty colors:

Could only have come from Heaven.

Anna Mason, Grade 9
Bellarmine Preparatory School, WA

Sing to Your Own Tune

Hark, this sweet sound,
Listen, the angels sing.
No voice could be heard so clear,
As yours.
None so sweet,
So true.
As others sing,
You go to your own tune.
Talented, strong,
Brave, noble.
Skilled at everything you do,
Ready at a moment's notice.
Stand tall,
Sing to your own tune.

Kelsey Pizac, Grade 8
Wasatch Jr High School, UT

My Heart

You can change my feelings
But you can never take my heart away.
Feelings change
But love stays forever.
So I will always love you
Even if it burns
Deep down inside me.
You will always be in my heart
Like everyone else.
But you will always be
At the top of the list
And most of my heart
Will always belong to you.

Jessica Baltzor, Grade 8
Floyd Light Middle School, OR

The One Girl I Love

In many different ways, I tried to express how I feel about you.
In many different ways I tried to get closer and closer to you.
In many different ways I tried to talk to you.
In all those ways I tried to get close to you,
I felt like I was getting father away.

Victor Lopez, Grade 8
Culver Middle School, OR

The Plants After the War

"Mankind must put an end to war, or war
will put an end to mankind." – John F. Kennedy, 1961

He stands
looking at the dead field
of his work, his shield
still by his side. No one understands

the pain he went through
to leave the farm alone
and travel far from his cozy home
and the meadow he knew.

War kills plants,
and he sees them lying, parched and dead,
like the soldiers in the war.

He was once with them. He took a chance
to see his home, only to find the empty words the soldiers said,
"that there was something worth fighting for."

Elaina Perpelitt, Grade 9
Delphian School, OR

I Am

I am slowly going insane
I wonder am I really annoying
I hear people telling me what to do
I see myself as an annoying person
I want to quit ruining people's lives
I am slowly going insane

I pretend there's nothing wrong
I feel like I am an idiot
I touch my feelings by writing them down
I cry because these assignments bring out my true feelings and
I don't like that
I am slowly going insane

I understand I made wrong choices in my life
I say everything is all right when people ask if anything is wrong
I dream I could change my past
I try to handle my situations in my life without help because I'm scared
people will not help me
I hope people understand what I'm going through
I am slowly going insane!!!

Thomas Adams, Grade 9
Buhl High School, ID

Pride Must Pass Away

When man attempts to know the secret things
And seeks celestial knowledge to obtain
He will at first look like he's in control.
It seems his thread of life he can ordain.
Yet soon will come to sudden steepling plunge.
Man's hubris is the reason for his fall.
He cannot be the ruler of his world.
Man's power doesn't order over all.
All man can do is take a humble place.
To freely live, his pride must pass away.
A willing servant he must gladly be.
He must be led in each and every way.
    When, calm content for others to be great
    Then man will smile and bless, not curse, his fate.

Henry Lewellen, Grade 9
Covenant High School, WA

No Matter Where I Go

People come and go throughout our lives
But our memories will always be with us
No matter where we go
Friends were lost, friends were made
Great bonds were made and will always stay

You can leave at any time, making a hole in my heart
Losing my love for you
But the hole will be filled with something better
Making no doubt,
The memories we had together will still stay in my heart forever
Memories of joy, laughter and friendship

The knowledge we have gained and the lessons we have learned
Will stay with us no matter where we go
Feelings can be changed
I can change
The world can change
But the memories we had together
Can never change
For the past is then
And the present is now
The future will hold greater moments

Nesley Bravo, Grade 7
Komachin Middle School, WA

Tina Tomato

Sometimes Tina Tomato has nightmares.
She remembers the other times,
When she had those dreams.
She is afraid to fall asleep,
Thinking about how other tomatoes are mushed into ketchup,
And squirted onto hamburgers or hot dogs.
Tina also has nightmares of being sliced.
When the refrigerator door opens and the light turns on,
She instantly wakes up and remembers she is still fat and alive.

Brittany Youngberg, Grade 7
Mears Middle School, AK

Jabberchorey*

'Twas snillig and the gorpy lads
Did chortle in slumberish euphor.
They conversed and guffawed 'bout times to be had;
Swamling and snoogling with no chores.
Then softly came the bribling phone,
On the CID it read Mom.
"Your chores should be done, I'm coming home,"
She muttered in sardonic gwam.
Chores! Only doof-dorfs do the chores!
Oh! The nasty jiberous jobs;
Woozle the toilets, shammy the dirty floors.
By the time you're done, ya can't play with Hobbs.
After much frazzment, I decided.
I grasped my mom, shammy, and bristle brush.
I squelched cleansing fluids undistracted.
Woozling, shammying, 'til the germs were hush hush.
I finished my woozling and such,
I'd conquered the nasty jiberous jobs.
All was moist and clean to the touch.
And best of all, I could still play with Hobbs.

Glossary

snillig — sunny; midday	gorpy — lazy, relaxed
swamling — swimming	snoogling — playing
gwam — tone of voice	doof-dorfs — wierdos
woozle — to scrub fiercely	frazzment — deep thought

Mark Woodbury, Grade 8
South Jordan Middle School, UT
*Inspired by "Jabberwocky" by Lewis Carroll

Love?

When you love someone,
You're willing to let them destroy you.

If you love someone you give up your power,
You allow yourself to become weaker,
You allow them into you,
You give them the power to hurt you.

If you love someone they can destroy you…
But they won't and if they do you keep them around…
Then you love them,
Far more than they love you.

If you're in love with someone,
Not having them around hurts you,
Thus no matter how much they hurt you before,
You fight to keep them around.

That is love…

Brie Baerg, Grade 9
Blaine High School, WA

What Is Forgotten?
What is forgotten?
Is it today, is it tomorrow?
Is it a feeling, or a sense of being?
Is it a noun, or a verb, or a phrase?
Is it something from the olden days?
Is it happiness, sorrow, or guilt, is it something that will wilt?
Is it a saying that's lost its touch, is it a person that's said too much?
Is it a book, or something that will look —
Into the ever-changing body and mind?
Here's another question, will it be kind?
Did it survive through the Ice Age, and wars?
Has it left its mark on Venus, or Mars?
Does it happen when the mind is full, or when the mind goes completely blank?
Has it floated, or has it sank?
Is it a memory of what has been, is it something that has yet to begin?
I think I know what the answer is, I think forgotten is something that will always be there.
Untouched and waiting, to have a next victim to strike!
To have forgotten is a terrible feeling, but to suddenly remember feels quite right.

Kristen Mitchell, Grade 7
Glacier Middle School, WA

Noises of Nature
As I walk along the cold windy mile long path,
I stop in the middle of the path and look at a tree that has a blanket of green moss.
The freezing wind talks to me as I stand there and says that only the sound of nature will calm it.
The birds are frozen as if they know I'm watching them,
But little do they know there are over ten kids behind them watching in amazement
There are geese making honking noises as they fly overhead in the shape of a V.
And my friends are behind me throwing rocks into the frozen pond as if they have never seen one.
As I'm watching the birds I realize that the sun is setting behind them and it is the most beautiful thing I've ever seen.

Bubba Johnson, Grade 7
Komachin Middle School, WA

If
If we were to fly, would we be birds or angels?
If we were to die, would we go to heaven or have heaven on earth?
If we were to cry, would we be crying for joy or of grief?
If we were to snicker, would it be kind or wicked?
If we were to sleep, would we be sleeping in fear or comfort?
If we were to eat, would we still be hungry or satisfied?
If we were to sing, would we be singing for pleasure or discomfort?
If we were to be a box of chocolates, would we be sweet or sour?
If we were to dream, would we be having good dreams or bad dreams?
If we were to write, would we be writing a story or a poem?
If we were to ask a question, would we think about it first or just say it aloud and maybe make
a fool out of ourselves?
If we were to judge someone, would we have time to love them or hate them?
If we were to cry, would it be happy tears or sad tears?
If we were to kill, would it be to concur or demolish?
If we were to stare, would we be prejudice or be in a daze?
If we were to hate, would it be of jealousy or hateful love?
If, is not the key to life, it is how you plan to live for the future and remember the past,
we should live our lives like there is no tomorrow. These are some of the things that we should
ask ourselves before we act, think, or persuade.

Amber Merry, Grade 7
Glide Middle School, OR

Overcoming the Moment
Final seconds or two outs in the bottom of the ninth inning,
It becomes your time to shine.
Whether you're an all-star,
Bench warmer or the average player,
The moments don't care,
They'll attack you the same way.

They'll attack you and
Try to rip you apart,
And expose you as
A person who just couldn't get it done.

Your heart beats faster,
Your body becomes numb
And you feel like you'll die if
You do something wrong.

But if you can overcome these moments,
With the walk-off hit, buzzer beater shot or
Field goal with time expiring,
Then you will be praised as a hero,
Who overcame the moment.
Sam Kinn, Grade 8
St Anne School, WA

Tombstones
I go to stand by the fresh-dug grave
The casket being lowered.
The dead soldier's mother
Is the only one standing there.

Quietly I approach,
Watching dirt cover the shiny casket lid.
Tears glisten in her eyes
I wonder who she is.

Next to her I stand
As she watches her son
Being lowered into the ground —
A final resting place.

I know the fear
And heartbreak
For I was here visiting my brother's grave —
The price of war is great.

I don't know who he is
Or she is
But I do know that hollow pain,
That utter loss.
Christine Dickson, Grade 8
Leota Jr High School, WA

Come Along with Me
There's a cloud in the sky,
A bird in the tree,
A fish in the water,
And a cricket in the weeds.
I walk around this world missing everything,
So come along with me.
Let's look at the blue sky,
The chirping birds in the trees,
The colorful fish in the water,
And search for crickets in the weeds.
The world around us is amazing,
Let's not miss it.
Let's search up and down,
Together.
Allyson Hamada, Grade 8
Wasatch Jr High School, UT

My Colors
Part of me is sky blue
calm and relaxed
happy and lazy,
drinking smoothies and talking with friends
maybe tomorrow I will feel much different.
Fiery red, like a volcano
energetic and excited
fierce and wild
running around crazy when nothing even happens
they are both fun to be
and they both fit me.
Oliver Ostler, Grade 8
Wasatch Jr High School, UT

After It's Stopped Beating
Can a heart still break,
After its stopped beating?
Well, I'm willing to find out are you?
'Cause it's what you deserve
After what you did to me
Breaking my heart like that
Without a care in the world
As long as you got what you wanted
And it wasn't me
Can a heart still break,
After your soul is lost?
Leaving you with no emotions?
I already found that out
Now, you need to, too
Can a heart still break,
After it's already been broken?
I don't want to know the answer
'Cause then I'll have no heart left
Could I break your heart,
Even when there's nothing there, but a big, empty hole?
I could but I won't 'cause I'm not as cruel as you are.
Jennifer Carlson, Grade 8
Mountain Home Jr High School, ID

Shark

Grey, massive, sharp teeth,
large large fin,
he likes to eat fish,
attacks from below,
most people fear it,
others study it,
he swims in the deep blue sea
but sometimes
you can find him swimming
in the aquarium.
He is a shark.

Parker Halliday, Grade 8
Wasatch Jr High School, UT

The Truth About Truth

What is truth? It's hard to know.
Only lucky ones can find
The meaning. It's one, I suppose,
Mr. Webster can hardly define.

"Correspondence to knowledge,"
Does that fit the description?
Is there really a distinct wedge
Between fact and fiction?

I think truth is like weather —
Sometimes good, sometimes bad.
Sunshine light as a feather,
Or frozen peaks, snowy clad.

Also, perceptions of truth
Are not always the same.
For example, joy can go, "POOF!"
When the sun isn't tame.

So truth can be friend,
Or it can be foe,
It all just depends
On what you need to know.

Rachel Pittenger, Grade 9
W F West High School, WA

Darkness Falls

Darkness falls after his light.
He paints the sky before he goes.
The water beneath him is his good night.
He comes and goes like daily shows.
His warmth is leaving us.
The cold blows over with a chill.
The water grasps the fiery mass
Expecting the sound of a sizzle.
Clouds are losing their surface glow.
The orange haze floats on the surface.
Night is here and what a show!

Stephanie Hawkins, Grade 8
Eugene Christian School, OR

I Am a British Soldier Fighting for a Lost Cause

I am a British soldier fighting for a lost cause
I wonder if the determined patriots are watching our every move
I hear the crackle of twigs in the forest
I see what must be their shadows
I am a British soldier fighting for a lost cause
I pretend that they aren't here and that we have won
But I feel their presence continually and wait to hear the alarm
I touch my musket ready to fire if I see the white of their eyes
I could worry if I only had time
I cry when I think of home and my family
I am a British soldier fighting for a lost cause
I understand Britain is angry
I say that Britain is the right in this war
I dream of the day I sail for home to my own country
I try to do my best in the war
I hope that it will all end soon
I am a British soldier fighting for a lost cause

Tyler Hillman, Grade 7
River HomeLink Program, WA

Daffodil

I can think back to the time I was little,
I had no cares and I roamed free.
One day, I was walking home from school, I was angry,
I knew I shouldn't, but I did.
I picked a yellow daffodil, it's yellow brightness glowing in the sun,
shouting to the world "Be happy!"
It was the last one the summer sun
had not touched with its golden rays.
I crushed it with my hands, I stomped it in the ground,
when my rage was gone, I looked down to see the beautiful yellow flower,
once happy, now sad and dead.
Gone from the world it once made joyful.
I picked up the dead flower, flat and wilting.
I don't remember if I cried,
but I did place it under the evergreens.
Every time I see the yellow flowers, I apologize.

Jamie Urry, Grade 8
Wasatch Jr High School, UT

Love

My heart is like a clock making a ticking sound.
My thoughts are my diary screaming out loud.
My life is an hourglass slowly running out of time.
You are like a memory that will always be mine.
My heart is full of love for any and everyone.
The starving kids in Africa skinny to the bone.
The homeless people in New Orleans devastated from the storm.
The people fighting for our country and the ones who have died.
I have love for everyone going through bad times.
My heart is like a porcelain doll, it can shatter if tampered with.
My thoughts are like a never ending wish.
My life is like a fire it can burn out at any time.
You are like a slippery bar of soap, but you will always be mine.

CJ Parker, Grade 7
Avery Elementary/Jr High School, ID

Wings of Silk

Wings of silk flutter about,
Colors of many paint them about.
Gracefully they fly as if a ballet,
Gliding to each flower they sip its sweet sap.

Mason Beck, Grade 7
Helper Jr High School, UT

Right Path

Teenagers traveling through life are like lizards
traveling through a dry desert not knowing where to go.
So many options; which way do we go?
How do we know?

Which way will lead us to the right path?
If what seems fun now
will it be fun later?
Will it be for the best?
How do we know?

Will we screw up our lives with one wrong turn?
Are we going the wrong way?
How do we know?

If we just take the safe path
how will we end up?
Will we live in regret for not exploring our options?
How do we know?

If what seems important now will it be important later?
Will we be the same later in life?
How do we know?

Tabitha Frey, Grade 9
Silver Creek Alternative School, ID

Hearts Beat

There's no other perfect match
It seemed like we finally won
The friend we've tried to catch
I'm here for you too. I swear.
There won't be a day I ditch you,
However that day you ditched me still burns in my head
I thought you had left me for the friends you made new
Traded me in like and old toy, dirty and used
I never thought you would be one to betray
And yet every time you did it, I would smile and shrug
Better to be in than out, right?
I think that's why we never hug
For a while I was filled with spite
But I knew that it wasn't the answer
So I've learned to accept it
Like someone learns to accept cancer
I wish it was as easy to press backspace or delete
Our hearts beat as one
Only just this once, they skipped a beat

Nicole Thai, Grade 7
Sylvester Middle School, WA

Friends

Even though we both have fought.
You still will always mean a lot.

I know its been hard for you and me.
But maybe its not as bad as it seems.

Though this friendship has been a race.
Lets take it step by step and pace by pace.

Rachael Gainer, Grade 9
Elk Ridge Middle School, UT

About Me

Jack
Happy, funny, quiet, handsome
Relative of Mark, my brother
Love of dirt bikes because they're fast, Maui because it's
    paradise, planes which have great food
Who feels angry at leaving Maui, funny when somebody
    tells a joke, and bored at school
Who needs a bed to rest in, a dirt bike to ride on, and a
    Playstation 2 to play
Who fears the doctor when something is wrong, shots that
    hurt, and getting knocked out again
Who gives directions to lost people, Kevin a hello in the
    morning, and a good bye to my mom when going to
    school
Who would like to see Kenny Bartrom in competition
    again, Ricky Carmichael, the professional dirt bike
    racer, and Travis Pastrana take first at the X-Games
Resident of a tan house with 9 or 10 dirt bikes in the
    garage in Culver, Oregon, the United States of
    America
Merrill

Jack Merrill, Grade 8
Culver Middle School, OR

Beach

A place for friends and me,
A place so I can get some fresh air.

A place for salt water I can swim in,
A place for the warm, soft sand where I stand.

A place for the wood I climb,
A place for the gorgeous horses I ride (so I'm not sad).

A place for ships I explore,
A place for fishing I do.

A place for the beach and I.

Rebekah DeForest, Grade 7
Walker Middle School, OR

Winter

Winter is like a day at school
School smartens up a complete fool
No matter what — you have to go
So you can learn stuff you don't know

You can take stuff for show and tell
At the end of recess you hear the bell
At the end of the day I watch the clock
It just turned three — oh what a shock
Tom Merkley, Grade 7
Mound Valley Rural School, NV

The Journey*

As dark as night, yet light as snow.
A double-edge sword.
It hovers silently over us
Bringing the old and the young,
Back home.
Do not be afraid of it, greet it.
Do not run from it, embrace it.
Do not fight it, accept it.
Because when God calls you home,
You must answer Him.
Tyler Sanford, Grade 7
Sylvester Middle School, WA
*Dedicated to Linda R. Matthews

Spanish Rose

Hear the music
Feel the beat
Smack my red lipstick
Turn up the heat

Shimmy to the back
Spin to the right
My fan is lacy black
Keep it up all night

Wave my skirt
Move my hips
This dance is made to flirt
We go into a dip

The look in your eyes
And the couples on the floor
On the lifts the audience cries
If we win we won't be amateurs

As the music ends
The judges start talking
The results are high on suspense
Us being the winner is shocking
Caitlin McKinnon, Grade 9
Idaho Arts Charter School, ID

Day at the Office

Clubs in the back
My Gatsby screwed on
Gloves pulled tight
Clubhouse to the right.

The clinging mist
The bright sun rays
First to tee
All the way.

The sky is clogged with clouds of gray
As they spit and spat on their way
In the cart I sit and wait
'Till it's clear enough to play.

The biting cold makes it harsh
The bitter weather spoils the day
The howling wind brings no joy
But still I play.
Evan Lantzy, Grade 8
Canfield Middle School, ID

School

I wonder why I have to go
To dull and boring school,
All we do is work
And it really isn't cool.
I stay up to do homework
And I work with all my might,
But still I have to stay up late
And do work every night.
I always am unhappy
'Cause I can hardly ever play,
But my mom says I can't
Unless I get an A.
After all these long, long years
I finally realize,
That if I put off all my work,
It just multiplies.
Jared Haviland, Grade 7
North Layton Jr High School, UT

Free Like Thee

Oh to be free, free like thee,
flying with the wind under your wings.
Oh to be free, free like thee,
as free as the drifting sea.
Oh to be free, free like thee,
like a roaming, wandering buffalo.
Oh to be free, free like thee,
just like a proud American.
Oh to be free.
Amanda Anderson, Grade 9
W F West High School, WA

The Place I Call Home

The place I call home
Is nice and neat
With a family I call my own!

So I wrote this beautiful poem
Of love and a heap!

Sweet scent filling the air
Of happiness and care
And love we share!

For this is my family,
My own,
The sweet love in the air,
And the caring we all do,
For it's my family!
My own!
Saije Bowler, Grade 8
King Cove School, AK

Storm Divorce

When the rain falls,
they are tears that
run down my face.

The lightning that strikes
is the pain that my heart feels

Thunder is the sound of
the voices yelling in the living room.

The storm is terrible
Storm in me.
When my parents divorced.
Angelica Scott, Grade 8
Molasky Middle School, NV

Friends

My friends are the coolest
My buddy is the best

We all like to talk
When we stand in a flock

People we do bother
Not like our father

We want to be famous star
When we learn to drive the car

We are doing what is fun
We like to play in the sun
Aspen Friend, Grade 8
Culver Middle School, OR

Growing Up

Each of us
Standing on the edge of that green valley
where we know each path
is safe.
Wishing we were still
the innocent little hatchlings we once were,
but at the same time longing
to be one
who has already flown away.

Edging toward a windy cliff,
alone,
staring at the great foggy mist
of the future.
Watching others jump too soon,
plunging into nothingness,
and seeing some soar off
into unknown territory
that we all know we must one day face.

Each of us
searching for
the dawn.

Eleanor Ellis, Grade 9
South Salem High School, OR

At the Oregon Zoo

You can spend a fun filled day at the Oregon Zoo.
There are different exhibits.
African,
Alaskan,
Rain forest,
any other animals you can think of.
They have larakeets.
Sometimes they will fly on your arm!
You can go to the petting zoo.

There are shows in 3-D.
Monthly shows anyone can enjoy.
Tickets are 4.50 per person.
Dinosaur shows,
Safari shows,
Even SpongeBob Squarepants.

You can buy a souvenir from the gift shop.
Stuffed animals,
handbags,
if you like those flatted pennies,
get one for 51 cents.
That is how you spend a day at the Oregon Zoo!

Kayla Loney, Grade 7
Ogden Middle School, OR

Mistakes

Everybody makes mistakes
Some worse than others
Even if we make one mistake
We still have to live with it
We regret regularly what we did
Last time I just hid
Every mistake is like a chip in the glass
It makes a bump in your life
Nothing's the same
It's such a shame

Every day walking down the street
Looking at your feet
You can feel the eyes on you
They are thinking, look at her remember?
You want them to stop
But they will never ever drop
A mistake is a chip in glass you can repair it
With all your might
Don't give up the fight

Everybody makes mistakes once in a while…and that's no lie
Mistakes make you want to just curl up and die

Danielle Newhouse, Grade 8
Sunnyside Christian Elementary School, WA

Skateboard

Some people skateboard some people don't
some people wish they could but won't
Some people are given with the skateboard skill
some people hate skateboarding still,
some people jump-and-grind and do tricks.
And some people only wish.

Justin Rebholz, Grade 7
Ogden Middle School, OR

Basketball

The resounding bounce
Hearts beating rapidly

My mind at ease
As my body begs to stop

There is a fierce rhythm
Entwined with a tenacious flow

Such energy and adrenaline
Trying to maintain composure

Achieving peace and harmony
With the flick of a wrist

It's right here on the court
Where I can take on the world at my own pace

Andrew Garratt, Grade 9
Shorecrest High School, WA

U.S. of A.

We've been through a lot
War after war
Sometimes we feel
Like our hearts are torn
We've fought for our country
Since our country began
All since Paul Revere ran
Civil war to Iraq
Between was 9/11
When the towers were attacked
Our great nation
Did not turn our backs
We stand by each other
'Till the wars end
I'll bet most, will do it again
We're not just separate states
Hawaii to Maine
We're the land of the free
Home of the Brave
We are the
U.S. of A.

Amanda Jones, Grade 7
Enterprise Middle School, WA

My Beautiful Horse

This is my horse,
My horse is a galloping fury,
My horse is as white as a snow flurry,
My horse is as calm as a soft rain,
My horse is as fast as a freight train,
My horse for caring,
My horse for loving,
My horse, my beautiful horse.

Emily Tolstrup, Grade 7
Ogden Middle School, OR

Fishing

Fishing on the boat,
From the harbor we go,
Set a net.
Catch the fish,
They wiggle,
Splish and splash.
Time to take them out.
Unhook the fish,
Put the net back in.
Fish, fish the whole time.
Work, work, the whole day.
Finally, the day is done.
Back to the harbor we go.
Sell the fish,
Feed our tummies;
Pay our bills.
Do it all again.

Zoya Kuzmin, Grade 8
Gerstle River School, AK

Kite!

We would go to the dollar store
and buy the one we wanted.
My friend's was striped, and mine spotted.
We ran to the backyard and struggled to get them into the air
Whoosh! Came the wind and took them without care
We held to the string and let them soar.
While bringing the kites down, our hearts tore.

Ashtyn McDermott, Grade 9
Elk Ridge Middle School, UT

Together

Together.
I changed myself for you, even though I didn't need to,
I changed myself for you, just because you wanted me to.
But then I realized, you're just like me very shy, you changed I see
You changed yourself because of me.
We may be alike, or we may not, you and I will never know.
This, is goodbye.
Because you changed, I do not know you. At least not for real.
Because I changed, you do not know me. At least not for real.
Together, we do not know each other.
Together, we will never know each other.
Together, and forever, we will not know for real.
This is goodbye.
We had our chance, but we both turned it down.
Once. Twice. And then for the last time.
We are sperate people, with separate minds.
We like each other at different times.
Together as a friendship hits the ground, two more friendships are surely bound.
Today was our last day, our last time, and now it's time to finally say,
Goodbye, Goodbye.

Julie King, Grade 9
Mount Si High School, WA

What One Woman Can Do

"Stop the violence, no put downs,"
Signs and banners tell the streets.
African-Americans were always being bound,
Sores all over their hands and feet.

Her husband right beside her, she is like a rock.
Proclaiming their freedoms and their rights,
With her voice loud and clear you couldn't keep her quiet, even though they mock.
Involved with the Civil Rights Movement, it's all just a big fight.

With one loud crash, boom!
You hear the sound of a gun.
Those responsible are fated for doom.
Never again will her husband look upon the face of their son.

With her name still loud and strong,
She soars high in the sky with her wings.
Still giving speeches, and singing songs
Her name is Coretta Scott King.

Marie Davidson, Grade 8
South Jordan Middle School, UT

Tea for Two

If tea is for two and two is for tea
Then why am I for you while you aren't for me?
You think I'm a paper and you are a pen,
I think you're an insect and I am a wren.
You think we go together like a left and right shoe,
I tell you you're wrong but you won't get a clue.
We are not a neck and the tie that goes 'round,
But you'd be that tie choking me, taking me down.
You and I are not in any way a pair,
I am a circle and you are a square.
Romeo and Juliet, we will never be,
More like I am a puppy and you are my flea.
In a Loony Toons show, you'd be Pepe la Pew,
And I'd be that poor little cat you pursue.
We aren't bread and butter, we aren't Chip and Dale.
I am a head, and you are a tail.
You're the pain in my head and the rock in my shoe.
If only forever I could wish you adieu.
In tea for two and two for tea,
I will not join you, I guarantee.

Michelle Fredrickson, Grade 9
Mountain Ridge Jr High School, UT

A Grandfather's Love

Grandpa has always been there
He is getting old, but still the same
Now he may leave my life
What do I do, I love him so much
Grandma's there too, but not the same
I love her just as much, but she is different from him
I love him and I will miss him
But if he goes, so will she
I have memories of us
Walking to get the mail, then sneaking off to the store
Going to lunch, just the two of us
I love him and I will miss him with all my heart
I will be lucky to keep him through the surgery.

Sarah Peterson, Grade 7
Adna Middle-High School, WA

Throughout the Years

School is out,
Hooray, hooray
No kids to pout

But soon, school will begin
The kids will mourn and shout
School should be a sin
All the students yell, "I want out!"

Thus all the students want summer to come
They are sick of learning math and the sum
But the year will end before you can count to three
Don't wish your life away; that is key.

Emma Stacey, Grade 7
St Anne School, WA

Snow

I look outside at the sky,
As white as it can be.
I fall asleep,
But soon arise and look out at my window
To see blistering winds blowing
Gleefully covering the ground in white.
What can it be glowing so brightly,
Shimmering in the sun.
I think, I think out loud,
I think to myself, what can this stuff be?
Aha, I got it, but can it be,
It has to be.
IT'S SNOW!

Alexander Dachsel, Grade 7
CLASS Academy, OR

Love

Two trains stand before me
Going in different directions
One will change, and one will be
Both have undying connections
Maybe one will go north, and the other south
Maybe one will go east, and the other west
But still they both will stop at the mouth
Of two different oceans where they will rest
Trains so beautiful as could be
And so astonishingly splendid
Bearing two wonderful paths for me
But very diversely ended
Which train shall I chose
One where I win, or one where I lose

Ashley Prentice, Grade 9
Wahtonka High School, OR

Good Bye

My dad left when I was three
He moved away, away from me
He has a girlfriend and kids too
I guess he just had too many things to do.

I guess he loves them more than me
because he never writes or talks to me
He doesn't love me
And he doesn't care
That I cry at night because I'm scared.

My grass is greener on the other side
Because I know I will be all right
And so I say…
Good bye…

Amy Lively, Grade 7
Union High School, OR

Finally

Finally it happened. Finally I'm free. Finally there is no more you and me. I've seen it coming from a mile away, but today it happened. I thought it would hurt. I thought we might cry, but today my eyes will remain dry. It was becoming way too stressful. A little way too much. So with no time to worry why, I have to say it was fun while it lasted but now it is goodbye. No more screaming. No more shouting. No more doubting when this will end. It has finally happened and I have to say that I am not sad yet a little disappointed yet a lot glad. You thought I was kidding. You thought it was a joke. You thought I would always hold on. But guess what? I have to tell you, you thought WRONG. A weight has been lifted off of my shoulders and it is so much better without you to bring all of my days down.

Monica Rengo, Grade 7
Sylvester Middle School, WA

The Robin

The wind was a cooling whisper, rustling the forest grove,
The sun was a sparkling diamond; the finest in the trove,
The river a laughing goddess, bantering with the breeze,
And the robin sat still, waiting, waiting, waiting,
The robin sat still, waiting, up in the lofty trees

She'd feathers of brown on her forehead, and feathers of brown on her back
Her ruby red chest shone resplendent; of beauty there was no lack.
Her plumage was smooth and perfect; her wings folded in at her sides,
And when she glided through the air she melded with the sky.

Amid the branches she sat and sighed enclosed in her neat little nest;
She tapped on her eggs with her small sharp beak but all seemed full of rest
But she whistled a tune to her unhatched young and what do you think happened then?
With a chirp and a twitter, a flap and a flitter, they hatched in their nest in the glen.

Kathleen Hoza, Grade 8
St Michael School, WA

Good-bye

It seems I don't know you anymore; you just walked right out the door.
I'm missing the smile that I once wore; I haven't seen you in forever, maybe more.

Since you've disappeared, it has been nothing but pain. I'm losing my mind. There's nothing to gain.
I have to remember I'm not to blame, but if it's true why do I feel the shame?

Why did you leave me? Why don't you need me? I'm crying so hard; can't you see me?
I felt so bad when I knew you were gone, I'm hurting bad but I must go on.

I must admit it feels wrong, but I've got to be strong and start moving on.
Whatever the case, I've got to hold on.

I've been broken hearted, since the day we parted.
It's so depressing, that we had to end what we started.

Why did you abandon me? I need you badly, can't you see?
I've dreamed of being together till the end. Now you think I'm only good enough for us to be just friends?

My heart took a beating, but my life is proceeding.
I'm torn and I'm bleeding, but I won't be defeated.

I'll spread my wings, and I will fly, I'll disappear into the sky.
You left me and I don't know why. I still care, but it's still good-bye.

Laura Lattin, Grade 7
West Valley Middle School, WA

Shadows Within

Darkness covers the Earth,
Waiting to bring some unknown dread.

They are waiting for you.
No peace will be given to these specters,
Not until we can create it.
But when will there be harmony?
It is these apparitions that forbid such hope.
Greed, fear, lust, they are all there,
Inside each mortal they lie,
Waiting to disrupt what serenity there is.

However, a voice inside advises and coaches.
Do we listen?
Some take that stand,
But others take a step away.
Anarchy takes the place of that fearful footstep.
Complete chaos.
Those who fight that bedlam may not live to tell the tale.
If everyone had taken that stand, fewer would have died.
If each person had listened to that voice
No fighting would have occurred.
Human nature prevents true peace.

Kaylin Halldorson, Grade 8
South Jordan Middle School, UT

Child of the Night

A child of the cimmerian night,
A dark waker and mother of silence untold
Do you envy chill winter's sight?
As you see it seep across the world?
A walker across the pools of ink
Above the silver ebbing clouds
Do you yearn for sun at the brink?
For a rope of golden shrouds?

Are you overjoyed and yet still sad?
Without a heart or friend?
Loyal, deserving, more to brag
Than just an outlet to an end.
As just predators and prey
You camouflage the burnished stars
A shield to keep the light at bay
Dimming cells behind closed bars.

Hard and cold you laugh at the day
Even when it eventually breaks down.
But, young suntaker, you never hear me when I say
That you too must lie dead in the ground
And fall apart to make way.

Stephanie Vargas, Grade 8
Pleasant Valley Middle School, WA

The Bay

down by the bay
where the children dare not play
the waves so tall
almost like a wall
my little brother running
to see it fall
he ran up not knowing
how the waves go a-flowing
as my mother saw the little boy
she screamed but not with joy
my grandpa ran there so quick
and a brother he a-pick
there he was so wet and cold
but so thankful that my grandpa's not that old

Sterling Emry, Grade 9
Idaho Arts Charter School, ID

The Frost and the Flame

The freezing strike of the flail
Sends beast and people across the field,
As the cruel grasp of death sweeps them clean.

The searing bite of the blade
Tears the carcass to bits,
Life flowing away from the murderous field.

The two face each other,
The Frost and the Flame,
Ready to take lives for their goal.

Fenrir and Phoenix,
Wolf and Tiger,
The Frost and the Flame.

The blade whistles, striking true
As the flail fall, disappearing behind the expanses of time,
The sun rises,
And summer, the victor, begins.

Braden Mauldin-Heiner, Grade 8
Canfield Middle School, ID

Children of the Holocaust

Nazis are coming we hear the guns,
Grenades going off we hear faraway hums,
Rome was falling into their hands,
Taking every Jewish boy, girl, woman, and man,
Beating every Jew in sight,
We are trying to survive with all our might.
Searching in every corner of the house,
Looking in hiding spots not even big for a mouse.
They took us by surprise,
They must have enjoyed the look in our eyes.
We were taken far away from Rome,
And I'm afraid that I'll never again see home.

Shawn Atkinson, Grade 8
South Jordan Middle School, UT

Good Bye

You look into my eyes,
And say it's time for good bye.
We stand and look at each other,
I say we shouldn't even bother.

I wish it could be different,
But know it could never be.
Our families are at war,
But one day they will see.

That true love can't deny,
The love in our hearts,
And the pain in our eyes.

So you go you your way,
And I'll go mine.
Left with memories,
In our minds.

Chelsea Riberal, Grade 9
Lowell High School, OR

Where Am I?

Where am I,
If you don't want me?
I know where I am,
At heart.
But where am I,
Physically?
Emotionally?
What about mentally?

Katie Marie Huffman, Grade 7
Marsing Middle School, ID

Welcome Back Mr. Winter

Low temperature
Gloomy atmosphere
Great grey clouds
Snowing, blizzard
Ice crystals cut like knives
Old man winter blusters
Silent, everything is still
Snowflakes silently swirl
Evergreens coated with frost.
Sunrise
Rosy red skies
No clouds in sight
Frosty air warms
Drip, Drip, Drip
Technicolor rainbows
White blankets shrink away
Inversions grip the valley
Fog, Smog
Clouds roll in and kick out the inversion
Welcoming back Mr. Winter.

Ryan Fuller, Grade 7
Indian Hills Middle School, UT

I Love Music

While I am hearing music
I often think of things
Like going to a concert and wearing my pair of rock n' roll jeans
Also blasting out my speakers, until my windows shatter
Or doing nothing all day long, because nothing else matters.
But most of the time I think of sitting on my comfy chair
And when I'm standing up on stage
and having fame blow through my hair.

Lindsay Powell, Grade 7
Ogden Middle School, OR

The War That Was Not Won Nor Lost

The captain sat behind his charts, eating a slice of apple pie,
His mate came in briskly then, he didn't knock, but why?
"Captain, you need to see this fast," Arthur jumped up and followed Cook.
The men climbed up the hatch to deck, the captain did not have to look.
His friend's behavior, loud and clear, Arthur had seen many times,
It bespoke danger very soon, the bell the crow's nest now did chime.
The captain's spyglass saw the worst, upon the horizon was a mast,
The Spanish flag he saw it fly, and the name came last.
"The Guerra Buena, dreaded ship." Arthur said to Cook,
Many English it had sank, the crew shivered and shook.
He said, "I want all crew, to the mess hall right away.
If we can fight them well enough, the Spaniards we may drive away."
His orders were, "man your guns, Cook, prepare to board.
Cannon crews, load them up. No miss we can afford."
The Spanish man-o-war drew near, declaring victory,
"Surrender now, puny English, or be sent to sea."
Arthur replied, "Not on your life, which won't be long.
Our men are elite, this fight will make them yawn."
The Spaniard said, "Our bluff has failed. Your ship's known far and wide.
But since we are three times your size, the fight's too risky for each side."

Dolan P. Murvihill, Grade 7
CLASS Academy, OR

Summer Days

Golden summer days, filled with butter yellow laughs,
A polished friendship bond, that was never to be broke.
We shared our coal dark secrets,
Our biggest problems and our brightest hopes,
Not to know that one day, this turquoise stream of ours,
Would fork into a deep dark river, and throw our lives apart.

Gold summer days, drifted foggy gray away,
But still our butter yellow hopes were oh, so very high.
We promised each other, with smiles, laughs and tears,
We would always be together, friends through and through the years.

Just like a turquoise stream, from which grows a deep dark river,
They are split by the land that once kept them bound together.
Our lives grew apart, no more butter yellow laughs,
And distance in between us is in classrooms and in halls.
A smile, a wave and then no more, the summer days are gone,
The stream has split, the path is chosen, and there is no more going back.

Brooke McDonald, Grade 8
Mountain Ridge Jr High School, UT

Wind
Wispy strings, waving politely.
Fast-moving, so stiff and cold.
"Don't breathe." said I.
"I can't," said he.
"I'm cold," said I.
"Take care," said he.
He felt my face with his smooth icy fingers,
And skipped around my melancholy heels,
All the while laughing in whisper.
He makes the trees bow,
As he skates through the woods.
His sudden appearance gives animals a shiver.
He and I are nothing the same.
He leaves as quickly as he came.
Kaisha Gauderman, Grade 8
Eugene Christian School, OR

Just…
It's so confusing being this age
We just get caught up in the moment
Not thinking what the consequences will be
Guys — girls — gossip — truth — friends
For some it may be just too hard
For some they just come to the end of the rope…
Hey…just…STOP
What are you thinking…
Just look around — look at all the good in our lives
What God has blessed us with
We take it so much for granted
Love — friendship — kindness — creation — life
Don't get down just look up and ahead
At all the beauty of what is to come
Julie Anna Long, Grade 8
Sunnyside Christian Elementary School, WA

A World Without Animals
Could you ever imagine the world without animals?
There would be no nothing like pigs or camels.
No dogs,
Not even frogs,
There'd be no chance to go to the zoo,
Or a pet to play with too.
The world would be quiet,
And you'd wish it were not,
Because having no animals would not be that hot.
It would be very boring,
You'd be snoring.
No animal movies to watch or see,
Old Yeller or,
Lion King,
Not even ducks to quack,
No seals to jump through hula rings,
Or birds to chirp or sing,
That's a world without animals.
Chelsea Roley, Grade 7
Ogden Middle School, OR

The Waterfall
The river is silent, not a sound to be heard
Floating gently downhill, floating quieter than a bird
Gentle ripples appear as the river grows faster
Just a single twig floats, just one leaf glides after
Little motion occurs as the river flows silent
Gliding down without end, unsoundly, nor violent
Then the rapids come upward as the waters travel farther
Mist is flying through the air as the rapids grow larger
Faster and faster the water will soar
Until the river bed, it is touching no more,
It glides through the air for a second or two
Then it falls through the air as if on cue
Flying fast through the sky, just awaiting its splash
Till it hits the rocks with a mighty crash
The waters gather together and float down the river's floor
Flowing quietly as ever, to repeat itself once more.
Andrew Doxey, Grade 9
Timberline Middle School, UT

Red
Red is blood, the stripes on the flag.
Red is courage, all the soldiers had.
Red is a color that means a lot.
Red is the war that all the men fought.
Red stands for the men who attacked us that day.
Red is for the people his men killed that way.
Matt Cooley, Grade 9
Buhl High School, ID

Come
"Come," says the river with a voice so smooth
"Come swim in waters fine.
Come catch a fish fill your empty belly."
"Come," it beckons
"Come walk with me;
come talk to me
like you did so long ago."
"I can't," I reply
"It is night and I must sleep now.
Tomorrow we can play."
"Then come," it says as before
"come lay by me
watch the stars
and drift off to
the sound of
my waters
o'er the rock and stone.
Come, rest with me.
And I shall wake you at dawn.
Come."
Amanda Frields, Grade 8
Eugene Christian School, OR

The Place with No Name
Sun shining, clouds whispering,
air breathing.
Flowers are swaying, dancing
in the wind.
Where glazed sunsets
are the frosting at the end of the day,
and you can count on bright rays
of moonlight every night.
Where rain is just a bath,
and the lake's ripples
are just chains of laughter.
There's a place you can go,
where nature, overlooked,
is waiting to help and watch you grow.
Hannah Bezdjian, Grade 8
Wasatch Jr High School, UT

New Love Is…
a young butterfly tickling
my stomach
an ocean with big waves
Going back and forth
New love is like being shy
or getting nervous in front of the class
New love is sadness
when your Heart is broken
when you're not loved back.
Samanta Corcuera, Grade 7
Spencer Butte Middle School, OR

Where I Belong
resting on this hillside,
gazing into the valley
below,
I see the lights of the city,
somewhere I never want
to go,
wondering up at the twilight sky,
stars twinkling their light
from above,
I never want
to leave this place,
that I so deeply love,
to take in this sweet, fresh air,
all around,
to know that this time of day
has no sound,
except for the crickets
chirping in the night,
absorbing
in the smell, sound, and sight,
this is where I belong.
Khouri Arnold, Grade 7
Dayton Jr High School, OR

Girls
Girls are like a puzzle,
They have to wear a muzzle
Why you ask?
They want massive things
they never use.
Financially you always lose,
the pain hurts like a bruise.
Alexa Orozco, Grade 8
St Patrick's Catholic School, WA

A Skate Park
On a hot steamy day
In the afternoon
Screaming in pain
Three sixties
Half pipes
People cheering
Grinding rails
I see kids falling down
Cars passing by
Friends walk by
I go to the half pipe
Skate my way down
In the hot flaming day
I'll be waiting 'till next time
Sonia Hernandez, Grade 8
Culver Middle School, OR

The Sunset
The sky is roaring with color.
Every shade of red and orange,
Green and blue,
Purple and pink,
Is screaming from the sky.
They flare and then fade,
To be replaced by a new color.
Each one more glorious than the last.
Then finally
The color fades,
And darkness casts its supreme shadow.
Those colors leave a searing mark
In my head.
And they linger on.
Laura Sigelmann, Grade 9
Shorecrest High School, WA

Friends
In my darkest hour
With love
Above money and power
By my side
Inside my heart
Lisa Jiang, Grade 7
Rogich Middle School, NV

You
You are the one who,
Lifts me up when I am down.

You love me as if,
I was your sister.

You keep me company when,
I am all alone.

You need me like I need,
Water on a hot summer day.

You are always there,
When I need you most.

You will always take care of me,
Through rough times.

You ARE my,
Best friend.
Tabatha Stewart, Grade 9
Priest River High School, ID

Aye, Aye, Captain!
There was a pirate named Frank.
He made people walk the plank.
When they fell,
He gave a yell,
And watched as the people sank.
Benjamin Rosenbaum, Grade 8
Mt Olive Lutheran School, NV

Rainbow
Blue means sad
Red means mad
or the love I give to you
Black is where night falls and no one
can be heard
Orange is the color of happiness
you give to me
Pink is the color of spice
in a person
Green is the color of plants
I grow for you
Gray makes us both depressed
when our love is too far
White is the color of frozen
memories that we share
Yellow is the color of the sun
that shines on us both
Mom I give you all the colors of the
Rainbow that is here, in the sky
Katie Ngo, Grade 7
Stoller Middle School, OR

Volleyball

Round, white, black, orange
Ref, players, net, fun
Coach is yelling!!!
"Get under the ball"
Fans yelling!!!
"Come on you can do it"
"Yea"
Ref calls the ball out
Point and ball goes to the other team
"Darn" the players say
"Come on we'll get it next time:
Or coach subbing people out
Fans saying "Come on!" "Yeah!"
Ball goes over the net to the other side
Oh no it comes back over
Someone calls help
Come on we can do it we can win this game
Serves up — silence
Goes over the net — score!!
We won! We won! We won!
Games over

Kaylinn Danford, Grade 8
Culver Middle School, OR

A Friend Looking In...

I'm just a friend looking in,
Yes, I know it's not a sin.
I don't want you to think I would criticize,
I'm simply telling you to recognize.

I can see it when you look in his eyes,
I can see it when you say your goodbyes.
You're in love with him I can tell,
And for that I wish you well.

Hold on dear friend I know times are bad,
But just remember I'll be here if you're sad.
You and him will grow up and be married,
Remember to live it up who knows when we'll be buried.

Hold on to him, don't let him slip,
He's a keeper so try not to trip.
Just hold him close and watch the snow,
Soon you'll see your relationship grow.

It'll bloom like a rose in a garden,
Soon enough it will crystal and harden.
'Till your love can cut like a knife,
That's a love that will last for life.

Miranda Ellars, Grade 8
Canfield Middle School, ID

Baseball

Feel the soft glove spread over your hand
See the ball flying at you
Hear the bat hit the ball
Smell the dirt on the baseball field
Taste the sunflower seeds when on the bench

Blake Stein, Grade 7
Ogden Middle School, OR

Our World

Can you see a place made for children to live?
People asking not what to take but to give?
Far off in a land not so far it seems,
There will be a place so much peace I could bring.
Our world will be something new,
Where hope is alive and our dreams will come true.
Our world is made up of love,
A world just right for you.
Will you take my hand?
Help all dreams be true?
Will you teach us truth,
In everything we do?
Please guide my way
Promise that you'll stay.
Always by my side.
There's nothing to hide.
Our world is a world just right for you.
Our world can make dreams come true!

Kaleigh Forster, Grade 7
Ogden Middle School, OR

Passion of Love

You sing the chorus of a thousand angels
You dance with elegant grace
You that I should love to kiss
I see her red rose soft lips and
Her hair that shimmers in the moonlit night
The passion of love begins

A destiny waiting to be unleashed
A secret kept so long captured
In the soul of passion
I see her moon lit eyes
Now is the time for the
Door of your deepest soul
To be opened

And came the harshest
Rejection for the soul to bear
For I realized love is not
Just a feeling but a strong
And lasting commitment
So true and sacred
For one day I wish to have it
And success in the Passion of love

Brandon Betty, Grade 7
Marsh Valley Middle School, ID

Old Pine
One hundred years of growing
and swaying in the wind.
The pine tree boughs
reach to the ground.
The needles spread all around
and then they cut me down

Zach Withers, Grade 9
Elk Ridge Middle School, UT

Pain
Scars haven't faded,
more pain has come.
Can't send it away,
it's burning through
    The walls around my heart
    are falling.
Scared to show my pain.
My burning need for release.
The pain inside, too strong.
    Everything's slipping,
    nothings fading.
    Don't step near my pains engulfing
Confinements breaking,
mask slipping,
    Scared to show my pain.
    Burning need for release.
    Pain inside, too strong.
Take it away,
can't stand it.
Afraid of what might
happen if my pains released.

Alischa Heinisch, Grade 8
Coffenberry Middle School, OR

Midnight Conversations
I'm walking down this line,
Wishing that I could see your smile,
Just one more time.
I keep thinking of the way,
You clench your fist, and hold your pain.
Thinking of the tears you cry,
I wish you didn't want to die.

Every day I am thankful,
That you are still alive.
I love you with all my heart,
For you, everything is what I'd give.

That last tear, that last drop of blood.
All I fear, just might come.
I hope it doesn't.
Just remember, remember this for you.
The never ending amount of love,
That I will always send to you.

Leigh Thompson, Grade 8
Central Davis Jr High School, UT

Flood
Rain, rain, glistening down.
Now buckets flow from the sky to the ground.
Rivers and streams now rise to their tips.
Over flowing it comes up to a house.
There it is running all around, until the sun drains it out.
It flows back to the rushing rapids until the rain pours again.

Karie DeGarlais, Grade 7
Lincoln Middle School, OR

Literature to Life
Life has got problems to be solved.
You have to think of how literature has made us evolve.
Why have we forgotten that life revolves around the Earth?
Or is it that literature makes us have a new meaning of the word "rebirth."
Life and literature have many things in common.
Fore example, literature can be expressed by falling from spring to autumn.
Life is different though.
It can be expressed as how to know which road to take and go.
Literature is to life as life is to literature, but can become a fixture.
Reasons? Do we need them?
No, because we have life to literature.
But yet, we try to hide from life.
When we hide, it is like a pipe; it burns and then quits the fight, dies,
Then flies to the heavens to regain the meaning of "swipe," or "put to flight."
Treason? Why defeat them?
For we have literature to life.
Literature can be expressed through fighting, biting, and realizing.
Please them? Why seize them?
For we have got life to literature.

Tory Sutton, Grade 9
Bonneville High School, ID

Self Swimming
The exterior is what sucks us in and makes us lose sight…
The exterior is our clothes, boyfriends/girlfriends, hair, toys, and gadgets,
    it is the labels of prep, goth, jock, and punk…
    the cars we drive and the houses we lay in every night.
To fulfill life we have to break through the surface and dive into ourselves.
Here in the interior we get to discover beneath it all.
This is our family, true friends, our talents and aspirations,
    our relationship with Christ and our souls.

Life has phases that we get to prepare and anticipate for
but we can't forget to take time to *live* between each one.
We can't forget to play before we work,
    and before we work we can't forget to dream,
    because without a dream, what will we work towards?

Before crying always remember to breathe
    and before giving up always remember to pray.
To figure out life is to look deep enough into our heart, soul and mind
    in order to see what our purpose is,
    what makes you happy and what your chosen path is.

Briana Nettles, Grade 9
Inglewood Jr High School, WA

Masterpiece

The world is my canvas
And I am the artist.
I may do with it what I wish
But my one goal is to create a masterpiece.
Until then, it is still blank
And my paints of emotion have not yet been poured.
Perhaps I shall paint abstract
Or a clear, summer's day
Or the murky sea waters
It all depends on my inspiration.
And though sometimes my easel of faith may grow weak
And seem to be unable to hold up the canvas
I shall not give up
For with the world as my blank canvas
It can be anything I desire
But for now, all I desire is to take these simple paints
And create a
   Masterpiece…

Jene' Johnson, Grade 8
Buhl Middle School, ID

My Trip Around the States

I went to Florida to see the gators,
But all I got were big, stinkin' tators.
I went to Oregon to find a nickel,
But to my amusement, a man-eating pickle.
I went to New York to ride a cab,
But instead an increase on my tab.
I went to Utah to ski the slopes,
But all I found were big fake popes.
When I get home at least I can say,
That from the popes, I learned to pray.
And about the tators,
They're better than gators.
I really liked the man-eating pickle,
I would have gladly paid my nickel.
New York was a waste of time,
Not even worth a little dime.
And now it's time to say goodbye,
And hope tomorrow that I fly.

James Miller, Grade 8
American Leadership Academy, UT

Guilt

Guilt is like a nightmare
When it catches up with you
It gnashes its teeth
And tears you apart

It's a monster in the darkness
Waiting for its chance
It pulls you into the depths of sadness
Until forgiveness like rays of sunshine
Breaks through the haze and saves

Renae J. Haringa, Grade 7
Sunnyside Christian Elementary School, WA

You and I

You say that you were born to laugh
With this I must agree.
'Cause every time we pass in class
You share your laugh with me.

You say you were born to be odd
This I say is fine.
'Cause every day I pass your way
You say a random line.

You say that you were born to die
And this I say is true.
But if you were to die next week
I'd be forever blue.

Now I see that you don't love me
It's on no list of crimes.
I'll be here to cheer you on
Cheering from the sidelines.

Oh my gosh! Look at the time!
It is twelve-o-clock!
There's school tomorrow, *you* tomorrow!
Hope we can still talk.

Rose Poelzer, Grade 7
Sylvester Middle School, WA

Ouch! My Leg!

I got pushed down at school one day,
It was a hot summer day in May.
I limped to the school phone,
All I got was a dial tone.
My mom said she'll be right there,
She was worried that I got a tear.
After hours of waiting,
And a lot of debating
The doctor said,
You'll have to stay in bed.
After my surgery, I was in this white thing.
I did not know the grief it would bring.
No running, no swimming, I couldn't even walk,
But the doctor said I could draw with chalk.
Six weeks passed, bye, bye cast!
I was on my way to the car,
When I realized my scar.
I wasn't paying attention,
When I fell into another dimension.
Good thing I didn't go into shock,
Or I would be going right back to the doc.

Amber Marlett, Grade 7
Mt Olive Lutheran School, NV

The Price to Pay

At the horizon arrives the tempest, swirling twisting her iron fist,
When the forces of the enemy swim in the mind, who knows in the end what we will find?
In the beginning of chaos on the darkest hour, the mastery will within our power,
On the day that the hungry are fed, the snow's gone and so is the red,
No it's too late it's left its mark, the glaciers melted there is nowhere to park,
Now here comes the deadly ascent, the chances of survival: lower than 20 percent,
Standing bravely we take a lifeless blow, fighting 'till our blood ceases to flow,
The yell of a plead of a whisper for help, shamefully tangled in kelp,
Hopefully help will soon come, to forgive us for being dumb,
The sky parched for air, now we have to pay for this outrageous dare,
Look what you have done to the newest generation, how wicked could be this federation?
Yes, we are fried but not enough; the struggle was merely a bluff,
No, no we're not ok, because here comes the price to pay.

Azrael Rempa, Grade 7
Whidbey Island Academy, WA

The Mind of an American Woman

Should we get in trouble for speaking our minds?
Do we need to be supervised like infants?
Are you too afraid to let us spread our wings and fly?
Is there more to you than you let be seen?
Are you scared that you may be wrong and the youth right?
Are you starting to realize that all you do is hurt and only help yourself?

Why do you make others suffer?
Did Daddy not give you all you ever wanted?
Like the love and compassion that you feel so strongly of for the American people?
But what about US?
Don't we get a say in what should go on?
I thought everyone has the right to exercise free speech?
Just because you don't have a one in front of an eight shouldn't determine when we can speak our minds and our hearts.

The right of the people to be secure in their persons, houses, papers, and effects,
Against unreasonable searches and seizures,
Shall not be violated.

What happened to that?

This makes me so frustrated!
How can a thirteen-year-old GIRL see this and you a fifty something MAN cannot!
Please…enlighten me.

Bekkah Perkins, Grade 8
Glacier Middle School, WA

My Favorite Place

My favorite place is where there is peace. It is where you can think, it is where you can be comfortable. My favorite place is where I can read. It is where I can write in my journal. My favorite place is where I can kick a ball around or juggle tennis balls on a racket. My favorite place is where I can take my best friend and tell her my latest crush. It is where I can sleep and listen to music. My favorite place is where I can eat and hang out because I have nothing to do. My favorite place is big and right by my house. It is a few steps from my front door, and has plenty of green and shade. My favorite place is fun to be at. My favorite place has a light breeze in the summertime and has a lot of shade and happy feeling to it. My favorite place is where I can hear birds chirping, kids having fun and the breeze in my ears. My favorite place gives me a sense of belonging and comfort. My favorite place is where I can sing or do my homework. It is a wonderful place to be. My favorite place is my chair under the oak tree with a blanket wrapped around me.

Chealsy Pond, Grade 8
Bonneville Jr High School, UT

Softball Monster

'Twas the summer and she was up to bat,
fear in her eyes as the first ball went back.
"1-0!" the ump yelled,
sweat in the air is how the softball diamond smelled.

As Bob came swirling by,
with a great smackle he hit her in the thigh.
With one down the rest of the team to go,
Bob was feeling good about his new steady flow.

Another one down,
the team was being bound.
The next girl stepped up with fear,
soon Bob was coming near.

SMACK went the bat against Bob!!!
As her team yelled, "a well done job!"
While trophies came to her team,
they all had on a big gleam!

With a smile on her face,
it was now a safe place.
With Bob now gone away,
that's all we can say.

Makenzie Quinn, Grade 8
South Jordan Middle School, UT

The Servant of a Stone Home

Your eyes are piercing, accusing.
You have given in to your fate,
To serve others when you were forgotten.
You help those in need whether old or young,
You care not.
You are learning to be at peace,
Yet you are in endless chaos.
You wonder what it would be like,
To live with your lost parents.
You wonder if it would be a better or a worse life,
You know not.
You depend on yourself while others depend on you as well.
You carry many burdens, yet not a burden to share.
Fate has taken your life and given you another;
This has changed you, for better or worse,
You know not.
You have a stone home, to live in and to meditate.
You are forever bound to this home,
For you serve it and worship it.
This is your life,
Your Fate.

Cameron Veblungsnes, Grade 9
Elk Ridge Middle School, UT

Lord of Honor

they say the one with the greatest rank
is the one with honor.
But sometimes it's the one with the greatest soul
and that is honor.

Billy Stockem, Grade 8
Culver Middle School, OR

Where Men Shall Trot

Man has always dreamt of a trek through the stars
A voyage to realms past our planet and Mars
So he built a great ship to propel through the black
He knew not if the brave men on board would be back

A trip was made to the white sphere in the sky
Those first few steps fill the U.S. up with pride
The spaceship returned to the planet of blue
It turns out the myths about cheese were not true

The success that was had made him cocky indeed
More ships were sent into the void with great speed
Until a launch ended in total disaster
There'd be no return for Columbia or Challenger

The chaos was caused by a single part flaw
When the ship blew, spectators all gaped up in awe
A small mistake was all that man had made then
'Twas a small part to fix. Could it happen again?

Man's dreams of success are sure not to end soon
The land less trot lay in the realm of the moon
He'll continue to soar through that ebony land
'Till the mysteries of space are all caught in his hand

Samantha Kopis, Grade 8
Horizon Middle School, WA

Sunrise Glow

Sunrise glow, sunrise shine,
Fill me with all your colors,
Orange and pink, yellow and red,
Not a cloud in the sky to take away your glory,
So shine and glow with all your might,
Fill everyone with your light,
Lift all the spirits of the gloomy,
Turn night into day,
Give us all something to look at,
With all of our tired eyes,
Amuse us, awe us, put us in a good mood,
Oh so short, but oh so beautiful,
A new day will come with you to greet us,
Oh Brother Sun, so strong and bright,
Light us day to night,
And when the morning comes,
Sunrise glow, sunrise shine,
Fill everyone with your light.

Matthew Chavarria, Grade 7
St Mary's Elementary School, AK

My Dad

My dad needed help,
He had this disease,
He got it in war,
It's called Hepatitis C.

My dad needed help,
To get a new liver,
He was offered a transplant,
And said "Yes" without a quiver.

My dad needed help,
But not anymore,
He's all better now,
He's the best you could ask for.

Mackenzie Hardinge, Grade 7
St Anne School, WA

Why?

Why Mom?
Did he have to go?
Why are you telling me this?
I'm only eight,
I want to meet him.
Did God need him to be with Him?
But why Mom?
Did you love him?
Did I meet him?
Dad

Krysha Tyree, Grade 9
Buhl High School, ID

Sugar Snow

Sugar snow
White blanket around you
Freezing, glowing
As cold as Zeus
Delicious

Shaina Godoy, Grade 7
Rogich Middle School, NV

The Trainer*

Old man on Colfax
Every type of training
Busted broncs
Trained reining champs
Found slow and gentle
Gave better results
Great knowledge
Much wisdom
Of these wonderful animals
Best horse now gone
Ted remains one of the wisest
I want to be just like him

Jake Jones, Grade 8
Culver Middle School, OR
*In honor of Ted Billingsley.

Self Portrait

My temper is like a stick of dynamite with a short fuse.
My airsoft guns are like extra arms.
My legs are like tank treads taking me into an airsoft battle.
My hobby is modeling WWII military models.
My heart holds love for history that is grey as smoke from the battlefield.
I live in a Pearshing tank and eat K-rations.

Austin Lee, Grade 7
Ogden Middle School, OR

The Photo on My Shelf

When I lay in bed at night, sometimes I have to hug myself tight.
To stop the flow of tears, I have grown over the years,
but I still have the memories I sit up and hug my knees,
You never seem to know what you have until it's gone.
It seems everything can go wrong.
The tears burn my eyes, I begin to rise,
but I fall back to my knees and once again I plead;
I need the strength for the next days. I feel the warmth of the sun's rays,
it instills peace and hope, I know I can and will cope.
I feel strong arms encircle around, I get up off the ground.
I know I will see her again someday, for I have chosen the best way.
I turn to the picture on my wall, a man sitting straight and tall.
His life seemed so tough, yet he loved us enough,
He sacrificed himself, this man in the photo on my shelf.
A love so deep, one I hope to keep. He was sinless, better than all the rest.
Yet ever so meek he always turned the other cheek.
He was the only one of this sort.
With his plan, I know that I can, be with her and my family, for the rest of eternity.
The man in the photo on my shelf leaning on the wall, he was "greater than us all."

Chelzie Snyder, Grade 9
Syracuse Jr High School, UT

The Tale of Icklepickle

I say this now, speaking to myself, "What is that doing on my kitchen shelf?"
High above the other mess, way up on the shelf, to rest,
Not knowing what could happen, not knowing what will befall,
Standing high upon a chair, reaching up that kitchen wall,
I stretch and reach to my final strands; I snatch the jar in my shaking hands,
What is this jar doing here? Among the dust and bottled beer?
With letters spelling out a word, that of which has never been heard,
I read it loud for all to hear, "Icklepickle" it says quite clear,
Icklepickle? What is that to mean? It sounds of a tongue which I am not so keen,
I quietly set the small jar down, upon the cold and dampening ground,
Although the story is extremely bent, I came to find what Icklepickle meant,
I may never know why it be in my home, but curiosity this tale has shone,
And once for all the whole world to see, I shall one day conclude this mystery.
When the sun shines, and the moon glows, and the world has things yet to know,
For I will keep it my secret, till my dying day,
Then I will tell my whole life away, and I will tell them of the story,
Of books and pens and morning glory, and finally after all is done,
I will mutter just a single one, a tiny word and what it meant,
"Icklepickle" and at last be sent, to a world of which I've always known,
Where the sky has shone and the wind has blown,
Now that I've concluded this mystery, I really do have places to be.

Claire Joko-Fujimoto, Grade 8
Lake Washington Girls Middle School, WA

Purple Dreams

Purple is the song of my heart
Simple and pure but longing of more
Purple is the color of destiny
Your future spread out
Upon skies of deep richness
Purple is the color that searches within
Searching for what you didn't know was there
Purple allows peace and tranquility
Yet it also causes
Heartbreak and sorrow
Purple is the color of moonbeams
A hope for the future
Purple is a pattern
Tiptoeing
Through shadows of our past
Purple is much more than the eye can see
It acts as a choice in life
A choice to dream

Nicole Simard, Grade 8
St Mark Catholic School, WA

Snow Boarding

Feel the soft bliss of fresh powder sifting through
the trees and landing on my face.

See the colorful, soothing sunset drop off beyond
the peak of Mt. Hood.

Hear the quiet green branches whiz by your head
while you rush through the mass of trees.

Smell the crisp clean mountain air
fill your lungs.

Taste the coarse cold crunch of snow while it
runs down your throat.

Mitchell Knable, Grade 7
Ogden Middle School, OR

The Hand of Friendship Has No Color

For the hand of friendship has no color,
So why do we all hate one another?
People hurt, abuse, and punch ones within
And it seems because of their race or skin.
They hiss and spit and call each other names.
When the good book says we are all the same.
Some people think that life is just a game.
And tease and cause each other lots of pain.
And if you are red, yellow, black or white.
We are all human beings in my sight.
Let's instead try to love and not to hate.
Our reward in heaven will be quite great.
Yes, the hand of friendship has no color,
We will grow and learn to love each other.

Emily Sulak, Grade 8
Horizon Middle School, WA

That's How We Roll

I am from…
"I'm not made of money"
and "holy smokes"
"Get it right" and "that's how we roll"
Sunday chores
and 6 neighborhoods
hot stoves and linen closets

I am from…
Spotlights, all eyes on me
breathing so fast hoping this excitement will last
my mom telling me I'm growing up way too fast

I am from…
Late night chat rooms
and weekend sleepovers
shopping sprees
heading to the movies at eleven at night
taking up two rows and laughing 'till we
all explode into tears

This is my life
it's what I'm all about
just another nook in my family tree

Yani Gallagher, Grade 7
Komachin Middle School, WA

The Libronster*

While quietly reading my librotsey,
There stood a libronster smiling with glee.
This miney young creature with short brownish hair,
Was wearing a bright blue and white striped tavare.
He had a small gleam in one devious blue eye,
And his smile was crooked, mischievous and sly.
With lightning quick movements for one of his height,
He snatched the librotsey with a smirk full of spite.
He grabbed up some snives as he ran out the door,
'Til he reached the library and ran no more.
He hid behind bookshelves, and what a surprise,
He cut up the librotsey right before my eyes.
I screamed in fright as he tore up a page,
And saw the librarian with eyes of rage.
When she finally calmed down,
She quickly pulled out a chrown.
She had slain the beast, the battle was won,
But this is not over, the story's not done.
The truth of the matter is really quite sad,
This monster's my brother a tiny young lad.

Brady Quinn, Grade 8
South Jordan Middle School, UT
*Inspired by "Jabberwocky" by Lewis Carroll

Blood, Sweat and Tears

Wrestling
      The sport of respect
The sweat cascading off my body
      Veins bulging
Heads bashing
      I thrust
Snatch his legs
      Lift his body
Slam!
      Massive struggle
The ref is counting
      One-one thousand Two-one thousand
Bam!
      As the refs hand cracks the mat
I rise
      For I am victorious.
                    Kyle Cardinal, Grade 8
Horse Heaven Hills Middle School, WA

Trees

                    A
                  Tree
                its green
          leaves rustling in
        a cool summer breeze.
      Gives us shade from the
    harsh sun rays, and cover
from the cold winter storms. They
keep us alive, and clean our polluted
air. Everywhere trees give us something
      to look up to. Strong, standing
            always, and not moving
                  providing homes for
                        birds, and others.
                  Holes in the
                trunk look
              like eyes
            looking at me,
          and the rough
        bark is like a
    mouth smiling at me.
              Brad Bennion, Grade 8
        Wasatch Jr High School, UT

I Wish

Sometimes I wish I was a bird,
So I could fly as high as the sky.
Sometimes I wish I was a fish,
So I could swim as deep as the sea.
Sometimes I wish I was a cloud,
So tears could run free.
Sometimes I wish I was free to be me.
                    Casie Dodd, Grade 8
          Chehalis Middle School, WA

Upon the Lake

Upon the lake
A midnight glow
A light to take
With might to row

To dip the oar
In the cool lake
And row to shore
And leave the lake

Stand on firm earth
To feel the ground
Full of light mirth
As the world goes 'round.
              Sarah Storniolo, Grade 7
        Corvallis Waldorf School, OR

Some Say

Some say I'm just a child
some say I have no clue
but if you step in my shoes
you'll find out that I do.

Some say I'm just a girl
Admit it you're wrong but you won't
I know things about the world
I know things that you don't

Some say how could I understand
When I am only a kid
But it is you who doesn't understand
I know things unseen.

Some say I'm just a kid
And haven't yet begun to live
Judge yourself and don't judge me
for it is life you must relive

Maybe I have no clue
But why is it up to you?
I am not a child
Not anymore
                    Ali Watson, Grade 7
        Naches Valley Middle School, WA

Let the Best Blood Win!

Baron, and Jaron are cousins.
They love playing poker.
Baron didn't want me to leave,
I was going to win.
But, this time he had
An ace up his sleeve.
                    Jaron Olson, Grade 8
        Mt Olive Lutheran School, NV

Bumblebee

      Bumblebee humming
    After dew, honeysuckle
  Warm sun, clear cool creeks
    Meadow glowing bright
  Soft sun on my eyes and cheeks
      Sweetly scented air
Audrey Beatrice Gudeman, Grade 8
Olympic Range Carden Academy, WA

The Sky Above*

I see a kite drift idly by
And oh I wish that I could fly
To fly like that red little kite
Would be to all of my delight
I wish I could with all my might

Way high up there the sky is blue
And that just reminds me of you
Your eyes that were so very blue
I know you've not been gone that long
To me it seems it's been lifelong

And though they said it was your time
Sometimes I don't think it was mine
To have you die so quick like that
I was so young, but you know that
I miss it now, you'd talk I sat

I guess I'll just leave off right there
I still can picture your white hair
Bright gleaming white, as clouds above
Like that one there shaped like a dove
I know you're way up there above
                    Eden Ramirez, Grade 7
        River HomeLink Program, WA
              Dedicated to Papa Jim

My Paper Adventure

Standing near a country lane
Watching Orville fly his plane,
Turn the page to Chapter Three
Climb with monkeys up a tree,
Change the scene and then you'll see
Winnie getting chased by bees,
Flip again and it will switch
To Harry and the flying snitch,
Close the book and you will find
Thoughts still floating in your mind,
Favorite scenes quickly appear
Memories to delight and cheer,
Now we want to read some more
And wander through another door.
                    Kaylee Boydstun, Grade 8
          Morgan Middle School, UT

Fever*

Coughing and sneezing,
Constantly wheezing,
Fever as hot as 120° Fahrenheit,
All because of a mosquito bite

Vomiting, sweating,
Will I ever get better?
I have a ten foot stack of get well letters
The doctor said I'd get better, but was wrong
A hospital is not where I belong,
I can't get up, I cannot bend,
Is this death, is it the end?
Good-bye Mom, good-bye Dad,
Good-bye life I've never had.

Melissa McGrath, Grade 7
Molasky Middle School, NV
*Inspired by West Nile — or Yellow Fever.

Somewhere

As the wind rustles my hair,
the leaves crunch beneath my feet,
the dog howls in my ear, the world is at peace.
Somewhere in the world a family sits at the table
talking about the day eating the meal before them,
somewhere kids are sliding on their sleds in the snow.
Somewhere in the world something is always happening.
Something wonderful and exciting,
something to bring joy to someone's face,
laughter to their ears,
happiness to their heart.
Somewhere in the world.

Alisha Haresnape, Grade 8
St Helens Middle School, OR

I Am Unique

I am unique like the lone comet.
I do not blend in.
I am the lone wolf at the mountain's summit.
You may know me if you are kin.
I am unique like the first snowflake.
You should get to know me.
For my appearance is only the icing on the cake.
Like the bark on a tree.
I am unique like Pluto.
Like the green flame.
Like the number zero.
This is my name.
CLINTON
I AM UNIQUE

Clinton Bullard, Grade 7
Union High School, OR

I Am

I am the sun
I see the unique wonders of Earth,
I hear the trees rustling blissfully in the wind
I'll always remember every precious moment
I am the sun
I wish I could be two places at once,
I cry when I feel unwanted
I am the sun
I pretend there is no hurt in me, and
I hope for things unknown
I wonder why we feel emotion
I want to be stress free
I am energetic
I feel like I could fly when I'm happy
I dream about the future and its surprises
I say "This is where the fun begins."
I can't wait to see the stars twinkle in my child's eye.
I try to do my best and live life fully
I care for my ancestors long ago
I am FREE.

Sharlee Eby, Grade 8
Wasatch Jr High School, UT

Richard, a Child from the Holocaust

Richard was a little boy,
When his family moved to France.
His mother, seeking greater joy,
Brought them there for a better chance.

Soon after, World War II broke out.
Their mother was taken away.
The children had to move about;
They left their beautiful home in Marseille.

The Nazis wanted to kill every Jew,
Even children, like Richard,
So innocent, so true.
To do such a thing would be so hard.

So many children in a chamber with gas
In May of 1944.
Then away, his innocent life passed.
Richard Benguigui was alive no more.

Brooke Saunders, Grade 8
South Jordan Middle School, UT

50 Flying

Anticipation
Fast start, streamlining, breakout
Watching your competition in the corner of your eye.
Speed,
Competitor is on your tail
Focus,
Victory!

Mariah Crockett, Grade 7
Sylvester Middle School, WA

The Mountain

Coming down the mountaintop,
as easy as it may seem,
will only get much harder
even though it seems like a dream.

He runs,
he bounds,
he falls…
and gets back up.

Sore and bleeding he slowly comes,
slower and slower as each knee grinds.
Fear of dying has begun to seep
slowly in as he goes to sleep.

His eyes are closing fast
with each pump of blood.
Coordination is leaving
and the hurt and light begins to fade.

Kyle Saari, Grade 9
W.F. West High School, WA

Sports

Football, basketball, track
I've played since way back
Running in a race
Trying to keep my pace
High jumping is like flying
I win first place, they'll be crying
Shooting the basketball
Remember all I recall
Dribble, dribble, shoot, score
You definitely will see a lot more
Guard, tackle, touchdown
We're so good we deserve a crown
The best sport is the hardest of all
Hold on tight, don't fumble the ball
Winning a game is a lot of fun
Enjoy it now before it's done
Winning or loosing we're still having fun
In my heart we're always number one

McKaylee Speas, Grade 8
Culver Middle School, OR

Love

Love is like a river
It flows this way and that
Love is like a roller coaster
It has its up and downs
Love is like a car
It goes and stops
Love can make you cry
Love can make you smile
So I wonder is love worth the while?

Riley Hansen, Grade 7
Kearns Jr High School, UT

Horse of my Dreams

My midnight maned, golden clad, high kicking beast,
My embodied west wind, bright sky of the east.
My brave charger of tales told long, long ago,
My spirited air sprite that darts to and fro.
My golden morning star, whose brilliance does gleam,
My swift footed, auburn eyed horse of my dreams.

Emma Dahl, Grade 7
Ogden Middle School, OR

Secrets

I hold my tongue to prevent what should be said from being said
I won't tell you my secrets, until I'm old and dead
You may be my friend, my teacher, or just a stranger
But my secrets are mine
Not yours to know
I hold my tongue and put on a smile
To hide from all
But behind it is true guile
I hold my tongue and hide from all
My secrets are mine
And only mine to know
But there are some times
When one wishes to know
That which they shouldn't
No matter how young or old
I turn and run
Until there is nowhere else to go
Then I turn again and try to be bold
But in the end I hold my tongue
Cry my tears and hide from all.

Ryan Stoddard, Grade 9
Bonneville High School, ID

Lida Mordehay

Lida and Nissim were Jews who lived in Bulgaria a long time ago.

A store as big as Texas their family owned,
where clothing and textiles were sold.

They had non-Jew friends and nannies too,
with plenty of servants, they laundry and cleaning to do.

Being the only Jewish family in the community,
Her parents were forced to wear yellow stars as bright as the sun.

Lida and Nissim to school they couldn't go,
were tutored by cousins at home.

While other Jews were deported to Poland,
many relatives were sheltered in their home.

The Bulgarian people had compassion for the Jew,
and began large-scale protests to protect the crew.

Dylan Harrison, Grade 8
South Jordan Middle School, UT

Love

You entrusted me with your heart.
Making it through every day together.
Hoping we would never be apart,
Getting through the worst and through the better.

What if I was to drop your heart?
Would your life just fall apart?
Promise me that you shall never hate me
And would love each other.

We call each other every day thinking it was love,
Was this planned from Heaven above?
Crying so loudly when we figure that it wasn't.
Does it work?
I was told that it doesn't.

Cheyenne Thayer, Grade 7
Central Davis Jr High School, UT

Air Dominance Fighter

Streaking through the sky
the F-22 Raptor flies
with high speed and great agility
this aircraft of endless capabilities

Going faster than the speed of sound
toward the enemy it's about to pound
The Raptor's AMRAAM missile brings it to the ground

Victory!

Safely the Raptor's pilot flies from this short dogfight
But his enemy's parachute is nowhere in sight.

Kevin Ratuiste, Grade 8
St Patrick's Catholic School, WA

Rabbit

We are rabbits,
We love to run and play,
Our favorite foods are vegetables,
We eat them every day,

We are selfish little animals,
Like our friends and family,
We steal our food from farmers who wish we would go away,

We are as fast as lightning,
Our hearing is super sonic,
We hide under ground,
And sleep until dawn,

And as the sun comes up,
We begin to wake up,
And we begin our daily routine until dusk.

Daniel Sendelbach, Grade 7
St Anne School, WA

I Want What I Want!!!

I can feel the wind and flowers blooming all around me
The more I see, the more I want
I want to have it all
The flowers
The skies
The wind itself
Past the obstacles in my way
I want to have everything
I was told to give up
I will not
I will take whatever I want regardless of other people
I want to have it all to myself
I will go insane
Crazy
Psychotic
If I don't get what I want
I'm going to blow
To do whatever it takes to have what I want
I want to see everything
I want to sail the seven seas
Just let me try to get and do what I want

Bret Geary, Grade 7
Fairview Christian School, WA

Athlete's Song

Nothing else mattered, in that moment, in that day.
My insides churned,
My cheeks burned
From racing all that way.

Nothing else matters when you give all you've got
When your heart beats fast
When you're not in last
And the sun beats scorching hot.

Nothing else can matter when you're adrenaline's got you going,
When you've won first place
In that long, long race,
And you're pride is overflowing.

Nothing else will matter when you've taken home the gold,
When your family laughs,
And chats and hugs,
And no good story goes untold.

Nothing else did matter when I won that race that day,
Such a wonderful,
And beautiful,
And oh so perfect day.

Jordan O'Masters, Grade 8
Canfield Middle School, ID

Mom

My mom is like a diamond to me
So precious and beautiful but still so fragile
My mom is like a leaf to me
Soaring through the sky like a freed soul
My mom is like a blank piece of paper to me
You can't describe her caring self for those whom she loves
My mom is like an eagle to me
So caring and protective over her young
But just to make this whole poem short
I just want to say to you mother
I love you with my whole heart
And that you'll be in my heart and memory 'till the day I have no more life in my veins
But just remember that Roxana will always *LOVE YOU*

Roxana Diaz, Grade 7
Kearns Jr High School, UT

My Refuge, My Kingdom

Many people don't believe in fairy tales.
I'm living one, breathing one.
Living a nonstop dream.
My refuge is my home.
My home is my kingdom, my room is my throne.
Not once have I moved, not yet have I tried;
my bond with this place is like touching the sky.
Memories live on, day after day, as I found those old treasures,
they put smiles on my face.
I'm breathing in hope, and feeling a cloud, day after day, living in royalty.
My guards are my family, my knights are my friends.
Watching, and protecting me on my journey through my dream.
Memories of times, memories of friends, memories await surrounding my royal chair.
From the time when I blossomed, to the time here on earth,
Memories have gathered, my dream cannot stop.
As I live in my sleep, my hope is my life.
Now I know that fairy tales are real,
And I am awake.

Colby Gabor, Grade 8
Komachin Middle School, WA

All About Life

Kevin
Funny, nice, giving, stubborn, easy going
Relative of Tanya Williams, greatest aunt
Lover of dirt bikes, challenging, BMX, it's enjoyable, fishing, it's relaxing
Who feels he needs to get good grades, people should stop bullying people, good about school.
Who needs new riding clothes — they're too small, a new bike — my mom ran over it, a nice day to ride my dirt bike
Who fear monkeys — had a horrible dream about them, heights — it's a long way down, and spiders — they're poisonous
Who give time to ride bikes with my brother, time to do my homework, time to spend time with friends
Who would like to see the OSU Beavers, Ricky Carmichael, a famous dirt bike rider, a four-stroke race bike — there is none
Resident of my annoying brother
Klopp

Kevin Klopp, Grade 8
Culver Middle School, OR

Tree

The tree looked so healthy,
So innocent
Big and strong,
With plenty of green leaves,

The neighborhood tree that all the kids played on,
The tree that has been in the city for many generations,
Just a tree to most people,
But to a little girl,
It was a connection.

Claire Downhour, Grade 7
Sylvester Middle School, WA

Obstreperous

He yells, he screams and spit does fly.
Onto the unfortunate people nearby.

He kicks and throws and yells some more.
He hits and bangs and slams the door.

What is the matter, do we know?
Is it the rain, the hail, the snow?

Or does he simply love to be,
So obnoxious to you and me?

Kylee Thompson, Grade 8
South Jordan Middle School, UT

Ceiling Feeling

Staring silently at the ceiling,
Alone and cold I know the feeling,

Room illuminated by the moon,
Softly sitting in night's gloom,

All I hear are silent screams,
Waking me up from my nightmarish dreams,

I once had a shining light,
That kept me safe through the long dark night,

But now it's gone lost in the past,
I'm back in the dark going nowhere fast,

In solitary silence as I lay in my bed,
I think about my love now dead,

It doesn't matter now as I stare at the ceiling,
Alone and cold I know the feeling.

Sarah Dineen, Grade 8
Lied Middle School, NV

I Am From…

I am from:
Purple and green…remembering routines
Coaches screaming…"Come on get it right"
Leotards…those were way too tight
Potato chips
Whip cream fights
Staying up all night
Talking to friends for hours and hours
Watching movies like Austin Powers
I am from:
Late night movies…shopping sprees
My mom getting so mad at me
Sneaking out…super loud
That is what I'm all about
I am from:
Ripped jeans…flip flops
Bathing suits when it's not even hot
Fast food…attitude
Pillow cases with stained on tears
Just beginning my teenage years

Morgan Williams, Grade 7
Komachin Middle School, WA

Waterfall

Your waters pure and clean flow,
Beautifully, splash the red rocks below.
You look like long strands of silver-white hair,
Such a breathtaking sight not found anywhere.
How smoothly and gracefully you fall to the Earth,
While you serenade others and give beauty a new birth.
You manipulate everything near to be green
Making everything else better than it would ever have been.
You're as loud as a drum, and wild as a bull,
But generate within us, feelings tranquil.
No matter the size, big or small,
Nothing is as majestic as a waterfall.

Brian Woodbury, Grade 8
Wasatch Jr High School, UT

Sad

The thoughts in my mind
Are cars on the freeway of my soul
Breaths are like stop lights
When I inhale the light turns red
And the feelings stop
I can think straight
Unlike the twisted road of life
But when I exhale
The cars hit their gas pedals
And BAM!
Sometimes there is a traffic jam
Right under the intersection
Of my heart

Hannah King, Grade 7
Lake Washington Girls Middle School, WA

My Friend

The sun rose late that day
When we saw
That my friend
Oh, my friend
My loyal friend
She has left
To another place
And time
Where no one returns
I wish she would
I wish she could
My friend shall,
Never return
The sun set that day
I was in tears
For my friend
My loyal friend
Is gone.

Priscilla Dorvall, Grade 8
Nikolaevsk School, AK

Sun

It's looking at me
It's yelling at me
It's ready to laugh at me when I do something wrong
It is warming me like a fresh-out-of-the-dryer robe
It is fooling me — fooling me into thinking it is warm
When instead it is a freezer ready to turn water into ice
It's looking at me
Making me screw up my face like a bolt
Its light gets into the crannies of the dark corners
And lights up everything to the point of blindness
So that even when you want to sleep in you cannot help but wake up
It is looking at me wherever I go
It laughs at me in winter when I look like a rock
Hunched over and cold
In summer it makes fun of me
Me being miserably hot and sticky all over
While it dances across the sky in its finely choreographed dance every day
It's looking at me, the sun; it's looking at me.

Elaine Speer, Grade 8
Lake Washington Girls Middle School, WA

True to Her Heart

Amelia Earhart flew her plane,
Over the Atlantic to gain her fame.
Americans celebrated; everyone came.
Her notoriety would never wane.

Her next big plan, so they say,
Was to fly the world all the way.
Boarding her plane that fateful day,
She waved to all and flew away.

Amelia Earhart flew in the sky.
She disappeared, we know not why.
The oceans below sense her there.
We still see her spirit in the misty air.

Kim Johnson, Grade 8
South Jordan Middle School, UT

I Am Willing

I wonder how the world would change if we all helped someone else.
I care about the future and the past; it's the present I can never figure out.
I hear Mother Nature. She's tired but willing to do more.
I give what I can, but I'm certain I could give more.
I want to see the world: its people, its hardships, its accomplishments.
I pretend to remember that one person can make a difference but it's hard.
I cry often. Crying cleanses the soul.
I worry all of the time about everything, but it's okay.
I feel time passing. It scares me.
I can't always be perfect. I know that. I just forget.
I see beauty from afar but can never get close enough.
I say things I don't mean because I don't understand.
I try to be myself, but who am I?
I dream of the day I am truly satisfied with myself.
I understand numbers. They can never be questioned.
I hope I've done enough before I leave.
      I am willing.

Caitlin Jensen, Grade 8
Wasatch Jr High School, UT

A Day at the Track

On a rebellious track
During a warm and cloudy day
In the late afternoon
Crowds cheering
Starting guns booming
Whistles blowing
Fans jumping up and down
Runners running
Racers crossing the finish line
I run down the lane
I race across the finish line
I jump with excitement
In the nice warm spring
I will be more determined

Dwight Selby, Grade 8
Culver Middle School, OR

How To Be A Nerd

This is how to be a nerd
Wear moon boots
Wear suspenders and pants that are too short and socks that are way long
Take your calculator everywhere with you and name it
Wear huge glasses that you do not even need
Write notes to yourself and talk to yourself
Carry around a handkerchief so you can blow your nose every five minutes
When you get home do homework then play with your calculator
Then go to school and tell people that you don't need friends
That you have your calculator and that is all that you need in life
That is how to be a nerd

Tawni Davis, Grade 8
Central Davis Jr High School, UT

I Can't Write Poetry When You Are Gone

How will I bloom
When my flower is cut
How will I love
When my love is missing from my life
How will I laugh
Without your deep, throaty laugh there with me
How will I cry
When my tears are all spent
How will I see
When all I see is you
How will I sleep
When I always dream of you
How will I smile
When I have forgotten how
How will I live
When you only live in my memories
How will I write poetry
When you are gone.

Hannah Rempel, Grade 7
Lake Washington Girls Middle School, WA

Volleyball

A cheer is said
A tear is shed
Fear is not an option
The scoreboard says it all
You shake so much you're about to fall
Fervor and passion, it's what the players feel
Our secrets for the game stay a-seal
The ball is tossed, a whack is heard
It soars so high, just like a bird
You're so nervous you can't stay a-stand
You charge for the ball, hands in hand
You hear your knee pads crash to the floor
Later discovered that they even tore
A centimeter away is where the ball lays
And that's where it stays
For just at that moment, that moment
You hear your team shout
"The ball's out!"

Justyna Kieko, Grade 7
St Anne School, WA

Learning Algebra

Algebra begins with unknown.
To solve a question, work must be shown.
Parentheses are added to make problems look harder,
But you can do it because you are still smarter.

The next day you learn coefficients and terms.
You get mixed up, and say you'll have to adjourn.
When you get back, you have a new mission,
Properties of numbers, using addition.

Jesus Flores, Grade 7
St Patrick's Catholic School, WA

Fear

When you're in the dark
You think of terrible things
Some don't
But most do
Your fear comes out
Your emotions show
You crack
You become pinned
Pinned to your fear of darkness
Your heart beats faster
Your body begins to shiver and twitch
Some may have tears rolling down their cheeks
The room may even change
The walls get closer
Your mind wanders further
When you get out
The light is blinding
Everything is back
But your fear is still inside your head
The thoughts are gone
Until you meet them again

Brandon Meyer, Grade 8
Komachin Middle School, WA

Your Fairy Tale

In this chamber lies your fate,
Few have found it, but few will try.
Use the strength that is hidden within,
To find the magic in your heart.
Though a door that none have seen
But those that have read these words.

Over to country that is hard to find,
Where the people dream of better days.
There creatures have a voice to raise,
But know not that it is there.

Unicorns and fairies are caged,
While dragons and giants roam free.
Danger lies on this great quest,
That is meant only for the brave at heart.

If you go and venture far,
Myths will unfold before your eyes.
There you will find the truth.
Unleash legends with your thoughts
You can never dream too big.
Try to find the fairy tale
That still exists within.

Lacy Christensen, Grade 8
Mountain Ridge Jr High School, UT

Gazing Night Stars

In the distance the stars gaze down
Sparkling through the empty night,
Jewels on a midnight crown
Tiny diamonds of powerful light;

Sprinkled across the evening sky
Shining so very bright,
Giving us the reason why
We wish upon their sight;

Everyone is like a star
Each has their own glow,
A firefly in a jar
Having nowhere else to go;

But when they look up at the night
They see that without each one,
The sky wouldn't be as bright
For each is like a sun.

Shalynn Stone, Grade 9
South Eugene High School, OR

War and Hope

Bombs are flying.
Blood everywhere is quickly spilled.
Soldiers' lives are soon snuffed out.

Filling every beat,
Hatred, it is everywhere.
Mans' war, who could withstand it?

Creator of War.
The ugliest thing on Earth.
How have we survived?

Hope, it is always there.
It's the creator of *love*.
It keeps us moving.

U.S.A. is hope.
"I pledge allegiance to the flag —"
Is a saying that helps build hope.

Soldiers keep fighting
For the goodness in the world.
Hope, it still survives.

Sara Marie Bass, Grade 8
Spanish Fork Jr High School, UT

Bird

I wish I were a bird
Flying high in the sky
Chirping as I go along.
To make the time go by.

Ashley Ogborn, Grade 7
Ogden Middle School, OR

The Dragon's Keep

My love is as strong as a valiant steed,
And I will ride that valiant steed 'till I'm at the dragon's keep,
With love to guide me on this leap of faith,
I shall go into the dragon';s keep,
This shall choose my line of fate,
I shall go on until I arrive at the dragon's feet,
And I'll fight that dragon as long as I can,
'Till I free you from this dreadful land,
And find you resting in my hands,
Onward and outward to my valiant steed,
To ride out in the sunset you and me,
For our love will last forever.

Andrew Silveria, Grade 8
Filer Middle School, ID

The Truth of Places

The ups and downs of my sideways town are easily mistaken.
Some streets are as dark as night,
Others as bright as the sun itself.
Watch your step for the ground cannot be trusted,
And the sky has serious mood swings.
No place is perfect,
I learned that early on.
But it's not the place itself that makes it great.
The very place no matter how big or small,
Is defined by its people.

Carolyn Craig, Grade 7
St Mary's Elementary School, AK

Sanity

How are you special to me?
You are my laughs, my good times, my glee
But who am I to act like I own you
You are not my leg to stand on
But I would gladly offer mine
Why do you stomp and trample me, when I only act accordingly
I may act immature at times
But what kind of person would make these rhymes
A person who feels let down I'd say and when I feel like no one cares
I turn to you who I know can share
Then when I turn to look to you
You turn me away like dirt on your shoe
You push me deeper into the ground which I thought you would not dare
And you go to someone else as if I were in your hair
Why should I keep my sanity?
When all but some has left me
Then people expect so much of me after people have left me hanging
I'm sorry to rave
But I just need to save
This little bit of sanity

Megan Nelson, Grade 8
Estacada Jr High School, OR

Man's Sinful Nature

The sinful nature man has in his heart
Induces him to seek the secret things,
He wants to rule his world for himself
And only dreams a life as that of kings,
Man's endless goal of trying to stand out.
The reason man has evil in his fate,
Is in his hasty conduct towards the Lord
And his desire to know his future state.
Since man refuses God and all His laws
He always falls and sin comes to embrace,
Then he is punished for his sins by God
Because he did not realize His great grace.
    The man that knows his fate destroys himself,
    Hence he should live a passive life for God.

Pavel Keptya, Grade 9
Covenant High School, WA

Untitled

As the sadness grows deep inside
The more you want to frown and cry
Between the injurious and melancholiac lines
You slip beneath the sands of time

You seem to be falling faster and faster
So fast, you're crumbling to a big disaster
Feeling so disfigured and tore up inside
Night after night the crying defines

Wishing to go back and start again
Hopefully to find a decent friend
So you can stop feeling so lonely and hurt
As you're crying here, lying in the dirt

Alyssa Martin, Grade 9
Sprague High School, WA

Snow

The snow is like marshmallows in hot chocolate.
They float through the air in peaceful daze.
Don't stop them, let them fall.
Wait, catch that one, it's the biggest one of all.
Now they are all getting big.
The snow is a blanket.
It covers the Earth.
But you don't want to cuddle in this one it's cold.
Look at the shapes.
They look like stars.
But stars don't float like these do.
Soon the sun will come up and melt them away.
Oh well, it will come again.

Amanda Bird, Grade 9
Buhl High School, ID

Confession

Once there was a boy,
About thirteen or so.
He really liked a girl, you see,
But he couldn't let her know.
As the months went by,
He did nothing but wish
About how much he wanted her,
To always be with him.
Many years went by,
But, still, she didn't know.
And so, one day, he decided
To be brave and tell her so.
So, with sweaty palms and shaking knees,
He told her how he felt.
And then, to his great surprise,
She liked him back herself.
So, to this day, the two are happy,
With all the love they share.
And are happy to know that
There was always something there.

Lindsey Corey, Grade 7
Sylvester Middle School, WA

Our Destiny

Every once in a while you have a transformation.
With a new sensation, alteration, modification,
And an incarnation with some celebration.

Every day there's a new equation.
Every day is a revelation.

With some information and anticipation,
Onto another destination.

Leilani Vallejo, Grade 7
St Patrick's Catholic School, WA

Basketball

Don't go to the mall, play basketball.
The exercise will make you feel great.
Don't pay your bills, work on basketball drills,
So what if you miss your date.
Don't eat a lot, practice making that shot.
You'll want to win this race.
Don't sit on your bum, play one-on-one.
It will help you pick up the pace.
Don't feed your dog kibble, work on your dribble.
You're bound to get it right.
Don't hang out with Tim, go to the gym.
You might have to stay there all night.
Don't scream and howl, you might just foul.
Keep working and don't get lazy.
Don't be a bore, just make that score.
If you don't play basketball you must be crazy.

Ryan DiMaio, Grade 8
Canfield Middle School, ID

Loving Life

Love is…
Not having everything in life be perfect
But having all the little things in life fit together
Love is…
Loving life like a llama loves lazy summer days
Sitting out in the summer sun's rays
Love is…
Listening to the bees buzz while sipping lemonade
And listening to a sweet serenade
Love is…
Living life on the edge
And never caring what other people think of you
Love is…
Lighting candles and taking a bubble bath
Well…what do you think love is?

Hilari Bosma, Grade 8
Sunnyside Christian Elementary School, WA

Index

Abbott, Han 32
Abbott, Lance 44
Abbott, Rebekah 55
Abby, Drew 166
Adam, Cody 39
Adams, Courtney 88
Adams, Thomas 184
Admire, Kayla 121
Agrusa, Angela 92
Alba, Ryan 160
Alcorn, Diandria 81
Alexander, Hilary 68
Altman II, Mark 101
Altree, Preston 148
Andersen, Jeff 10
Anderson, Amanda 190
Anderson, Carly 86
Anderson, Emily 73
Anderson, Ian 160
Anderson, J.C. 121
Anderson, Kolten 167
Anderson, Matt 183
Andrews, Shawna 66
Angell, Missy 51
Anglen, Bailey 118
Aquino, Geoclyn 167
Arnold, Khouri 198
Arteaga, Aleksndr 155
Artig, Abby 46
Ashmore, Allison 135
Asmussen, Brittanie 128
Atkinson, Shawn 195
Ax, Savannah 59
Bade, Kielley 126
Baerg, Brie 185
Baggett, Dustin 20
Baker, Brittainy 98
Baker, Dalton 118
Baker, Katie 121
Baltzor, Jessica 184
Banks, Jessica 149
Barlow, Thomas 181
Barnes, April 92
Barney, Ryan 25
Barrett, Michaela 129
Barrington, Riley 45
Bars, Danielle 69
Bass, Sara Marie 214
Bates, Chelsea 77
Batterman, Jennifer 60
Bazzano, Kendra 47

Bean, Cassie 141
Beattie, Ingrid 125
Beatty, Lauren 70
Beauchamp, Victor 88
Beck, Brooke 53
Beck, Mason 189
Becker, Charis 23
Becker, Isaac 126
Belicina, Arlene 183
Bell, Maddi 83
Belnap, Lindsay 63
Benavides, Alicia 72
Bennion, Brad 206
Bergland, Stephanie 76
Bertram, Kenzie 145
Bestwick, Fiona 123
Betty, Brandon 199
Betty, Monique 56
Bewley, Jacob 131
Bezdjian, Hannah 198
Bicchieri, Sage 125
Bijelic, Lizzy 129
Bilden, Karla 99
Bird, Amanda 215
Black, Jessica 97
Blackham, Sterling 54
Bland, Jessica 11
Blas, Candace 74
Bliss, Natalie 150
Blott, Erin 158
Bohus, Allie 22
Boman, Karli 156
Booth-Killian, Vanessa 88
Bosma, Hilari 216
Bove, Christine 23
Bowler, Saije 190
Boydstun, Kaylee 206
Brady, Chase 32
Branca, Annie 175
Bratt, Nick 27
Bravo, Nesley 185
Brevak, Ashley 166
Brewster, Kevin 62
Briggs, Kristeen 80
Brimley, Tyler 128
Brklacich, Tyler 53
Brooks, Elizabeth 120
Brown, Jason 177
Brown, Kya 162
Brudevold, Ally 166
Brueske, Spencer 143

Brundage, Brittany 65
Bryant, Jillian 181
Bryner, Parker 117
Buck, Jody 133
Bugni, Sarah 85
Bullard, Clinton 207
Burns, Abby 87
Burt, Lindsay 52
Burton, David 41
Burton, Jennifer 20
Busig, Melissa 82
Butler, Darren 153
Butler, Heather 27
Butzer, Baylee 163
Bygland, Trevor 73
Byington, Kyler 128
Caldwell, Kayleigh 59
Calvi, Tyler G. 24
Campbell, Jeff 27
Campbell, Kyle 173
Cannon, Jessica 91
Canul, Sarah 140
Cardenas, Mercedes 80
Cardinal, Kyle 206
Cardoso, Lena 170
Cardoza, Paul 134
Carlisle, Stephanie 153
Carlson, Dana 132
Carlson, Jennifer 187
Carlston, Paige 142
Carman, Shaila 100
Carter, Jessica 106
Castillo, Briana 131
Castle, Josephine 183
Castro, Juan 21
Castro, Kassey 182
Catucci, Jessica 177
Cha, Tong 161
Chase, Alicia 76
Chase, Alicia 172
Chase, Chris 79
Chavarria, Matthew 203
Chavez, Crystal Lynne 146
Chen, Ivy 147
Chesley, Hannah 137
Chinn, Corey 60
Christensen, Jennifer 49
Christensen, Lacy 213
Christensen, Michele Marie 64
Clapp, Jessica 28
Clark, Daniel 59

Clark, Kalsin 171
Clarke, Jennifer Irene 160
Clawson, Kellie 160
Clawson, Mychelle 35
Clements, Morgan 134
Clemons, Kary 141
Clifton, Raquel 116
Cloud, Mariesa 38
Coats, Nick 36
Coday, Adam 165
Coffey, Alisha 176
Coleman, Chris 173
Conley, Maggie 23
Conner, Eric 44
Cooley, Matt 197
Copling, Ashlee 143
Corbridge, Bailey 35
Corbridge, Brittany 92
Corcuera, Samanta 198
Cordova, Maria 181
Corey, Lindsey 215
Coughlin, Samantha 44
Coulter, Tim 33
Covington, Taylor 152
Cowan, Allison 52
Cox, Travis 60
Craig, Carolyn 214
Crane, Margo 165
Creech, Joyce 31
Crites, Tyler 157
Crockett, Mariah 207
Cromar, Alexandra 149
Crooke, Jenae 173
Cross, Meg 39
Crouse, Chris 142
Crowther, Kyle 147
Crump, Kenny 72
Cubitt, Rebecca 142
Cullen, Jesse 63
Cundick, Lauren 36
Curriden, Morgan 141
Dabney, Brittany 59
Dachsel, Alexander 193
Dahl, Emma 208
Dailey, Melissa 124
Dalgliesh, Shayla 43
Dambi, David 102
Danford, Kaylinn 199
Daniels, Asa 84
Dashiell, Katie 156
Davidson, Marie 192
Davies, Marina 134
Davies, Paige 67
Davis, Cherie 78
Davis, DeAngela 40
Davis, Tawni 212
Dawson, Misty 91

Day, Brandy 162
Dayhuff, Ashton 182
Deacon, Dominic 133
Deaton, Alyssa 178
DeForest, Rebekah 189
DeGarlais, Karie 200
deJong, Jessica 128
DeJong, Kevin 159
DeLaCruz, Alyx 166
Delgado, Laverne 89
Della Iacono, Christina 64
Demitropoulos, Deanna 170
DePina, Maxwell 153
DeRosso, Jacqueline 131
Dettmann, Jessica 52
Diaz, Roxana 210
Diaz, Roxy 96
Dickson, Christine 187
Diederich, Tori 158
DiMaio, Ryan 215
Dimbi, Andy 90
Dineen, Sarah 211
Diskin, Evan 169
Doble, Ryan 134
Dodd, Casie 206
Dodd, Nicol 158
Doremus, Callie 149
Dorrenbacher, Kassondra 56
Dorvall, Priscilla 212
Downhour, Claire 211
Doxey, Andrew 197
Draxton, Jonathan 37
Drury, Randi 76
Duever, Alison 45
Dunn-Hartman, Carmella 107
Eby, Sharlee 207
Edayan, Jasmine 51
Edwards, Clark 51
Edwards, Krystal 81
Egan, Marilee 177
Ellars, Miranda 199
Ellis, Eleanor 191
Ellsworth, Nikki 65
Emry, Sterling 195
Engerran, Nick 78
England, Eric 144
Erickson, Elizabeth 79
Erlewine, Roslyn 168
Escamilla, Darcey 173
Eskelson, Ashley 76
Espe, TeJay 102
Esquela, Tristine 67
Estes, Jacqueline 134
Evans, Angela 62
Evans, Lauren 152
Fader, Brigitta 141
Farrell, Michael 90

Fefelov, Cassie 175
Fefelov, Mark 137
Feldman, Danielle L. 36
Felt, Catherine 169
Ferguson, Robert 149
Fernandez, Alana Marie 81
Feroah, Ali 31
Filipe, Devereaux 121
Findlay, Ryan 41
Finley, David 77
Finley, Kysa 123
Firch, Will 159
Fisher, Kris 44
Fishman, Tristan 48
Fitzgerald, Joe 174
Fitzpatrick, Geoff 156
Fleck, David 153
Floodman, Marissa 49
Floor, Carsten 118
Flores, Jesus 213
Fong, Alayna 32
Fong, Brennen 55
Forsgren, Lance 58
Forsgren, Tammy 62
Forster, Kaleigh 199
Foster, Brittany 68
Fowler, Jaime 163
Fox, Amy 21
Fox, Tischa 75
Fratto, Alysa Jo 118
Fraughton, Seth 24
Frazier, Trisha 167
Frederick, Kevin 25
Fredrickson, Michelle 193
Freeman, Amanda Kay 134
Freeman, Savannah 177
Frey, Tabitha 189
Friedman, Ashley 27
Frields, Amanda 197
Friend, Aspen 190
Fuller, Ryan 196
Gabbard, Amanda 94
Gabor, Colby 210
Gainer, Rachael 189
Gaines, Annie 179
Gallagher, Yani 205
Garcia, Claudia 40
Gardner, Boston 176
Gardner, Jazmin 68
Gardner, Jessica 184
Garner, Samuel 86
Garratt, Andrew 191
Gaston, Brooke 103
Gauderman, Kaisha 197
Gayer, Troy 129
Geary, Bret 209
Geer, Alex 103

Gemlich, Jackie 53
George, Allen 144
George, Eddie 57
German, Ben 49
Giang, Lena 134
Gidley, Chuck 174
Gilbert, Kayla 12
Giles, Christopher 165
Gingrich, Madison 46
Glasgow, Nichelle 58
Goddi, Issa 30
Godoy, Shaina 204
Golightly, Clover Elizabeth 48
Gollofon, Kristin 150
Gomez, Oraliz 89
Gonzales, Theresa 30
Gonzalez, Jeanette Juarez 22
Gooby, Bobbi 47
Goodsell, Emily 13
Gordon, Brittany 143
Gorecki, Sasha 167
Gould, Myriah 142
Gourneau, Kayla 87
Graham, Beth 163
Graham, Zoe 35
Granados, Eduardo 173
Grannis, Ammon 23
Gray, Ali 47
Gray, Amy 24
Gray, Christina 93
Green, Daniel 95
Greene, Jade 95
Greenlea, Michael 97
Greer, Lauren 88
Gren, Ashley 142
Gresham, Hannah 93
Griffin, Dusty 174
Grogan, Austin Howard 93
Gubbe, Jennifer 62
Gudeman, Audrey Beatrice 206
Gudewicz, Rachael 126
Gudjonson, Jaime 85
Gutierrez-Vargas, Marlen 116
Ha, Jeffrey 169
Ha, Thao 129
Hachenberg, Robbie C. 174
Hahn, Kelcie 176
Hales, Travis 145
Hall, Amber L. 33
Halldorson, Kaylin 195
Halliday, Parker 188
Hamada, Allyson 187
Hammer, Justin 46
Hancock, Holly 42
Hand, Cortney 41
Handy, Corissa 88
Hankins, Fallon 50

Hanna, Zach 71
Hansell, Sarah 122
Hansen, Dillon 182
Hansen, Riley 208
Hanson, Erika 76
Harabedoff, Arthur 43
Haralson, Stephanie 94
Hardinge, Mackenzie 204
Hardman, Bethany 60
Hardy, Ryan 118
Haresnape, Alisha 207
Haringa, Renae J. 201
Harris, Marissa 141
Harris, Taylor 60
Harrison, Dylan 208
Harrison, Sky 44
Hart, Eva 116
Hartshorn, Robert 92
Haslam, Megan Lynn 62
Haslip, Jessica 150
Hatch, Collette 64
Hatch, Megan 55
Haviland, Jared 190
Hawkins, Stephanie 188
Hawley, Zach 70
Hayes, Jordan 75
Hayward, Jocelynne 98
Heinisch, Alischa 200
Hemsley, Ryan 168
Henderson, Austin 178
Henkel, Anna 50
Henning, Mary 61
Henriksen, Landon 179
Hepworth, Desiree 159
Hernandez, Sonia 198
Hess, Harrison 38
Hestir, Megan 145
Hill, Jennifer 133
Hill, Sarah 29
Hillis, Sean 56
Hillman, Tyler 188
Hiltbrand, Patrick 47
Hinojosa, Carla 31
Ho, Alan 94
Hodapp, Hannah 40
Hoffman, Sierra 153
Hoj, Taylor 117
Holcomb, Sierra 117
Holdiman, Devin 131
Holt, Chandra 79
Hood, Evangeline 134
Hooper, Krystal 84
Hoover, Erika 136
Horn, Marty 127
Horton, Sarah Marie 14
Hoskinson, Josh 32
Hostetler, Lauren 41

Hostetler, Trisha 156
Houk, Hannah 25
Houskeeper, Gary 35
Housley, Kevin 15
Howard, Kara 55
Howe, Chenin 180
Howell, Natalie 46
Hoza, Kathleen 194
Huffman, Chelsea 136
Huffman, Katie Marie 196
Hughes, Nate 139
Hunsaker, Aleigh A. 135
Hunsaker, Alyssa 100
Hunsaker, Kristin 46
Hunt, Joshua 68
Hunt, Richard 57
Hutcheson, Hanna 120
Hutchinson, Jenna 121
Hutnik, Kayla 147
Hylkema, Tiffany 120
Ibarra, Ana 27
Ifrim, Raluca 180
Imani, Noelia 147
Ingvalson, Abby 179
Ireland, Katie 86
Isaacson, Rebecca 62
Ivanov, David 180
Jackson, Abel 171
Jackson, Asher 69
Jackson, Christian 160
Jackson, Tony 29
Jacobson, Gabe 174
Jahnsen, Katie 148
Jake, Brittany 130
Jeffries, Kori 126
Jenkins, Marci 53
Jennings, Emma 152
Jennings, Mallory 108
Jensen, Caitlin 212
Jenson, Carolyn 86
Jepperson, Jordan 166
Jewett, JD 77
Jewkes, Wacey 53
Jiang, Lisa 198
Jim, Charmayne 33
Johnson, Alex 63
Johnson, Bubba 186
Johnson, Jene' 201
Johnson, Kayla 96
Johnson, Kim 212
Johnson, Marquea 95
Johnston, Lydia 133
Joko-Fujimoto, Claire 204
Jolley, Tiffany 117
Jones, Allison 147
Jones, Amanda 192
Jones, Caitlin 54

Jones, Channing 168
Jones, Crystal 45
Jones, Jake 204
Jones, Sean G. 127
Jones, Sterling 94
Jordan, Cody 169
Jordan, Sarah 131
Jorgensen, Jennifer 41
Josi, Ashley M. 54
Judd, Adam 54
Kadinger, Jenny 82
Kaelin, Michael 149
Kamenz, Ali 180
Keith, Lisa 86
Keller, Lauren 140
Kelley, Drew 37
Kelly, Kurran 126
Kennedy, Joe 16
Kenworthy, Kasey 93
Keptya, Pavel 215
Kieko, Justyna 213
Kile, Timothy 17
Kindell, Hayley 157
King, Hannah 211
King, John R. 56
King, Julie 192
Kinn, Sam 187
Kirby, Samantha 102
Kirstine, Sara 34
Kisch, Tian 158
Kitto, Heather 101
Klein, Kalli 158
Kleinhans, Austin 181
Klippel, Kirstin 139
Klopfer, Emily 134
Klopp, Kevin 210
Knable, Mitchell 205
Knefel, Greg 150
Knight, Krystle Lauree 69
Knowlton, Celeste 71
Koester, Luke 166
Kolin, Kaylee 155
Konnerup, Ricki 20
Kononova, Yuliya 127
Kontgis, Lexi 164
Kopetzky, Christi 121
Kopis, Samantha 203
Kotzen, Hannah 151
Kretschmer, Carina 81
Kunde, Kelsey 126
Kuner, Billie 63
Kuzmin, Fektista 61
Kuzmin, Zoya 192
Laboca, Kim 144
Lamb, Josh 56
Landa, Maria 158
Lane, Cjaristy 125

Lantzy, Evan 190
Lapham, Melanie 102
Larsen, Brian 150
Larsen, Ricky 181
Larson, Kaylee 140
Larson, Trevor 156
LaRue, Katie 123
Lattin, Laura 194
Lawler, Dalila 76
Lee, Alisa 123
Lee, Austin 204
Lee, Madeline 125
Lee, Sammy 37
Leen, Jackie 62
Leen, Kyler 87
Lefkowitz, Sabine 109
Lehman-Carter, Matisse 133
Lemley, Chris T. 124
Lensch, Benjamin 31
Leonard, Madison 110
Letourneau, Stephanie 129
Lev, Elana 27
Levy, Emma 146
Lewellen, Henry 185
Lewis, Alisha 132
Lewis, Beau 139
Lewis, Whitney 135
Liang, Maria 62
Librande, Jason 126
Lim, Katrina 84
Linroth, Emily 71
Lively, Amy 193
Locker, Christine 84
Loney, Kayla 191
Long, Julie Anna 197
Longacre, Lauren 32
Lopez, Palmis 174
Lopez, Veronica 144
Lopez, Victor 184
Loredo, Jaime 29
Love, Becky 29
Lovelace, Larissa 59
Loveless, Hillary 165
Lowber, Katie 73
Lowe, Amanda 80
Lowen, Kate 132
Luke, Brooke 30
Luna, Marisela 49
Lund, Brody 57
Lundell, Kody 161
Lustig, Adeline 43
Luthy, Rachel 97
Lyles, Raissa 42
Lyman, Jay 57
Madaus, Jeremy 89
Main, Jordan 62
Major, Lloyd 164

Malard, Julien 182
March, Kirsten 154
Marcial, Regina 88
Marlett, Amber 201
Marriott, Emily 94
Marshall, Brittany 30
Marshall, Cassandra 55
Martin, Alyssa 215
Martin, Holly 23
Martinez, Amelia 70
Martinez, Cristian 28
Marzluff, Zoe 182
Mason, Anna 184
Mason, Lauren 180
Matranga, Amanda 32
Mattila, Vance 139
Maughan, Chelcey 37
Maughan, Kylie 144
Mauldin-Heiner, Braden 195
May, Kali 24
McBride, Savannah 99
McComas, Hannah 175
McCorkindale, Lydia 125
McDermott, Ashtyn 192
McDonald, Brooke 196
McEntee, Stephanie 124
McGee, Justin 165
McGrath, Melissa 207
McGrew, Monica 33
McKane, Marisa 38
McKillop, Lacey 73
McKinnon, Caitlin 190
McKinnon, Conner 99
McManamon, Erin 102
McMaster, Heather 132
McMillan, Ashley 36
McMonagle, James 167
McMurray, Grant 170
McNeely, Julie 52
McWilliams, Kate 118
Mead, Nicholas 175
Medina, Isamar 95
Meek, Kaylee 131
Meeks, Lindsay 158
Meldrum, Markus 97
Melugin, Anna 39
Mendiola, Mercedes 40
Merkley, Tom 190
Merrill, Jack 189
Merry, Amber 186
Mesenbrink, Emily 62
Meyer, Brandon 213
Meyer, Patrick 168
Migita, Michael 91
Milano, Nichole 127
Miller, Amy 155
Miller, James 201

Miller, Josh 183
Miller, Sarah 88
Miller, Talicia 179
Miller, Thomas 120
Mills, Mackenzie 74
Miner, Robert 119
Ming, Melissa 21
Mitchell, Deborah 87
Mitchell, Kristen 186
Mitchell, Mia 88
Moake, Scott 116
Moini, Ariana Nicole 183
Mojumder, Rogina 52
Moll, Kyle 75
Montgomery, Rylan 180
Moody, Spencer 157
Moore, Adam J. 56
Moore, Molly 118
Moosman, Amanda 70
Moran, Sarah 158
Moreno, Joseph 48
Morin, Kathryn 136
Morrissette, Grace 155
Morrow, Sandra 49
Mortensen, Kaylin 77
Muehlheim, Trevor 174
Muhlestein, Kathryn 18
Munyan, Spencer 67
Murray, Evangeline 179
Murvihill, Dolan P. 196
Myer, Brittany 151
Myrick, Mitchell 158
Myung, Claire 38
Nelson, Megan 214
Nelson, Nick 80
Nettles, Briana 200
Newhouse, Danielle 191
Newton, Kellie 40
Ngo, Katie 198
Nguyen, Kha 176
Nice, John 148
Nisbet, Hailee 152
Nitiprawoto, Phian 152
Noonan, Chelsea 182
Normandin, Randall 96
Norris, Briana 91
Nozue, Ayaka 92
Nuss, Alyssa 127
Nuttall, Jordan 83
O'Brien, Lila 103
O'Crowley, September 161
O'Donnell, Meghan 135
O'Gorman, Sarah 136
O'Masters, Jordan 209
O'Mealy, Caitlyn 128
O'Neil, Chelsea 91
O'Neill, Marie 48

Oakley, Justin 63
Oechsle, Jenny 37
Ogborn, Ashley 214
Okpeaha, Tommy 46
Olsen, Amanda Ellen 149
Olsen, Travis 32
Olson, Jaron 206
Orozco, Alexa 198
Orr, Carrie 101
Osborne, Victoria 138
Ostler, Oliver 187
Otley, Brenda 183
Owings, Jessica R. 69
Paauw, Matt 145
Pacheco, David 134
Page, Amber 65
Palladina, Lena 160
Palmer, Kysen 101
Park, Serena 20
Parker, CJ 188
Parker, Jonathan 138
Pashakhan, Sasha 181
Passey, Jennifer 79
Paxson, Richael 166
Payne, Kimberleigh 145
Peckham, Alex 166
Pedersen, Kade 45
Pegram, Andrew 140
Pelham, Becca 124
Penalosa, Kristine 96
Pendell, Alex 171
Penfield, Braz 116
Perekurenko, Vicka 142
Perkins, Bekkah 202
Perpelitt, Elaina 184
Peters, Alyssa 65
Petersen, Angie 30
Petersen, Emily 174
Peterson, Erica 43
Peterson, Nicholas 100
Peterson, Sarah 193
Peterson, Zack 93
Phanmanivong, Tina 150
Phillips, Katie 20
Phillips, Lynette 45
Pickens, Elizabeth 169
Pierson, Josh 163
Pimper, Kory 172
Pintado, Ashley 79
Piper, Kibbee 99
Pittenger, Rachel 188
Pizac, Kelsey 184
Plaster, Forrest 39
Poelzer, Rose 201
Pol, Sabrina 163
Pollaehne, Nathan 30
Pollard, Lyndsey 96

Pond, Chealsy 202
Pont, Robert 64
Porter, Keoasha 26
Porter, Matthew Douglas 93
Potter, John 46
Poulsen, Christine 160
Powell, Lindsay 196
Powers, Katie 118
Powers, Melissa 130
Prengel, Becca 137
Prentice, Ashley 193
Price, Collin 177
Prince, Carl 136
Proulx, Keelie 137
Puffe, Rochelle 178
Quick, Austianna 161
Quinn, Brady 205
Quinn, Makenzie 203
Quitoriano, Clare 119
Ramirez, Eden 206
Ramirez, Zuleima 75
Ramos, Brianne 140
Rasmussen, Bryce 75
Ratuiste, Kevin 209
Rawson, Katelyn 156
Raymond, Rocky 139
Rebholz, Justin 191
Redding, Chelsea 77
Reddish, Dallon 86
Redkey, Jeremy 157
Reece, Telisha 63
Reed, Ashley 28
Reed, Miranda 124
Reeder, Kelly 123
Rees, Micah 72
Reese, Emily 173
Reisher, Jordan 125
Reister, Emily 78
Rempa, Azrael 202
Rempel, Hannah 213
Rengo, Monica 194
Renninger, Christina 164
Reoch, Miranda 119
Reynolds, Jamie 120
Rhea, Shane 75
Riberal, Chelsea 196
Richardson, Joseph 171
Richardson, Tyler 33
Ricks, Krystle 61
Riser-Kositsky, Maya 161
Robbins, Caitlyn 89
Robert, Cristian 166
Roberts, Chris 122
Robinson, Brandon 122
Robinson, Rikki Lee 25
Rock, Kyle 83
Rodriguez, Danielle 38

Rodriguez, Maddison 66
Roe, Ethan C. 118
Roley, Chelsea 197
Rominski, Brian 95
Rose, Katie 155
Rosell, Bonnie 46
Rosenbaum, Benjamin 198
Rosner, Jannalee 171
Rouse, Travis 26
Rowbal, Kayla 111
Rowen, Lyla 137
Rumsey, Kellianne 61
Ruske, Christian 158
Russom, Greg G. 46
Saari, Kyle 208
Salazar, Tae'Lor 83
Saldana, Raymond 96
Salinas, Makiah 119
Salvada, André 117
Salvino, Ali 175
Sanchez, Desiree 58
Sanders, Katie 50
Sanders, Sara 26
Sanford, Tyler 190
Sapienza, Felecia 132
Saunders, Brooke 207
Savage, Joe 151
Sawyer, Charlotte 147
Saylor, Matthew 172
Scarborough, Tyson 90
Scarbrough, Mercedes 140
Schafer, Willis 150
Schier, Nick Allen 83
Schilling, Katie 32
Schilling, Tessa 117
Schmitz, Michael 157
Schmunk, Ky Lee 23
Schoborg, Sherra 28
Schoenbachler, Adrienne 101
Schonbrun, Jackie 21
Schuster, Matthew 24
Scott, Angelica 190
Scott, Nadya 168
Scott, Richard 162
Scroggins, Jessica 74
Seamons, Aaron J. 24
Selby, Dwight 212
Sendelbach, Daniel 209
Serrata, Alyssa 153
Sershon, Cody 92
Shapley, Olivia 154
Sharp, Gabriel 67
Sharp, Talia 62
Shaw, David 112
Shaw, Kathryn 179
Shelden, Rosemary 71
Shepherd, Ty 161

Sherman, Miles 97
Shinn, Kollin 143
Shipka, Erin 19
Shulman, Talia 138
Shulock, Samantha 72
Sides, Matt 148
Sigelmann, Laura 198
Silveira, Brian 42
Silveria, Andrew 214
Simard, Nicole 205
Simon, Jacob 54
Simpson, Lauren 22
Sinderson, Daniel 25
Sines, Brendan 60
Sirosh, Dar'ya 116
Sitterud, Chelsie 53
Sivertson, Sierra 119
Sizemore, Jessica 120
Skiles, Megan 157
Smith, Amanda 166
Smith, Betsy 182
Smith, Derek 22
Smith, Ryan 119
Smith, Scout 174
Snow, Reagan 87
Snyder, Chelzie 204
Soderberg, Corey 142
Sorensen, Kaleey 154
Sorensen, Tanner 172
Sorg, Jeanna 100
Sotelo, Eunice 52
Sparks, Jackie 151
Speas, McKaylee 208
Speer, Elaine 212
Sperry, Alyssa 54
Sprague, Lindsey 36
Springli, Ben 159
St. John, Emma 73
St. John, Zach 61
Stables, Megan 34
Stacey, Emma 193
Stagner, Hannah 35
Steele, Jordan 85
Steele, Joshua Benson 76
Steele, Zachary 43
Stein, Blake 199
Stephenson, Tasheena 70
Stewart, Kate 113
Stewart, Tabatha 198
Stipek, Jesse 59
Stockem, Billy 203
Stoddard, Ryan 208
Stone, Shalynn 214
Storniolo, Sarah 206
Strohm, Deanna 51
Stuhlsatz, Greta L. 29
Stutesman, Erin 48

Sulak, Emily 205
Sullivan, Dana 144
Summers, Jamie Lynn 57
Sutton, Tory 200
Svistunova, Rita 73
Swain, Tyler 79
Swars, Breanna 116
Swiger, Kendra 98
Swofford, Devon 164
Synsteby, Kyle 101
Szymanski, Anna 36
Tanalega, John 72
Terranova, Donavan 130
Thach, Phang 42
Thai, Nicole 189
Thayer, Cheyenne 209
Theofelis, Marika 175
Thingvall, Anthony 118
Thoma, Marie 148
Thompson, Alisha 100
Thompson, Alli 34
Thompson, Kelvin 38
Thompson, Kylee 211
Thompson, Leigh 200
Thonney, Cheryl 151
Thurman, Stephanie 20
Tillotson, Keeley 126
Toland, Sara 35
Tolstrup, Emily 192
Toussant, Krista 128
Tripp, Preston 39
Tucker, Micaela 78
Tupper, Kasey 143
Turner, Chad 64
Turner, Jordin 78
Tyree, Krysha 204
Ufkes, Patrick 164
Ulmer, Anna 114
Uptain, Amanda 172
Urry, Jamie 188
Vallejo, Leilani 215
Van Arnum, Cory 141
Van Gelder, Kaylee 94
VanLeuven, Rylee 76
Vargas, Melissa 102
Vargas, Stephanie 195
Vasquez, Francisca 57
Vaughn, Ashley 77
Veblungsnes, Cameron 203
Veerappan, Raman 164
Vega, Joel 118
Veja, Daniel 80
Verbon, Brad 174
Verhei, Samantha 57
Veriga, Leonisa 84
Vermilyea, Sofie 148
Viado, Kevin 32

Vidales, Israel 51
Viklund, Sam 137
Vilgalys, Tauras 129
Vineyard, Annie 139
Voss, Josh 152
Walker, Shawntelle 22
Wallace, Bethany 37
Wamsley, Kaitlin 127
Washburn, Lacey 135
Washington, Roshonda 81
Wasser, Brenna 172
Watkins, Meghan 132
Watson, Ali 206
Watson, Tabitha 155
Webb, Caitlin 100
Webb, Kailey 176
Webb, Mary 124
Webber, Christine 39
Weigley, Leah 33
Weller, Francis 28
Welshans, Tosh 49
West, Phar 150
Westenskow, Emilee 102
Wheeler, Dioni 76
Whipp, Anna 47
Whisler, Braly 149
White, Cody 146
White, Emily 85
White, Kasey 102
Whited, Trista 47
Whitelock, Amy 182
Whiting, Scott 21
Wickstrom, Tyler 65
Wike, Regina 41
Williams, Kiera 136
Williams, Morgan 211
Williams, Nick 136
Willmore, Brent 71
Willows, Aaron C. 69
Wilson, Alea 126
Wilson, Elliott 142
Wilson, Kyle 31
Wilson, Luke 151
Wilson, Peter 80
Wilson, Robert 25
Wilson, Wesley 182
Winsor, Anson 148
Winward, Greg 31
Winward, Tyler 29
Winwood, Brandon 21
Wiser, Stacey 68
Wishon, JoDanna 71
Withers, Zach 200
Wolf, Billy 133
Wolfley, Aaron 84
Wolkoff, Bill 22
Womack, Lauren 44

Wong, Alice 135
Woodbury, Brian 211
Woodbury, Mark 185
Woodhouse, Madeline 28
Woods, Mirjum 45
Woolsey, Megan 171
Woolstenhulme, Bree 89
Woolstenhulme, Trevor 72
Wren, Klarissa 150
Wright, Carly 68
Wrye, Nadine 43
Xu, Zihao 51
Yacapin, Emmy 159
Yakunin, Jonah 176
Yardley, Justin 88
Yates, McKenzie 159
Yeager, Jace 55
Ylst, Ashley 67
Yoder, Laryssa 123
Yokel, Robin Bonneau 115
Youngberg, Brittany 185
Yturbe, Autumn 164
Yusuf, Abdullahe 78
Zabka, Olivia 143
Zander, Corinne 142
Zayed, Amal 142
Zemler, Rhiannon 85
Zhang, Sherry 167
Zomchek, Jennifer 99
Zwick, Katrina 69

Author Autograph Page

Author Autograph Page

Author Autograph Page

Author Autograph Page

Author Autograph Page

Author Autograph Page

Author Autograph Page

Author Autograph Page